Serendipitous Adventur   ...m Britannia

and

Burnt Orange Britannia (2005)

SERENDIPITOUS ADVENTURES WITH

BRITANNIA

Personalities, Politics and Culture in Britain

Edited by Wm. Roger Louis

I.B.Tauris
London · New York

Harry Ransom Center
Austin

Published in 2019 by I. B. Tauris & Co Ltd
50 Bedford Square, London WC1B 3DP
a division of Bloomsbury Publishing
In the United States of America and Canada, distributed by
Bloomsbury USA
1385 Broadway, Fifth Floor, New York NY 10018
www.ibtauris.com

Harry Ransom Center
University of Texas at Austin
P.O. Drawer 7219
Austin, Texas 78713-7219

ISBN 978-0-75569-330-6 hardcover
ISBN 978-0-75569-331-3 paperback

Library of Congress Control Number: 2019949093

Print production by Studio AZUL, Inc., Austin, Texas

Table of Contents

List of Authors

Paul Addison studied at Pembroke College, Oxford, and then at Nuffield College for postgraduate study. In 1967 he was appointed to a lectureship at the University of Edinburgh, and later became a Visiting Fellow at All Souls College, Oxford. His books include *The Road to 1945* (1975), *Now the War Is Over: A Social History of Britain, 1945–1951* (1985), *Churchill on the Home Front* (1992), *Churchill: The Unexpected Hero* (2005), and *The Bombing of Dresden* (2006).

Elizabeth Baigent is the University of Oxford's Reader in the History of Geography. From 1993 to 2003, she was research director of the *Oxford Dictionary of National Biography*, one of the largest British humanities research projects ever undertaken. Outside biography, her research interests lie in the histories of cartography and geography. She is a Fellow of the Society of Antiquaries, the Royal Historical Society, and the Royal Geographical Society.

Richard Davenport-Hines is a former Visiting Fellow of All Souls College, Oxford. His book *Traitors: Communist Espionage and the Making of Modern Britain* (2018) is based on secret service sources. He has written biographies of W. H. Auden, Marcel Proust and Maynard Keynes as well as socio-medical histories of drugs (*The Pursuit of Oblivion*) and sex (*Sex, Death and Punishment* and *An English Affair*).

Joseph Epstein is the author of more than twenty-five books. Two recent works are *The Ideal of Culture* (2018), a collection of essays, and *Frozen in Time* (2016), a selection of his short stories. *Snobbery: The American Version* was published in 2002. He was the Editor of Phi Beta Kappa's *American Scholar* magazine, 1974–98. In 2003 he won the National Humanities Medal of the National Endowment for the Humanities.

John D. Fair teaches and does research at the Stark Center for Physical Culture and Sports at the University of Texas. His career has spanned the fields of British history, physical culture, and the American South. He taught at Auburn University–Montgomery, 1971–97, and at Georgia College and State University, 1997–2012. His books include *British Interparty Conferences* (1980), *Harold Temperley* (1992), *Muscletown USA* (1999), *The Tifts of Georgia* (2010), and *Mr. America* (2015).

Alan W. Friedman is Thaman Professor of English and Comparative Literature at the University of Texas, where he has received the Civitatis Award for distinguished teaching and service. He specializes in modern British, Irish, and American literature, the novel, and Shakespearean drama. His books include *Surreal Beckett: Samuel Beckett, James Joyce, and Surrealism* (2017) and *Party Pieces: Oral Narrative and Social Performance in Joyce and Beckett* (2007).

Max Hastings was the first journalist to enter liberated Port Stanley during the 1982 Falklands War. He then served ten years as editor-in-chief of the *Daily Telegraph*. His military histories include *Nemesis: The Battle for Japan, 1944–45* (2007), *All Hell Let Loose: The World at War, 1939–1945* (2011), and *Vietnam: An Epic Tragedy, 1945–1975* (2018). His biographical studies include *Finest Years: Churchill as Warlord, 1940–45* (2009).

Rosemary Hill is an historian of art and ideas. Her biography *A. W. N. Pugin: God's Architect* (2007) won the Wolfson History Prize. She is a contributing editor to the *London Review of Books,* a Fellow of the Royal Society of Literature, a Quondam Fellow of All Souls College, Oxford, and a member of Historic England's Blue Plaques Committee. Her current research is on antiquarianism in the Romantic period.

George Kelling served in the U.S. Army from 1958 to 1978. On retiring, he entered graduate school, earning a doctorate in history at the University of Texas in 1988, with a dissertation dealing with Cyprus in the period 1939–55. He has had a second career as a civilian historian with the U.S. Air Force. He has maintained a vigorous interest in the history of the British Empire, particularly Cyprus and the eastern Mediterranean, during the Second World War.

Kevin Kenny is Professor of History and Glucksman Professor in Irish Studies at New York University. His books include *Making Sense of the Molly Maguires* (1998), *The American Irish* (2000), *Peaceable Kingdom Lost* (2009), *Diaspora* (2013), and *Ireland and the British Empire: The Oxford History of the British Empire Companion Series* (editor, 2004). He taught at the University of Texas from 1994 to 1999 and at Boston College from 1999 to 2018.

Robert D. King, from Hattiesburg, Mississippi, has spent his career at the University of Texas. He at various times has been Rapoport Chair of Jewish Studies; Professor of Linguistics, Germanic Languages, and Asian Studies; and a member of the Academy of Distinguished Teachers. He was Founding Dean of the College of Liberal Arts, a position he occupied from 1976 to 1993. He provided material support to Roger Louis in getting the British Studies Seminar off the ground in the 1970s and 1980s.

David L. Leal is Professor of Government at the University of Texas and an Associate Member of Nuffield College, Oxford. His research interests include Arthur Conan Doyle as well as Latino politics, religion and politics, and immigration policy. He is the co-editor of the *Oxford Handbook of Racial and Ethnic Politics in the United States* and *Migration in an Era of Restriction and Recession* (2016). He teaches courses on British government and politics.

Derek Leebaert's books include *Magic and Mayhem: The Delusions of American Foreign Policy* (2010); *To Dare and to Conquer: Special Operations and the Destiny of Nations* (2006); and *The Fifty-Year Wound: How America's Cold War Victory Shapes Our World* (2002). He is a former Smithsonian Fellow, an editor of *International Security,* and a founder of the National Museum of the U.S. Army. He is a partner in the global consulting firm Management Alignment Partners AG.

Margaret MacMillan is a former Warden of St. Antony's College and Professor of International History at Oxford. Her books include *Women of the Raj* (1988), *Paris 1919: Six Months That Changed the World* (2001), *Dangerous Games: The Uses and Abuses of History* (2009), and *The War That Ended Peace: The Road to 1914* (2013). In 2018 she delivered the Reith Lectures on the history of war and society.

Al Martinich is Vaughan Professor in Philosophy and Professor of History and Government at the University of Texas. He is the author of *The Two Gods of Leviathan: Thomas Hobbes on Religion and Politics* (1992). His book *Hobbes: A Biography* (1999) won the Robert W. Hamilton Award. He is co-editor, with Kinch Hoekstra, of *The Oxford Handbook of Hobbes* (2016). His edited volume *The Philosophy of Language* (6th ed., 2013) has been a standard text for thirty years.

Sandra Mayer is a Research Fellow in English Literature at the University of Vienna and Wolfson College, Oxford. She is the author of *Oscar Wilde in Vienna: Pleasing and Teasing the Audience* (2018). She coedited special issues of the journals *Life Writing* ("Life Writing and Celebrity," 2018, with Julia Lajta-Novak), *Persona Studies* ("Persona

Studies and Theatre," 2018, with Mary Luckhurst), and *Comparative Critical Studies* (forthcoming, 2020, with Clément Dessy).

Jeffrey Meyers is a biographer and literary, art, and film critic. Thirty-three of his fifty-four books have been translated into fourteen languages and published on six continents. In 2012 he gave the Seymour lectures on biography at the National Library of Australia. His most recent books include *Thomas Mann's Artist-Heroes* (2014), *Robert Lowell in Love* (2016), and *The Mystery of the Real: Correspondence with Alex Colville* (2016). His present chapter represents his 1,000th article.

Edward Mortimer is a Distinguished Fellow of All Souls College, Oxford. He was a journalist on *The Times* (1967–85) and the *Financial Times* (1987–98). He served as chief speechwriter and director of communications for UN Secretary-General Kofi Annan (1998–2006), and chief program officer of the Salzburg Seminar (2007–12). His books include *France and the Africans* (1969), *Faith and Power: The Politics of Islam* (1982), and *The World That FDR Built* (1989).

Nigel Newton is an American-born British publisher originally from San Francisco. He studied English at Selwyn College, Cambridge. He then stayed in England, learning the book trade first at Macmillan and then at Sidgwick and Jackson, where he became deputy managing director at age twenty-seven. He first thought of creating a new company in 1984, and launched Bloomsbury in London two years later. The firm quickly became prosperous, and its success was ensured when it published J. K. Rowling in 1997.

Jane Ridley studied at St. Hugh's College, Oxford, and Nuffield College, Oxford. She is an English historian, biographer, author, and broadcaster, and Professor of Modern History at the University of Buckingham. She won the Duff Cooper Prize in 2002 for *The Architect and His Wife*, a biography of her great-grandfather Edwin Lutyens. Her other books include *Bertie: A Life of Edward VII* (2012) and *Queen Victoria* (2014). She is working on a biography of George V.

Peter Stansky was educated at Yale, Cambridge, and Harvard. He has spent his career as a Professor of British history at Stanford University. His writing on modern Britain includes two books on William Morris as well as studies of Bloomsbury, George Orwell, and British participants in the Spanish Civil War—and, not least, the arts in Britain during the Second World War. With Fred Leventhal he has written a biography of Leonard Woolf (in press).

Philip Waller is a Fellow of Merton College, Oxford, where he has served as History Tutor, Sub-Warden, and Acting Warden. He is the author of *Writers, Readers, and Reputations: Literary Life in Britain, 1870–1918* (2006), which, while heavyweight in scale (1,181 pages!), and lauded as the "defining literary history of the period," is consistently entertaining. He has also written urban history and on religion and politics. He is a past editor of the *English Historical Review.*

Bernard Wasserstein has taught at the University of Glasgow and the University of Chicago. A Guggenheim and British Academy Fellow, he has been a recipient of the Golden Dagger and Yad Vashem book awards. His books include *The British in Palestine* (1978), *Israelis and Palestinians* (2003), *On the Eve: The Jews of Europe before the Second World War* (2012), and *Gertrude van Tijn and the Fate of the Dutch Jews* (2014).

Geoffrey Wheatcroft is an English journalist and historian who writes for American as well as British newspapers and magazines, including the *New Republic* and the *New York Review of Books.* His books include *The Controversy of Zion* (1996), which won a National Jewish Book Award, and *The Strange Death of Tory England* (2005). He has also written a history of the Tour de France and, as a regular visitor to Austin, counts himself a long-distance Longhorn fan.

Paul Woodruff has taught at the University of Texas since 1973. His publications include *The Necessity of Theater* (2008), *The Ajax Dilemma: Justice and Fairness in Rewards* (2011), *Reverence: Renewing a Forgotten Virtue* (2014), and *The Garden of Leaders: Toward a Revolution in Higher Education* (2019). He has translated (with Peter Meineck) all of Sophocles's plays, as well as Plato's *Symposium* (with Alexander Nehamas). He has recently edited volumes on Oedipus and on the ethics of philanthropy.

The editor, Wm. Roger Louis, is Kerr Professor of English History and Culture and Distinguished Teaching Professor at the University of Texas at Austin, an Honorary Fellow of St. Antony's College, Oxford, and a past President of the American Historical Association. His books include *Ends of British Imperialism* (2006). He is the Editor-in-Chief of the *Oxford History of the British Empire.* In 2013, he was awarded the Benson Medal of the Royal Society of Literature, and in 2016 he delivered the Weizmann Memorial Lecture.

Introduction

WM. ROGER LOUIS

In introducing another volume of adventures—*Serendipitous Adventures*—I am once again reminded of the wisdom of the Cambridge mathematician G. H. Hardy, who wrote that the pain of having to repeat himself was so excruciating that he decided to end the agony by offering no apology. In the spirit of the adventurous refrain—more, still more, yet more, penultimate, ultimate, resurgent, irrepressible, resplendent, effervescent, and now serendipitous—I once again follow his example. This book consists of a representative selection of lectures given to the British Studies seminar at the University of Texas at Austin. Most of the present lectures were delivered in the years 2017–19.

Lectures are different from essays or scholarly articles. A lecture presumes an audience rather than a reader and usually has a more conversational tone. It allows greater freedom in the expression of personal or subjective views. It permits and invites greater candor. It is sometimes informally entertaining as well as anecdotally instructive. In this volume, the lecture sometimes takes the form of intellectual autobiography—an account of how the speaker has come to grips with a significant topic in the field of British Studies, which broadly defined means things British throughout the world as well as things that happen to be English, Irish, Scottish, or Welsh. The scope of British Studies includes all disciplines in the social sciences and humanities as well as music, architecture, and the visual arts.

Most of the lectures in this collection fall within the fields of history, politics, and literature, though the dominant themes, here as previously, are literary and historical. Occasionally though rarely, the lectures have to be given in absentia. In such cases, the lectures or at least substantial parts of them are read and then critically discussed. The full sweep of the lectures will be apparent from the list at the end of the book, which is reproduced in its entirety to give a comprehensive idea of the seminar's evolution and substance.

In 2019, the British Studies seminar celebrated its forty-fourth year. The circumstances for its creation were favorable because of the existence of the Humanities Research Center, now the Harry Ransom Center, at the University of Texas. Harry Ransom was the founder of the HRC, a Professor of English and later Chancellor of the University, a collector of rare books, and a man of humane vision. Through the administrative and financial creativity of Ransom and subsequent directors, the HRC has developed into a virtually unique literary archive with substantial collections, especially in English literature. Ransom thought a weekly seminar might provide the opportunity to learn of the original research being conducted at the HRC as well as to create common bonds of intellectual interest in a congenial setting of overstuffed armchairs, Persian carpets, and generous libations of sherry. The seminar was launched in the fall semester of 1975. It has remained consistent in its dual purpose of providing a forum for visiting scholars engaged in research at the HRC and of enabling the members of the seminar to discuss their own work.

The sherry at the Friday seminar sessions symbolizes the attitude. The seminar meets to discuss whatever happens to be on the agenda, Scottish or Indian, Canadian or Jamaican, English or Australian. George Bernard Shaw once said that England and America were two great countries divided by a common language, but he understated the case by several countries. The interaction of British and other societies is an endlessly fascinating subject on which points of view do not often converge. Diverse preconceptions, which are tempered by different disciplines, help initiate and then sustain controversy, not end it. The ongoing discussions in British Studies are engaging because of the clash of different perspectives as well as the nuance of cultural interpretation. Though the printed page cannot capture the atmosphere of lively discussion, the lectures do offer the opportunity to savor the result of wide-ranging research and reflection.

I am grateful to Philippa Levine, the Co-Director of British Studies, for help in sustaining the program. The seminar has two University sponsors, the College of Liberal Arts and the Harry Ransom Center. We are indebted to the Dean of Liberal Arts, Randy Diehl, for his support and especially for allocating resources for the program of Junior Fellows—a few assistant professors appointed each year to bring fresh blood, brash ideas, and new commitment to the program. We are equally grateful to the Director of the HRC, Stephen Enniss, for providing a home for the seminar. I wish also to thank Frances Terry, Holly McCarthy, and Marian Barber, who have handled the week-by-week administrative detail from early on in the seminar's history. I am indebted to Kip Keller for his steadfast assistance in many ways.

The seminar benefits especially from the support of the Creekmore and Adele Fath Foundation. When Creekmore Fath was an undergraduate at the University of Texas in the 1930s, he valued particularly the chance to exchange ideas and become friends with faculty members. The Fath Foundation has enabled the seminar to offer undergraduate and graduate scholarships and generally to advance the cause of the liberal arts. The students appointed to scholarships are known as Churchill Scholars. The Churchill Scholars, like the Junior Fellows, not only contribute to the vitality of the seminar but also extend its age range from those in their late teens to their late nineties.

For vital support we continue to thank the late Mildred Kerr and Baine Kerr of Houston, John and Susan Kerr of San Antonio, Custis Wright and the late Charles Alan Wright of Austin, Althea Osborn, and the two dozen stouthearted members of the seminar who have contributed to its endowment. We are indebted to Dean Robert D. King for his help over many years. I again extend special thanks to Sam Jamot Brown and Sherry Brown of Durango, Colorado, and Tex and Charles Moncrief of Fort Worth.

THE CHAPTERS—MORE PRECISELY, THE LECTURES—are clustered together more or less chronologically and thematically. Winston Churchill perhaps reached his symbolic apex of fame when President George W. Bush placed a bust of him in the Oval Office, thus enhancing the "Churchill cult" in America. Yet as **Paul Addison** points out in a perceptive study, the British leader's critics included Irish, Australian, and Indian iconoclasts who remembered him as the arch-representative of the British Empire, with its racial hierarchies and assumptions of superiority. Neither friends nor enemies identified the subtle duality in Churchill's intellect that resulted in an obscure "flaw in the metal." Churchill was a brilliant politician of exceptional drive and ability, but he lacked judgment. He was self-centered and arrogant. Yet he possessed insight. In much of the interwar period, he was remembered for his part in the catastrophic Dardanelles campaign of the First World War and his notorious

unreliability in party politics. In the Second World War, General
Alan Brooke, his Chief of Staff, found it virtually impossible to get
Churchill to see the war in its complexity, because of his obsession
with single problems. Churchill identified Hitler as the principal enemy but failed to see that Japan posed a fatal threat to Singapore.
Nevertheless, he was the right man at the right time. His contemporaries continued to believe that he lacked judgment, but were forced
to acknowledge that his insight about Hitler proved to be right.

Kevin Kenny assesses the controversial career of Éamon de Valera, whose life as an Irish patriot and statesman extended from
the Easter Rising of 1916 to the turn of the 1960s. He lived to the
age of ninety, leading some of his contemporaries later to compare
him with Charles de Gaulle. He was divisive, self-righteous, and
dogmatic; yet he had a critical significance in the national and cultural revolution of Ireland in the twentieth century. He played only
a minor part in the Easter Rising, but was the last commander to
surrender and narrowly escaped execution by the British. He subsequently visited the United States to collect funds for the cause
of Irish independence. He opposed a peace treaty with Britain because it would require the Irish to swear an oath of allegiance to the
British Crown. As *Taoiseach,* or Prime Minister, he severed connections with Britain and imposed a program of severe national self-
sufficiency. He believed that a strong single-party government was
indispensable. Though there was a ruthless side to his personality,
his views evolved from militant republicanism to social, cultural,
and economic conservatism. During the Second World War, he upheld Ireland's neutrality as the foundation of national sovereignty.
Upon Hitler's death, he sent condolences to the German Embassy
in Dublin. Kenny judges that de Valera achieved a certain measure
of economic stability; yet at the time of his political retirement, in
1959, Ireland was "bleak and narrow-minded," a country marked by
de Valera's legacy of "cultural backwardness."

Richard Davenport-Hines describes the life and five-percent fortunes of the industrial and oil magnate Calouste Gulbenian. He
was known as "Mr. 5 Percent" because of his ingenuity in acquiring
that percentage of the Turkish Petroleum Company, which in 1929
was renamed the Iraq Petroleum Company. Of Armenian origin, he
was born in Constantinople but obtained a British passport in 1902.
When he died, in 1955, he was the second-richest man in the world,
after J. Paul Getty. His skill derived in part from his early training
in physics and petroleum engineering, but he acquired stupendous
financial success by playing a critical part in putting together the
consortia of oil companies with holdings in the Middle East. Temperamentally, he was reclusive and possessive yet immensely gener-

ous. As a collector of art and a shrewd connoisseur of books, coins, and carpets, he endowed museums and art galleries in London and Paris with such beneficence that at the time of his death he was compared with Cecil Rhodes and Ferdinand de Lesseps.

Lord Beaverbrook (Max Aitken) built the *Daily Express* into the largest-selling daily newspaper in the world, with a circulation of 3,855,000 in 1948. **Jane Ridley** explains the reasons for his success in journalism and to some extent in British politics. He was originally from Canada, where he became a millionaire at an early age. In England, he became a foremost champion of Imperial Preference, the economic system designed to promote free trade within the empire—and in many ways the precursor of Brexit. He was active in politics during both world wars, favoring appeasement in 1939 but in 1940 taking on the critical job of supervising aircraft production. He was widely disliked, yet he cultivated friendships and influenced prominent politicians, including Churchill. He performed a service to historians by collecting the political papers of such figures as David Lloyd George and Bonar Law for the Beaverbrook Library, of which the famous historian A. J. P. Taylor was the first director. Ridley refers to Taylor's "sycophantic biography" of Beaverbrook, and she is right. It is his worst book.

Recording a hilarious yet serious episode involving Randolph Churchill and Evelyn Waugh, **Jeffrey Meyers** describes their military mission during the Second World War from mid-1944 to early 1945. The purpose was to ensure friendly relations with Marshal Tito's partisans in German-occupied Yugoslavia. The Prime Minister chose his son, Randolph, to command the contingent in order to indicate British support for the guerrilla force. Randolph in turn recruited Evelyn Waugh, at that time a Royal Marine. Both were members of the same London club, White's. Recalling their boisterous conversations at the bar, Randolph believed that Waugh was "just the chap for me" because he seemed to be a man of "adventurous spirit." Although eight years older than Randolph, Waugh leapt at the chance to serve under his command in a dangerous mission. Neither knew anything about Yugoslavia, and neither spoke a word of Serbo-Croatian. Both were frequently drunk. It did not take long for these two flamboyant men to be completely at odds. The account of the unavoidable explosive friction between Randolph and Waugh is best left to Meyers, but a hint of it can be gathered in Waugh's complaint about Randolph's "constant farting." The reader is certain to enjoy what is surely one of the oddest episodes of the war.

Explaining the major issues in the complicated life of Alan Turing, **Robert D. King** from the outset makes clear that he was one of the distinguished mathematicians of the twentieth century. Turing was renowned above all for breaking the secrets of the Enigma machine, which encrypted German ciphers during the Second World War. He may be regarded also as the father of computer science and artificial intelligence. During the war, he worked for the Government Code and Cypher School at Bletchley Park, between Oxford and Cambridge. The work at Bletchley was highly classified, and he never received recognition for his achievements, though he was appointed to the Order of the British Empire and was elected to the Royal Society. The lecture deals also with the espionage case of Guy Burgess, but the emergent theme is Turing's ordeal as a homosexual at a time when homosexuality in Britain was a crime. (It was decriminalized in 1967.) He was prosecuted in 1952 for "gross indecency" but granted probation on the condition that he submit to chemical castration. He killed himself in despair shortly thereafter. In 2009, Prime Minister Gordon Brown made a public apology for the way in which Turing had been treated. He further received a Royal Pardon in 2013—but to those of a later generation, the apology and pardon hardly compensated, in Bob King's words, for "the tragedy, the uselessness, the sadness of it all."

John D. Fair sketches the life Louis George Martin, a weightlifter from Jamaica. He was born in Kingston in 1936; in school there he developed a lifelong love of poetry. In 1956 he immigrated to Britain, where he found a home in Derby and worked as an electrician. Dedication to his work helped him avoid color prejudice. Discovering a gym behind a local pub, he began weight training. Within a year, he was able to enter the Mr. Universe contest, in which he placed fourth in his weight class. His reputation then soared. He defeated prominent Russian and Polish opponents in weightlifting and won world championships in the 1960s. He became famous as well for his melodramatic performance while lifting—"with nostrils flaring," he would glare at the weight bar before lifting it to his chest. From the mid-1960s onward, he could not compete with eastern European opponents, because of their use of steroids; but in 1966 he nevertheless won a gold medal at the Commonwealth Games in Jamaica, a victory that fortified his reputation as one of Britain's all-time great athletes.

Sandra Mayer develops as her theme the similarities between Benjamin Disraeli and Oscar Wilde as novelists. As a young man, Wilde was fascinated with Disraeli's *Vivian Grey,* in which the protagonist attempts to gain political power through the manipulation of a Member of Parliament. As if inspired by Byron, Disraeli develops the theme of a dual personality, the poet and the man of action, both with dandyish lifestyles. In *The Picture of Dorian Gray,* three-quarters of a century later, Wilde writes against the background of a society that glamorizes celebrity. He pursues the hedonistic view that beauty and sensual fulfillment are the goals of aristocratic life. *Dorian Gray* proved to have a timeless appeal in its perceptive contemplation of debauchery—and more seriously for its take on elite society, on art and fashion, and on double lives for public and private worlds. Both Disraeli and Wilde saw themselves as outsiders, Disraeli as a Jewish politician and novelist, Wilde as an Irish poet and playwright. Wilde no less than Disraeli expressed a subtle subversion of social convention. Disraeli was remarkable in his time for flashy dandyism that concealed political acumen. Wilde in the late nineteenth century became notorious for flippancy and frivolousness aimed at exposing the hypocrisy of public attitudes toward homosexuality. Both proved to be shrewd observers of English society.

Peter Stansky sketches the life of William Morris as a Victorian craftsman and designer. He was also a poet, painter, architect, publisher, and political activist. Morris believed that Victorian mass production was a consequence of the Industrial Revolution. Capitalism threatened the quality of England's arts and crafts. He produced wallpaper, textiles, tapestries, furniture, and stained glass, thereby bringing about a virtual revolution in public taste. Each innovation bore his personal stamp because he made sure that no work would be produced in his shops until he had mastered the technique of production. Among his other achievements was the adaptation of Gothic style to nineteenth-century architecture. In 1890 he founded the Kelmscott Press, for which he designed typefaces as well as ornamental letters and borders. Kelmscott stood for unpretentious yet excellent craftsmanship, in a word, "Englishness." In the political dimension of his career, Morris gradually came to believe that the scandalous circumstances of the "underclass" and "class divisiveness" would need to be addressed by Marxist socialism—and by revolution if necessary. In the mid-1880s he was at the center of political protest, urging virtual insurrection. His political influence extended to founders of the post-1945 welfare state, including R. H. Tawney and Clement Attlee. Yet he is remembered mainly as a champion of craftsmanship. All in all, Stansky concludes, Morris stands as one of the most successful cultural figures of Victorian England.

Ida John was the wife of the famous painter Augustus John. **Rosemary Hill** sympathetically recounts the ordeal of their marriage. They met at the Slade School of Fine Art, marrying in 1901 against the will of her family. She plunged readily into the bohemian life of an artist's wife, in which, she hoped, her family would prosper, but the odds of enjoying a full life were against her from the beginning. In only seven years of marriage, she bore Augustus five children. To maintain her husband and the babies, she had to adjust to housework that often lasted from dawn to dusk. She gave up her own painting. Augustus, who had always been interested in Gypsies, bought a horse-drawn cart. With his mistress as well as Ida, he traveled in the country in Gypsy fashion. Rosemary Hill relates the painful story of Ida as an "emotionally sophisticated, morally honest woman" who struggled to cope with the "monstrous" Augustus, who was apparently unaware of the pain and loneliness suffered by his wife. Shackled to grueling domesticity, Ida wrote to a friend: "You know that we are not a conventional family . . . my only happiness is for [Augustus] to be happy."

The substantial Arthur Conan Doyle archive at the Harry Ransom Center includes some of his furniture. His desk can be found in the British Studies office. **David Leal** has studied Conan Doyle's papers and manuscripts to see whether his belief in spiritualism can be explained in relation to the supremely rational Sherlock Holmes. Readers of the Holmes stories might ask of Conan Doyle's preoccupation with the supernatural, how could he have believed this stuff? Trained as a physician, Conan Doyle saw his investigations of spiritualism as grounded in science. Yet in the last decade of his life, the 1920s, he quietly dropped the scientific dimension. There was no evidence. But he persisted in the belief that life continued much the same after death as before, indeed without some of its inconveniences and annoyances. At one point, he even suggested that whisky might be available. His faith in spiritualism allowed him to point out that he managed to console a dozen mothers who had lost sons in the First World War. Perhaps he found solace that way himself, since his son died of pneumonia in 1918. He was as consistent in his spiritual beliefs as in his writing. In contrast with his credulous creator, Holmes, from his first appearance, was persistently skeptical. Conan Doyle wisely knew that he could not convert him. Holmes once remarked about his detective practice that it stood flat-footed on the ground: "Ghosts need not apply."

Within a few pages, **Joseph Epstein** achieves the equivalent of a sharp-witted short biography. With no shortage of sense of humor himself, he contemplates the reasons why the ninety-five novels of P. G. "Plum" Wodehouse remain witty, popular, and extraordinarily enjoyable. Wodehouse was distant from his parents because his father worked as a magistrate in Hong Kong. But in England he had no fewer than twenty aunts. His most famous comic figure, the imperishable Bertie Wooster, continually faces female tyranny. Bertie's sagacious factotum, Jeeves, is perhaps Wodehouse's greatest creation. He possesses infallible common sense and surprising knowledge. When Bertie asks Jeeves about Nietzsche, he replies, "Fundamentally unsound, sir." Epstein straightforwardly relates Wodehouse's blunder of making broadcasts from Berlin after his capture by the Nazis. In Wodehouse's own words, "I made an ass of myself." But he took the harsh public criticism in stride, and was later knighted by Queen Elizabeth. He wrote imaginatively, with clarity and precision. Epstein provides a persuasive explanation why Wodehouse is the most widely read of twentieth-century English humorists.

Samuel Beckett often gives readers and audiences a sense of disconnected pessimism and black humor. **Alan W. Friedman** explains the underlying continuity of his work by discussing his writings from the late 1920s to 1945, when Beckett lived mostly in Paris until forced to flee from the Gestapo. These are the years of his Surrealist period—Surrealist in the sense, at least to some readers, that his novels and plays convey unnerving and illogical ideas juxtaposed with everyday objects. Friedman points out that Beckett was born in 1906 and was thus too young to take part in the First World War. But its consequences directly affected him. His Surrealist predecessors depicted bodily decrepitude and a devastated landscape; Beckett represented isolated body parts or truncated objects in settings that seemed abstract. Yet there are also recognizable locales, for example, streets and houses in Paris and London. Beckett underwent psychotherapy, which perhaps helped him with an almost pathological shyness. He also gained an understanding of dreams and the unconscious. He was inspired by his friend James Joyce, a fellow Irishman, though he steadily found his own distinctive voice. In the 1930s he could be seen in the cafés on the Left Bank in the company of friends such as Nancy Cunard and Peggy Guggenheim. He gradually made it clear that he regarded the world "as a cosmic joke." The best one could do was to face reality directly and "courageously defy it."

The founder and chief executive of Bloomsbury Publishing, **Nigel Newton**, relates the improbable birth of the *Harry Potter* series. Having had the manuscript recommended by his children's editor, he gave it to his daughter Alice to read. Alice was eight years old. She read the manuscript quickly and then came down the stairs full of enthusiasm, saying that it would be the best children's book Bloomsbury ever published. The first printing contained an error and had to be withdrawn—or rather, shipped to Australia. The Australians who bought those copies thus have an invaluable first edition. The series went on to sell 500 million copies worldwide and still sells hugely. There were many remarkable experiences along the way, including a launch at King's Cross station on Platform 9¾ and a tour of the country by steam-powered train. The success of the series can be found in Harry himself. He is intelligent and resourceful, and he experiences friendship and camaraderie at school. Readers can imagine that they too can be Harry Potter!

A classicist as well as a philosopher, **Paul Woodruff** inquires into the question how the Regius Professor of Greek is appointed at Oxford. He studies a critical case from the 1930s. The incumbent was Gilbert Murray, world-renowned as a founder of the League of Nations as well as a formidable scholar. His book on ancient Greek tragedies had sold a half-million copies. He chose to retire in 1936. Two candidates hoped to succeed him as Regius Professor. One was Maurice Bowra, a scholar of long-standing fame in Oxford as a buoyant personality as well as an acknowledged authority on ancient Greek. Bowra had served in the First World War, twice narrowly escaping death. The other was E. R. Dodds, at the time Professor of Greek at the University of Birmingham. Unlike Bowra, Dodds had not fought in the war. He was an Irishman who had supported the Easter Rising of 1916. Murray faced a consequential choice. Ancient Greece was the polestar of Oxford intellectual life. His successor would officially be appointed by the Prime Minister, but there was no doubt that Murray would actually make the decision. Woodruff builds suspense before explaining Murray's assessment of the two candidates and his choice. Readers will discover the reasons why it proved to be an excellent decision.

Al Martinich discusses five favorite books, four on Stuart England and one on China. Collectively, they convey the themes of freedom, authority, and obedience. The Stuart period of British history, when religious strife led in 1642 to civil war and the execution of the King, Charles I, was a crucible for intense consideration of questions of liberty and duty. The first book Martinich considers is the Bible, replete with examples of obedience and disobedience. Next is *Leviathan* by Thomas Hobbes, which was published two years after King Charles's execution. The social contract, for which Hobbes is famous, can be understood also as a "covenant" between ruler and ruled, and the Bible's two testaments as the "Old Covenant" and the "New Covenant." The third book, *Puritanism and Liberty*, looks closely at the question of obedience in relation to promises. Ordinary soldiers under Oliver Cromwell had defeated the King but, contrary to what had been guaranteed them, received nothing in return. When their pleas to Parliament—the subject of the book— were ignored, they mutinied and were suppressed. The fourth book,

Christopher Hill's *Intellectual Origins of the English Revolution,* develops a clear theme that revolutionary ideas were a cause of the English Civil War. A comparison with the English Civil War can be found on the other side of the world in the last book, *Wild Swans* by Jung Chang, which relates the origins and consequences of twentieth-century Chinese history as experienced by three generations of a single family: a grandmother, a mother, and a daughter. Martinich writes: "No book has had a greater emotional impact on me."

The *Dictionary of National Biography* was first published in 1885. A standard work of reference, it is the legendary and indispensable source covering an array of individuals representative of all walks of British life. The subjects of some entries are recognizable at a glance because they are historically famous. Others are more obscure but nevertheless played a significant role in British history. **Elizabeth Baigent** traces the *DNB*'s development as a reflection of national identity and an "imagined community" from its late nineteenth-century origins to its present scope, including individuals from former British colonies (yes, the colonies in North America before independence) and the Commonwealth. Since 1917, Oxford University Press has published the work as the *Oxford Dictionary of National Biography.* Its point of recent transformation occurred when Colin Matthew was editor in the 1990s. He digitized the series and significantly expanded the scope of entries by including notorious as well as influential figures from the entire canvas of British life, especially previously neglected women. Readers of the *Adventures with Britannia* series will be interested in reading the entry on Britannia as a patriotic allegory of the British nation and emblem of the British Empire. As painted by Rex Whistler in 1928, her iconic figure appears on the jackets of the series as a buxom Britannia traveling in a hansom cab with Union Jack–covered wheels. The cab is pulled by a unicorn and driven by a lion, symbolizing links with the British monarchy. Other fictitious characters with their own entries include John Bull, the epitome of Englishness and British imperialism.

Taking note that "contested statues" in the United States often are connected with slavery and the Civil War, **Edward Mortimer** makes the contrast with memorials in Britain, where it is not only slavery but also the British Empire that "comes back to haunt us." Yet the legacy of empire in Oxford became a public matter only recently. In 2016 the "Rhodes Must Fall" movement protested Rhodes's statue at Oriel College. Yet the governing body of the college decided to keep the statue in place after experiencing "overwhelming support" for retaining it (and perhaps taking into account the possible loss of £100 million in gifts). A similar protest at All Souls

College demanded that the statue of Christopher Codrington be removed from the college library. A student stood at the college entrance with chains around his neck and "All Slaves College" painted on his chest. Codrington was an eighteenth-century benefactor of the College whose huge family fortune derived mainly from slave labor on his sugar plantations in the Caribbean. The statue remains in place, but to commemorate the suffering of slaves, All Souls has endowed a scholarship each year (not attached to All Souls) for a student from the Caribbean and has installed by the entrance to the library a tablet commemorating "those who worked in slavery on the Codrington Plantations in the West Indies." A Fellow of All Souls himself, Mortimer concludes that the debate about memorials needs to continue—and he makes far-reaching suggestions.

The social history of the Raj is often a controversial subject. **Max Hastings** attempts a balanced approach by dealing equally with corrupt soldiers as well as officers in the Indian Civil Service, who had a reputation for exceptional probity. Lord Cornwallis, who became Governor-General after his defeat at Yorktown, played a critical part in creating two traditions with radical consequences, one malign and one benign. He decreed the exclusion of Indians from all senior military and civil posts; but he laid also the foundation for a civil service based on honesty and decency. Hastings emphasizes family tradition in India by quoting Kipling: "Certain families serve India generation after generation." Kipling's tribute continued to be true even after independence in 1947—often because Indian bungalows were far preferable to the dreary multistory houses in postwar England. Hastings writes of the Raj's "indisputable racism, cultural condescension, exploitation and dreadful periodic cruelties." But he describes also the rule of law, an impartial judiciary, and the universities. He achieves a balanced and memorable assessment.

The comparison of Versailles in 1919 and the end of war in 1945 by **Margaret MacMillan** is clear, compelling, and complex. Dealing briefly with the part of her argument about Woodrow Wilson and his legacy may help clarify the main points. Wilson's vision of a postwar world contained a contradiction between reparations and a new European order. Assuming that he could arbitrate to find a fair-minded balance, he made significant mistakes. One was to negotiate with the German civilian government rather than the generals, thus giving rise to the myth of the "stab in the back" by politicians. Another was misplaced optimism that the creation of a parliamentary government in Germany would make reparations less necessary. On the American side, his campaign for the League of Nations alienated Republicans. Franklin Delano Roosevelt, by contrast, attempted to build a postwar order by bipartisan enterprise. Truman and Eisenhower continued to counter the isolationists. They were helped by the specter of communism, which alarmed even the isolationists, but in any case they and their successors worked to support allies in both Europe and Asia. If a domestically divided United States turns inward to secure only its immediate interests, there is a risk of underestimating the danger of populist and aggressive dictators. The mistakes of a century ago should be ensconced in public memory as somber warnings to the United States in 2019.

After the German occupation of Greece in 1941, it seemed entirely likely that Cyprus would face invasion next. German control of Cyprus as the key strategic point in the eastern Mediterranean would threaten Egypt and the Suez Canal. But the island's defense posed difficult problems for the local colonial administration. Though Greek and Turkish Cypriots enlisted in the British Army, the British did not trust the Cypriot populace; later in the war, King George VI and Churchill were publicly denounced—"booed"—in movie theaters and elsewhere. **George Kelling** argues that the colonial administration assumed that there would be no "people's war" against a German invasion, as there had been in Crete. The British developed a plan of eleven fortifications on high ground called "keeps"—latter-day Crusader castles that would serve as bases for mobile columns engaging the enemy. The Governor, (Sir) William Battershill (who later prepared Tanganyika for independence and then retired to Cyprus), did not know that the Germans had no intention of invading the island. He remained ignorant of the breaking of the Ultra code. Had he been informed, he would have noted that German signals made no reference to Cyprus. The German attack on the Soviet Union, not Cyprus, proved to be the landmark of the war in the summer of 1941. Yet on the island there developed a long-range danger to the British. Later in the same year, the Greek Prime Minister proclaimed Cyprus to be among the daughters of Greece. Cyprus remained a Mediterranean stronghold that the British had no intention of relinquishing. But the war ineradicably invigorated the *enosis* movement, in which Greek Cypriots sought the union of the island with Greece.

In May 1948 the British abandoned Palestine without handing over authority to a successor government. **Bernard Wasserstein** describes a colonial administration attempting to preserve the semblance of a planned military withdrawal against the background of the intensifying civil war between Arabs and Jews. There were some 55,000 British soldiers in Palestine (only 3,000 more than the number of undergraduates at the University of Texas). How did they respond to changing circumstances of towns and villages controlled by one side or the other? In general the British assisted whichever side happened to be dominant in each locality. As the struggle between Jews and Arabs intensified, the British in the last stages of evacuation tended simply to go along with events. There was one major exception. In Haifa the British continued to control the port area. The Arabs in Haifa "fled in British army and navy convoys." On this point Wasserstein makes a harsh judgment: "Here the British not only acquiesced in partition; they colluded in what we would now call ethnic cleansing." In the rest of Palestine, the Arabs were badly trained and poorly armed except for King Abdullah's Arab Legion, commanded by British officers. The part of Palestine adjacent to Jordan was absorbed into the Kingdom of Jordan. Elsewhere the author addresses the question of British motivation during the last weeks of withdrawal, noting, "The actions of British soldiers were dictated neither solely by political partisanship nor by greed." The dominant impulse among the soldiers was simply to get home as soon as possible.

Derek Leebaert aims to shatter the preponderant myth that Britain ceased to be a world power after 1945. Were the British too weak and dispirited to sustain global influence? They certainly did not believe so themselves. They possessed the second-strongest military force as well as the largest colonial empire. They upheld political and military commitments in Asia, the Middle East, and Africa. On the American side, Leebaert was the first historian to use National Security Council Report 75, issued in 1950 (he himself had it declassified), which concluded that the British remained robust. They were still ahead of the United States, for example, in civil nuclear energy, jet aviation, and many of the sciences. British intelligence services were engaged worldwide and had a high degree of competence. The United States depended on the British to stabilize areas extending from Malaya to tropical Africa. Yet Britain had plunged into the first of its postwar financial crises in 1947. Two years later the British were forced to devalue the pound sterling by 30 percent. In 1951 the Iranian government nationalized the Anglo-Iranian Oil Company. Yet it was only in 1956, in the aftermath of Britain's Suez fiasco, that—in the judgment of the British as well as the Americans—Britain's strength as a world power began to fade. Leebaert resoundingly concludes that at the same time—only in the mid-1950s—did the United States emerge as a superpower.

It would spoil the fun to give more than a few examples from "Light Reading for Intellectual Heavyweights" by **Philip Waller**. Honesty is essential. If asked to choose a "desert island" book and you said *Finnegans Wake*, no one would believe you. A. J. P. Taylor proclaimed it "gibberish." He himself would have responded immediately with *The Good Soldier Schweik*. To those who are tired of reading the "100 Best Books," Waller recommends Jerome K. Jerome's *Idle Thoughts of an Idle Fellow*. The famous late-Victorian journalist W. T. Stead went down with the *Titanic*. But since he believed that the dead can communicate with the living, he might one day still report on his queries, made shortly before his embarkation, to twenty-nine Members of Parliament on their favorite reading. Waller uncovers some astonishing facts. Isaiah Berlin could rattle off the titles and plots of fifty Jules Verne novels. But perhaps the serendipitous prize would go to H. H. Asquith. To relieve the pressures of office while Prime Minister, he would sit in bed and translate Kipling into Greek. "Surely that was an effort," his wife once commented. "Not at all," he responded, "it was a relaxation."

Left to right: General Sir Alan Brooke, General Dwight Eisenhower, and Prime Minister Winston Churchill, in Eisenhower's headquarters camp near Rheims, France, 14 November 1944. Photograph by Ron Harvey. Everett Historical Collection / Alamy Stock Photo.

1

How Churchill's Mind Worked

PAUL ADDISON

When David Lloyd George succeeded Herbert Asquith as Prime Minister, in December 1916, Winston Churchill was out of office and in disgrace. Almost everyone, Lloyd George included, blamed him for the tragedy of the Gallipoli campaign, in which 132,000 British and Allied troops were killed or injured. Lloyd George, however, understood that although Churchill was down, he was far from out. Recognizing him as a politician of exceptional drive and ability, and potentially a dangerous opponent if excluded from office, he decided in July 1917 to bring Churchill into the government as Minister of Munitions. As he describes in his memoirs, it was a decision that provoked howls of protest from colleagues:

> Some of them were more excited about his appointment than about the war. It was a serious crisis. It was interesting to observe in a concentrated form every phase of the distrust and trepidation with which mediocrity views genius at close quarters.
> They admitted he was a man of dazzling talents, that he possessed a forceful and a fascinating personality. They recognised his courage and that he was an indefatigible worker. . . . His mind was a powerful machine, but there lay hidden in its material or its make-up some obscure defect which prevented it from always running true. When the mechanism went wrong, its very power made the action disastrous, not only to himself but to the causes in which he was engaged and the men with whom he was co-operating.[1]

This notion of Churchill as a man of great brilliance with a tragic flaw predated the First World War. At the height of the Ulster crisis in 1914, Sir Almeric Fitzroy, the clerk to the Privy Council, observed: "It is no disparagement of Winston's extraordinary qualities to say that his judgement is not quite equal to his abilities, nor his abilities quite equal to his ambitions. His defect is that he sees everything through the magnifying glass of his self-confidence."[2]

Though Churchill inspired doubts and fears, he also inspired something very like a sense of awe in his contemporaries. According to Samuel Johnson, the hallmark of genius was abundance, and no one was more abundant than Churchill. No one in public life could rival his literary achievements, nor—with the exception of Lloyd George—was there a more powerful orator and rhetorician. It also had to be admitted that he had substantial achievements to his name. In partnership with Lloyd George, he shared the credit for the introduction of national insurance. There was almost universal praise for his work in preparing the Royal Navy for war in 1914. But whatever the items on the credit side, they were outweighed by the notion that sooner or later he would career off the rails and crash into a ditch. Such was the justification that Stanley Baldwin and Neville Chamberlain gave for excluding him from office during the 1930s. As Baldwin put it, in conversation with his sidekick Thomas Jones in May 1936: "When Winston was born lots of fairies swooped down on his cradle with gifts—imagination, eloquence, industry, ability—and then came a fairy who said 'No one person has a right to so many gifts', picked him up and gave him such a shake and a twist that he was denied judgment and wisdom."[3]

The notion that Churchill lacked judgment was superseded by the conviction that he had been right about Nazi Germany when almost everyone else was wrong. It would be hard to overstate the damage inflicted on the reputations of Baldwin, Chamberlain, and the appeasers by the calamitous events of 1940, when France fell and Britain was threatened with invasion. They were vilified as the "Guilty Men" who, deceived by Hitler and the Nazis, had failed to rearm in time. The Munich Agreement of September 1938 became a badge of shame. Churchill, meanwhile, was hailed as the prophet and hero of the hour, a verdict he sought to carve in stone in the six volumes of war memoirs published between 1948 and 1953.

The historical debate over Churchill stemmed initially from the contradictions between these two competing narratives, the one rooted in the popular patriotism of the Second World War and Churchill's egocentric version of events, the other in the skepticism of the pre-war establishment, which began to bubble to the surface again after his death. Decades later there remains a spectrum of opinion on Churchill, with substantial differences between Churchillian loyalists (mainly in the United States), who see him as a paragon of leadership and statecraft; critical admirers (mainly in the United Kingdom), who see him as a great man with feet of clay; and iconoclasts (mainly in Ireland, India, and Australia), who denigrate his record and character. Iconoclasts, as a general rule, detest him too much to weigh the merits of his ideas. Loyalists think of him as exceptionally wise and perceptive, with a mind like a searchlight illuminating past, present, and future. Critical admirers are more likely to agree with Clement Attlee, a man of few words: "Fifty per cent of Winston is genius, fifty per cent bloody fool."[4] One of the keys to the assessment of Churchill is therefore to understand, or at any rate to describe, how that exceptional mind worked.

AT SCHOOL CHURCHILL WAS A PERSISTENT rule breaker: insubordinate, self-centered, arrogant, and conceited, a solitary boy unpopular with his peers. He excelled in English and history, subjects he enjoyed and put his mind to, but refused to make an effort with subjects that bored him—notably, Latin. As he matured into an adult, his intellect grew to reflect these egocentric traits and he began to detect in himself the promptings of genius. As he confided to Asquith's daughter Violet, at a dinner party in 1906: "We are all worms. But I do believe that I am a glow-worm."[5] He attributed his many narrow escapes from death on the battlefield to the fact that Providence was preserving him to fulfill some heroic destiny. One weekend, about 1910–11, Lloyd George and Churchill were motoring down to Lloyd George's home in Brighton in the company of a civil servant, Ralph Hawtrey, when Churchill began to speak of the next war. As Hawtrey recalled: "He described how, at the climax, he himself, in command of the army, would win the decisive victory in the Middle East, and would return to England in triumph. Lloyd George quietly interposed, 'And where do I come in?'"[6]

Ironically, Churchill's hopes of triumph were to be dashed, and his career all but wrecked by Gallipoli, while Lloyd George emerged as the great war leader. The middle-aged Churchill seems to have lost faith in his destiny, only to recover it as war drew near again in the late 1930s. In a famous passage in his war memoirs, he wrote of his emotions on his appointment as Prime Minister on 10 May 1940: "I felt as though I were walking with destiny and that all my past life had been but a preparation for this hour and for this trial."[7] One evening in London during the Blitz, he was out for a stroll with his detective, Inspector Thompson, when a bomb dropped where they had been walking only twenty seconds before. That night Churchill took Thompson by the arm and confided in him: "There is somebody looking after me besides you, Thompson." Thompson asked whether he was referring to Sergeant Davies. "No Thompson," Churchill replied, pointing a finger upward to heaven. "I have a mission to perform and That Person will see that it is performed."[8]

Churchill freely acknowledged that he was actuated by a thirst for fame and glory, and he was never ashamed of the fact, nor did it contradict his belief that he was serving a higher purpose. In February 1908, he told his friend Charles Masterman that he felt called upon by Providence to come to the rescue of the poor. Masterman questioned his sincerity: "You can't deny that you enjoy it all immensely—the speeches and crowds, the sense of increasing power." "Of course I do," Churchill replied. "Thou shalt not muzzle the ox when he treadeth out the corn. That shall be my plea at the day of judgment."[9] It was like the claim of a great painter or composer to be granted, in recognition of the unique importance of art, a license for self-indulgence.

Like other professional politicians, Churchill sought office and power. His creed was action, and he strove above all to perform great deeds for which he would be acclaimed in history. At a weekend house party in January 1915, Margot Asquith heard him exclaim: "My God! This is living History. Everything we are doing and saying is thrilling—it will be read by a thousand generations—think of that!"[10] According to Attlee, who was a member of Churchill's War Cabinet from 1940 to 1945: "If there was one thing that marked him out from the comparable figures in history, it was his characteristic way of standing back and looking at himself—and his country—as he believed history would."[11]

It is hard to imagine what would have become of Churchill in an age of stability, peace, and progress. He rejoiced in crises and conflicts and longed to be at the center of events. As Attlee remarked, he was always searching for a finest hour, and inclined to manufacture one if none could be found.

Uniquely among the politicians of his day, Churchill believed that he was endowed with the ability to command great armies in the field. As a cavalry subaltern, he had fought in India, Sudan, and South Africa. Fascinated by war and steeped in military history, he had come to the conclusion that an intelligent civilian could run military operations as well as or better than the generals. His two great heroes were his ancestor John Churchill, the first duke of Marlborough, and Napoleon, with whom he was often mockingly compared in the years before 1914. The journalist A. G. Gardiner, a radical commentator alarmed by Churchill's tendencies toward militarism, wrote in 1913:

> He is himself his most astonished spectator. He sees himself moving through the smoke of battle—triumphant, terrible, his brow clothed with thunder, his legions looking to him for victory, and not looking in vain. . . . It is not make-believe, it is not insincerity: it is that in that fervid and picturesque imagination there are always great deeds afoot with himself cast by destiny in the Agamemnon role.

Gardiner also struck a warning note: "Remember, he is a soldier first, last and always. He will write his name big in our future. Let us take care he does not write it in blood."[12] Although Churchill was always a parliamentary politician, there were times, as in the Second World War, when the politician was all but superseded by the generalissimo.

In party politics, Churchill was notoriously unreliable. First elected to Parliament as a Tory in 1900, he changed parties from Tory to Liberal in 1904, and from Liberal to Tory again in 1924. As Violet Bonham-Carter recalled in her memoirs, he was temperamentally neither a Tory nor a Liberal. Too untrammeled by convention to be a true Tory, "he never shared the reluctance which inhibits Liberals from invoking force to solve a problem."[13] He expected, in any case, to lead a party rather than follow it, and resented the restrictions placed on the freedom of action of Cabinet ministers by party dogmas.

HERE THEN WAS A MAN OF COMPULSIVE ambition, imperious independence of spirit, and ceaseless dynamism. If we are to understand the claim that he "lacked judgment," we need to observe him closely, through the eyes of his contemporaries, in the throes of decision making.

Our first witness, already mentioned, is Charles Masterman, a Liberal politician and friend of Churchill's who worked closely with him at the Board of Trade (1908–10) and the Home Office (1910–11). Masterman was astonished by the sight of his mental processes at work:

> In nearly every case an idea enters his head from outside. It then rolls round the hollow of his brain, collecting strength like a snowball. Then, after whirling winds of *rhetoric*, he becomes convinced that it is *right*, and denounces everyone who criticises it. He is in the Greek sense a Rhetorician, the slave of the words which his mind forms around ideas. He sets ideas to Rhetoric as

musicians set theirs to music. And he can convince himself of almost every truth if it is once allowed thus to start on its wild career through his rhetorical machinery.[14]

Our second witness is Neville Chamberlain, writing in August 1928 to his friend Lord Irwin, later Lord Halifax. Baldwin was Prime Minister, with Chamberlain as Minister of Health and Churchill as Chancellor of the Exchequer. Having collaborated with some difficulty over the expansion of social insurance, they were now fighting a series of battles over Churchill's plans to lower taxes on industry. Chamberlain wrote:

> One doesn't often come across a real man of genius or, perhaps, appreciate him when one does. Winston is such a man and he has *les defauts de ses qualites*. . . . Then as you know there is no subject on which he is not prepared to propound some novel theory and to sustain and illustrate his theory with cogent and convincing arguments. So quickly does his mind work in building up a case that it frequently carries him off his own feet.
>
> I have often watched him in Cabinet begin with a casual comment on what has been said, then as an image or simile comes into his mind proceed with great animation, when presently you see his whole face suffused with pink, his speech becomes more and more rapid and impetuous till in a few minutes he will not hear of the possibility of opposition to an idea which only occurred to him a few minutes ago.[15]

Another member of Baldwin's Cabinet, First Lord of the Admiralty William Bridgeman, recorded his impressions of Churchill, with whom he had clashed over the Chancellor's attempts to cut the naval estimates:

> The most indescribable & amazing character of all my colleagues. His fertile brain turned out ideas by the score on all subjects, very few of which bore the test of analysis, but that did not prevent the continuance of production. He laid eggs as rapidly as a partridge & if his nest was disturbed quickly started another, but the proportion of his eggs that came to maturity was small . . . He lives entirely in the present & takes his colour entirely from the particular office he happens to be holding at the time. A big navy-ite at the Admiralty, & the reverse as Chancellor of the Exchequer.[16]

Our next witness is Field Marshal Alan Brooke, the Chief of the Imperial General Staff, who chaired the Chiefs of Staff Committee from March 1942 until the end of the war. One of the most notable omissions from Churchill's war memoirs was any reference to the frequent rows between him and his military advisers, who spent much of the war resisting his proposals for military "sideshows." Brooke believed that Churchill was indispensable as a popular leader but incapable of strategic planning. After a discussion between the Prime Minister and the Chiefs of Staff on strategy in the Far East in May 1943, he noted:

> He [Churchill] again showed that he cannot grasp the relation of various theatres of war to each other. He always gets carried away by the one he is examining and in prosecuting it is prepared to sacrifice most of the others. I have never . . . succeeded in making him review the war as a whole and to relate the importance of various fronts to one each other. . . . We were intended to discuss the Mediterranean strategy, but it was not long before we were drawn off again to his pet of the moment in the shape of an attack on Northern Sumatra or Penang!![17]

Our final witness is Desmond Morton, a civil servant who supplied Churchill with secret intelligence about the German economy in the 1930s and served in wartime as a liaison officer between the Prime Minister and the security services. Having fallen out of favor with his master, he was a jaundiced witness but not necessarily a false one. Writing to the author R. W. Thompson in 1960, he suggested that

> more might be made of W's factual knowledge, which was astonishingly superficial and sketchy, even in matters in which he really thought himself something of an expert. He carried this off by a remarkable capacity for acquiring almost instantaneously the technical terms of the "science" concerned, together with an ability to memorise effective phrases in papers or conversations with real experts. . . . The things on which only a supreme expert could challenge him, and even might be rash to do so, were the English language, English and American history and, less so, the history of Western Europe.[18]

Churchill was patently lacking in most of the qualities that marked a politician out as a sound administrator and a "safe pair of hands." The question was whether the streak of genius in him compensated for the deficiency, or even perhaps eclipsed it altogether. Much depended on the skill of his advisers in managing him. In every office Churchill held, his fertile imagination gave rise to a stream of new ideas, some of them a great deal more practical than others. During the twenty-one months in which he was Home Secretary (1910–11), he won the admiration of the Permanent Secretary, Sir Edward Troup, and they made an effective team. As Troup recalled: "Once a week or perhaps oftener, Mr Churchill came down to the office bringing with him some adventurous and impossible projects: but after half an hour's discussion something was evolved which was less adventurous but no longer impossible."[19]

One of the most ill judged of Churchill's decisions was the appointment in October 1914 of Admiral Sir John Fisher as First Sea Lord and principal naval adviser. "Jackie" was as famous a public figure as Churchill himself, with an ego to match. "Volatile, emotional, duplicitous, secretive and inconsistent," he proved quite incapable of managing Churchill and more interested in intriguing against him.[20] Fisher was no less responsible for Gallipoli than Churchill, but his resignation in May 1915 ensured that it was Churchill who shouldered the blame. Fisher claimed that he resigned in protest against a decision by Churchill to overrule him on an operational matter, which, though technically true, made Churchill's position untenable. Churchill learned an enduring lesson. Though he often pressed the Chiefs of Staff hard in the Second World War, he never overruled them.

Unlike Fisher, most of Churchill's Whitehall advisers were conscientious gatekeepers, blocking ideas they thought dangerous or unworkable and encouraging him to practice the art of the possible. Chamberlain, as we have seen, wrote that "he wears out his guardians with the constant strain he puts upon them," and Brooke thought of himself as Churchill's long-suffering nanny. Churchill has to be seen as part of a collective process of decision making in the course of which many of his brainwaves were suppressed and others adapted for Whitehall consumption. An assessment of him also has to allow for his own acceptance of the process. Although he often argued a point of view with passion, and with anger when it was opposed, he had the common sense to abandon or revise it when confronted with a solid wall of opposition. There was always a sense in which he was trying out and testing ideas rather than seeking to impose them. Did he perhaps suspect that there was indeed something amiss with the hyperactive workings of his brain?

On the public stage, Churchill presented himself as a bold and consistent statesman, expert in the issues he was dealing with and logical in the path he was pursuing. Behind the mask lay a restless, more protean character who reached his decisions on the basis of impressions and rhetoric. His long political life was punctuated by a series of intuitive leaps from one position to another. Neither he nor anyone else could predict the direction he would take next. He would first shift his ground and then rationalize the change by arming himself with the facts and the rhetoric needed to justify his new position. In 1930, when he broke into rebellion against the leaders of his party over India, he knew very little about the affairs of the subcontinent. He sensed, however, that the promise of Dominion status for India would mark the end of the British Empire. He sensed also that Baldwin, the leader of the Conservative Party, was vulnerable to attack. Only after these considerations had prompted him to rebel did he turn to old India hands for information about the ethnic, religious, and constitutional problems of India,

The psychiatrist Anthony Storr identified Churchill as an "extraverted intuitive," one of eight psychological types defined by Carl Jung in a seminal work of 1921. "The intuitive," Jung wrote,

> is never to be found in the world of accepted reality-values, but he has a keen nose for anything new and in the making. Because he is always seeking out new possibilities, stable conditions suffocate him . . . Neither reason nor feeling can restrain him or frighten him away from a new possibility, even though it goes against all his previous convictions. Thinking and feeling, the indispensable components of conviction, are his inferior functions, carrying no weight and hence incapable of effectively withstanding the power of intuition.[21]

When Jung described the extraverted intuitive as always seeking out new possibilities, he might almost have been referring to Churchill, who was forever probing the ground ahead and exploring the shape of things to come. One of the recurrent features of his long political life was a vein of prophetic of utterance, sometimes looking forward with optimism to the "broad sunlit uplands," sometimes with foreboding to Armageddon. A passage in a speech delivered to the House of Commons in May 1901 still has the power to startle by its deadly accuracy:

> I have frequently been astonished since I have been in this House to hear with what composure, and how glibly Members, and even Ministers, talk of a European war. . . . In former days, when wars arose from individual causes, from the policy of a Minister or the passion of a King, when they were fought by small regular armies of professional soldiers, and when their course was retarded by the difficulties of communication and supply, and often suspended by the winter season, it was possible to limit the liabilities of the combatants. But now, when mighty populations are impelled on each other . . . when the resources of science and civilisation sweep away everything that might mitigate their fury, a European war can only end in the ruin of the vanquished and the scarcely less fatal commercial dislocation and exhaustion of the conquerors. Democracy is more vindictive than Cabinets. The wars of peoples will be more terrible than the wars of kings.[22]

Until the Second World War, Churchill was more likely to be written off as an alarmist than acclaimed for his foresight, but his warnings of the menace of Nazism in the 1930s established his enduring fame as a prophet. Rightly so, but it is salutary to recall that his judgments on defense policy and his predictions of the character of the next war were often wrong in detail. His campaign for "parity in the air," fueled by information secretly supplied to him in defiance of the Official Secrets Act by civil servants and officers in the RAF, was based on highly exaggerated estimates of the strength of the Luftwaffe. The numbers appeared to show that Britain had lost "air parity" in 1935 and had failed to recover it before the outbreak of war. Richard Overy's researches have shown, on the contrary, that between 1933 and 1937, nearly two-thirds of the aircraft produced for the Luftwaffe were noncombat planes. In principle, Churchill was right about Hitler's intention to build up a massive German air fleet, but until 1939 "the German air force was no real threat to Britain."[23]

Nor did secret intelligence enlighten him about the Luftwaffe's strategic intentions. Like every one else in the British establishment, he assumed that Hitler was building up his air force with the intention of mounting a "knock-out blow" against London. The Luftwaffe, however, was designed to act in support of the army and the navy. There was no plan at any time in the 1930s for an air offensive against Britain or an all-out attack on London. It was only as a consequence of the defeat of the British and French on land in 1940, a disaster that took Churchill and almost everyone else by surprise, that the Luftwaffe was in a position to mount an air offensive against Britain. Nor was this the only earth-shattering development that he failed to anticipate. Intensely preoccupied with the threat from Nazi Germany, he failed to spot the danger posed by Japan to the British Empire in the Far East. In a memorandum on sea power he sent to Chamberlain in March 1939, he wrote: "Consider how vain is the menace that Japan will send a fleet and army to conquer Singapore. It is as far from Japan as Southampton from New York . . . One can take it as quite certain that Japan would not run such a risk."[24]

DID CHURCHILL LACK "JUDGMENT"? The scientist and novelist C. P. Snow, himself a wartime civil servant, recognized both the truth of the claim and its limitations. In a shrewd survey of the problem, he drew a distinction between the virtues of judgment and insight:

"Judgement," to people concerned with political decisions, means two things—one which most of us would think bad, one good. . . .

> The good thing in "judgment" is the ability to think of many matters at once, in their interdependence, their relative importance and their consequences. In this sense, I don't think there is any burking the fact Churchill's judgment was, on a great many occasions in his life, seriously defective. . . .
>
> Judgement is a fine thing: but it is not all that uncommon. Deep insight is much rarer. Churchill had flashes of that kind of insight, dug up from his own nature, independent of influences, owing nothing to anyone outside himself. Sometimes it was a better guide than judgement: in the ultimate crisis when he came to power, there were times when judgment itself could . . . become a source of weakness.
>
> When Hitler came to power, Churchill did not use judgement, but one of his deep insights. This was absolute danger, there was no easy way round . . . Not many men in conservative England had such insight. Churchill had.[25]

It was Churchill's intuitive qualities that transformed him, in the summer of 1940, into a great war leader. Never had the need for inspirational egotism been greater. At a time when unity was imperative, Churchill was a politician who transcended party, and a sublime orator with the skill to express the will of the people. His burning passion for war was reinforced by the conviction that he was uniquely qualified to direct it. He believed that he was acting with divine help and guidance. His war aims were the defeat of Nazi Germany, the liberation of the occupied nations, and the preservation of the British Empire. How victory could be won he did not know, but intuition told him that it could be, and his imagination strode ahead of reality in seven-league boots. Perhaps it was Churchill's "lack of judgment" that saved the nation.

Fall Semester 2017

1. David Lloyd George, *The War Memoirs of David Lloyd George* (1934), III, pp. 1070–71.

2. Quoted in Andrew Roberts, *Churchill: Walking with Destiny* (2018), p. 176.

3. Quoted in Martin Gilbert, *Churchill: A Life* (1991), p. 556.

4. Quoted in Lord Moran, *Winston Churchill: The Struggle for Survival, 1940–1965* (1966), p. 777.

5. Violet Bonham Carter, *Winston Churchill as I Knew Him* (1965), p. 16.

6. Quoted in Martin Gilbert, *In Search of Churchill: A Historian's Journey* (1994), p. 175.

7. Winston S. Churchill, *The Second World War*, I, *The Gathering Storm* (1948), p. 527.

8. Tom Hickman, *Churchill's Bodyguard* (2005), p. 106.

9. Lucy Masterman, *C. F. G. Masterman: A Biography* (1939), pp. 97–98.

10. Quoted in Gilbert, *Churchill: A Life*, p. 294.

11. Lord Attlee, "Churchill: The Man I Knew," *Observer*, 31 Jan. 1965.

12. A. G. Gardiner, *Pillars of Society* (1913), pp. 57–58, 68.

13. Bonham Carter, *Churchill as I Knew Him*, p. 197.

14. Quoted in Robert Rhodes James, *Churchill: A Study in Failure, 1900–1939* (1973 edn.), pp. 33–34. Rhodes James does not give the source of the quotation, which I have not been able to find elsewhere.

15. Chamberlain to Halifax, 12 Aug. 1928, in Martin Gilbert, ed., *Winston S. Churchill: Companion Volume V, Part 1, The Exchequer Years, 1922–1929* (1979), pp. 1328–29.

16. Philip Williamson, ed., *The Modernisation of Conservative Politics: The Diaries and Letters of William Bridgeman, 1904–1935* (1988), pp. 233–34.

17. Field Marshal Lord Alanbrooke, diary entry for 10 May 1943, in *War Diaries, 1939–1945* (2001), ed. Alex Danchev and Daniel Todman, p. 401.

18. Morton to Thompson, 16 Aug. 1960, in R. W. Thompson, *Churchill and Morton* (1976), pp. 71–72.

19. Quoted in Masterman, *C. F. G. Masterman*, p. 135.

20. Christopher Bell, *Churchill and the Dardanelles* (2017), p. 9.

21. Anthony Storr, "The Man," in A. J. P. Taylor et al., *Churchill: Four Faces and the Man* (1973), p. 213; C. G. Jung and John Beebe, *Psychological Types* (1921; 2017 edn.), pp. 340–41.

22. Churchill, speech in the House of Commons, 13 May 1901, in Robert Rhodes James, ed., *Winston S Churchill: His Complete Speeches, 1897–1963; Volume I: 1897–1908* (1974), p. 82.

23. Richard Overy, "German Air Strength, 1933 to 1939: A Note," *Historical Journal*, 27, 2 (1984), p. 469.

24. Churchill, "Memorandum on Sea Power, 1939," 27 Mar. 1939, in Martin Gilbert, ed., *Winston S. Churchill: Companion Volume V, Part 3, The Coming of War, 1936–1939* (1982), p. 1415.

25. C. P. Snow, *Variety of Men* (1969 edn.), pp. 136–38.

Éamon de Valera, c. 1922–30. Photograph by the National Photo Company. Digital ID cph 3b15291, Prints and Photographs Division, Library of Congress.

2

Éamon de Valera

KEVIN KENNY

É amon De Valera was the dominant figure in Irish politics
for almost half a century, from his role in the Easter Rising
of 1916 to his last term as *Taoiseach* (prime minister), which
ended in 1959. After that, he served two seven-year terms in the ceremonial but influential office of President of Ireland. The architect
of the Irish state, de Valera is also the most controversial and divisive figure in modern Irish history. It is fair to say that he is currently
more disliked than liked in Ireland, for two main reasons. First, his
rejection of the Anglo-Irish Treaty of 1921 contributed in significant measure to the civil war that directly followed. The treaty split,
rather than a conventional left-right spectrum, has defined Irish
party politics ever since. While de Valera remains a hero to some
hard-line republican nationalists, his role in the treaty negotiations
and the civil war earned him an enduring reputation as dogmatic,
self-righteous, and anti-democratic. Second, because de Valera was
the dominant political figure in Ireland for so long, retiring from
the presidency only at the age of ninety, when he was almost fully
blind, he is generally perceived as having overstayed his time and as
embodying an Ireland beset by an economic and cultural backwardness of which he seemed at best dimly aware. De Valera believed in
economic self-sufficiency more than development. He did nothing
to stop the massive emigration that characterized Ireland throughout the twentieth century as much as it had in the nineteenth. And
he clung to a deeply conservative approach on social questions. Add

to this the censorship he introduced during and after the Second
World War, and de Valera's Ireland emerges as a bleak and narrow-
minded place.

The case against de Valera, then, is a strong one. But so, too,
is the case in his favor. When he returned to power in the 1930s,
a decade after the treaty split, he drafted a new constitution that
made Ireland a republic in all but name. And he carved out a space
for Irish neutrality that carried Ireland through the crisis of world
war. In these two ways in particular, Éamon de Valera created modern Ireland as a sovereign state.

Biographies of Éamon de Valera have ranged from initial hagiography, through bitter criticism, to more recent, well-balanced
appraisals. The official biography published by Lord Longford
and Thomas P. O'Neill (*Éamon de Valera*, 1970) was by the nature
of its genre long on praise and short on critical judgment, being
told largely from its protagonist's perspective. Tim Pat Coogan, a
well-known Irish newspaper editor, set out to provide a corrective in
his 700-page *Éamon de Valera: The Man Who Was Ireland*, published
in 1995. Coogan had previously published a biography of Michael
Collins, de Valera's chief antagonist in the civil war, whom Coogan regarded as the legitimate architect of the Irish state. In the
film *Michael Collins* (1996), the eponymous hero—played by Liam
Neeson—and the craven, duplicitous figure of de Valera—brilliantly
though surely inaccurately portrayed by the late Alan Rickman—
largely conformed to Coogan's interpretation.

Coogan's biography of de Valera, though comprehensive, is something of a hatchet job. "Was he a Lincoln or a Machiavelli?" Coogan
asked at the outset. "A saint or a charlatan? A man of peace, or one
who incited young men to hatred and violence?"[1] The very terms of
this inquiry virtually ensured that the latter attributes in each pair
would not only get a serious airing but would, on balance, win out.
Coogan's de Valera was vain, self-righteous, petulant, dogmatic, de-
vious, and always angling for power. Coogan found de Valera's handling of the treaty negotiations "irresponsible" and "born out of a
reckless pride." As a result of de Valera's actions, Coogan concluded,
"Ireland's course was set in bitterness and small horizons."[2] And "on
the great challenges" that confronted him in office—partition, the
economy, and emigration—"de Valera did little that was useful and
much that was harmful."[3]

Recent biographers, by contrast, have emphasized de Valera's accomplishments as a nation-builder. Professor Diarmaid Ferriter of
University College Dublin began the process of revising the revision-
ists in 2007, with his thoroughly documented and lavishly illustrated

Judging Dev: A Reassessment of the Life and Legacy of Eamon de Valera.[4] Professor Ronan Fanning, also of University College Dublin, offered a short, subtle, and sophisticated account in 2015, *Éamon de Valera: A Will to Power.* Recognizing de Valera as the most significant figure in the political history of modern Ireland as well as the most controversial, Fanning sought "to define the magnitude of his political achievement."[5] Most recently, the broadcaster and historian David McCullagh, drawing extensively on de Valera's personal archives, along with Irish, British, and American official records, produced a comprehensive, well-balanced, and accessible two-part biography, *De Valera: Rise, 1882–1932* (2017) and *De Valera: Rule, 1932–1973* (2018), which will remain the standard work for quite some time. Like Coogan, Fanning and McCullagh are harshly critical of de Valera's intransigence over the treaty negotiations and his culpability in Ireland's civil war. But they lend much greater weight to his subsequent political and diplomatic contributions, especially in the 1930s and 1940s. Drawing on these recent, more judicious appraisals, this essay interweaves an assessment of Éamon de Valera's achievements into a political biography that examines his strengths and weaknesses as a political leader, his role in the treaty split and the civil war, his crafting of a new constitution that paved the way for a full-fledged independent republic, and the question of neutrality, which he saw as the key to national sovereignty.

Éamon De Valera was born in New York City in 1882, the only child of an Irish immigrant named Catherine Coll (b. 1856) and a Spanish sculptor named Juan Vivion de Valera (b. 1853). Catherine Coll emigrated in 1879 from Bruree, County Limerick, to Brooklyn, where, like many Irish women of her generation, she entered domestic service. The details of Vivion de Valera's background are obscure; he may have been born in the Basque country, the son of an army officer who moved his family from Spain to Cuba. According to Éamon de Valera's account, as told to him by his mother, his parents were married in New Jersey in 1881. No documentary evidence of the marriage survived, and his political opponents occasionally raised the specter of illegitimacy. But in general, de Valera used his exotic surname to cultivate an aura of being above the fray of Irish politics. Known early on as the "Spaniard," he was sometimes referred to as the "Long Fellow" (because of his height, six feet one inch), and eventually and universally as "Dev."

Like many of his generation, de Valera was radicalized by the Home Rule crisis that broke out in 1912. He joined the paramilitary Irish Volunteers at their inaugural meeting, in Dublin in November 1913, and his diligent attendance at weekly drill meetings, combined with his interest in advanced military exercises, won him promotion to captain of his own company. With the Lords' veto over the House of Commons reduced in 1911 to a three-year moratorium, the Home Rule bill was finally passed in September 1914. But war had just broken out in Europe, and the measure was suspended for the duration of the conflict. John Redmond, the leader of the dominant, moderate, nationalist Irish Party, sensing a chance to demonstrate the compatibility of Home Rule with imperial loyalty and unity, recommended that the Irish enlist and fight. Although 210,000 Irishmen eventually served in the British Army during the war and 35,000 died—including Redmond's brother Willy—the result was a split within the Irish Volunteers. The great majority sided with Redmond, but about 7,500 men broke away—among them Éamon de Valera—and this extremist group played a central role in the lead-up to the Easter 1916 rising.

De Valera played only a minor part in the rising, commanding an isolated outpost (at Boland's Mill), but the events of Easter week made his reputation and laid the foundation for his political career. He was one of ninety leaders sentenced to death by a military court (of whom fifteen were executed). De Valera's wife, Sinéad (his Irish teacher when they met, in 1908), asked the American consul to intervene on the grounds that he was a U.S. citizen. But de Valera may have been saved partly by a stroke of luck. Despite a telegram from Asquith calling for a halt to the shootings, Maxwell proceeded with the execution of the socialist leader James Connolly on 12 May. He then asked the Crown prosecuting officer (W. E. Wylie) whether the next prisoner on the list, Éamon de Valera, was of any importance. "No," said Wylie. "He is a school-master who was taken at Boland's Mill."[6] McCullagh places less weight on this story than Coogan, suggesting that the timing was crucial. All but two of the men who were executed faced court-martial before de Valera, and he too would have been shot, McCullagh concludes, if he had been sentenced.

De Valera spent the next year behind bars, first in Mountjoy Jail in Dublin and then in four English prisons (Dartmoor, Lewes, Maidstone, and Pentonville). It was in prison that—like many subsequent colonial leaders, especially in Africa—he made the transition from soldier to politician, establishing himself as the undisputed leader of the Irish revolution. Older than most of his companions and enjoying military seniority as a surviving commanding officer of the Easter Rising, de Valera defied the authorities, insisted on political prisoner status, embraced solitary confinement, and won the unequivocal respect of his fellow prisoners. Selected as the candidate for a by-election in the constituency of Clare East before his release,

Figure 2.1. Éamon de Valera under arrest in Richmond Barracks after the 1916 Easter Rising.

he agreed to run on the Sinn Féin ticket and was elected by a two-to-one majority (commencing forty years of uninterrupted victories in that seat). De Valera returned to Ireland in June 1917 a popular hero, and was elected in October as president of both the new revolutionary party Sinn Féin (a post he held until 1926) and the Irish Volunteers (known as the Irish Republican Army, or IRA, from 1919 onward).

De Valera consolidated his leadership by leading a successful campaign against conscription, during which he skillfully secured the support of the Irish hierarchy. The bishops' proclamation that the Irish people had the right to resist conscription by every means consonant with God's law was a critical step toward legitimacy for Sinn Féin as a political party. Faced with this opposition, the British government backed down on extending conscription to Ireland, but de Valera and seventy-two Sinn Féin leaders were arrested in May 1918 on trumped-up allegations of plotting with German agents. De Valera spent eight months in Lincoln Jail, during which time he was returned unopposed for Clare East in the general election of December 1918, when Sinn Féin ousted the old pro–Home Rule Irish Party and Ireland's self-declared parliament, Dáil Éireann, met for its inaugural session, on 21 January 1919.

De Valera escaped from Lincoln Jail in February 1919 and considered going straight to the United States, in the belief that he could best advance Ireland's case for self-determination by bringing pressure to bear on President Woodrow Wilson. He was persuaded to return to Dublin, where he attended Dáil Éireann and was elected president of that body on 1 April. He nonetheless left Ireland in June 1919 for an eighteen-month tour of the United States, where he eventually grew impatient with Irish American efforts to lobby Wilson, concentrating his energies instead on raising funds to support the Irish republic. In de Valera's opinion, Ireland did not need to be granted the right of self-determination by any council of international powers; it had already exercised that right, of its own volition, in the insurrection of 1916 and the election of 1918. Irish Americans, he concluded, should stop devoting their time and money to opposing the Versailles Treaty and should instead help Ireland in its war of independence against the British. To secure control over American funds, de Valera bypassed the existing Irish American nationalist societies in 1920 and set up his own organization, the American Association for the Recognition of the Irish Republic. During his time in the United States, he issued up to $5 million dollars in bond certificates whereby Americans could support the war for Irish independence.

De Valera returned to Ireland on 23 December 1920, the same day that Parliament enacted the Government of Ireland Act, partitioning the island into two unequal parts. The six northeastern counties constituting Northern Ireland remained part of the United Kingdom; the status of the remaining twenty-six counties would soon be up for negotiation. After a truce came into effect on 11 July 1921, de Valera met David Lloyd George four times at 10 Downing Street but rejected an offer of effective Dominion status with safeguards for British defense interests. The two leaders continued to correspond until September, when de Valera accepted an invitation for an Irish delegation to attend a conference in London to determine the nature of Ireland's association with the empire. The conference began on 11 October.

De Valera himself refused to attend the conference, and his decision to send a delegation led by Arthur Griffith and Michael Collins has been a source of endless criticism and recrimination ever since. He claimed subsequently that he remained at home to avoid compromising the republic, to evade any trickery by Lloyd George, and to ensure that any final decision would be taken in Dublin rather than London. Based on his previous meetings with Lloyd George, however, he knew how inexperienced the Irish team would be compared with their British counterparts, who included Winston

Churchill as well as Lloyd George. And in retrospect, it seems clear that he ought to have explained clearly to the Irish delegates that, in his view, they did not have full plenipotentiary power to agree to a treaty. But de Valera's authority in Ireland had been so unquestioned since 1916 that he apparently saw no need to offer any such explanation. He did not anticipate that the Irish delegates would bond as a team during their journeys back and forth to London by sea and rail, that they would be worn down by the British negotiators, or above all that they would eventually sign an agreement without his approval, which they duly did on 6 December.[7]

Collins remarked pragmatically and presciently that the treaty, while it did not grant full independence, gave Ireland the freedom to achieve freedom. De Valera, however, rejected the agreement out of hand. Instead, he proposed his own version of "external association" in the so-called Document Number 2. The treaty negotiated in London provided for the Irish Free State to become a Dominion of the British Empire in which the King would be the head of state, with a governor-general as his representative. Members of the Irish parliament would swear an oath of allegiance not only to the constitution of the Irish Free State but also to the King, in virtue of the Irish people's common citizenship with the British, and the state's membership in the Commonwealth. But de Valera, insisting that the only source of authority over Ireland was the Irish people, could not accept this arrangement. Under his alternative plan, Ireland would cooperate with other Commonwealth powers on matters of common concern, but representatives to Dáil Éireann would swear an oath only to the constitution of the Irish Free State, rather than to the King as head of that state, while recognizing the monarch as head of the Commonwealth, an association to which Ireland voluntarily belonged.

The issue at stake, in short, was the sovereignty of the twenty-six counties (rather than partition, which was now a fait accompli). Would southern Ireland constitute an independent republic? Or would it retain an allegiance to the British Empire that required the members of its government to swear an oath of loyalty to the Crown, with the King remaining Ireland's head of state? For de Valera, moreover, there could be no sense in which the Irish Republic was seceding from the empire. Ireland had nothing to secede from: the union had been imposed, not chosen, and Ireland had reasserted a national sovereignty in 1916 that stretched back through time immemorial. The only secessionists in the Irish case were the Ulster Unionists, who supported the partition of a nation whose territorial sovereignty was inviolable.

De Valera expected to win majority support for his alternative formulation, but the Dáil approved the treaty, 64–57, on 7 January 1922. He resigned as president of Dáil Éireann, stood for reelection to that office, and was defeated by the even narrower margin of 60–58 on 10 January. Unable to accept this outcome, de Valera took the profoundly undemocratic step of withdrawing from the Dáil with his supporters. Like Coogan, Fanning sees a large element of wounded pride here. Having enjoyed almost unquestioned deference since 1916, de Valera seemed unable to deal with defiance of his will. "He opposed the treaty," as Fanning puts it, "not because it was *a* compromise but because it was not *his* compromise—not, that is, a compromise that he had authorized in advance of its conclusion."[8] There would have been armed conflict over the treaty even without de Valera, since republican extremists were determined to resist its implementation. He was caught between the pro-treaty forces and extremist forces he had never controlled, who supported him only insofar as it benefited their hard-line cause to do so. But de Valera's pronouncements as the crisis escalated certainly enhanced the chances of war and shaped the course it would take. On St. Patrick's Day 1922, he declared that if the treaty were accepted, the IRA "would have to wade through Irish blood, through the blood of the soldiers of the Irish government, and through, perhaps, the blood of some of the members of the government in order to get Irish freedom."[9] The following month, anti-treaty forces occupied the Four Courts in Dublin, and the storming of that building by the Irish Free State army on 28 June ignited a war that lasted until 27 April 1923.

In the general election of August 1923, de Valera's Sinn Féin candidates won 44 of the 155 Dáil seats contested. But they refused to take their seats, on the grounds that the Irish Free State was invalid. De Valera was arrested by Free State troops on 15 August 1923 and detained until 16 July 1924. This was the low point of his career. But he was already planning his slow return to power.

IN 1926, ÉAMON DE VALERA RESIGNED as president of Sinn Féin and announced the formation of a new political party, Fianna Fáil, with the stated objectives of securing the political independence of a united Irish Republic, restoring the Irish language, and implementing a social system of equal opportunity, land redistribution, and economic self-sufficiency. In the 1927 general election, Fianna Fáil won 44 seats, and the government party declined from 63 to 47. But the Fianna Fáil deputies still would not take their seats if they had to swear an oath of allegiance to the Crown. Following the IRA's assassination of the prominent Free State politician Kevin O'Higgins, the government introduced a bill requiring candidates for the Irish parliament to declare their intention, before nomination, to take the oath if elected. De Valera advised Fianna Fáil's national executive that they had to choose between entering the Dáil or forsaking political action. He issued a press release explaining that the required declaration was not really an oath but simply an empty political formula carrying no obligation of loyalty to the English Crown. Why he could not have seen the matter in this way in January 1922 remained unexplained. (McCullagh points out that taking the oath in 1922 involved an individual roll call before an official acting as the representative of the governor-general, whereas five years later it merely required signing the parliamentary clerk's book.) De Valera and his Fianna Fáil deputies signed their names in August 1927, denying that their signatures involved any transfer of allegiance to the Crown and entering the Irish parliament as the party of republican opposition.

In the general election of 1932, Fianna Fáil secured a majority with the support of the Labour Party and some independents. In the context of recent Irish and European politics, the transition of power was strikingly peaceful and democratic. Along with head of government (*Taoiseach*), de Valera took on the position of Minister for External Affairs. De Valera wanted to remove the remaining impediments to Irish independence and, on that basis, to carve out a position for Ireland as a neutral state in a world beset by growing ideological divisions. He moved quickly to enact his agenda, introducing legislation to abolish the oath on 20 April 1932 (though it was not enacted until the following May because of opposition in the senate). In 1935, de Valera began working on a new constitution for Ireland, taking advantage of the British abdication crisis the following year to implement its central features. On 10 December 1936, the day that Edward VIII stepped down, the Irish cabinet agreed to delete all mention of the King and the governor-general from the existing constitution. By 12 December, de Valera had pushed through legislation to this effect. Ireland's new constitution, approved by the Dáil on 14 June and endorsed by the Irish people in a referendum on 1 July, came into effect on 29 December 1937.

The Constitution created an independent Irish state, though without using the word "republic." Article 1 affirmed the Irish nation's "inalienable, indefeasible, and sovereign right to choose its own form of government, to determine its relations with other nations, and develop its life, political, economic, and cultural, in accordance with its own genius and traditions." Article 5 declared that "Ireland is a sovereign, independent, democratic state." But de Valera chose the name *Éire* (Ireland) rather than *Poblacht na hÉireann* ("The Republic of Ireland"), thereby retaining a vague relationship with the

Commonwealth, in part because he feared that Irish-born citizens might be deprived of their rights in Britain or that the safety valve of emigration might be closed. He also claimed subsequently that the term "republic" should not be used for the twenty-six counties alone, but only for the thirty-two counties of Ireland when they were duly reunited.

Article 44, conferring a "special position" on the Catholic Church, is among the most controversial aspects of de Valera's constitution. He drafted this article himself and did not reveal its wording until he shared the text of the full document with his cabinet on 28 April, the day before it went, unchanged, for printing. Article 44 was roundly criticized by later generations for favoring the Catholic Church, but in context it can be seen as a compromise. Given the power of the Catholic Church in Irish society, the hierarchy had wanted exclusive, not merely special, recognition. De Valera was personally sympathetic to the hierarchy's view, but he realized that the idea of an established church was politically unfeasible. The Constitution not only avoided so extreme a formulation, but also took pains to make explicit references to the rights of Protestants and (significantly in the context of the late 1930s) Jews.

Satisfied that his new constitution had reconciled sovereignty with majority rule—a formula he had signally failed to arrive at in 1922 when he rejected democracy in favor of national integrity—de Valera moved to repudiate the IRA. Now that the Irish people had established a state in accordance with their own wishes, he regarded any attempt to overthrow that state as sedition. The Treason Act of 1937 was passed with extremist republicans in mind. When the IRA, as the self-styled "government of the Irish Republic," launched a bombing campaign in England in 1939, de Valera reinforced the Treason Act with a new Offences Against the State Act. And in 1940, aware that IRA overtures to Hitler's Germany threatened to give Britain a pretext to infringe on Irish neutrality, he enacted draconian emergency-powers legislation under which IRA prisoners were interned without trial. Among those who were tried, some were executed by military tribunal and others were allowed to die on hunger strikes. By 1940, then, de Valera had distanced himself decisively from his erstwhile extremist republican allies, but in pursuit of an agenda that had remained strikingly consistent over time—the creation of an independent Ireland.

De Valera's second great accomplishment in the 1930s was to lay the ground for Irish neutrality, which helped the country survive the Second World War. The sole remaining restriction on Irish sovereignty, under the defense annex to the 1921 treaty, was Britain's retention of the harbor defenses at Berehaven, Cobh (Queenstown), and Lough Swilly. Unlike the oath and the governor-generalship, de Valera could not dismantle this restriction unilaterally: he would have to persuade the British to depart. After negotiations with Neville Chamberlain's government, it was agreed in April 1938 that all defense facilities retained by the British would be handed over to the Irish government. Even as the ports were being formally transferred, however, the Irish and British intelligence services cooperated closely on counterespionage and other security matters. De Valera had long believed that an independent Ireland would never threaten Britain. On the contrary, Irish independence would benefit both countries. Provided that Britain respected Irish sovereignty, Ireland would have a vested interest in its neighbor remaining strong. And Britain would benefit from Ireland's refusal to cooperate with enemy powers. In de Valera's mind, therefore, neutrality entailed mutual cooperation with Britain and a commitment to prevent Germany from using Irish territory in the event of war.

De Valera maneuvered Ireland, for the most part expertly, through the challenges of the war. An outward display of absolute neutrality was essential to preserve Ireland's sovereignty. But at the same time, aware that a German victory would destroy that sovereignty, Ireland furnished considerable assistance to Britain in secret, including permission for overflights of Irish territory, transmission of coast-watching and meteorological reports, and shared intelligence. Censorship prevented the public from knowing the extent of this cooperation. Chamberlain in 1940, and Churchill in 1941, offered a united Ireland in return for the abandonment of neutrality and use of the treaty ports. But de Valera, refusing to compromise Irish independence, rejected these proposals out of hand. Nor, of course, was he naïve enough to assume that Chamberlain or Churchill had the intention or the ability to follow through on their wartime overtures.

De Valera's pursuit of neutrality significantly enhanced his position as a statesman. He rather spoiled the effect on 2 May 1945 with his insistence that strict neutrality required him to visit the German envoy in Dublin, Edouard Hempel, to pay his condolences on the occasion of Hitler's death—a gesture that infuriated the British and, even more so, the Americans. Yet by his own punctilious standards, de Valera believed that he had behaved "correctly" and "wisely."[10] He was merely extending basic diplomatic courtesies; he had called on the U.S. ambassador, David Gray, two weeks earlier when Roosevelt died, and it was incumbent upon him to do the same in the German case. Yet given what de Valera knew about the Holocaust by

Figure 2.2. Éamon de Valera, President of Ireland, c. 1964. Wikimedia Commons.

this time, Fanning is correct that de Valera's action was "grotesquely ill-judged."[11] McCullagh, while he shows that de Valera was provoked to act as he did by Gray's insistence that Ireland turn over the archive of the German legation, sees the visit to the legation as "his biggest blunder of the war."[12] This one notorious incident aside, de Valera's policy on neutrality was notably successful. He emerged victorious from an exchange of radio broadcasts with Churchill two weeks later when the British Prime Minister, congratulating himself for his self-restraint at not having reoccupied the treaty ports, made several sneering references to the Irish leader and his policies. De Valera, in a dignified response regarded as one of his finest speeches, calmly reiterated that neutrality was the sine qua non of Irish independence.

Éamon de Valera went on to serve three terms as *Taoiseach* and two as president. But it is primarily on the period through the end of the Second World War that he must be judged. He may have been authoritarian, pedantic, and self-righteous, but these same qualities were the key to the unshakeable self-confidence that defined his political leadership. "Whenever I wanted to know what the Irish peopled wanted," he declared on the eve of the treaty split, "I had only to examine my own heart, and it told me straight off what the Irish people wanted."[13] This formulation entailed consigning large numbers of Irish people to the category of "un-Irish"—not only a million Northern Protestants, but also those in the rest of Ireland who disagreed with de Valera on politics, culture, or anything else. Yet if de Valera's self-confidence was his greatest weakness, contributing to the calamity of the civil war, it also allowed him to create a new Irish nation-state. His style of leadership was so skilled and self-assured that it made him seem like Ireland's only natural leader—in his own eyes and in the eyes of most Irish voters. In this respect there is perhaps a partial comparison with General de Gaulle. The two men had very different personalities, of course, the one extroverted and volatile and the other introverted and reserved. What they had in common was unshakable self-confidence in matters of state. They met in 1969 in the twilight of their careers, when President de Valera hosted the former French president in Dublin. Each of them, for better and for worse, saw himself and his country as one and the same.

Fall Semester 2018

I would like to thank Professor Wm. Roger Louis for inviting me to give the first draft of this essay as a lecture at the British Studies Seminar on 26 October 2018, and Professor Toyin Falola for his insightful comments on that occasion

1. Tim Pat Coogan, *Éamon de Valera: The Man Who Was Ireland* (New York, 1995), 1.
2. Ibid., pp. 695, 696.
3. Ibid., p. 693.
4. Diarmaid Ferriter, *Judging Dev: A Reassessment of the Life and Legacy of Eamon de Valera* (Dublin, 2007).
5. Ronan Fanning, *Éamon de Valera: A Will to Power* (London, 2015), p. 1.
6. Wylie quoted in Coogan, *Éamon de Valera*, p. 78.
7. Fanning, *Éamon de Valera*, pp. 103–7.
8. Fanning, *Éamon de Valera*, p. 265.
9. Fanning, *Éamon de Valera*, p. 133.
10. Éamon de Valera to Robert Brennan, quoted in Fanning, *Éamon de Valera*, p. 197.
11. Ibid., p. 610.
12. David McCullagh, *De Valera: Rule, 1932–1975* (Dublin, 2018), p. 252.
13. Éamon de Valera, speech on 6 Jan. 1922, quoted in Fanning, *Éamon de Valera*, p. 128.

Calouste Gulbenkian, c. 1900.

3

Calouste Gulbenkian
Mr. Five Percent

RICHARD DAVENPORT-HINES

When Calouste Gulbenkian died, in 1955, *The Times* compared him to Ferdinand de Lesseps and Cecil Rhodes, two business visionaries who created commercial kingdoms. In the first half of the twentieth century, Gulbenkian made deals in the international oil business, took percentages, and accumulated a vast fortune.

Gulbenkian was a man of astounding self-reliance, with almost invincible willpower. He managed his vast interests with a very small staff. He was, said his daughter, "a Special Number" who lived on his own terms and behaved as he wanted. Rules, including taxation regulations, existed for him to evade or defy. Without any trace of conscious eccentricity, he was different from other people; his manners, his methods, and his moods were fascinating.

He was born in 1869 in the Constantinople suburb of Scutari. His father, of Armenian heritage, was a trader in kerosene. He studied physics at the École de Commerce in Marseille and at King's College London before making an expedition to Baku in 1888. This was his sole visit to an oil-producing area in his long business life. The duplication of extraction facilities and the hopeless waste that he saw there gave him the mission that dominated the rest of his life: to lead, in the words of Jonathan Conlin, "the orderly development and consolidation of a fragmented oil industry through vertical integration and international cartels." Conlin's *Mr. Five Per Cent: The Many Lives of Calouste Gulbenkian, the World's Richest Man* (2019), outshines all previous accounts of its subject's life. A calm, lucid, fair-minded writer, Conlin resists every temptation to indulge in cheap sensation or glib judgment, and he refrains from making a burdensome heap of every detail and statistic. He does Gulbenkian proud.

In his twenties, when the world market was dominated by Russian and American oil producers, "Gulbenkian saw the potential for cartels to take the politics out of upstream activities (that is, production), by ensuring that no single power predominated," writes Conlin. "Empires and states, diplomats and statesmen, spheres of influence and national champions, all were distractions to Gulbenkian: to be ignored if possible, or else coached and coopted." He dedicated his working life to negotiating deals, to forming international consortia and cartels, to managing share issues, to lawyers and litigation, and to chasing profit. Gulbenkian worked like a Stakhanovite. His idea of relaxation was to check his children's accounts. Indeed, his office mantra, as Conlin reminds us, was "check, check, check." By temperament he was possessive, studious, reclusive, and mistrustful.

In 1912, Gulbenkian took a 15 percent stake in the Turkish Petroleum Company, which was formed under his aegis to develop and exploit the oilfields of Mesopotamia. When this was reconstituted in 1929 as the Iraq Petroleum Company (IPC), Gulbenkian was allotted 5 percent of the profits. Huge income accrued to him after the opening of Iraq's first oil pipeline, in 1934. In the last years of his life, as a result of the IPC's Big Inch pipeline coming onstream, he became the richest man in the world, rivaled only by J. Paul Getty.

Gulbenkian was admirably disdainful of nation-states and of prating about national identity. His attitude was shared by Sir Robert Waley Cohen of Royal Dutch Shell: "If by transferring control to the Hottentots we could increase our security and our dividends, I don't believe any of us would hesitate for long." London and Paris provided his ambits. Gulbenkian never visited Iran, Iraq, or the United States. Many of his negotiations were conducted in French resorts. By the 1920s he was an international celebrity, all the more talked about because he discouraged publicity and therefore seemed mysterious. In this he resembled another boy from Constantinople who had become a Paris millionaire, the arms dealer Basil Zaharoff. Clamoring journalists nicknamed him "Mr. Five Per Cent."

Gulbenkian moved to a house on the north side of Hyde Park in 1899 and obtained a British passport in 1902. Thereafter he traveled like incognito royalty between London and Paris. In both cities he was a habitué of the Ritz hotels, where he could avail himself of nymphets, away from the prying eyes of his wife. In 1922 he bought a Paris *hôtel particulier* at 51 Avenue d'Iéna that had been built for the Franco-German banker and art collector Rodolphe Kann. He had the house gutted and rebuilt over the course of four years. In its final form, the interior was stupendous Louis XVI. Gulbenkian's private suite on the third floor contained a bedroom with a single bed, an aviary (he loved birds), and a bathroom conceived by the art nouveau designer René Lalique. At the center of the bathroom was a high-pressure hose that Gulbenkian's valets would squirt over their master as he stood naked in a niche lined with silver leaf.

Once he had the time and money, Gulbenkian became an ardent collector and indeed a discerning connoisseur. He expected *un prix amical* (friendly terms) from his dealers rather than *marchandage* (hard bargaining). In return, he gave his dealers lucrative investment tips: "*Stick* to your shares [in Mexican Eagle oil] and find something very fine for me," he told the dealer Joseph Duveen in 1920. Houdon, Rodin, Canaletto, paintings, statuary, Islamic art, Egyptian antiquities, Roman gems, Greek and Sicilian coins, books, manuscripts, carpets, English Pre-Raphaelites, and other artifacts were arrayed in his house on Avenue d'Iéna. They were, he said, his "children." In Normandy, he bought hectares outside Deauville and hired Achille Duchêne, "the Napoleon of *paysagistes*," to lay out sumptuous gardens and pleasure grounds, but he never bothered to build a house on the site. Gulbenkian felt ardent love for the picturesque, and for sunrises and sunsets. When, in his mideighties, he sank into contented dotage, he liked to be taken daily to watch the birds and animals at the zoo in Lisbon, where he had moved during the war.

Fall Semester 2017

A version of this lecture appeared in the *Literary Review,* December 2018– January 2019.

Max Aitken, Lord Beaverbrook, in his office, 11 June 1964. Photograph by Associated Newspapers. Shutterstock.

4

Lord Beaverbrook

JANE RIDLEY

Max Beaverbrook was widely disliked during his lifetime as a newspaper owner and backstairs politician who used the *Daily Express* to further his own interests. Nonetheless, it is hard not to admire the young Max Aitken's rise from rags to riches. One of six children of a Scots Presbyterian minister who had immigrated to Canada before Max was born in 1879, he endured a hard, joyless childhood in remote New Brunswick. He did badly at school, failed the entrance exam to Dalhousie University, and then fooled around, getting into debt. All this changed when, at age twenty-one, he took a job in Halifax, Nova Scotia, with an established financier named Stairs. Aitken worked hard, learned quickly, and showed a marked talent for making money. Attaching himself to an older and more powerful man was to become a pattern.

At twenty-six, Aitken made a loveless but socially ambitious marriage to Gladys Henderson Drury, the daughter of a lieutenant colonel. By the time he was thirty, he was a millionaire, having amassed a fortune during the Canadian boom of the 1900s by driving through industrial mergers. Of the forty massive Canadian mergers that took place between 1896 and 1913, the largest three were promoted by Aitken. One of these, a merger of cement firms, led to a financial scandal. To escape a potential lawsuit, Aitken sailed to London, in search of new excitements.

Upon his arrival in London, Aitken went to see the hang-dog Unionist MP Andrew Bonar Law, like himself a successful businessman and the child of a New Brunswick manse. This connection transformed Aitken's life. Scouting for candidates who would support tariff reform (the Edwardian equivalent of Brexit) to stand at the December 1910 election, Bonar Law put Aitken forward for the seat of Ashton-under-Lyne. Aitken ran a brilliant campaign and won. He instantly regretted it: Parliament bored him, and he toyed with the idea of returning to Canada.

Over the course of the next year, he shuttled back and forth across the Atlantic on the *Lusitania,* dodging scandals in Canada and running away from tedious constituency duties in Britain. Thanks to Bonar Law, he got a knighthood. (For what?) He eventually put down roots in England, buying Cherkley Court, an ugly, ostentatious house in Surrey. He began to build a newspaper empire, secretly investing in and then acquiring control of the failing *Daily Express.*

When Bonar Law became Conservative leader in 1911, Aitken gained access to the inner circle of British politics. How much influence he really had is debatable. J. L. Garvin of the *Observer* called him a "hermit crab," insinuating himself into Bonar Law's ear. Aitken hosted secret talks between Asquith and Bonar Law over Irish Home Rule in 1914. In Aitken's later writings, he exaggerated his own importance.

The First World War gave Aitken the sort of opportunities he relished. He was appointed official war correspondent by the Canadian government, and this allowed him to escape the British newspaper censors and file sensational reports revealing what was really happening at the front. But the war also exposed his shortcomings. Appointed British Minister of Information in 1918 (by which time he had been created Lord Beaverbrook), he appears to have seen the job as yet another business venture. He tried to gain control over all war intelligence, predictably incurring the fury of government colleagues. He didn't last long in the office.

Beaverbrook's real role was to support Bonar Law. Some detected "a touch of the feminine" in his relations with his patron; he frequently acted as companion to the widowed leader, especially after the deaths of two of Bonar Law's sons in the war. When Bonar Law, who became Prime Minister in 1922, was forced to resign after just seven months in the job on account of throat cancer, Beaverbrook put him in touch with his doctor. (Loyalty to friends in trouble was one of his more attractive characteristics.) Law's death a few months after his resignation left Beaverbrook rudderless and without a direct line to the top of government.

Beaverbrook's dealings with women were generally shabby, and Charles Williams, in *Max Beaverbrook: Not Quite a Gentleman* (2019), perhaps let him off too lightly in this respect. The small man with a big head and a wide urchin's grin bedded a string of women, most of whom he treated badly. He neglected and cheated on his long-suffering wife, who died young from a brain tumor. Jean Norton, the wife of the future Lord Grantley, was installed as Beaverbrook's mistress at Cherkley, but he was constantly unfaithful to her too.

Beaverbrook's judgment was often wrong. The only thing he cared for in politics was free trade within the British Empire, which became a lost cause after 1914. During the abdication crisis, he backed Edward VIII. He managed to keep the press quiet about Wallis Simpson's divorce and tried to organize a king's party. He was very slow to see the dangers of appeasement, campaigning in his newspapers for a policy of isolationism. In January 1940 he met the Duke of Windsor to discuss making a peace offer to Hitler.

The Second World War brought Beaverbrook back into government, this time through his friendship with Winston Churchill. A. J. P. Taylor, Beaverbrook's sycophantic biographer, claimed in the 1970s that as minister of aircraft production, Beaverbrook had been responsible for the acceleration in the construction of fighters that ultimately led to the defeat of Germany in the Battle of Britain. This was untrue. The increase in production had already been planned before Beaverbrook was appointed in May 1940, but he took the credit. He refused to work at the ministry's offices in Harrogate, instead setting up his own headquarters at his house in St James's. The result was chaos.

Perhaps the most important thing that Beaverbrook did during the war was to play Falstaff to Churchill's Prince Hal. Churchill depended upon him for companionship and conviviality, as a sounding board and as a dinner companion. To perform this role, Beaverbrook need to know what was going on, and for this reason he had to be given a Cabinet position. In his correspondence with Churchill, Beaverbrook grumbled, whinged, and constantly threatened resignation, often at moments of crisis. He was self-pitying and petulant, and he quarreled with his ministerial colleagues, but Churchill needed him. Ernest Bevin remarked, "Well, you see it's like this; it's as if the old man [Churchill] had married an 'ore. He knows what she is but he loves her."

As Charles Williams shows, Beaverbrook's influence did not ultimately depend on his newspapers, his money, or his political judgment, but on his ability to act as a crony of greater men.

Spring Semester 2018

A version of this lecture appeared in the *Literary Review,* April 2019.

Evelyn Waugh and Randolph Churchill in the Balkans, c. 1944.

5

Evelyn Waugh and
Randolph Churchill in Yugoslavia

JEFFREY MEYERS

Evelyn Waugh and Randolph Churchill served on a military mission to Marshal Tito's Partisans in Yugoslavia from July 1944 to February 1945. Earlier in the war, Waugh had been insubordinate and unable to adjust to regimental life; Randolph, as always, had been notoriously drunk, belligerent and offensive. Like fierce ferrets confined in a cage, two of the most difficult and disagreeable officers in the British army acted out a disastrous vendetta. Their caustic clash alienated Tito and damaged the relations between Britain and its crucial ally during the German occupation of Yugoslavia.

One hundred and twenty pages of unpublished material from the National Archives and the Public Record Office in Kew, England, and from Churchill College, Cambridge University, cast new light on British policy in Yugoslavia, its military contacts with Tito, and the contrast between his communist Partisans and the pro-Nazi Ustashe; on Randolph's work, constant complaints and offensive behavior as well as his courage under fire; on Waugh and Randolph's near-fatal air crash, their English comrade Stephen Clissold and Waugh's support of the Catholic Ustashe in opposition to official policy. This archival material explains why these tragicomic adventurers wound up in wartime Croatia, why they quarreled bitterly in an isolated village and why their important mission was doomed to failure.

Randolph (1911–1968) and Waugh (1903–1966), an odd couple and odd choice for this mission, were anticommunist, had no experience in Yugoslavia and no knowledge of Serbo-Croat. They had first met socially in the early 1930s, had many friends in common and maintained an intermittent, often hostile friendship. Both men had made calamitous first marriages to unfaithful wives. Randolph had all the qualities that the snobbish Waugh lacked and craved. He was descended from John Churchill, Duke of Marlborough, one of the greatest soldiers in English history, and was the son of Winston Churchill, the all-powerful wartime Prime Minister. Tall, handsome, wealthy and influential, he was educated at Eton and Christchurch, Oxford, and was Member of Parliament for Preston, Scotland, from 1940 to 1945. In April 1942 he joined Major David Stirling's elite commandos in the Libyan Desert where he injured his back in a serious road accident. Randolph and Brigadier Fitzroy Maclean first parachuted into Drvar, Croatia, on 19 January 1944; Waugh arrived by plane, six months later, on 10 July. Though eight years younger than Captain Waugh, Major Churchill outranked him and led the operation.

Christopher Sykes, a friend of both men and biographer of Waugh, described Randolph's habitual behavior. He recalled an outrageous 1939 luncheon party at a local country house where "Randolph did everything he knew, and he knew a lot, to distress, anger, exasperate and make miserable his host and every one of his fellow guests!" After the war the unregenerate Randolph "still insisted on laying down the law, still resented any show of opposition, still bullied his audience into submission and was still incapable of controlling his temper." Though more horrified than amused, friends continued to court the well-connected and influential social lion.

The son of a middle-class publisher and critic, Waugh was short, baby-faced and burdened with an effeminate name. He had gone to Lancing, a distinctly less impressive public school, and to Hertford College, Oxford, where he was frequently drunk, passed through an intense homosexual phase and left without taking a degree. He joined the Royal Marines in December 1939 at the age of thirty-six, when he seemed too old to enlist yet fancied himself a military man. But he was irritable and sarcastic with his men and lost his command of a company. He participated in the failed raid on Dakar, in Vichy-controlled French West Africa, in September 1940. He fought with Colonel Robert Laycock's elite commando force during a failed mission to Libya in February 1941, and took part in the evacuation of Crete after the Greek island was captured by German paratroopers in May 1941.

Like the left-wing Loyalist factions who had fought each other as well as their fascist enemy in the recent Spanish Civil War, Tito's communist Partisans, Draza Mihailovic's Serbian Chetniks and Ante Pavelic's pro-Nazi Ustashe were fighting a savage ideological war, during the German occupation, for postwar control of their country. Michael Davie, editor of Waugh's *Diaries,* explained how early in 1944 Brigadier Fitzroy Maclean and Major William Deakin, serving behind enemy lines in Yugoslavia, effected a radical change in British policy: "Their reports on Tito's anti-German zeal, and the ruthlessness of his guerrillas, were enthusiastic. Mihailovic, by contrast, appeared to be less interested in fighting the Germans than in waiting his chance to restore the fortunes of Serbia [and the exiled King Peter II]. The British accordingly abandoned Mihailovic and put their full support behind Tito." Maclean's mission, whose headquarters were in the southern Adriatic city of Bari, Italy, was to assist Tito's irregular army with supplies and weapons in order to defeat the Germans.

Secret reports sent from English agents in Yugoslavia to Bari in July and September 1944, while Waugh and Randolph were serving in Croatia, revealed the complexity of Yugoslavian politics. Captain D. C. Owen thought the Partisans were more anti-Nazi than fanatically communist and emphasized their brutal warfare. Since the Partisans did not take prisoners, the Ustashe fought fiercely to avoid being captured:

> The majority of the Partisan forces, when asked, say "I am fighting for the Partisans now because I wish to help get rid of the Germans, but I have different political ideas after the war." This is the general trend and the general colour of the political instruction within the Corps is more "pink" than "red." . . . The USTASHI are determined fighters, as they know they will be killed anyway—no quarter given on either side. The Partisan leaders say that about 20% of the USTASHI have either been conscripted unwillingly or have no blood on their hands, and if captured would be given trial [i.e., summary execution], but front line troops difficult to persuade to take prisoners.

After Tito won the civil war Draza Mihailovic was executed. Ante Pavelic survived an assassination attempt in Argentina and died in Madrid.

Lieutenant J. H. Gibbs reported that the Yugoslavs—struggling for survival and aware of their ideological opposition to the British—both needed and exploited the ally who provided essential war materiel. They were naturally suspicious and resentful of political and military interference by the country that had recently backed their enemy Mihailovic. But distrust had subsided and relations improved after the successful Allied landings in France on 6 June 1944 made victory in Europe seem likely:

> General impression, after 10 months with 6 Corps and 3 months with 10 Corps: we are of use to the Partisan movement for stores and propaganda—and last autumn, not even for stores. If they could get the same benefits without our presence they would not want us. They have no reasons for pinning us down (don't have after public professions of friendship), yet they are uneasy to set us free. Suspicious if we make friends. I know of one Partisan who was cross-questioned by the Corps Commandant as to what he talked about with the BLO [British Liaison Officer] and told to watch his step.
>
> One sometimes gets the feeling, when asking them for collaboration, that they have orders from a higher level to obstruct, but will not put their cards on the table and say so. This refers, of course, only to relations with the higher officers, who incidentally are invariably correct and cordial and the above impression only slowly takes form. Outside that narrow circle, their relations are usually excellent. The BLO is welcomed and popular either as an individual or as an 'Englishman' (very hard on the Scots)—both in peasant cottages and with ex-ZAGREB townspeople. Since the opening of the 'Second Front' and the march through FRANCE, which has staggered the most hardened critics, pro-British and American feeling is very high.

Winston Churchill sent his only son to Yugoslavia to show his solidarity with and personal commitment to Tito's Partisans. On 28 June 1944, before leaving London, Randolph rampaged through the bar in White's club and shouted: "Where the hell is Evelyn Waugh? I've tried everywhere! No one can tell me! I need him immediately! . . . I've been commissioned to undertake a subordinate mission under Fitzroy Maclean in Jugoslavia. . . . I told Fitz before I left that I must have officers I can talk to and he agreed with me that Evelyn was just the chap for me. It's all very secret," he added, his voice rising in volume.

Ignoring Waugh's contentious personality, Randolph thought the former commando had the right adventurous character and military experience to fortify the mission. Waugh's biographer Martin Stannard noted that "in civilian life Waugh often found Churchill stimulating, an eccentric eager for life, volatile, courageous, sentimental. In wartime this preposterous schoolboy seemed sadly diminished . . . unable to crawl from the weight of his father's fame." Stannard added that Waugh intensified their volatile mixture, "When drunk Waugh could be amusingly offensive; sober, he was caustic and melancholy."

Randolph also believed that Waugh, like a powerful medieval pope, would "be able to heal the Great Schism between the Catholic and the Orthodox churches." In fact, Waugh damaged relations with the Partisans by contacting the pro-Nazi Croatian Catholics, and was nearly expelled by the communists for interfering in their internal conflict. Brian Roberts, Randolph's biographer, expressed astonishment that he and Waugh had been recruited for such an important and sensitive task: "the choice of two such tactless, intolerant, quick-tempered and heavy-handed men for what was obviously a delicate diplomatic mission is incomprehensible. Neither of them had the slightest sympathy with Communism and they never attempted to pretend otherwise. Two more unlikely ambassadors to a peasant people is difficult to imagine." Both men felt they were entitled to special treatment: they ignored military regulations, disobeyed their superiors, and were hated by their fellow officers and men.

When Maclean met Randolph in Cairo in November 1943, he was recovering from his crash in the desert, was boorishly drunk, insulted generals and embarrassed his father. Nevertheless Maclean, who outranked Randolph and could control him, praised his social graces and wrote: "I began to realize what a marvelous companion Randolph could be. Maddening, of course, in a dozen different ways, but endlessly stimulating and entertaining." But Maclean was quite mistaken in thinking Waugh could control Randolph and was far off the mark in stating that Randolph could consider Waugh his social equal: "Here, at last, was someone well qualified to contain Randolph, someone whom, with major adjustments, he might even regard as his social and intellectual equal."

In his autobiography *Eastern Approaches,* published in 1949 when his poor judgment had become obvious, Maclean stubbornly and unconvincingly justified his choice:

> Randolph would make a useful addition to my Mission. . . . For my present purposes he seemed just the man. On operations I knew him to be thoroughly dependable, possessing both endurance and determination. He was also gifted with an acute intelligence and a very considerable background of general politics. . . . I felt, too—rightly, as it turned out—that he would get on well with the Jugoslavs, for his enthusiastic and at times explosive approach to life was not unlike their own. Lastly I knew him to be

a stimulating companion, an important consideration in the circumstances under which we lived.

In fact, Randolph, who could be rather dim, did not get on with the Yugoslavs or with Waugh, and his explosive approach to diplomacy created a tense atmosphere.

On 25 May 1944, two months before Waugh arrived, Randolph showed the best side of his character. Though his mission did not include actual combat, he was awarded an MBE (Member of the British Empire) for outstanding leadership and courage under fire:

> Major CHURCHILL was with the British Military Mission in DRVAR when the Germans made a sudden airborne attack on 25 May. After marching for many hours throughout that day, he was sent off during the night to a Partisan Corps some miles away. He successfully accomplished this journey, which was through enemy occupied territory, and transmitted some most important messages which had been entrusted to him. He then took charge of the mission attached to this Corps and, in very difficult circumstances, kept ITALY well informed of the progress of operations, so that the maximum Allied assistance could be given to the Partisans. Later he was placed in charge of a British and Russian party which was to be evacuated to BARI. Although continuously harried and kept on the move by the enemy, he kept the party together until an opportunity occurred for them to be evacuated by air. It was largely due to his efforts that this evacuation was successfully accomplished.

Frank McLynn, Maclean's biographer, tried to explain the twisted motives behind his choice: "[Waugh] was a character of some distinction, and Fitzroy liked such people. . . . Fitzroy was dazzled by Waugh's reputation and thought it would add to the aura of the mission. . . . [He] had received an advance copy of *Put Out More Flags* [1942], liked it and thought it would be interesting to have a writer on the mission, especially one Randolph had requested." Waugh's novel included a flattering "Dedicatory Letter to Major Randolph Churchill" and was signed "Your affectionate friend, the Author." Maclean, choosing literary over military qualities, saw himself as a fictional Waugh hero and sought literary fame.

Though Maclean had chosen him, Waugh disliked his new commander at first sight and rather harshly described the Scotsman, dedicated to British interests, as "dour, unprincipled, ambitious, probably wicked; shaved head and devil's ears." Stannard called Waugh "a fake hard man"; real heroes, Maclean and Tito, "shocked him in their toughness." When Wilfred Thesiger, an equally tough

explorer and soldier, met Waugh in Abyssinia in 1930, he immediately perceived Waugh's weakness and recalled, "he struck me
as flaccid and petulant and I disliked him on sight." When Waugh
asked if he could accompany him on a dangerous mission, Thesiger
refused and fiercely remarked, "Had he come, I suspect only one of
us would have returned."

Freddy Birkenhead, the son of the earl who was Winston's greatest friend, had been Randolph's superior at Eton. He was sent to
Croatia as an emotional buffer when relations between Waugh and
Randolph had reached the breaking point, and wrote that "the duties of the British missions in Yugoslavia were mainly to liaise with
the Partisan military headquarters and the political commissars,
and to spread with tact and care as much pro-British information
as possible to counteract the . . . [influence of] Russia to whom they
were attached by political and historical association." Soon after arriving Randolph confirmed, "I am now with Fitzroy Maclean. My job
is to look after propaganda (a) about us to the Partisans and (b) to
the outside world about the Partisans." But on 27 January 1944, the
Minister of State's Office in Cairo had warned the Foreign Office in
London to proceed with great caution: "We conceive that any overt
attempt at propaganda penetration of Partisan movement would
raise objections on the part of Tito and that this problem must be
properly approached and with full information."

On 10 July 1944, Waugh and Randolph flew from Bari to meet
Marshal Tito on the Adriatic island of Vis, which was protected
by British planes based in Italy. As Britain's main ally in German-
occupied Yugoslavia, Tito had to be treated with the greatest deli-
cacy and tact, yet Waugh made him the target of a relentless joke.
Stannard explained the origin of Waugh's amusing but provocative
behavior: "In the early days of Maclean's mission, over a year before,
no one had been certain whether Tito even existed, let alone whether
this mythical figure were male or female. This tiny seed of gossip fueled years of Waugh's malice and, far from retracting the slander, he
took every opportunity to embellish it." Waugh expressed his hostility to the communists by calling their leader a woman and even a lesbian, and tried to divert his colleagues by continuing to repeat that
dangerous absurdity. Birkenhead recalled, "he never referred to the
Yugoslav leader except as 'Auntie,' and claimed that the Marshal had
been seen emerging from the sea off the island of Vis in a wet bath-
ing dress and that there was no possible question about 'her' sex. . . .
We became much concerned that the Yugoslav members of the staff
would overhear him and that our work might be seriously imper-
illed." Warned by Birkenhead, Waugh cheekily replied, "Her face is

pretty, but her legs are *very* thick." When Waugh was introduced to
the unmistakably virile Tito, the heroic leader ignored the insult,
stared at him and said, "Ask Captain Waugh why he thinks I am a
woman." Waugh, for once, was reduced to silence. The Croats called
Waugh Captain "Vo," which means "ox" in their language.

After the unfortunate meeting with Tito, Waugh and Randolph
returned to Bari. On 16 July 1944 they flew at night to Partisan headquarters in Topusko, Croatia (about forty miles south of Zagreb), an
important escape route for crews of downed Allied bombers and ex-
prisoners of war. But their propeller-driven Dakota transport plane
crashed from about 400 feet and burst into flames in the remote
village of Gajevi. Waugh recalled:

> I was conscious by my ears that we were descending and circling
> the airfield, then we suddenly shot upwards and the next thing I
> knew was that I was walking in a cornfield by the light of the burn-
> ing aeroplane talking to a strange British officer about the prog-
> ress of the war in a detached fashion. . . . I had no recollection of
> the crash nor, at the time, any knowledge of where I was or why,
> but a confused idea that we had made a forced landing during
> some retreat.

The pilot, who misjudged the length of the landing field, tried
to gain altitude, lost speed, stalled and crashed. Nine passengers
freed themselves from the rear of the plane; ten in the front were
killed. On 17 July, Randolph cabled Winston, "asking him to inform
Mrs. Joan Sowman that her husband Douglas Sowman [Randolph's
batman] was killed in a plane crash in Yugoslavia and to send her
his deepest sympathy and inform the wives of [the war correspon-
dent] Philip Jordan and Evelyn Waugh that they are safe."

Randolph, escaping from his second near-fatal accident, had
both legs crushed and could barely move. Waugh's head, arms and
legs were burned but, anesthetized by the shock of the crash, he
felt no pain. He recorded that when they returned, wrapped like
mummies, to recover in the hospital in Bari, Randolph was "drinking, attacking the night nurse, wanting everyone's medicine and all
treatment, dictating letters, plastering the hospital with American
propaganda photographs with Serbo-Croat captions."

After a two-month convalescence in Bari, Waugh and Randolph
flew to their base in Topusko, where enforced proximity with few
duties set off their intense antagonism. They lived in a four-room,
rat-infested farmhouse, the only cottage in town that had an indoor
toilet, and were looked after by two local servants. Waugh, who had
been granted unusual wartime leave to write *Brideshead Revisited*

(1945), had a room to himself that allowed him to correct the proofs of the novel and afforded a temporary refuge. He loathed the fiery local *rakia* brandy that stank of sewage and glue and remained sober, which made Randolph's habitual inebriation all the more difficult for him to endure.

Topusko had been a spa before the war, and the machine that pumped water into the bathhouse was still in working order. Waugh recorded, "we go there daily & sit in the radio-active hot water which I find very enervating. The town has been laid out entirely for leisure, with neglected gardens and woodland promenades. It suits our leisured life well." In a photo taken in Topusko, Waugh—indoors, framed by the window and lit by the sun—looks shy, slim and boyish. The dissipated Randolph, standing outside in the shadow with his right arm on the windowsill and left hand on his hip, has a confident, devilish smile and looks older than Waugh.

By September 1944, however, Waugh minimized their mission's achievements: "We do very little & see little company except a partisan liaison officer, the secretary general of the communist party, the leader of the Peasant party & such people. We also arrange for the evacuation of distressed jews," an event that played an important part in his wartime *Sword of Honour* trilogy (1952–61). Fleeing the Ustashe genocide, the Jews felt unsafe in Europe and wanted to emigrate to Palestine. But the intricacies of Yugoslav politics were quite beyond Waugh's comprehension. A fanatical Catholic convert, Waugh defiantly sympathized with the pro-Nazi Catholic Ustashe and undermined the anti-German alliance between the godless communists and the Christian British. He completely misread the situation and recorded, "There is no gratitude to us among the Jugoslavs nor need there be, for we have no generosity to them. We pursue a policy of niggardly and near-sighted self-advantage and then whine when we fail to secure universal love and esteem." Britain certainly needed the military support of the Partisans, but did not expect to win their universal love.

Bored in Topusko, Waugh annoyed headquarters in Bari by sending trivial cables with a secret prefix that meant only senior officers could decode them. Famous for his wicked wit, Waugh was quick to retaliate when provoked. Randolph—a perfect target—gave him plenty of provocation and then complained about his satiric barbs. Neither was willing to change the habits of a lifetime to satisfy the whims of the other. When Randolph asked Waugh to agree that Winston's *Life of Marlborough* was a great work, Waugh, wounding his family pride, savagely replied: "As history it is beneath contempt, the special pleading of a defence lawyer. As literature it is worthless."

Randolph retorted by asking, "Have you ever noticed that it is always the people who are most religious who are most mean and cruel?" To which Waugh, claiming that faith was the only thing that held him in check, said, "But my dear Randolph, you have no idea what I should be like if I wasn't [religious]."

Randolph's biography, written by his son (another Winston Churchill), minimized the conflict between his father and Waugh. He quoted Randolph's praise of Waugh's bravery and criticism of his self-destructive impulse, a judgment that applied with equal force to himself: "Waugh possesses both physical and moral courage in a very high degree. He has seen action in this war at Dakar, in Crete, and in Jugoslavia. His courage, coupled with his intellect, might have won him a distinguished military career. But he was usually more interested in driving his immediate superiors mad than in bringing about the defeat of the enemy. One of his superiors, an officer of high standing, had a nervous breakdown after only two months of having Waugh under his command."

In Croatia Randolph was equally difficult, quarrelsome and inefficient. Tito's high-ranking comrade Milovan Djilas disdainfully wrote that Randolph "revealed through his drinking and lack of interest that he had inherited neither political imagination nor dynamism with his surname." No wonder the Partisans took what they could from the British and rejected them politically. After three months with Randolph, Waugh had wondered "how long I could bear his company, even he I think faintly conscious of strain. . . . [He made] it plain to me that he found the restraints of my company irksome." On 5 February 1944 the Resident Minister in Cairo had written to the Foreign Office in London suggesting that an expert join the mission: "We are all in agreement here that it is most important to have Clissold in Yugoslavia since we are not obtaining adequate political intelligence in the present circumstances." On October 13, 1944, the unexpected and fortunate arrival of Major Freddy Birkenhead and Major Stephen Clissold—a gentle former teacher from Zagreb, fluent in Serbo-Croat and political advisor to Maclean—prevented an outbreak of feral violence between Waugh and Randolph.

When Waugh first appeared Randolph publicly mocked him and incited another bitter confrontation. Birkenhead recalled, " 'There he is!' roared [Randolph]—'there's the little fellow in his camel-hair dressing-gown! Look at him standing there!' Evelyn directed on him a stare cold and hostile as the Arctic Ocean, and remarked with poisonous restraint: 'You've got drunk very quickly tonight. Don't send any more signals.' " That same day Waugh wrote to his confidante Nancy Mitford (who was related to Randolph's mother) about

Birkenhead's appearance: "It is a great joy having him not only for his own sour & meaty company but as a relief from perpetual watch with your cousin Randolph whose boisterous good nature, after weeks of solitary confinement with him, has begun to exhaust me." Birkenhead wrote favorably about Waugh in a 1973 volume of tributes but later, when he discovered that Waugh had portrayed him in his *Diaries* and *Letters* as drunk, boring and ineffective, he called Waugh "an odious, indeed a psychopathic character."

Waugh's personal writings, enlivened by the novelist's eye for telling details, contained a litany of comic complaints about his claustrophobic connection with Randolph, amusing to read but no doubt painful to endure. When talking to the Partisan liaison officer, Waugh noted, "Randolph got drunk in the early afternoon and had an endless argument with [Leo] Mates, going round in ponderous circles, contradicting himself, heavily humorous, patronizing, appalling." Waugh lamented "how boring it was to be obliged to tell Randolph everything twice—once when he was drunk, once when he was sober . . . . His American slang, his coughing and farting make him a poor companion in wet weather."

The best time of Waugh's day was the first two hours of daylight when Randolph was still asleep. Once awake he became cantankerous and belligerent, then inebriated and comatose—and acted like a character in Waugh's satiric comedies. Waugh rejected Randolph's pleas for kinder treatment, condemned his cowardly abuse and tried to restrain his own short temper: "[He] left me unmoved for in these matters he is simply a flabby bully who rejoices in blustering and shouting down anyone weaker than himself and starts squealing as soon as he meets anyone as strong. . . . I must exercise self-control and give him the privileges of a commanding officer even though he shirks his responsibilities." He then cut to the core of their relations by confessing they were both unpopular officers and unemployable misfits: "No one else would have chosen me, nor would anyone else have accepted him."

Choosing hostility rather than restraint, Waugh wrote, "I have got to the stage of disliking Randolph which is really more convenient than thinking I liked him & constantly trying to reconcile myself to his enormities. Now I can regard him as one of the evils of war." He remarked that in an effort to control Randolph, who liked to gamble, rose to a challenge, and was fortified by brandy and cigars, "Freddy and I have bet him £10 each that he will not read the Bible straight through in a fortnight. He has set to work but not as quietly as we hoped. He sits bouncing about on his chair, chortling and saying, 'I say, did you know this came in the Bible "bring down my

grey hairs with sorrow to the grave"? ' Or simply, 'God, isn't God a
shit?'. . . Instead of purchasing a few hours silence for my £10 I now
have to endure an endless campaign of interruption and banter."

When Randolph—sounding like a character in Beckett's *Waiting for Godot*—complained about Waugh's cruel treatment, Waugh
hardened his heart, threatened to leave and mocked him: "[While]
Freddy was talking gibberish to himself in the earth closet, Randolph broke into maudlin reproaches of my failure of friendship
and cruelty to him. 'It can't go on. It can't go on.' 'All right then I'll
go back to Bari.' 'I'm still fond of you. In spite of all your beastliness
to me. I am wounded and grieved.'"

Randolph sent Bari a torrent of complaints about not receiving
the supplies he had requested. But Robert Bruce Lockhart (who
coordinated all British propaganda against the Axis powers) told
Brendan Bracken (the Minister of Information) that "in point of
fact Randolph has been getting all possible material for some time."
Nevertheless, Randolph's most vituperative explosion, which almost
led to fisticuffs, provoked a furious response from the journalist,
radio broadcaster and diplomat Ralph Murray in Bari. He sent
Lockhart a three-and-a-half-page, single-spaced typed letter, "MOST
SECRET AND PESONAL," about a disturbing episode when a Yugoslav
major was present. Murray's letter revealed what Waugh had also
been forced to tolerate. In unusually fierce and undiplomatic language, the deeply wounded Murray described Randolph's torrent of
filthy abuse and horrible insults:

> I think it necessary to give you a short account of an incident with
> Randolph Churchill for your most confidential information. . . .
> It is difficult to write soberly of Churchill's behaviour. . . . He re-
> ferred to our ignorance of his appointment, status and functions,
> and [forced us] to listen to a minor diatribe from him. . . .
>
> At the end of the meal, during which he had been rude to his
> American neighbours, he strove to pick a quarrel—I am being
> conservative in my expression—with me personally. He declared
> that . . . I had lied and obstructed him. . . . For nearly two hours we
> were treated to a violent and insulting diatribe of a degrading and
> shifty and horrible kind. . . . His insults to me in particular were
> of a character foul and deliberate. . . . I (who was, in sum, a filthy,
> scheming, obstructive little careerist) had intrigued against him,
> tried to get him out of Jugoslavia, to supplant him with Clissold,
> to hinder the war effort, the whole elaborated with degrading in-
> sults. . . . I understand that among his acquaintances such behav-
> iour is treated lightly, and there is perhaps nothing else for them
> to do. [But] there can be no question of putting up with another
> such outburst of filth.

Though reprimanded by his angry superiors, Randolph repeated his abusive attack on Murray and offered a feeble but arrogant defense. Anyone else would have been immediately relieved of his command and sent home in disgrace but Randolph, the son of the Prime Minister, managed to survive. (Murray, 1908–1983, was later knighted and became ambassador to Greece.)

Not to be outdone by Randolph, Waugh was willing to risk his life to enrage and insult his adversary. During a German air attack on their farmhouse in Topusko on 22 October 1944, when the Heinkels dropped bombs and fired machine-guns, Randolph thought the enemy had discovered his hideout and were trying to kill him in order to hurt his father. Birkenhead recalled:

> In the middle of this attack, the small figure of Evelyn, somehow overlooked, emerged from the Mission, clad in a white duffel-coat which might have been designed to attract fire, and which gleamed in leprous prominence in the dawn. At this sight, Randolph's face, empurpled with rage, appeared over the trench and in tones verging on hysteria he screamed: "You bloody little swine, take off that coat.! TAKE OFF THAT ***** COAT! It's an order! It's a military order!" Evelyn did not seem to regard even this dire threat as binding, and without removing the coat lowered himself with leisurely dignity into the trench among the bullets, pausing only on his way to remark to Randolph: "I'll tell you what I think of your repulsive manners when the bombardment is over." Evelyn's behaviour was difficult to forgive, and we shared Randolph's annoyance. It seemed to us that Evelyn had either chosen this extremely hazardous method of irritating his friend, or else been seized by some obscure death-wish. In either case, his action had endangered all of us. After the attack Randolph, "drawing Evelyn aside, apologised if his manners had been abrupt . . . reminding him that as the Mission Commander he was responsible for the safety of all its members." Waugh, putting the knife in, replied: "My dear Randolph, it wasn't your manners I was complaining of: it was your cowardice."

On 14 May 1945—after the Partisans had conquered Zagreb, capital of Croatia—the British Mission reported to Bari that the political situation remained complex and uncertain, and there would be a lot of bloodshed before victory in the civil war was finally achieved: "It is difficult even to say whether the liberation of Zagreb is popular with the majority of citizens or not. In view of the number of them who must be aware that they have collaborated to some extent with the Ustashi Government it is probable that the proportion of people who are profoundly relieved that the Germans have gone is about equal to the number who feel uneasy that the Partisans have arrived."

The unpublished archival material reveals that Maclean mistakenly chose Randolph for the mission to Croatia, Randolph mistakenly chose Waugh, and both men did more harm than good. Randolph, a Member of Parliament, represented Winston and carried his tremendous prestige. But he behaved boorishly and obstructed the British mission, offended both the Partisans and the American allies, and stirred up a lot of unnecessary trouble at high levels in Bari and London. The pro-Catholic, anticommunist Waugh was supposed to entertain Randolph and support the Partisans, but constantly fought with him and made three disastrous mistakes. He openly courted the Ustashe fascists, publicly insulted Tito and endangered his comrades by flaunting his whitecoat during the air attack. Waugh was most amusing when filled with hate. In 1964, when Randolph had a tumor removed that turned out to be benign, Waugh remarked that the doctors had found "the only part of Randolph that was not malignant."

Fall Semester 2017

Alan Turing. Wikimedia Commons.

6

Alan Turing
Genius, Patriot, Victim

ROBERT D. KING

In 1950, life was looking good for Alan Turing. He was coming to be recognized as the most brilliant mathematician England had produced in the mid-twentieth century. His wartime work in breaking the German Enigma cipher machine was still classified—which delayed his recognition as a world-class mathematician—but he was known by those who mattered, by Winston Churchill, for example, as the major contributor to the hugely successful code-breaking operation at Bletchley Park, and as an extraordinary mind by John von Neumann, generally regarded as the foremost mathematician of his time.

After treading water during the funding uncertainties of postwar England, he decided not to return to his fellowship at King's College, Cambridge, instead taking what was presented as a cutting-edge assignment involving computers and mathematical biology at the University of Manchester. It wasn't the perfect job, but Turing was easygoing about such matters. Give him some toys, like a computer or a chess puzzle, a few congenial people to pal around with, and let him practice his running, and he was generally content.

Four years later, on 7 June 1954, Turing, at night and alone, dipped half an apple in cyanide, ate most of it, and died. They found his body the next day. He was not quite forty-three years old.

In my earlier life as mathematician and computer programmer at Cape Canaveral, I knew who Turing was—you couldn't help knowing about him in those days of ALGOL and COBOL, FORTRAN, base 2 arithmetic, machine-language programming—but I didn't know until much later how he died. I still flinch at the tragedy, the uselessness, the sadness of it all, this modern variant of Socrates and the hemlock.

Turing, an unapologetic homosexual, was charged with gross indecency under Section 11 of the Criminal Law Amendment Act of 1885 (the statute under which Oscar Wilde had been sentenced to prison). He was given probation with the proviso that he "submit for treatment by a . . . qualified medical practitioner at Manchester Royal Infirmary." In short, Turing was sentenced to a form of chemical castration by hormones ("organotherapy"), thought at the time to be a cure for homosexuality—electric shock treatment was also recommended. The side effects were brutal and humiliating, and he decided apparently that life under those conditions was not worth living.

Many issues intersect in the Turing case: genius, homosexuality, the British class system, public schools, Oxbridge snobbery, and bureaucratic infighting. And the personal: he had a dark side, from his early days onward, that could never be completely concealed.

England had vicious legal penalties against homosexuality, which were applied to males more often than to females. Queen Victoria spoke for her country of shopkeepers when she was told of lesbians and asked: "But what on earth do they *do*?" Most European countries had harsh laws, too, as did America and Canada. France was the exception, which was why so many upper-class Englishmen took their holidays across the Channel. Two to ten years in prison was the usual sentence in England, though until 1861 the death penalty was still on the books. Homosexuality pinched some existential nerve in the psyche of the English middle class.

The laws were enforced through the 1950s. Nothing changed until the Wolfenden Report, which recommended in 1957 that "homosexual behaviour between consenting adults in private should no longer be a criminal offence." The report eventually led to the passage of the Sexual Offences Act of 1967, which in effect decriminalized almost all moral offenses in England and Wales.

But that was not the world Alan Turing lived in. He was born in 1912 into what George Orwell described as his own social class: the lower upper-middle class. Turing's father, whom he liked, was largely absent in India. He could have wished for a different mother, but she wasn't completely bad as mothers go. She worshipped her son even if there was a peculiar distance between them; she described him in her memoirs after his death as "a strange study in light and shade."

Children of Turing's social status were expected to attend pub-lic—that is, private and, on the whole, expensive—schools, which usually meant competing for a scholarship. Orwell got one to Eton. Turing had more trouble (Latin was his bugaboo), but eventually got a scholarship to attend Sherborne, a public school of the mid to upper ranks in Dorset, one of whose old boys is the spy novelist John le Carré.

Turing had most of the usual genius problems, plus some uniquely his own. He wasn't very good academically, but made up for it in what Sherborne called "the sciences." He detested the team sports and canings that made up a large part of the sadistic under-tow of an English public school. He became a serious runner and remained one up until the end—he almost qualified for the 1948 British Olympic marathon team. He claimed that he became a fast runner so that he would never have to be near the ball and be ex-pected to do something with the thing. (I totally sympathize. No matter the sport, I was always picked last, my brother first.)

By his last years at Sherborne, his affection for the place had grown; he had made friends, some of them for life; and he realized as soon as he understood anything about himself at all that he was attracted to boys, not girls. He was homosexual and almost mathe-matical about it. The statement "Some men are attracted to women" can be generalized to "some men are attracted to men." QED.

TURING WAS A PRODUCT OF THAT wondrous alchemy by which the English used to take middle-class types with brains, give them scholarships, send them to a decent Oxbridge college, and then turn out—well, an Alan Turing or a George Orwell, a future Prime Minister or a servant of the empire. Turing had outlasted the can-ings and humiliations dealt out by Sherborne. He came out of it with wounds, none disabling, and a few lifetime friends, but not the slightest disposition to write an essay striking back at his former tormentors, as Orwell did with "Such, Such Were the Joys." (Orwell and Turing remain two of my dwindling number of cultural heroes. Orwell as an Etonian in his school uniform—well, the thing simply cannot be imagined. Nor Turing in his.)

After a few uncertain moves, Turing was accepted into King's Col-lege, Cambridge. King's wasn't his first choice—Trinity was—but Tu-ring never cared much about things like that. He just plowed ahead. And King's turned out to be the right choice for him because of its eminence in mathematics.

Turing was elected a Fellow of King's at the young age of twenty-two in 1935. He wrote a paper, published in 1937, titled "On Comput-able numbers, with an Application to the Entscheidungsproblem,"

which, after a slow beginning, eventually made world-class mathematicians such as John von Neumann sit up and take notice. This
paper established a fundamental principle of theoretical computer
science and, more importantly, of software engineering: no algorithm can prove that any other algorithm terminates. It sounds
straightforward, but it took a genius to think this. (The American
mathematician Alonzo Church published independently a similar
paper on the *Entscheidungsproblem* ["decision-problem"] at almost
the same time.)

Though not at first universally acknowledged as a mathematical genius of the first order, Turing knew how good he was, and he
knew his time would come. To use a phrase of our day that he would
have hated (as I do), he was comfortable in his own skin. That applied particularly to his homosexuality, a preference that was easy
to satisfy at King's. Many of the dons were gay, as were many of the
students, and an Oxford or Cambridge college has always been a
shelter from the outside world.

At King's, he could be as eccentric and bizarre in his behavior as
he wanted to be. Cambridge was a masterwork of eccentricity, especially among its mathematicians. Its leading light, the cricket-crazy
G. H. Hardy, was said never to have missed a test match at Lord's
Cricket Grounds. In January 1913, Hardy had been sent a famous
letter by the self-taught but impoverished Indian mathematician
Srinivasa Ramanujan, asking for support. The theorems Ramanujan offered were so compelling that Hardy concluded: "I had never
seen anything in the least like them before. A single look at them is
enough to show that they could only be written down by a mathematician of the highest class." And in a characteristic Hardy flourish,
he added: "They must be true because, if they were not true, no one
would have the imagination to invent them."

One time Hardy visited Ramanujan in the hospital and commented to him that he had ridden over in taxi cab number 1729,
and being British and clever, Hardy added that the number seemed
to him a rather dull one. "No," Ramanujan replied, "it is a very interesting number; it is the smallest number expressible as a sum of
two cubes in two different ways." (The two solutions are $1^3 + 12^3$ and
$9^3 + 10^3$. One of the reasons I fled my career as mathematician for
easier fields to plow, such as linguistics, is stories like that one: great
mathematicians emit an otherworldly glow of intellect.)

The Hardy-Ramanujan collaboration in number theory is one
of the most famous in mathematics. It ended sadly, in a way that
reminds me somewhat of Turing's death (though homosexuality
played no part in it). Ramanujan fell ill of a mysterious wasting ail-

ment that probably was tuberculosis but might have been something more akin to loneliness, isolation, and starvation. As a Brahmin of the strictest observance, he could eat only what he or another Brahmin cooked, and Cambridge did have not enough Brahmins or enough *pukka* Indian food to keep him healthy. He returned to India and died in 1920, age thirty-two.

Turing was definitely odd. He held up his trousers with string, wore his pajamas under his sports coat, and affected a teddy bear—shades of Sebastian Flyte in *Brideshead Revisited*—named Porgy. During tutorials, he often propped up Porgy by the fire and greeted his students with "Porgy is very studious this morning." Turing once showed up for a tennis match wearing nothing but a raincoat.

Then there was the voice, high-pitched and likely to stall in mid-sentence with an "Ah-ah-ah-ah." The words, when they came, could have been polysyllabic monstrosities, a wild scheme, or a rude suggestion. Apart from the voice, what people remembered about Turing were his hands, with odd ridges on his fingernails, never cleaned or cut.

Odd as all this might have been outside the college gates, it was hardly noticed inside Cambridge. Some of the older dons may have looked down their noses at Turing and his personal habits, but the undergraduates liked him. Above all, he was not a snob—unusual for an Oxbridge Fellow—and that was refreshingly novel. Also, he liked to talk to students about mathematics and just about anything else, though not his love life.

THE SECOND WORLD WAR ARRIVED just as Turing's research career was about to take flight. When war was declared, Turing announced that his patriotic duty was to join the war effort. Britain wasn't going to make the same tragic mistake it had made in the First World War, when everybody was subject to conscription, meaning that budding scientists, writers, painters, and poets alike were sent to France and Gallipoli to end up as cannon fodder. A generation of talent died in stinking, putrid trenches or, like the poet Rupert Brooke, of sunstroke. T. S. Eliot got it right: the 1920s were a waste land indeed.

The military is known for giving its personnel ridiculous assignments: they saw my math degrees and put me to work as a clerk-typist. In a miracle of good sense, Turing was recruited to work on code breaking at the British center in Bletchley Park, north of London and midway between Oxford and Cambridge. His mathematical work fed easily into code and cipher breaking.

It was a brilliant appointment. Turing, more than any other single person, was responsible for the hugely successful assault on the

Figure 6.1. The Enigma machine, showing the plugboard. Wikimedia Commons.

German enciphering machine known as the Enigma. He made dazzling contributions to both pure and applied mathematics and pioneered what today we call artificial intelligence.

Turing was not put administratively in charge of Bletchley. England might have lost the war if he had been. He had no talent for administration. His gift was for seeing connections that other human beings couldn't see or even imagine, for thinking of solutions (like the computer) to problems that were beyond the ken of everybody else. Plus, he was handy. If a light socket didn't work, Turing was the go-to guy to get it fixed in a hurry.

He felt very much at home in the shadow world of Bletchley. There was no time for academic snobbery or all the class nonsense of British soceity. There was a war to win. The code breakers were an eccentric lot: winners of crossword puzzle contests, chess masters, linguists, math wizards. With Turing's funny laugh and unappealing fingernails and unconventional clothing, he fit right in. Churchill, who loved the romance of the spy world, called the code breakers the geese who laid the golden eggs but never cackled. Once, on a tour of Bletchley, seeing all the odd-looking creatures with their peculiar mannerisms, he whispered to the director "When I told you to leave no stone unturned in finding people to work here, I didn't expect you to take me literally."

David Kahn, the dean of historians of codes and ciphers, once wrote that Bletchley's success in breaking the German Enigma shortened the war by up to two years. Probably six months to a year is more like it, but by any measure it was a towering accomplishment. Because the work at Bletchley was classified and most of it would remain so for almost half a century (some of it is still kept secret), Turing did not receive any public acclaim when the war ended. But he was secretly elected a Fellow of the Royal Society and made an Officer of the Most Excellent Order of the British Empire.

After the war, Turing created one of the first designs for a stored-program computer, the ACE (Automatic Computing Engine). In 1948 he joined the Computing Laboratory at Manchester University, where he assisted in the development of computers and became interested in mathematical biology. One of his lifelong interests was in the Fibonacci sequence of numbers, in which each number in the series is the sum of the previous two: 0, 1, 1, 2, 3, 5, 8, 13, 21, 34, 55, 89, etc. He argued that branching patterns in shrubs and plants followed the Fibonacci sequence. The idea sounds strange: why would a numerical sequence derived formally from a number system be reflected in nature? But there is something to it; for example, the outsides of pineapples are typically covered by scales arranged in three spirals, the number of scales in each corresponding to consecutive Fibonacci numbers, such as 8, 13, and 21.

As MENTIONED EARLIER, THE TREATMENT that Turing received as a homosexual involved entrenched notions of snobbery and the British class system. The intersection of class and sexuality can be seen in sharp focus by contrasting how Turing was punished with how Guy Burgess (1911–1963), Turing's contemporary and one of the most infamous traitors in British history, went unpunished for the same infraction. Burgess was a member of the Cambridge Five—along with Donald Maclean, Kim Philby, Anthony Blunt, and John Cairncross—a spy ring that passed every important secret they could get their hands on to the Soviets. Besides intelligence about military plans and atomic weapons, they revealed the names of British agents, often people they themselves knew or had recruited, who were quickly rounded up by the KGB and shot in the head after being tortured.

Burgess worked in the Foreign Office, and he was homosexual. In the Cambridge of the 1930s, he had been the embodiment of a type, perhaps of an era: handsome, blue eyed, curly haired, conversationally brilliant, politically engaged. He was recruited by the Soviets while a student. He later served as the model for the mole (Bill Haydon) in John le Carré's great spy novel *Tinker, Tailor, Soldier, Spy* (1974). At the Foreign Office, Burgess had a sensitive position with access to top secrets.

He became a heavy drinker and a slob infamous on three continents for deficiencies in his personal habits. And he was aggressively and publicly homosexual. He had to be relatively careful in England about his homosexuality, but abroad he could run wild. The British ambassador in Egypt had to reprimand him for getting drunk and chasing a young man down a hotel corridor shouting, "I must have this delicious boy!" The ambassador said he was disturbing the other guests. Burgess was too much even by the louche standards of Cambridge, and the Soviets eventually had to spirit him away to Moscow.

Burgess once was arrested in a men's lavatory at Victoria Station in London, having passed a note inviting the man in the next stall to have sex. The recipient happened to be a vice officer, who promptly arrested Burgess and took him down to the constabulary. There he called some of his influential friends, notably Lady Rothschild of the Rothschild banking family, to intercede on his behalf, which they were more than happy to do.

Burgess's disingenuous explanation was that he had been sitting on the toilet reading a borrowed copy of the novel *Middlemarch* when a note he had been using as a bookmark fell out and sailed onto the floor of the next stall. The utter implausibility of the lie was a nice touch, altogether typical of the outrageous Burgess, and the police hastened to swallow this preposterous story and be done with the whole thing. He was sent home without a stain on his record.

But that kind of good-natured treatment of homosexuals was a privilege reserved for the ruling class, not for those caught in homosexual encounters who didn't know Lady Rothschild's phone number. In other words, people like Alan Turing. Turing was Burgess's opposite in about every way. He was not well born, and although a Fellow of King's, he was too ungainly and too much an odd duck to have made the right connections at university. Alan Turing—FRS, OBE, Quondam Fellow of King's College, Cambridge—was a loner, all the establishment markers notwithstanding. He didn't belong, didn't have the right friends; he was only an eccentric mathematical genius who had served his country with distinction and quiet valor. No civilian, apart, I suppose, from Winston Churchill, did more to beat the Germans than Turing. He was a bona fide war hero.

When Turing was arrested, did *no one* feel an obligation to intervene and get the charges dropped? Couldn't someone have let Churchill, recently back in as Prime Minister, know? Why bother to have an old-boy network if you're not going to use it to save someone like Alan Turing?

THERE HAS BEEN INCREASING RECOGNITION of what Turing accomplished. Since 1966, the Turing Award has been given annually by the Association for Computing Machinery to a person for technical contributions to the computing community. It is considered to be the computing world's highest honor, almost equivalent to the Nobel Prize.

In 1994, a stretch of the A6010 road around Manchester was named Alan Turing Way. A bridge on this road was widened and carries today the name Alan Turing Bridge. A statue of Turing was unveiled in Manchester on 23 June 2001. It is in Sackville Park, near the Canal Street gay village. The statue depicts the "Father of Computer Science" sitting on a bench in the park, where he often went to be alone.

Turing is shown holding an apple—a symbol classically used to represent forbidden love, the object that is said to have inspired Isaac Newton's theory of gravitation, and the means of Turing's own death. The cast-bronze bench carries in relief the text "Alan Mathison Turing 1912–1954" and the motto "Founder of Computer Science" as it would appear if enciphered by an Enigma machine: IEKYF ROMSI ADXUO KVKZC GUBJ. (To be pedantic, Enigma would have enciphered the last group, GUBJ [four letters], as a five-letter group by adding a dummy letter such as Q, giving GUBJQ.)

On 10 September 2009, following an Internet campaign, Prime Minister Gordon Brown made an official public apology on behalf of the British government for the way in which Turing was treated after the war. America has done its bit, too. The *Princeton Alumni Weekly* named Turing the second-most significant alumnus in the history of Princeton University, second only to President James Madison. (Turing attended Princeton for two years in the 1930s.) A 1.5-ton life-size statue of Turing was unveiled on 19 June 2007 at Bletchley Park, having been commissioned by the American billionaire Sidney Frank, who made his money in Grey Goose vodka. In 1999, *Time* magazine named Turing one of the 100 Most Important People of the 20th Century for his role in the creation of the modern computer. Queen Elizabeth issued a Royal Pardon to Turing in 2013.

Turing had extraordinarily good luck in the man who became his biographer, Andrew Hodges. *Alan Turing: The Enigma* came out in 1983, and a subsequent edition in 2012, on the centenary of Turing's birth. Hodges is a distinguished mathematical physicist who is gay.

He had access to all of Turing's papers, plus many people who knew Turing in life. His authoritative biography is a beautifully written tour de force. I relied on it heavily for this lecture.

Turing reminds me of Ramanujan in being profoundly different from most great mathematicians: both were strange geniuses, outsiders. But there the resemblance ends. Turing was a war hero. His work at Bletchley saved countless lives and shortened the war. He can claim joint fatherhood of the computer (along with von Neumann). The open embrace of his homosexuality took courage that can hardly be imagined today, and he died for it. We still do not understand the man and probably never will: his life was lived in what in a different context has been called "a wilderness of mirrors."

Iain Stewart, a Conservative Member of Parliament who was involved in the campaign to secure a Royal Pardon, said: "Alan Turing was an incredibly important figure in our history. He was the father of computer science and the originator of the dominant technology of the late 20th century. He made a huge impact on the world he lived in and left a legacy for the world of today and tomorrow. This royal pardon is a just reward for a man who was stripped of his honour, his work, and the loyalty he showed his nation."

Fall Semester 2018

Louis George Martin

7

Louis George Martin
Champion Weightlifter

JOHN D. FAIR

Louis George Martin (1936–2015), weightlifter and physical culturist, was born on 11 November 1936 in Kingston, Jamaica, the son of Ita Stanford (Frank) Martin, saddle maker and chef, and his wife, Valeeta. His parents had met in Cuba and lived there for over a decade. They provided a middle-class home on Oliver Road, Kingston, where education was a priority for Louis and his older siblings, Joyce and Frank. He thrived in school. The excellent teaching and English-style examination system enabled him to skip some grades, and he developed a lifelong love of poetry.

After leaving school, Martin, who was also proficient in sports, started weight training to improve his appearance. In the warm Jamaican climate, bodily exposure was the norm, and a well-developed male physique was highly prized. Each day, Martin worked as an apprentice electrician and then trained with his brother in their backyard gym in the evenings and at the beach on weekends.

Encouraged by the cosmopolitan outlook of his parents, Martin immigrated to England in May 1956, settling with a friend in Derby. Within two days, he had secured another apprenticeship and found a gym in the back of a pub, where he was enthusiastically welcomed. It was a seamless relocation, providing Martin with immediate financial and emotional security. His engaging personality and work ethic enabled him to make friends easily and avoid racial prejudice.

With encouragement from other weightlifters, Martin started entering and winning local physique competitions and attracting press coverage. Only four months after arriving in England, he was the "sensation" of a show at Langley Mill, Derbyshire, and received favorable notice from Oscar Heidenstam, who headed the National Amateur Bodybuilding Association (NABBA). Winning the Mr. Midlands title at Newark enabled him to compete in the prestigious Mr. Universe contest in 1957, where he placed fourth in his weight class. Concurrently, the Scottish weightlifting champion Bill Orbin urged him to try the Olympic lifts (press, snatch, and clean and jerk), with an eye to competing in the British Empire and Commonwealth games in Cardiff in 1958. At that competition, representing Jamaica, Martin missed all of his presses. He contemplated a return to bodybuilding, but with support from fellow lifters and coaches, he continued to train for the Olympic lifts, eventually winning the Midlands championships and setting several British Commonwealth records as a middle heavyweight. Martin was named NABBA sportsman of the year in 1958 and sports personality of the year in 1959, and his pictures frequently graced the pages and covers of *Health & Strength* magazine.

Popular acclaim for his athletic achievements became international in 1959 when Martin, representing Great Britain, hoisted a 303-pound press, 292-pound snatch, and 385.75-pound clean and jerk to upset the great Russian champion Arkady Vorobiev at the world championships in Warsaw. With enthusiastic crowd support, he lifted 15 pounds more than he had ever done, and claimed the world title by having a lower body weight than Vorobiev. Martin's charismatic platform manner had a special appeal. His coach David Webster described it in a 2015 reminiscence: "On the platform he would stalk backwards and forwards behind the bar—glaring at it with nostrils flaring and muttering self-hypnotising phrases before slapping his hands together and raising a cloud of chalk." Then he would pounce on the bar and rip it to arm's length. Martin won a bronze medal at the Rome Olympics in 1960. Hampered by training injuries, he was defeated by Vorobiev and Trofim Lomakin, another Soviet weightlifter. Hoping for a comeback in 1961, he beat Vorobiev at the world championships in Vienna, but both were bested by the Polish champion Ireneusz Paliński, who had moved up from the light-heavyweight division. At Budapest in 1962, Martin turned the tables, defeating Paliński for both the European and world titles with a world-record (three-lift) total of 1,056 pounds, a feat he repeated in Stockholm in 1963. These multiple victories against the world's best weightlifters marked the high point of his athletic career.

At the Olympics in Tokyo in 1964, Martin won a silver medal, beaten by the Russian lifter Vladimir Golovanov. (Paliński took bronze.) Undeterred, Martin reached another milestone in his life a month later by marrying Ann Robinson (1940–2007), a seamstress who was the daughter of Richard Henry Robinson, a florist; he met her while working as an electrician for British Rail. Their mixed-race union at the Victoria Street Congregational Church in Derby on 14 November 1964 attracted national attention when Lord Snowden, then married to Princess Margaret, photographed the couple at their home for a *Sunday Times* color supplement. They had two sons, Louis Martin Jr. (b. 1967) and Richard (b. 1971), who pursued successful careers in higher education and public health, respectively.

Meanwhile, Martin re-established his renown as the best middle-heavyweight weightlifter by overtaking Golovanov at the world championships in Tehran in 1965. Owing to a dramatic increase in anabolic steroid use and correspondingly higher lifting totals, however, Martin could no longer compete on an equal basis with the Eastern Europeans. In a desperate bid to secure a bronze medal at the Mexico City Olympics in 1968, he failed on three attempts to negotiate a 424.25-pound clean and jerk. But he returned as a local hero to Jamaica to win a gold medal at the Commonwealth Games in 1966, a feat he repeated in Edinburgh in 1970, after which he retired from competition. Although knowing he could no longer win world titles, he was consoled by the immortal lines of Omar Khayyam: "The Moving Finger writes; and, having writ, / Moves on."

For the next several decades, Martin operated a small weightlifting and bodybuilding gym in Derby that was free for underprivileged youths. Having little direct experience of racial prejudice, he believed most Britons confused class prejudice with racism. He challenged both preconceptions and sought to give voice to underrepresented immigrants and minorities in Derby. Though unsuccessful in a bid for a local council seat in 1971 and 1972 as a Conservative candidate, he remained active in public life and later served as president of the British Weightlifting Association.

In 1962, Martin became a British citizen, and in 1965 he was appointed MBE for his services to weightlifting. In 2012 he served as an Olympic torchbearer in the Midlands before the London games. A highly cultured man, he recited from memory (often at competitions) the works of Shelley, Longfellow, and Shakespeare, and had a fine singing voice. He had a deep appreciation for English culture and the educational values that had been instilled in him as a youth. He died on 16 January 2015 of the asbestos-related cancer mesothelioma, at the home of his son Richard, 2 Castle Court, Heanor, Derbyshire. His burial on 19 January at the Nottingham Road cemetery in Chaddesden was followed by a celebration of his life at the Heanor Conservative Club on 2 February.

Fall Semester 2017

A version of this lecture appeared in the *Oxford Dictionary of National Biography.*

Benjamin Disraeli, 1868. Photograph by W. and D. Downey. NPG x662. © National Portrait Gallery, London.

8

Benjamin Disraeli and Oscar Wilde

SANDRA MAYER

In 1886, five years after Benjamin Disraeli's death, Oscar Wilde reviewed two newly published editions of the former Prime Minister's correspondence. In the midst of refashioning his own public persona from hyped prophet of the Aesthetic movement to a critically acclaimed writer with serious literary credentials, Wilde noted admiringly: "Lord Beaconsfield played a brilliant comedy to a 'pit full of Kings,' and was immensely pleased at his own performance." Like many of his contemporaries, Wilde was struck by how Disraeli's public image effortlessly combined the roles and personae of bestselling novelist, flamboyant dandy, eminent statesman, Jewish-born upstart, and icon of Conservative politics in a remarkable feat of perpetual migration between different sociocultural fields and contexts. For Wilde, as for many others who remained eternally puzzled by the elusiveness and mercurial quality of Disraeli's reputation, the writer-*cum*-politician's "life was the most brilliant of paradoxes."[1] It certainly served as a model for someone who, as an Irishman and aspiring literary celebrity, shared Disraeli's outsider status, his flashy Byronic dandyism, his mastery of the quotable epigram, and his self-fashioning strategies in the quest for fame and acceptance among the British establishment.

Wilde's only novel, *The Picture of Dorian Gray* (1890), with its heady mix of scandal, sensationalism, celebrity, and autobiographical revelation, likely drew inspiration from Disraeli's equally explosive literary debut, *Vivian Grey*. Published anonymously by Henry Colburn in

1826, the novel was a silver-fork potboiler that combined romance and realism, political satire and Gothic suspense, and catered to the voyeuristic desires of a reading public increasingly obsessed with the glittering social world of the rich, beautiful, and alluringly notorious. The work owed its best-selling succès de scandale in no small measure to the marketing strategies of the publisher, whose advance notes and keys to the characters cleverly suggested that the novel had been written by an author of high social standing with privileged access to the social elites depicted. Cunningly aware of the growing impact of celebrity culture in Regency England, Disraeli found success in turning out silver-fork novels for a burgeoning, commercialized literary marketplace, though he realized that such endeavors risked turning an aspiring author into a "literary prostitute," as he complained in a letter to his patron, Benjamin Austen, in 1829.[2]

Both Disraeli and, half a century later, Oscar Wilde skillfully exploited the mechanisms of media celebrity. They became famous authors of a recognizable type in an age that saw the proliferation of mass markets and new media, revolutionary advances in communication technology, the arrival of flourishing commodity and consumer cultures, and the exponential growth of literate mass audiences. By the mid-Victorian period, celebrity culture had made significant inroads in virtually every sphere of public life, including art, entertainment, politics, and royalty, prompting one of the narrators in Wilkie Collins's 1868 novel *The Moonstone* to observe with barely disguised incredulity: "In our modern system of civilization, celebrity (no matter of what kind) is the lever that will move anything."[3] The comment points to the demographic, social, economic, and technological transformations that contributed to a more democratic attainability of fame through dexterous image management and the successful cultivation of a ubiquitous or, in many cases, notorious public persona. At a time when mass-mediated visibility, self-fashioning, and public display became the key ingredients in the accumulation of "celebrity capital," Benjamin Disraeli and Oscar Wilde calculatedly formed and performed their celebrity personae across a range of social fields and contexts, challenging traditional social categories and leading to charges of insincerity and the prioritizing of style over substance. Rather than indicating a lack of "authenticity," however, each man's symbiotic mingling of his many parallel lives was part of a carefully staged performance of the self that was attuned to the desires of an increasingly pervasive Victorian celebrity culture, which, paradoxically, could function as a social leveler within a traditionally class-based society.

Few nineteenth-century literary figures can be considered more adept at exploiting the late-Victorian culture industry to his advantage than Oscar Wilde, whose celebrity status preceded his success as a writer. The fact that "fame would *launch* Wilde's career, not cap it,"[4] identified Wilde as a prototypical modern celebrity, disparagingly described by Daniel Boorstin in the early 1960s as a "person who is known for his well-knownness":[5] the representative of a type of renown associated with a distinctive public persona founded on notoriety or outrageousness rather than any specific talent, merit, or achievement, and that gains significance primarily by being circulated in the mass media. Wilde's formative self-publicizing performance is visually encapsulated in William Powell Frith's painting *A Private View at the Royal Academy, 1881* (1883), which might be read as a satirical commentary on the mechanisms at play in the production and consumption of celebrity (plate 1). Here, at the opening of the 1881 Royal Academy summer exhibition, the dandy-aesthete and would-be poet features prominently in a panoramic vision of late-Victorian fashionable society. Unmistakable amidst a crowd of aristocrats, clergymen, politicians, actors, artists, writers, and professional beauties, he can be seen preaching the gospel of Aestheticism to a rapt audience of (largely female) star-struck admirers while being eyed with a mix of wonder and suspicion by the doyens of the Victorian establishment. The painting presents the young Oscar Wilde busily engaged in inventing himself as the self-declared "apostle" of the Aesthetic movement. Absorbed in a blatantly performative act of self-display, Wilde willingly makes himself available for consumption and turns himself into a commodity, an object of art to be gazed at and scrutinized in much the same way as the paintings on the walls. Wilde's pose as a self-styled arbiter of taste and an eccentrically dressed, quick-witted conversationalist was part of a carefully choreographed self-advertising campaign that transformed him into a universally recognized figure long before he made his name as a writer. This transformation was facilitated by the advent of a public culture that no longer viewed lineage, wealth, or achievement as the necessary cornerstones of public pre-eminence, and instead rewarded an entrepreneurial genius for attention grabbing and self-commodification. "Life has been your art," Lord Henry Wotton tells the static, immaculately ageless Dorian Gray toward the grim denouement of Wilde's novel, which eerily echoes the famous Wildean quip, reported by André Gide: "I've put my genius into my life; I've put only my talent into my works."[6]

The spectacular success of Wilde's 1882–83 North American lecture tour—instigated by the theatre impresario Richard D'Oyly

Figure 8.1. Oscar Wilde, 1883. Photograph by Napoleon Sarany. NPG P1133. © National Portrait Gallery, London.

Carte as a publicity stunt to promote the New York City production of the Gilbert and Sullivan operetta *Patience*—has frequently invited fairy tale analogies. By all accounts, it triggered a remarkable metamorphosis during which "a young nobody becomes a somebody." As Wilde found himself courted by literary coteries and political grandees and besieged by journalists and admirers of both sexes, "the transformative events of 1882 would divide his life sharply into Before and After," as Michèle Mendelssohn argues in her recent book on Wilde's path to global iconicity.[7] "Nothing like it since Dickens, they tell me. I am torn in bits by Society," Wilde boasted.[8] But while the enormous scale of attention received by the flamboyant aesthete hardly rested on a reputation as a giant of English literature, Wilde certainly matched Dickens when it came to the latter's aptitude for carefully choreographed public performance and diligently managed publicity. With his shrewd sense of what today would be called self-branding, Wilde turned himself into an artifact of consumption to be traded and marketed through cartoons, satires, popular songs, and "aesthetic advertisements" that used his image and the emblems of Aestheticism to sell a wealth of goods, including cigars, corsets, and stoves. A playful letter sent home in May 1882 reveals Wilde's crucial awareness that in an emerging mass-media society, celebrity capital could be made and unmade by the forces of commerce and media circulation: "I am now six feet high (my name on the placards), printed it is true in those primary colours against which I pass my life protesting, but still it is fame, and anything is better than virtuous obscurity, even one's own name in alternate colours of Albert blue and magenta and six feet high."[9]

Wilde found forerunners among fictionalized self-fashioning dandies and aspiring men of letters. Writing to George Curzon, a prominent Conservative politician whom he knew from his days at Oxford (and a future Viceroy of India), he described the powerfully gratifying sensation of being a universally fêted lion: "As for myself, I feel like Tancred or Lothair. I travel in such a state, for in a free country one cannot live without slaves." Three years later, when Curzon was about to become assistant private secretary to Prime Minister Salisbury, Wilde addressed him in a letter as "you brilliant young Coningsby."[10] Playfully ironic as they might be, Wilde's evocations of Coningsby, Tancred, and Lothair, the eponymous heroes of three of Benjamin Disraeli's novels, published in 1844, 1847, and 1870, suggest a certain affinity for the novel-writing statesman and his work. Charting the spiritual pilgrimages of dashing, fabulously wealthy, and naïve but pure-hearted heroes in the throes of religious and constitutional struggles, the novels present an eclectic mix of bildungsroman, romance, fantasy, roman à clef, satire, allegory, and fairy tale that appealed to a reading public fascinated with their potent syntheses of Eastern mysticism, dark political conspiracy, salacious gossip, and autobiographical disclosure.

OFFERING A COMMENTARY ON THE distinctive manifestations and contours of late-Victorian celebrity culture, Frith's painting subtly points to the irony of an art exhibition—the display of objects created by artistic mastery, skill, and achievement—becoming an arena for the unbridled display, exhibition, and objectification of the self. At the same time, it sets up a contrast between celebrity as a lesser type of fame, one that is transitory, ephemeral, inseparably linked with mass mediation and commodification and therefore of no lasting cultural value, and, on the other hand, enduring, posthumous greatness, defined by the traditional markers of genius, heroism, and merit. While the former is represented by shamelessly self-promoting social climbers like Wilde and Lillie Langtry, mingling with the illustrious crowd to see and, even more crucially, to be seen, the latter appears to be the prerogative of those immortalized by art. Recently deceased, in April 1881, Disraeli is a looming presence by absence in Frith's painting; two portraits of him, one by John Everett Millais and posthumously completed at the request of Queen Victoria, mark his imminent transformation into a national and political icon, the center of a myth-making cult of memorialization under the banner of the primrose, said to be Disraeli's favorite flower and about to become a populist emblem of his political values and patriotism.

Many of Disraeli's contemporaries saw his career as progressing straightforwardly from the chimerical celebrity of the literary lion to the venerable gravitas of the distinguished elder statesman. A more complex picture emerges when one considers how Disraeli shrewdly responded to the growing impact of celebrity culture, which can at least partly be explained by his indebtedness to the Romantic traditions of artistic self-conception and public-image construction. Though lacking a title, personal wealth, and a university education, Disraeli grew up in a literary and scholarly household, presided over by his father, Isaac D'Israeli, whose friends included some of the major figures of English Romanticism: John Murray, Tom Moore, Samuel Rogers, Lady Blessington, Robert Southey, William Godwin, and his daughter, Mary Shelley. Their firsthand anecdotes and tales nurtured in the future author a lifelong fascination with Lord Byron, who, along with Percy Bysshe Shelley, is the thinly veiled subject of Disraeli's 1837 novel *Venetia,* a highly complex fictional engagement with his own Romantic idealism. Frequently dismissed by nineteenth- and twentieth-century critics as a potboiler hastily composed to make money to fend off the bailiffs, the novel has more recently been reassessed as Disraeli's attempt at realigning his youthful fascination with second-generation Romanticism with his newly created public persona as a respectable Tory MP and statesman. The novel indeed presents more than a straightforward exorcism of Romantic political and social radicalism in favor of Victorian respectability, order, and pragmatism. Like his other literary works, the book served Disraeli as a "workshop of the self," a safe testing ground for developing, articulating, and negotiating his public and private identities and trying to come to terms with the constant tension he experienced between art and action, the visionary and the expedient.[11] While such interpretative approaches contribute to a timely rethinking and acknowledgment of the complexity of Disraeli's literary work, its more pragmatic aspect must not be overlooked: the engagement with celebrity culture as one of the most enduring legacies of the Romantic era in the Victorian age. *Venetia* features a range of phenomena in which early-nineteenth-century literary celebrity culture manifested itself, including literary lionism, fan worship, literary tourism, and the veneration of material artifacts associated with an idolized author. The novel's underlying theme is the public's obsession with the author's private life, notorious personality, physical presence, and scandalous sexuality, fed by the reading public's desire to forge a closer emotional and physical bond with its literary heroes.

As Andrew Elfenbein suggests, Disraeli's admiration for Byron was "more complicated than [mere] fan-worship"; from Byron's career, "he learned . . . something about becoming a celebrity."[12] Since fame was no longer the exclusive prerogative of those commanding high rank and position, ambitious young men like Disraeli could hope to build a career on a capital of notoriety by performing a sexually risqué pose of effeminate Byronic dandyism. The young Benjamin Disraeli pictured by Daniel Maclise in the May 1833 issue of *Fraser's Magazine*'s "Gallery of Literary Characters" is a truly Byronic disciple in elaborately coiffed ringlets and fashionable frills and laces: a social climber languidly propped against a cluttered mantelpiece and appropriately accessorized with Turkish slippers and a Turkish pipe. His carefully cultivated act of Byronic self-fashioning served as a means of gaining public attention and successfully "operated as a form of symbolic capital that might compensate for the lack of more conventional forms of social capital."[13] Disraeli's Byronic allegiance was also firmly rooted in his identification with the boundary-breaking, and hence shamefully wronged and ostracized, rebel-genius, who steadfastly defied convention and

AUTHOR OF VIVIAN GREY.

Figure 8.2. Benjamin Disraeli. Drawing by Daniel Maclise, *Fraser's Magazine*, May 1833.

morality and transgressed social norms. Indeed, Byron's scandalous celebrity served Disraeli as a blueprint for turning the potential obstacle of his own social, political, and ethnic outsider status into an asset and for reinventing himself as a chosen prophet-hero and visionary who would react to anti-Semitic sneers and antagonism with haughty arrogance.

Disraeli's personal notebooks and diaries provide an intriguing insight into his self-affirming identity construction, laying bare an urgent need to perform the self in line with the "autobiographical life"—the "life lived in anticipation of one's biographers."[14] Disraeli's 1842 commonplace book, for instance, offers striking evidence of this performance of the self in a curious chronicle that follows the principle of compulsive name-dropping. It lines up historical figures and contemporaries alongside one another in bizarrely themed categories, including "Eccentric Characters," "Second class, but remarkable," "Dandies," "Female Adventurers," and "Literary-Political," in which Disraeli includes fellow author-*cum*-politicians Thomas Macaulay, Edward Bulwer-Lytton, and John Cam Hobhouse. Another category, "Spirit of the Times," comprises an eclectic mix of individuals ranging from Alexander the Great, Julius Caesar, and Jesus Christ to Shakespeare, Pope Julius II, and Byron; it reveals Disraeli's need to place himself within a tradition of convention-defying great men, visionaries, and transgressive Byronic heroes as identity-shaping models to emulate and, eventually, to overcome.[15]

Modeling himself on someone like Byron also meant embracing and negotiating a double act of art and action. Disraeli's life and career reveal the close intersections of the literary and the political, and together with the celebrity-enhancing possibilities of his social and ethnic Otherness, they became mutually sustaining factors in the shaping of his reputation. Recent scholarship has demonstrated how, for Disraeli, literature and politics represented closely interconnected arenas of self-invention and self-projection through which he tried both to gain public acclaim and attention and to align the life of action with that of creative imagination. In his 2013 literary biography of Disraeli, Robert O'Kell acknowledges the intimate relationship between the two spheres of Disraeli's career as "enactments of the same urgencies and purposes," stressing how he treated "politics as a form of fiction" and theatrical self-display, and "fiction as an expression of politics."[16]

The Byronic socialite and flamboyant dandy causing a sensation in Lady Blessington's literary salon; the fast-selling silver-fork novelist; the political opportunist and rabble-rouser responsible for Peel's fall; the Jewish-born upstart reinventing himself as an enigmatic

Eastern oracle—the curious mingling of Disraeli's multiple public
roles and personae presented a blurring of boundaries that many
of his contemporaries found highly puzzling. Critical responses to
his late novels *Lothair* (1870) and *Endymion* (1880), published in the
wake of his first and second terms as Prime Minister, suggest that
literary production, with its whiff of flippancy and frivolousness, sat
uneasily with the gravitas and dignity of respectable statesmanship
and potentially undercut Disraeli's trustworthiness as a Tory party
leader. At the same time, the novels were considered extraordinary
literary coups for which their author received huge advance pay-
ments and publicity, and the elusiveness and mercurial quality of his
public image crucially contributed to his fame and exceptional position in the popular imagination. While many Victorians still looked
upon Disraeli's career as a natural and teleological ascent up the social ladder from Byronic poseur to internationally venerated senior
statesman, a growing counter-tendency accepted his complex and
sustained border crossings as the key to his public pre-eminence.
At a time when celebrity culture had firmly taken root in both the
"world of fancy" and the "world of Blue Books," his dual commitment to literature and politics only added to his allure. In an 1874
review titled "Mr. Disraeli's Novels," Leslie Stephen offered a poignant analysis of Disraeli's complexly tangled literary and political
lives, which, Stephen insisted, needed to be regarded in light of a
"theory of a double consciousness" and which required Disraeli's
readers to "pray with the mystic and sneer with the politician."[17]

OSCAR WILDE MAY NOT HAVE LAUNCHED a political career, but he
tried out different avenues that would lead him straight into the
public limelight as a lecturer, flamboyant dandy-about-town, art
critic, journalist, and academic. Someone like Disraeli was certainly
a role model: an outsider who, throughout his life, continued to be
confronted with anti-Semitic prejudice, who was routinely portrayed
in contemporary cartoons as an essentially un-English impostor, a
sleazy Oriental flatterer, and a sinister conjuror, and yet who, brush-
ing aside all adversity and personal antagonism, managed to scram-
ble his way to the "top of the greasy pole."[18] Just as Disraeli's Jewish
origins enduringly defined his character and identity in virtually all
his public representations, Wilde's own alienness as an Irishman uneasily positioned him at an isolated vantage point on the edges of
the English establishment. It ultimately turned him not only into
a shrewd observer of English society but also a skilful operator and
networker who was aware of the crucial importance of a carefully
managed public profile and the ready embrace of consumerist aesthetics. Wilde, much like Disraeli, actively and cunningly partici-

pated in an "economy of sensation," in which a whiff of notoriety or scandal was not necessarily detrimental to becoming a much-noted public figure, even if they found themselves beleaguered by charges of plagiarism, immorality, insincerity, or literary inconsequentiality.[19] In one of the most famous epigrams in *The Picture of Dorian Gray*, a novel whose timeless appeal can be related to its perceptive meditations on the modern condition of celebrity, Lord Henry muses, "There is only one thing in the world worse than being talked about, and that is not being talked about."[20]

The celebrity capital accumulated by Wilde was rooted in performance, self-display, commodification, and the construction and cultivation of his public persona, but it was also connected with his calculated negotiations between elitism and populism, art and fashion, intellectualism and entertainment, public and private worlds, whose results are reflected in his works and their potential for multiple significations and interpretations. His pursuit of literary celebrity, his craving for critical acclaim and commercial success as a dramatist, demanded a certain degree of accommodation to market dynamics and rendered him susceptible to artistic compromise; ever the pragmatist, even while treading a precariously thin line between conformity and subversion, he was willing to make concessions to bourgeois sensibilities and the mainstream tastes of late-Victorian upper-class and upper-middle-class theatergoers. Wilde's popularity as a dramatist in the 1890s thus firmly rested on his versatility and chameleon-like ability to adapt. He masterfully understood not only how to please by taking the edge off the rebellious anti-philistinism propagated in his critical essays, but also how to tease by way of the subtle subversion of social gesture and convention.

VERSATILE AND AMBIGUOUS PERFORMANCES of the self across a variety of social fields, media, and genres, marked by the ability to change guises and resist rigid categorization, necessarily raise questions of authenticity and sincerity. *What Is He?* was the self-reflexive title of a best-selling 1833 pamphlet in which Disraeli set out to justify his seemingly opportunistic switching of political allegiance from Radicalism to Toryism. It was a legitimate query that continued to preoccupy nineteenth-century biographers and critics, especially when it came to Disraeli's migration between the literary and the political fields. But what challenged norms of clear-cut categorization ultimately contributed to a process of celebrity making that resulted from the dynamic interaction of Disraeli's multiple personae. They colluded in the shaping of his public profile, as alluded to in a commemorative verse tribute that appeared at the time of Disraeli's death: "Sage, patriot, warrior, statesman, writer, friend, /

Peer, Viscount, all harmoniously blend."[21] Similarly, from the very
beginning, Wilde's career was built on his remarkable capacity for
mask switching and role play and his playful collapsing of boundaries between art and life, depth and surface, authenticity and performance. Vacillating between bitter self-castigation and the desire to
salvage a vestige of self-respect from the dregs of a shattered existence, he wrote in 1897, in his long prison letter, *De Profundis:* "I was
a man who stood in symbolic relations to the art and culture of my
age. . . . I treated Art as the supreme reality, and life as a mere mode
of fiction: I awoke the imagination of my century so that it created
myth and legend around me."[22] What appealed to the imagination
and myth-making tendencies of his own century is also what makes
the author a cultural icon of and for our times: a defiance of essentialist notions of a fixed and stable self and the playful celebration
of individuals as "complex multiform creatures."[23] His resistance to
fixity and finite interpretation, his tightrope act balancing innovation and conventionality, provocation and appeasement, perpetually invite audiences to become coauthors in the ongoing process
of adapting and reinventing his mercurial public image. This is a
point worth stressing, for even if Wilde, in a desperate attempt at
cathartic self-affirmation, rather overemphasized his own agency,
his remarkable life and no less dramatic afterlives yield poignant
evidence that he was not the sole author of his reputation. In the
project of controlling his public persona, his individual agency got
hopelessly embroiled in a knotted web of ideology, social convention, sexual politics, and cultural mythmaking, drawing attention to
the porous lines between fame and infamy, celebrity and notoriety.
There is a certain timeless truth in Lord Henry's observation that it
is "personalities, not principles, that move the age."[24] Both Disraeli
and Wilde, as they navigated the vast territory between the poles
of pragmatic calculation and idealistic vocation, knew the powerful impact of a successful performance of the self. Their lives and
careers, however, also forcefully reveal the interplay of person and
process, self-invention and appropriation, that results in a multi-authored and multi-authoring public persona.

Spring Semester 2019

A version of this lecture appeared in "Portraits of the Artist as Politician,
the Politician as Artist: Commemorating the Disraeli Phenomenon," *Journal of Victorian Culture* 21, 3 (2016): 281–300.

1. Oscar Wilde, "Amiel and Lord Beaconsfield," in *The Complete Works of Oscar Wilde*, ed. John Stokes and Mark W. Turner (Oxford, 2013), VII, pp. 577, 578.

2. Disraeli to Benjamin Austen, 8 Dec. 1829, in Benjamin Disraeli, *Letters, 1815–1834*, ed. J. A. W. Gunn, John Matthews, Donald M. Schurman, and M. G. Wiebe (Toronto, 1982), I, p. 113.

3. Wilkie Collins, *The Moonstone* (London, 1998), p. 439.

4. David Friedman, *Wilde in America: Oscar Wilde and the Invention of Modern Celebrity* (New York, 2014), p. 31.

5. Daniel Boorstin, *The Image: A Guide to Pseudo-Events in America* (New York, 1961), p. 57.

6. Oscar Wilde, *The Picture of Dorian Gray* (London, 1985), p. 256.

7. Michèle Mendelssohn, *Making Oscar Wilde* (Oxford, 2018), pp. 43, 3.

8. Wilde to Norman Forbes-Robertson, 15 Jan. 1882, in *The Complete Letters of Oscar Wilde*, ed. Merlin Holland and Rupert Hart-Davis (London, 2000), p. 127.

9. Wilde to Norman Forbes-Robertson, 2 May 1882, in ibid., p. 168.

10. Wilde to George Curzon, 15 Feb. 1882, in ibid., p. 139; Wilde to Curzon, 20 July 1885, in ibid., p. 264.

11. Charles Richmond, "Disraeli's Education," in *The Self-Fashioning of Disraeli, 1818–1851*, ed. Charles Richmond and Paul Smith (Cambridge, 1998), p. 41.

12. Andrew Elfenbein, "Silver-Fork Byron and the Image of Regency England," in *Byromania: Portraits of the Artist in Nineteenth- and Twentieth-Century Culture*, ed. Frances Wilson (Basingstoke, 1999), p. 80.

13. Andrew Elfenbein, "Byronism and the Work of Homosexual Performance in Early Victorian England," *Modern Language Quarterly*, 54, 4 (Dec. 1993), p. 544.

14. Carl Pletsch, "On the Autobiographical Life of Nietzsche", in *Psychoanalytic Studies of Biography*, ed. George Moraitis and George H. Pollock (Madison, 1987), p. 415.

15. Bodleian Library, University of Oxford, Dep. Hughenden 30/1-2.

16. Robert O'Kell, *Disraeli: The Romance of Politics* (Toronto, 2013), pp. vii, 504.

17. Leslie Stephen, "Mr Disraeli's Novels," *Fortnightly Review*, 16 (1874), p. 444.

18. Disraeli quoted in William Fraser, *Disraeli and His Day* (London, 1891), p. 52.

19. Clara Tuite, "Tainted Love and Romantic Literary Celebrity," *English Literary History*, 74 (2007), p. 78.

20. Wilde, *Picture of Dorian Gray*, p. 24.

21. J. M. Milner, *In Memoriam the Right Hon. Benjamin Disraeli, Earl of Beaconsfield, Viscount Hughenden* (London, 1881), n. p.

22. Oscar Wilde, *De Profundis*, in *The Complete Works of Oscar Wilde* (Glasgow, 1994), p. 1016.

23. Wilde, *Picture of Dorian Gray*, p. 175.

24. Ibid., p. 80.

William Morris, London, 1874. Photograph by Frederick Hollyer. NPG x3758. ©
National Portrait Gallery, London.

9

William Morris
Artist, Businessman, and Radical

PETER STANSKY

William Morris established the Arts and Crafts movement and thereby changed the look of our world. A man of many and varied accomplishments, Morris was brought up and trained by an upper-middle-class society that he nonetheless sought radically to change. In fact, Morris wished to destroy it and replace it with a socialist world. Like other English radicals, he extolled the past as a model for the future. He was inspired by what he saw, whether historically correct or not, as the comradeship and sense of equality in the medieval guilds that created artifacts ranging from jewelry to great cathedrals.

John Ruskin was an artist, but not a major one. Nor was art his primary commitment. Rather, it played a major role in his voluminous writings that dealt with "the condition of England" question and much else besides: how the Industrial Revolution was creating a world of ugliness and how such a world should be corrected. Eventually, and Ruskin should be given much credit for this, the look of the world changed, although the deeper transformations that he wished for either did not take place or did so to a far lesser degree than he hoped. William Morris was the single most important figure in moving Ruskin's ideas forward.

Morris was born on 24 March 1834 in Walthamstow, in Essex. As his name suggests, his family was originally Welsh, and its story was a

typical nineteenth-century success. His father rose from modest circumstances to become a very successful stockbroker, acquiring considerable holdings in a copper mine, which was the central part of
the family's fortune. Although he died young, he left his family well
off. William, as the eldest son, might have been particularly favored.
When he turned twenty-one, he had an annual private income of
£900, a considerable sum at the time. The freedom resulting from
that income allowed him to explore several career possibilities; he
did not earn any money until he was twenty-five. As he wrote in 1883,
"If I had not been born rich or well-to-do I should have found my
position *un*endurable, should have been a mere rebel against what
would have seemed a system of robbery and injustice." And Morris,
contrary to what some thought, was a very good businessman: he
ran a profitable design firm and, toward the end of his life, a small
publishing house. A practical man, he realized that it was necessary
to earn the money that would allow him to work toward subverting
the system that made his income possible.

He had a happy childhood. When he was six, the family moved
to its grandest house, Woodford Hall, with fifty acres of park and
a hundred acres of farmland. He was a young romantic, saturat-
ing himself in the novels of Walter Scott and riding about nearby
Epping Forest, frequently dressed in a suit of armor. In his early
days, he was fairly religious, influenced by his mother and his favorite sister; until the end of his Oxford years, he thought he might become an Anglican priest. After his father's death, the family moved
to a smaller but still grand house, Water House in Walthamstow
(now the William Morris Gallery). He received what was becoming
the traditional education for boys of his class: at thirteen he went
to Marlborough, one of the up-and-coming new boarding schools
founded to serve the ambitions of the middle class to educate its
sons appropriately. Fortunately for Morris, the school was not yet
well organized, and he was able to wander in nearby Savernake Forest, enriching his sense of nature, which would contribute greatly to
his later designs.

In 1851, his aesthetic sensibility was already evident: he refused
to attend the Great Exhibition, based on what he had heard about
it. The exhibition stood for the international industrial triumph of
Britain. But many of the British objects on display were examples of
overly elaborate design meant for ostentatious display rather than
practicality and simplicity. The latter qualities would become characteristic of the Arts and Crafts movement, which he led.

He entered Exeter College, Oxford, in 1852. His experiences
there were crucial for his future, less because of his formal studies

than because his multiple interests took shape and he made friends that he would have for the rest of his life, most notably the artist Edward Burne-Jones, then plain Edward Jones. He became a poet and helped pay for the journal that published his work. In his lifetime, his greatest fame was as a poet, most notably for his multi-volume work *The Earthly Paradise* (1868–70). (From time to time he was referred to as the Earthly Paradox.) He might well have become Poet Laureate at the time of Tennyson's death if not for his politics. Today his poetry tends to the least studied of his extraordinary range of accomplishments; his rather splendid, earlier poems are of the greatest interest.

Morris and Burne-Jones dedicated themselves to fighting what they called "shoddy" in the world. The question was how best to do it. They first considered becoming Anglican priests. Ironically, being overwhelmed by the beauty of the cathedrals of northern France convinced them to try to change the world through art, not religion. Morris's reading of Thomas Carlyle and, even more, John Ruskin strongly shaped his ideas. Carlyle's *Past and Present* (1855) gave Morris an admiration of medieval guilds, putting him in the tradition of English radicalism that looks backward in order to go forward. Ruskin was even more significant in directing Morris's thoughts. "The Nature of Gothic," a chapter in Ruskin's *The Stones of Venice* (1853), was so formative that years later Morris reprinted it as the fourth book issued by his Kelmscott Press. In the preface, he wrote that "in future days it will be considered as one of the very few necessary and inevitable utterances of this century." Ruskin advanced an idea that became crucial to Morris's thinking: there was virtue in the lack of perfection or roughness in Gothic craftsmanship, since it reflected the humanity of the art and the pleasure that the maker took in the work. It is too easily assumed that Morris hated machine work. He thought machines should be used when appropriate, to aid in manufacture and to cope with its more tedious aspects.

But how was Morris to implement his way of attacking shoddy in the world about him? As an architect? He went to work in the Oxford office of the prominent and progressive architect G. E. Street. That was unsuccessful, although it was there that he met Philip Webb, who became the leading Arts and Crafts architect and a very close friend. Street was important for instilling in Morris the idea that a building was to be a total work of art and that one needed to take into consideration everything that went into it, including its furnishings. It was also at this time that he became part of Dante Gabriel Rossetti's circle of Pre-Raphaelites. He took a flat in Red Lion Square in London, and finding no worthy furniture, he designed his own. In 1857, led by Rossetti, Morris and others embarked on an unsuccessful project to paint frescoes in the Oxford Union.

More significantly, Rossetti spotted what he called a "stunner" at the Oxford Music Rooms: the beautiful Jane Burden, the daughter of a groom. Morris's one major painting was a full-length portrait of her, although he was not satisfied with the result, commenting that he loved her but could not paint her. Though Rossetti may have spotted her first, Morris and Burden were married in 1859. It was not a happy marriage, although they stayed together and had two daughters, the epileptic Jenny and the powerful May, who was very active in her father's activities and the editor of his *Collected Works*. One suspects that Morris loved Jane more than she loved him. He turned from painting to poetry, and in 1858 he published his first book of poems, *The Defence of Guenevere,* in many ways now regarded as his best, although poorly reviewed at the time. The poems are marked by their interest in medieval scenes, their sense of decorativeness, and their honesty in facing the grimness of medieval life rather than romanticizing it. They surge with erotic energy.

In a sense, his marriage precipitated the next step in his career, and a critical event in his relation to the Arts and Crafts movement. Though he had moved to a larger flat in London, it was too small for a married couple. He decided to build a house, and hoped it would serve as a sort of commune shared with the Burne-Joneses. (That did not happen.) Red House in Bexleyheath, outside London, was designed by Philip Webb in 1860. Some have seen it, perhaps with exaggeration, as the beginning of modern architecture because of its comparative plainness, almost austerity. It is a beautiful house that looks both medieval and modern, an L-shaped two-story building with a faint feeling of the monastic, although Morris believed in jolly dinners with lots of wine. Morris lived there only until 1865, since his business required him to move back to London. It was the only house he built for himself. Eventually, he rented Kelmscott Manor, a beautiful old house in Kelmscott village near Oxford, and the handsome Georgian Kelmscott House on the Thames in Hammersmith.

MORRIS CAME TO SEE BUILDINGS AND BOOKS as exemplary, total works of art. To that end, he and his friends felt that they needed to design their own furniture and that the walls of their houses needed to be painted in patterns designed by Morris. The aim was not to impress others but rather to provide comfort and beauty for those who lived there. An ordinary person could not afford to build such a house, but it suggested a direction that domestic architecture and interior design might take. To transform the look of everything about them, Morris and his friends in 1861 established the firm Morris, Marshall, Faulkner & Company. Morris was always the major figure, and that was recognized in 1875 when the company was reorganized as Morris & Co. Rossetti and Burne-Jones were very much involved in the business. Morris wrote in 1883 about the firm's goals: "All the minor arts were in a state of complete degradation especially in England, and accordingly in 1861 with the conceited courage of a young man I set myself to reforming all that: and started a sort of firm for producing decorative objects." He was incredibly prolific; in the 1870s he created more than six hundred designs, mostly for textiles and wallpapers. His first wallpaper design, *Daisy,* was made in 1862, and his last, *Compton,* in 1896 (plates 2 and 3).

They were virtually all inspired by the natural world. At first they were hand-produced by his firm, as he noted—"Almost all the designs we use for surface decoration, wallpapers, textiles, and the like, I design myself. I have had to learn the theory and to some extent the practice of weaving, dyeing, and textile printing, all of which I must admit has given me and still gives me a great deal of enjoyment"— but eventually many of them were done by machine by Jeffrey & Co. Morris was perhaps the greatest pattern designer of the nineteenth century. Ironically, although Morris was not religious, the firm profited greatly from the manufacture of stained-glass windows, mostly ones designed by Rossetti, Ford Madox Brown, and Burne-Jones, although Morris designed 150. Six hundred churches in Britain have windows designed by the Morris firm, as do others abroad. Charles Sewter, a historian of the company, regards its production as the greatest manufacture of stained glass since the sixteenth century. Morris also revived the making of tapestries. (He would weave while composing poetry.)

There was a paradox in Morris's career as a businessman. He was not particularly radical when he began the business, but he became increasingly so in later years, ultimately believing that capitalism should be replaced by Marxist socialism, by revolution if necessary. But to finance his political activities as well as his life, he needed to make money, particularly since his private income was in decline. He paid his one hundred or more workers well, and there was some profit sharing, but they were by necessity part of the commercial system that he abhorred. What he called a profit-grinding society made it impossible for him to function as he might have done in the medieval past and as he hoped others would do in the socialist world of the future. He envisioned this utopia in his greatest novel, *News from Nowhere* (1890).

In the 1860s, he returned to poetry with book-length poems such as *The Life and Death of Jason* (1867). In 1868 he started publishing the four volumes of *The Earthly Paradise*. It consists of twenty-four alternate tales told by Norse seafarers and descendants of ancient Greeks. Morris became strongly interested in the Icelandic sagas and translated quite a few of them with the help of a distinguished native speaker. He traveled to Iceland in 1871 and 1873, in part to escape the pain of his wife's affair with Rossetti. (Though he professed to believe that people should follow the pull of their emotions.) He vastly enjoyed what he regarded as the relatively primitive world of Iceland, and even brought back a pony, "Mouse," to England. At this time he also took up calligraphy, creating approximately fifteen hundred pages. The range, quality, and quantity of his talents were breathtaking.

IN THE MID-1870S, MORRIS'S ATTENTION turned to politics, and he began his pilgrimage leftward. He first became an ardent Gladstonian Liberal, swept along by the dramatic denunciation of the Turkish massacre of Bulgarians in William Gladstone's *The Bulgarian Horrors and the Question of the East* (1876). In a letter to the press in 1876, Morris referred to the Turks as "thieves and murderers." As a wealthy activist, he became the treasurer of the Eastern Question Association and later of the National Liberal League. But as the 1870s progressed, he became increasingly disillusioned with traditional politics. Once Gladstone and the Liberals were back in office in 1880, he was disturbed by their coercion of Ireland and the bombing of Alexandria.

The multifaceted Morris made one of his greatest contributions in 1877 as the major founder of probably the first group of its kind, the Society for the Protection of Ancient Buildings, nicknamed Anti-Scrape. It is still an active and important organization. And still somewhat controversial. Morris was horrified by the tearing down of older buildings of merit. But he approached the problem somewhat unusually in that he hated restoration. His enemy was the great Victorian architect Gilbert Scott, who rebuilt ancient buildings as reproductions, not genuine articles, untrue both to the time when they were built and to the present age. Morris believed that to stay true to the original building, the minimum should be done to keep it in good repair, and that if that weren't possible, the building should be allowed to have a decent death.

The society made him a public figure and turned his attention to the public sphere. He gave talks on art and politics. As he remarked in 1883: "I have only one subject on which to lecture: the relation of art to labour." The need for revolutionary change became a major preoccupation. He wanted to foster a society of small semi-independent units that were not centrally controlled. He came to believe that the elimination of private ownership was essential. His growing disdain for traditional politics was shown in *News from Nowhere,* in which the disused Houses of Parliament serve as a storehouse for manure. During the political unrest of the 1880s, he helped finance political organizations that became precursors of the Labour Party. Ironically, he was too individualistic to be a good party man. He first joined the Social Democratic Federation, whose membership card he designed. Under the leadership of H. M. Hyndham, it had a Marxist orientation, which Morris supported. But in his view, it was too committed to parliamentary politics. He read *Das Kapital* in a cheap French edition, although he claimed he never quite understood its economics. Yet like Marx, he became a profound critic of the alienation of laborers from their work. He felt that art could not flourish under capitalism. He announced his conversion to socialism in 1883, rather incongruously in a lecture at Oxford chaired by John Ruskin, much to the irritation of the university authorities: "So long as the system of competition in the production and exchange of the means of life goes on, the degradation of the arts will go on." In 1889 he declared himself a communist.

Fed up with the traditional politics of the Social Democratic Federation, he moved in an anarchistic direction and formed a new group, the Socialist League. He was its leader until 1890. Its membership card, designed by Walter Crane, depicted Morris as a blacksmith at an anvil. He hoped that there would soon be real revolutionary change in Britain, but his hopes ended on Bloody Sunday, 13 November 1887, when 30,000 socialists, radicals, and Irish were dispersed and beaten by police in Trafalgar Square. Morris wrote "Death Song" for Alfred Linnell, one of the two men killed at the demonstration, the proceeds from its sales to benefit his children. The more parliamentary-inclined members of the Socialist League, led by Eleanor Marx, withdrew from the group when they were outvoted. Morris found the now-dominant, more anarchistic wing uncongenial and formed a small local group that met in his coach house: the Hammersmith Socialist Society. Morris passionately believed in group action, yet he was a deeply Victorian individualist and a natural leader who couldn't stay in groups, even as leader, if they went in directions he disfavored. His continual aim was to bring about an England where classes and private property were abolished, where workers could enjoy their work and the fruits of their labor, and where exploitation would no longer take place.

But he knew that it was a continual process and that permanently achieving it would be almost impossible.

While engaged in all these political pursuits, he was also extremely active in his design firm, which continued to do well. He began to influence a group of younger disciples. A. H. Mackmurdo and Herbert Horne founded the Century Guild in 1882, the Art Workers' Guild was established in 1884, and C. R. Ashbee formed the Guild of Handicraft in 1888. That same year, the Arts and Crafts Exhibition Society had its first show. The bookbinder and printer T. J. Cobden-Sanderson coined the phrase "Arts and Crafts," a now-canonical term suggesting that the so-called lesser arts are on the same level as the higher arts. The society had annual exhibitions that promulgated the style. The movement became increasingly active in the United States and was influential on the Continent as well. Morris gave these guilds and other organizations his somewhat grudging blessing; he regarded them as palliatives that did not get to the heart of economics and politics.

Morris wrote continually. Among the best of his later books are *A Dream of John Ball* (1888) and *News from Nowhere*. The former had a splendid frontispiece by Burne-Jones, with the rhyme "When Adam delved and Eve spanned / who was then the gentleman?" The novel recounts, through John Ball, the rebel Lollard priest, the failed peasant uprising led by Wat Tyler in 1381. (The rhyme on the frontispiece is attributed to Ball.) As Morris wrote: "How men fight and lose the battle, and the thing they fought for comes about in spite of their defeat, and when it comes turns out not to be what they meant, and other men have to fight for what they meant under another name."

News from Nowhere begins with the Morris figure returning disillusioned from a meeting of the Socialist League at which the six attendees presented six divergent views. The next day he wakes up in the twenty-first century; a two-year violent revolution that ended in 1952 had brought about a victory for socialism. Law courts and prisons have been abolished, and the central government has been replaced by direct, participatory democracy in a series of self-governing, loosely coordinated communes. For government and the economy, small is beautiful. It is a world where it appears that Morris & Co. designed everything and where its inhabitants have learned the lesson that pleasure in work results in the production of more beautiful objects. Everything in people's houses is either beautiful or useful, preferably both. Material progress is of little concern; at some point there was a turn from "useless toil" to "useful work." As

Old Hammond, who lived through the revolution, explains to the narrator, "The production of what used to be called art . . . has no name amongst us now, because it has become a necessary part of the labour of every man who produces."

Morris in his later years also published six prose romances, several of them about splendid German tribes, which gained renewed popularity in the 1960s, since they were seen as similar to Tolkien's tales of Middle-earth. Two further ones were published after his death. Morris claimed somewhat disingenuously and inaccurately that these works were apolitical, that they were meant to be tales "pure and simple."

Though in declining health, Morris kept up to a considerable degree with the firm and his political activities right up to the end. Much of what he produced as a designer (and later as a publisher) was available only to the well off. He felt that circumstance wouldn't fundamentally change without a revolution. Nevertheless, by changing the public's taste and setting new standards of beauty and craftsmanship, his design work might still have good effects. As he wrote: "To enjoy good houses and good books in self-respect and decent comfort, seems to me to be the pleasurable end towards which all societies of human beings ought now to struggle."

Morris became an avid book collector, particularly of early printed books and illuminated manuscripts. And in a related move, in 1892 he founded the Kelmscott Press. He was inspired to launch the venture by a lecture by Emery Walker on type at the first Arts and Crafts Exhibition in 1888. (Morris had lectured on tapestry and carpet weaving.) He regarded each book he published as a total artistic entity, with equal care given to its contents and its design. The books were printed in one of the three typefaces that he designed. He worked out the needed relationships between, as he wrote, "the paper, the form of the type, the relative spacing of the letters, the words, and the lines; and lastly the position of the printed matter on the page." As usual, his work was inspirational, providing the major impetus for the spate of private presses that followed in his wake, such as Doves, Vale, Ashendene, and Essex House. The press published fifty-three books, three after Morris's death, many of them reprints of poetry, including his own. Its masterpiece was the Kelmscott Chaucer, finished in June 1896. Burne-Jones, who did eighty-seven woodcut illustrations for it, called it a "pocket cathedral." Morris designed the decorative aspects of the book, such as initial words and borders.

Morris caught a cold while speaking in December 1895 in the open air at the funeral of Sergius Stepniak, the Russian anarchist.

He died on 3 October 1896; after a simple funeral, he was buried in the churchyard at Kelmscott under a raised Viking-like tombstone designed by Philip Webb. Morris's ideas and activities were so widespread that it is possible to see his life as extremely diffuse, even unfocused. But a strong consistent line runs through his thought and activities: the idea that we might be able to live better and more fulfilling lives. After his death, interest in him tended to decline somewhat and to be divided among his fields of action, with perhaps the most attention being paid to him as a Victorian poet. Many of those interested in his poetry or designs were put off by his politics. But that changed after the Second World War, when the conception of an integrated Morris gradually became more dominant. This was marked, among other indications, by the formation of the William Morris Society in 1955 and by the publication of E. P. Thompson's great *William Morris: Romantic to Revolutionary* in the same year. Interest in his political ideas greatly increased as many on the left became disillusioned with the failures of the Soviet Union and of state socialism. Morris became something of a hero of the counterculture, both stylistically and politically, as well as for many others who appreciated his art, his writings, and his political views. His design work helped improve our world, and perhaps at some point in the future, it might help make a better world. As the last line of *News from Nowhere* puts it: "If others can see it as I have seen it, then it may be called a vision rather than a dream."

Spring Semester 2019

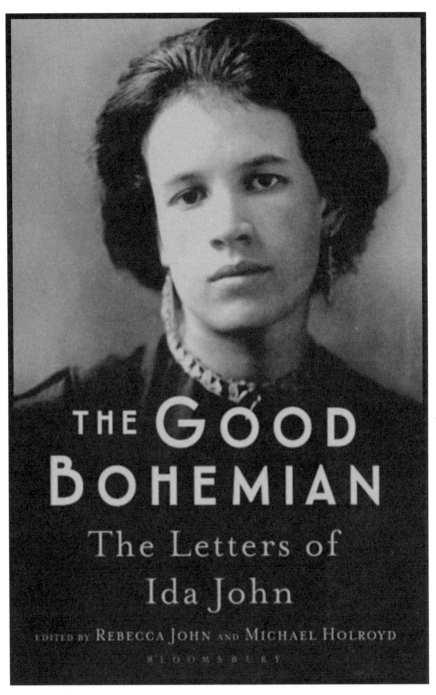

Ida John, pictured on the cover of *The Good Bohemian: The Letters of Ida John* (2017), edited by Rebecca John and Michael Holroyd. Bloomsbury Publishing Plc.

10

Ida John
Portrait of the Artist's Wife

ROSEMARY HILL

Bohemia was never a safe country for women. If they didn't all die of consumption in a garret, many of them might as well have done. In the 1890s, when the "new woman" sprang, as Max Beerbohm put it, "fully armed from Ibsen's brain," their cases tended to follow a pattern. Attracted by the idea of freedom from social and sexual convention and the chance to live among artists, even to be artists, they found themselves not in a new world but in a mirror image of the old, with as many constraints but fewer comforts. The hoped-for careers rarely developed. The bohemian man may have idealized women as muses and models, but he was unhampered by bourgeois obligations to be faithful or to earn money, though rarely was he so unconventional as to undertake any housework or child care. The bohemian woman with children was as much shackled to domesticity as any solicitor's wife, but without the staff that a middle-class household would command, or the security. Meanwhile, the door to a respectable life had slammed shut behind her.

Such, more or less, was the story of Ida Nettleship, the first wife of Augustus John, who died of puerperal fever at the age of thirty in 1907 and was soon lost to view. In John's unfinished mural *Lyric Fantasy*, painted soon after Ida's death, she stands to one side of

the group of women and children who make up the extended John
ménage, a monumental figure in deep shadow. In his memoir,
Chiaroscuro, published in 1952, John made no mention of her. Her
five sons, the eldest of whom was five when she died, seem to have
known little about their mother. The recent publication of her letters, edited by Rebecca John and Michael Holroyd, goes a long way
to recovering her. They tell a painful story of an emotionally sophisticated, morally honest woman struggling with the trap in which she
found herself, trying by turns to escape and to take control of the
situation. To different correspondents she showed different facets
of her predicament, and the result is a portrait both fragmentary
and poignant.

The Nettleships were an artistic family. Ida's father, John Trivett,
was a painter of some repute, though remembered by W. B. Yeats
chiefly for his "melodramatic lions"; her mother, Adaline, was a
dressmaker and theatrical costumer. She created the famous iri-
descent gown, covered in beetle wings, in which Ellen Terry played
Lady Macbeth and in which Sargent painted her in 1889. The picture, "the sensation of the year" according to Terry's diary, shows
her snakelike in her glistening robe, holding the crown of Scotland
above her head, an embodiment of dangerous female sexuality.
When it was painted, she was forty-one with three marriages behind
her. Ida was twelve, and whether or not she saw the painting, she
grew up in a milieu where such lives were known to be possible.
It was this, perhaps, that made her mother determined to keep a
tight rein on her three daughters. Adaline's moral code was worked
out in what Michael Holroyd memorably termed the "moral gymna-
sium" of the last Victorian decades. He characterized it, too harshly,
as a culture of "conceit and condemnation . . . complacency and
fear of change," but it was a period when conventions hardened in
reaction to the fin de siècle stirrings of the Aesthetic movement, *The
Yellow Book,* and talk of votes for women. Increasingly, one was either
in or out of respectable society.

Ida was fifteen when she enrolled at the Slade School of Fine Art,
where her father had studied, arriving just in time for the Slade's
golden age, at the heart of which were Augustus John and his sister Gwen. They had come to London to study under the irascible
but inspiring Henry Tonks and soon attracted a group of talented
students around them. "Those Johns you know have a hold that
never ceases," Ida wrote to a friend. She stayed for six years, working hard to be an artist and making friendships that lasted all her
life. Among her fellow students were some of the fourteen children
of the wealthy Salaman family, whose father had made a fortune in

the "feather boom" of the 1880s when fabulous prices were paid for ostrich plumes. Ida became engaged to Clement Salaman. She liked him perfectly well. He was reliable, suitable, and fond of her. They might have been happy enough had not her "beautiful warm face" caught the eye of Augustus John. Then she knew what it was to have a grand passion and to be on the horns of a dilemma. Her parents would not agree to a marriage, and she would not agree to sex without one. Augustus visited the Nettleship home in Wigmore Street, thereby making matters worse. His long-haired Gypsy-ish appearance was against him, and since he was afraid of saying the wrong thing, he said nothing. He and Mrs. Nettleship regarded each other in hostile silence until, in 1901, the deadlock was broken with a discreet trip to the St. Pancras Register Office.

Ida's letters before her marriage suggest a lively mind emerging from the chrysalis of late-Victorian girlhood and its peculiarly prescribed emotional range. Like many of her contemporaries, she wrote to other women in extravagant terms: "I am so lonely," she told her fellow student Edna Waugh, "I love you dear *dear*—& please love me." But there are also flashes of Wildean sensibility: "Wouldn't it be lovely to be free . . . just be a beautiful mind growing from outward impressions. I think self-consciousness is like gin—it stops the growth." Beyond the warm world of female confidences, growth was inhibited in other ways. Edna Waugh had been spotted at the age of fourteen by a friend of her father, a barrister named William Clarke Hall, who urged him to send her to art school. By the time she was sixteen, Hall was "determined" to marry her, and she and Ida were in fraught correspondence about what to do. Ida sensibly argued with both parties that Edna was simply too young to know her own mind, which may well have been precisely the reason why Clarke Hall and so many other nineteenth-century men wanted to marry teenage girls. Ellen Terry was sixteen when she married the forty-six-year-old artist G. F. Watts; Ruskin was the same age when he proposed to the eighteen-year-old Rose La Touche. More than the obvious attractions of youth or the anachronistic charges of pedophilia sometimes leveled against the Victorians, there was something like a desire to preserve that quality of indeterminacy, to keep a woman like a bonsai specimen, clipped at the root to be perfect and miniature for ever.

Ida advised her friend to stick to her course and be an artist: "Don't get down side paths . . . Look the thing in the face and be a man for a time." In the end, however, their paths forked. Edna married Clarke Hall, and Ida, having broken her engagement to Salaman, went to Florence, where she stayed in a pensione full of

"Americans & poets & grey haired spinsters who drink hot water," blew smoke rings, and painted the Arno, before going to Paris, where she embarked on the true *vie de bohème*. The "very excellent" flat she shared with Gwen Salmond and Gwen John had "a charming studio room and nice spots of drawings & photographs on the walls" and "two . . . Jap prints" bought for two pence from the bouquinistes by the Seine. "Gwen John is sitting before a mirror carefully posing herself," Ida wrote. "She has been at it for half an hour. It is for an 'interior.'" The letters themselves are a series of still lifes of Paris in the Belle Époque. Ida, who inherited her mother's interest in clothes, debated what to wear to a dance at Whistler's studio, thinking of white muslin with old gold ribbons; she discovered a restaurant "where anarchists go & seem to live an intense life in common" and concluded that altogether this was "the most interesting time" she had ever spent. Her parents seem to have been untroubled by her independence and to have hoped that she was forgetting Gwen's brother, but Augustus was never far in the background. He seemed to embody all that Ida was enjoying of the artistic life, the alternative to the Clarke Halls of the world.

After their marriage, which Ida's father glossed to friends as having been "private" rather than clandestine, things went well at first. Augustus got a job teaching art at University College, Liverpool, and they found the city lively and cosmopolitan. Ida painted, using "an old man model" who sat "like a rock." They made friends. By the autumn, she was pregnant and adapting her wardrobe. Adaline was asked for a "loose black lace evening blouse . . . with long sleeves but not transparent—& a little low neck cut round—and perhaps streamers down the front?" For the baby, she made petticoats and asked whether "the thing will have to wear two garments at night." As the tone suggests, she was ambivalent about children before she had them, and their arrival did nothing to change her mind. David Nettleship John was "a comic little fellow," she reported, "but he grumbles such a fearful lot. I think he would very much rather not have been created." As one pregnancy followed another, she gave up painting, and since their income did not grow, she took up housework, which, at the turn of the century, meant heavy manual labor. Ambivalence was from now on to be her almost permanent state. Mary Dowdall, a novelist with a flair for comedy, whom Ida nicknamed "the Rāni," was the friend to whom she wrote with the least inhibition, displaying moods that shifted from one paragraph to the next. In 1903, pregnant again, she told the Rāni that "there are times like tonight, when I think no place could be better . . . our life just now flows so evenly and regularly," adding, "but I'm afraid Gus finds it rather a bore." Four sentences later she explains that since the laundry bills were so large, she was doing it herself—"it is such a proud moment when one puts on one's self-washed drawers"—but at the same time, she "should like to live on a mountain side & never speak to anybody." The letter ends with a clear-eyed summary of the new woman and her fate: 'I think to live with a girlfriend & have lovers would be almost perfect. Whatever are we all training for that we have to shape ourselves & compromise with things all our lives? It's eternally fitting a square peg into a round hole & squeezing up one's eyes to make it look a better fit—isn't it?'

That year a further and permanent complication arrived in the form of Dorothy McNeill, known as Dorelia, a twenty-one-year-old secretary who spent her evenings at the Westminster School of Art. It was Gwen John who met her first, and soon she and Augustus were captivated and determined to have her for themselves. They painted her repeatedly and, as she sometimes felt in the early days, relentlessly. What it was about Dorelia that exerted such fascination is difficult now to know. Perhaps like Janey Morris she had to be seen to be believed, though the effect was due only partly to her looks. Nicolette Devas, who was later absorbed as a child into the John household, recalled the impression she made on a sharp but innocent eye: "Hers was a fierce beauty, a dark, austere beauty with something of the peasant . . . She frightened people. If the visitor was lucky he received a repressive "Hello" in that deep, husky voice her children have inherited. Her silences were unforced by theory; she was incapable of small talk, and only spoke in short barks, and disappeared again, wrapped in her mystery and protected by her dignity."

Ida, with her bothersome babies and her domestic "serfdom," stood little chance against the Johns' shared passion. From then she was the awkward third in two triangles. In her marriage, she shared her husband with Dorelia. Outside it, she shared him with the "impitoyable" Gwen. The siblings generated a force field, as they had at the Slade, and their obsession with Dorelia drew her to them; though reluctant at first, she was soon sucked in and digested like an insect in a Venus flytrap. Ida found ways of squeezing up her eyes to make it look a better fit. She and Augustus had taken a house at Matching Green in Essex, from where Ida wrote defensively to Alice Rothenstein, a friend from Liverpool days: "You know that we are not a *conventional* family. You have heard Dorelia is beautiful and most charming, and you must learn that my only happiness is for [Augustus] to be happy and complete, and that far from diminishing our love for each other it appears to augment it. I do have my bad times . . . She is *so* remarkably charming. But those times are . . . not the truth."

The bad times were heard more often in the letters to the Rāni, in which Ida seemed to go back to the most interesting time of her life and imagine the different routes she might have taken from that point: "It suddenly strikes me how perfectly divine it would be if you and I were living in Paris together. I can imagine going to the Louvre and then back to a small room over a restaurant." Alternating regret, defensiveness, and a determination to become the hero of her own life characterize most of the letters, but those to Dorelia have their own peculiar tone, in which the emotionalism of Edwardian female friendship is laced with something like emotional sadomasochism: "O my honey let me say it—I *crave* for you to come here . . . I heard from Gwen 'Dorelia writes she has given in.' Were you holding out against Gus, you little bitch? You are a mystery, but you are ours."

Meanwhile Ida insisted that everyone, including her mother, had to accept the situation. Mrs. Nettleship, on whom Holroyd is remarkably hard, maintained a conversational rapport with her son-in-law, which was surely heroic in the circumstances. Ida hoped at times for "a different life later on," and in the summer of 1905 she set out the case to Dorelia: "We have neither the peace of mind of the wife nor the freedom (at least I haven't) of the mistress. We have the evils of both states for the one good, which belongs to both—a man's company. Is it worth it? Isn't it paying twice over for our boon?" What, if anything, the laconic Dorelia said in reply is not explained, but clearly even Augustus dimly sensed that all was not well. He came up with what perhaps only he could have considered a practical solution. Explaining that their household had become too conventional, and that what was needed was "an ever-changing outdoor life," he bought a horse and a covered wagon. While Dorelia, who was now pregnant, went with Augustus to see it, Ida, who was also pregnant, despite "violent efforts" to bring on a miscarriage, turned her bravest face to Alice, assuring her that "it will be lovely to be camping." It wasn't, really. Dorelia had her baby, and they called him Pyramus. Ida had her fourth child, "another beastly boy," called Edwin, and for all the romance of the gypsy life, depicted in its many ideal permutations in John's paintings and sketches, she was exhausted, washing and looking after the children "from 6 or 7 until 9" while Augustus "when not painting lies reading or playing with a toy boat," which, Ida explained to the Rāni, was quite understandable, because 'how could he paint if he had to be on duty in between—duty is so wearing & tearing."

Ida, who had tried to live the free life, found herself the embodiment of convention. To her husband, she represented "the dull home . . . the gruesome dinner table." "I was the chain," she told Dorelia, "you were the key." Dorelia had the right temperament for bohemia: "You are a wanderer—you would hate safety"—while Ida was caught between two worlds. In 1905 she decided to move to Paris with Dorelia and their children; Augustus stayed in London. But it was not the same as before: how could it be with six babies? It was difficult to meet people or go out. "I crave for a time when the children are grown up," she told the Rāni, "& I can ride about on the tops of omnibuses as of yore in a luxury of vague observation." She had given up any idea of painting. "It has cost me much pain," she confessed to her sister Ursula, adding: "but it doesn't matter!" Gwen was also in Paris, living alone, painting, and "becoming indispensable" to Rodin. "It must be a pleasure," her brother thought, "to be at the service of such a man." To her sister-in-law, however, Gwen remained "always the same strange reserved creature." Alice's husband, William, visited and was appalled by the sight of the assembled infants "rolling around the floor." Ida considered leaving Augustus, but there wasn't enough money, and anyway she was pregnant for the fifth time. After her third son, Robin, she had told a friend: "I am going to climb an apple tree and never have another baby." If only she had. In the early spring of 1907, she wrote to her mother to say that she was going to have this baby in hospital. On 9 March she gave birth to yet another boy, Henry. Five days later, having suffered an infection from an abscess, she died.

The publication of her letters rights a number of wrongs, but there are frustrations. The reasons for the editors' many excisions are not explained, and there are odd misprints and mistakes, such as the confusion of Yeats's father with his brother. The account of Augustus John in the accompanying text is generous, understandably so, given that Holroyd, as his biographer, knows him from his more attractive angles, and Rebecca John is his granddaughter as well as Ida's, yet he is given the benefit of too many doubts. Describing how he began a double portrait of Ida and Dorelia and later painted Ida out, a note assures us that he did it "without realising the pain he gave her," which, if true, makes him even more monstrous. Like Ida herself, Holroyd and John are inclined to blame everyone but Augustus, and poor Adaline Nettleship especially, who is accused of using "aggressive tactics" to try to get access to her grandchildren after her daughter's death. She can hardly be blamed.

Without Ida, the John ménage rolled on before coming to rest in Dorset, where a picturesque convoy of horse-drawn carts and wagons pulled up in the summer of 1911 at Alderney Manor, "a rambling red brick bungalow" in what Nicolette Devas considered "the worst pseudo-Gothic style." Dorelia's sister Edie joined them as a "much needed Martha" in the household. Everyone dressed in handmade clothes so that Augustus's paintings "walked about" before him. He and Dorelia had two more children together, and he had another four, each with a different woman. Offered a knighthood in the 1940s if he would regularize his life by marrying, he proposed to Dorelia, who had the integrity to turn him down—he had to make do with the Order of Merit. Neither of Ida's sisters married, but they kept in touch with their nephews. Rebecca John knew her great-aunts well in their old age, but she learned nothing about Ida from them, recalling that "they never mentioned her to us, and we never asked."

Fall Semester 2018

A version of this lecture appeared in the *London Review of Books*, 29 June 2017.

Arthur Conan Doyle, 1920s. Photograph by Armand Luigi Cigarini. NPG x8038. © National Portrait Gallery, London.

11

Arthur Conan Doyle and Spiritualism

DAVID L. LEAL

We walk upon the shore of a mysterious ocean and the boldest of
us are but ankle-deep.

Arthur Conan Doyle

Rarely has an artist been more thoroughly eclipsed by his art
than was Arthur Conan Doyle. He created a character that
escaped from his control, shaped his public image, sustained
him financially, and thoroughly obscured his other work. Conan
Doyle came to loathe his most famous creation, pondered "slaying
Holmes" in what would have been only the twelfth short story in the
series, and wrote that "he takes my mind from better things."[1] He
tried to throw Holmes off Reichenbach Falls, but a sputtering career and a declining bank balance forced the character's return.

As a consequence, few people today—especially fans of the Great
Detective—care very much about Conan Doyle. He is seen largely
as a Victorian caricature: a decent and honorable but pompous and
unreflective man. Further tarnishing his legacy is his advocacy of
spiritualism, which led a book reviewer in the *Sunday Express* to ask,
"Is Conan Doyle Mad?"[2]

To better understand his life and legacy, and particularly to help
reconcile the creator of the arch-rational detective with the believer
in fairies and séances, this chapter examines a trove of documents
in the Arthur Conan Doyle archive at the Harry Ransom Center.
The collection, which was assembled over time from varied sources,
includes letters, speeches, and draft manuscripts as well as artifacts

such as his golf clubs and his Ouija board. It is therefore particularly valuable for those with interests in Conan Doyle beyond Sherlock Holmes, in areas such as religion, the Victorian and Edwardian
literary worlds, material culture, letter writing, and magazine and
book publishing. Most importantly, it allows Conan Doyle to speak
directly about the topic that generated the most controversy during
his life—spiritualism—and his explanations may prove surprising
to Sherlockians who see his interest in the other world as irrational.
Conan Doyle saw spiritualism as a scientific pursuit, and his views
not as a "faith" but rather as propositions that had been empirically
tested and verified.

BEFORE CREATING SHERLOCK HOLMES, Conan Doyle was a highly
productive—although not overly successful—producer of all sorts
of fiction and nonfiction. He was essentially throwing lots of literary
spaghetti against the wall and hoping that something would stick.
His goal was to leave medical practice and become a full-time writer,
which he ultimately did, but he needed a reliable income because he
and his first wife were not independently wealthy, and he had financial obligations to members of his immediate and extended family.

His success came with Holmes, a creation that made everything
else in his life possible. The popularity of these stories reflected his
characters, plots, and a writing skill that had been honed for years,
but it also followed a decision to move away from novels and publish
a series of short stories in magazines appealing to the growing, literate middle classes.

Today, Sherlock Holmes is among the best-known individuals
in world history, perhaps rivaled only by religious figures such as
Moses, Jesus, Mohammed, and the Buddha, but the general public
has only the vaguest ideas about Conan Doyle's life. And the most
devoted fans of Sherlock Holmes, far from honoring his creator's
memory, conspicuously ignore or even denigrate him. Imagine if
the admirers of *Pride and Prejudice* and *Northanger Abbey* denounced
Jane Austen as a rather mediocre talent who never appreciated her
characters and may not have written any of those novels anyway.

Why this antipathy? Because Conan Doyle was no fan of Sherlock
Holmes. The Holmes-Doyle relationship might be seen as a sort of
Thirty Years' War, one that Holmes resoundingly won. Conan Doyle
grumbled about Holmes, showed little affection toward his creation,
whined about how his historical novels were being overshadowed
by this "penny dreadful" character, and plotted to kill him. Conan
Doyle saw Holmes largely as a source of revenue rather than as the
greatest cultural creation of the Victorian and Edwardian eras.

Imagine if Jane Austen had grown sick of her characters and dispatched a unit of French soldiers to cross the Channel, invade her country houses, and massacre Mr. Darcy, Elizabeth Bennet, and the rest so that she would have more time to write historical fiction and talk to the dead. The fans of her novels today might then understandably have less regard for her.

The difficult Doyle-Holmes relationship was recognized during the writer's lifetime. A famous 1926 *Punch* cartoon portrays Conan Doyle with his head in the clouds, a reference to his spiritualism, and his leg chained to Holmes. For his part, Conan Doyle may have seen himself as the Dr. Watson prototype—a loyal, honorable, steadfast trooper who could be counted on in a crisis. While Sherlockians do not entirely disagree, they also see an element of comedy. Instead of the Watson portrayed by Edward Hardwick in the Jeremy Brett television series, Conan Doyle is remembered more as the version of Watson portrayed by Nigel Bruce in the Basil Rathbone film series—a none-too-bright and pompous bumbler who is a pale shadow of the man he chronicles. Conan Doyle's gravestone at All Saints Church in Minstead, Hampshire, is inscribed "Steel True, Blade Straight," which seems a bit much for someone who was primarily a writer.

The reality of Conan Doyle, however, is more complicated. In particular, his arguments for spiritualism are more interesting than might be expected, since he made scientific and even populist arguments in its favor. Spiritualism allowed him to combine the religious impulse of his youth (Catholicism) with the scientific career of his adulthood (medicine). An examination of Conan Doyle's spiritual journey in his own words offers a more sympathetic perspective, one that contradicts much of his public image.

ARTHUR IGNATIUS CONAN DOYLE was born in Edinburgh in 1859 to Irish parents who were devout Catholics, especially his father. Conan Doyle had two aunts who became nuns, and his early education was at the Catholic public school Stoneyhurst. It is helpful to understand him as someone born into a minority religion that in much of the nineteenth century was subject to formal, legal discrimination and informal social sanctions.

He claimed to have lost his Christian faith as a young adult, but he later took up a new creed, spiritualism. As the Conan Doyle biographer Andrew Lycett noted, "Becoming a spiritualist so soon after creating the quintessentially rational Sherlock Holmes: that is the central paradox of Arthur's life. It seems strange for someone steeped in Edinburgh's empirical tradition to take what amounted to a leap of faith. For Arthur there was no discrepancy, however. He regarded spiritualism as a science or, at least, a natural extension of science."[3]

The arguments in his essays, lectures, and debates about spiritualism are complex, but many Sherlock Holmes fans see Conan Doyle the spiritualist as a dupe. For instance, the actor and writer Stephen Fry was dismayed by "such a strong disconnect between the writer-creator of Sherlock Holmes and the dupe who could be fooled by plausible mountebanks"; for Fry, Conan Doyle resembled "the ordinary, gullible man who swallowed such nonsense whole."[4] Others more sympathetically saw him as drawn to spiritualism out of grief after his son died in the First World War. His writings indicate that neither story is exactly true.

Lycett's biography of Conan Doyle argues that he could no longer follow the Catholicism of his youth but retained a romantic nature that wanted to reconcile religion with science. He was of the generation hit hard by Charles Darwin and earlier critical thinkers and writers, and in spiritualism he found the answer: a system of belief that allowed for life after death while also being amenable, he thought, to scientific scrutiny. Conan Doyle stated in lecture notes, "I have known in my own person what it is to be without belief, and how much is gained when one finds something which one can reconcile with facts and reason."[5]

The role of scientific inquiry in Conan Doyle's spiritual beliefs is critical, and he saw spiritualism as a science that had been proved. In a letter, he refers to "psychic science," which may seem like a contradiction but gets to the core of his attraction to it.[6] He saw the claims of spiritualism as testable in the modern scientific way and once referred to the séance table as "our laboratory." Fry argued that he "refused in the face of all evidence to give up his belief" in spiritualist phenomenon, but it was evidence that created and sustained his spiritualism.[7]

Conan Doyle used scientific comparisons to make his points. In "The New Revelation," he explains: "If you use a telescope you can see the moons of Jupiter. If you don't you won't. That does not mean that the moons are not there. It means that you have yourself been at fault. If instead of 'telescope' you say 'medium' the argument is still the same."[8] He further claims that no "scientific man" who had impartially studied spiritualism had doubted it, and that its detractors violated "the first law of science" by substituting their prejudices for evidence.[9] In a lecture titled "The Proof of Spiritualism," Conan Doyle argues that spirits are part of the scientific world. He says that they must follow the laws of the universe and the laws of matter, and that psychic science is working on discovering these laws.[10] The spiritualist is therefore a type of scientist, and spirits are within the natural world rather than without or above it. His conclusion is firm: "The time has come when we need no more evidence as to survival and communication after death. It is a waste of time and energy."[11]

He denied that spiritualism was a "faith"—his writing refers to "facts" and "proofs" and "evidence"—and he was scornful of "mere belief."[12] Knowledge had replaced faith: "It is no use to speak of faith. There are too many faiths and not enough proofs. The age of faith is past . . . But there is something better than faith. It is knowledge. To know is better than to believe. We think that if the age of faith is past, the age of knowledge is begun." He also thought that scientists could not disprove spiritualist findings: "I am not aware of any man of high scientific reputation who has thoroughly examined the phenomenon and decided against them."[13]

Conan Doyle believed not only in communicating with the dead, but also that he had done so: "I have spoken with my 'dead' son and brother about intimate family matters. I have seen in the séance room my mother's face and that of my nephew as plainly as ever in life . . . I had got in touch with eight out of ten relatives whom I had lost in the war."[14] And he claimed to have personal proof of phenomena such as ectoplasm, which he says he held in his hands.[15]

Conan Doyle claimed to have had psychic experiences with family, friends, and strangers, and many people wrote to him about their contacts with the spirit world. For example, he received in 1919 a letter from a William Holmes, who describes himself as a British civil servant in India who subsequently moved to Canada.[16] He makes no mention of his shared name with the Great Detective but notes that he had psychic episodes in both nations. Most dramatically, he believed he had received a communication from a son who was killed at Ypres; the message involved "no voice" but "a bright light like the flow of an electric light" in the daytime. Today, many might doubt the reality of such events, but Conan Doyle noted that spiritualism provided unique comfort for the bereaved.[17]

While Conan Doyle is often thought to have become a spiritualist after the death of his son at the end of the First World War, his interest appears to have developed much earlier—in the same year he published his first Sherlock Holmes story. In the transcript of a radio broadcast, he notes that "in 1887 some curious psychic experiences came my way and especially I was impressed by the fact of telepathy which I proved for myself by experiments with a friend." He then wonders whether a living mind could communicate with a "discarnate" mind; he says that he examined the evidence for twenty years and came to a favorable conclusion "beyond all doubt."[18] He refers to additional evidence he found and experiments he conducted. He says that he went public with his beliefs in 1916, two years before his son died, "when all the world was asking, 'Where are our dead boys?' and getting un-satisfactory answers, both from the church and from Science."[19]

His scientific interest in spiritualism seems to have been well known at the time. A 1924 invitation from the Oxford Union to Conan Doyle notes that "theological subjects are technically barred by our Constitution," so they ask him to discuss "the scientific realities [rather] than . . . the religious aspect of the question."[20] The letter was from Gerald Gardiner, the future Lord Chancellor who had survived the First World War with the Coldstream Guards and would survive an IRA assassination attempt in 1981. In 1925, the Oxford Junior Scientific Society invited him to speak, noting that it had "an excellent lantern and a skilled operator," a likely reference to his use of spirit photography in his public presentations.[21] (I have found no evidence that he spoke before this group or the Oxford Union.)

The odd position of spiritualism in the religious ferment of the time is illustrated by his public debates with both bishops and humanists. He found battling on two fronts to be frustrating, claiming that "spiritualism is bringing the evidence in favor of religion that skeptics have been demanding all along."[22] And he was annoyed that while he was debating the irreligious, "the clergy are ready to attack us from behind."[23] In notes that Conan Doyle took for a debate with Bishop Karney of Johannesburg, he makes a surprising, almost populist attack on the authority of the Anglican Church, not the sort of thing expected from such an old-fashioned man. In discussing spiritualism, he emphasizes the knowledge of laypeople in contrast to the ignorance of the church hierarchy: "Is it not strange therefore that this study is left entirely to laymen. I don't know a single Bishop who is a member of a S.P.R. [Society for Psychic Research]. It is really rather scandalous. At present the laymen know more than the Clergy & the Clergy know more than the Bishops."[24]

Conan Doyle claimed that spiritualism, especially in its evidence for life after death, was not an attack on existing religions. In a radio address on psychic photographs, he said, "We are not against any religion. Our knowledge is for the world. Use it as best you can. Add it to the religion you already have, and you will find that religion all the better."[25] But he doubted the divinity of Jesus and the existence of hell, and he had unusual views of heaven, believing that the soul advanced through stages.[26] He also believed that deathbed repentance was meaningless, that people would be called to account for their sins: "And one thing we have got clearly from the other side. It is that a man has to pay his own bills and cannot shuffle them off on some one else, holier than himself."[27] Spiritualism, he claimed, would "reform the religions of the world" and "combine science with religion, to replace faith with knowledge, and to give us firm ground upon which to build the social system of the future."[28] Understandably, perhaps, Christian bishops did not see any need for reforms, additions, or revelations at the hands of the talking dead and their apostle Conan Doyle. And skeptics would have found little appealing about his faith in the spirit world and life after death. Nevertheless, that Conan Doyle so doggedly and for so long took on both ends of the religious-scientific divide deserves some respect.

IN ADDITION TO HIS EXTENSIVE public lectures on spiritualism around the world, Conan Doyle started the Psychic and General Book Shop, in London. Its telegraph address was "Ectoplasm, Sowest, London." This venture cost him considerable money and time, and one eyewitness account describes him as engaged in everyday store tasks like packing books for mailing. One of the account books for the store includes his handwritten notation of "a deficit of £167," but adds, "I have paid in new capital of nearly £400 and taken nothing out."[29] The building was destroyed during the Blitz, bringing to an end what Conan Doyle saw as an important part of his legacy. He might have been happy, though, to know that an Arthur Conan Doyle Centre operates today in Edinburgh. The center describes itself on its website as "formed to provide for the physical, emotional and spiritual well-being of society and community needs in Edinburgh." It is the current home of the Edinburgh Association of Spiritualists.

Despite all their criticism of Conan Doyle, Sherlockians are grateful that he never allowed his spiritualist beliefs to influence his characterization of Sherlock Holmes. He could have easily converted Holmes to spiritualism or portrayed him as using spiritual powers to solve crimes. One reason for his forbearance may be that he had an alternate fictional universe, that of Professor Challenger. Conan Doyle noted in a letter that the character was "founded upon one of my old tutors at the University"[30]—but not the same one who was the model for Sherlock Holmes. Spiritualism becomes an essential part of the third, and last, book in the Challenger series, published in 1926, and the professor becomes a convert. Perhaps Conan Doyle introduced spiritualism there because the series was relatively new, while Sherlock Holmes was already well established. In addition, the

latter had a formidable readership that might have objected to any
fundamental changes in Holmes. The critic Richard Jenkyns saw
Conan Doyle's continuation of a rational Holmes in more practical
terms, as "some instinct of literary self-preservation."[31]

Conan Doyle nevertheless wrote about the potential of mediums
to solve real-life crimes. The essay "The Detective of the Future" was
originally titled "The Psychic Detection of Crime."[32] In it, he imagines clairvoyants assisting the police, tracking down the location of
dead bodies or giving clues about suspects—psychic bloodhounds
following invisible tracks. But he notes that spirits from the other
world may not cooperate with the police in some cases, since they
are opposed to capital punishment.

He also has encouraging news about pets in the other world, a
subject of debate even today among Christians: "All pet animals
continue to live with us. Mutual love holds them . . . I have heard
the barking of dogs in the séance room and have felt their heads
on my knee."[33] For this touching passage alone, even critics of
Conan Doyle's spiritualism might wish to extend "amnesty in that
direction."[34]

While Conan Doyle is often portrayed as a dupe of spiritualist
frauds, most prominently in the case of the faked fairy photographs,
he was well aware of such problems. In a letter to a William Strachey,
a relation of Lytton Strachey, he writes, "I have been attending some
séances in the North of London and have grave doubts of their honesty." And he was a friend of Harry Houdini, who sought to expose
fraudulent mediums.

Conan Doyle wrote about controversial spiritualists of the day, including the theosophist Madame Blavatsky, who had supporters and
detractors throughout her life, with Conan Doyle in the detractor
camp. He also noted in a lecture that the séance room's "necessity
for darkness has unfortunately been taken advantage of by rogues
in order to do fraudulent tricks."[35] But he wrote that the existence
of fake mediums was no more a problem for spiritualism than Judas
was a problem for Christianity.

On the other hand, he did believe in the famous, faked Cottingley
fairies. This credulity is not entirely surprising, since Conan Doyle
generally believed in photographic evidence of spiritualism. Drafts
for his lectures feature photographic images, and the Oxford Junior
Scientific Society invitation letter, as noted above, makes clear that
his use of photographs in lectures was well known.

Conan Doyle thought that spiritualism could solve serious problems in the world. In his writing, he repeatedly points to materialism as a dire temptation. In a lecture, he claims: "[Spiritualists]

Figure 11.1. Frances Griffiths and the Cottingley fairies, 1917. Photograph by Elsie Wright.

believe that materialism is the great curse of the world, and that it will destroy the world if it is not checked. The old religions have failed to check it. It increases continuously. It is clear that if we are not to despair some new force is needed. It is a force which we believe that we can supply."[36] He elaborated in notes on the back of envelopes, possibly for a lecture. It is titled "Watchman, what of the night?"—a line taken from Isaiah, but perhaps doing double duty as a cricket metaphor:

> In more than a century, since the Napoleonic Wars, we have looked out upon an ever darkening night. A night of grinding industrial competition. A night of coarse materialism. A night of gold worship. A night of overdrinking and overeating. Materialistic life, materialistic negative philosophy, materialistic churches, so sunk in matter that they could not understand spirit when it was just before them.[37]

On a more optimistic note, an intriguing outgrowth of spiritualism was the possibility that the great writers of the past might provide new works through mediums. In "The Alleged Posthumous writings of Great Authors," Conan Doyle complains that critics unfairly dismiss this as absurd and therefore ignore the textual evidence. He examines four cases—Charles Dickens, Oscar Wilde, Jack London, and the publisher Lord Northcliffe. Overall, he finds "the case for the genuine character of these writings is an exceedingly strong one."[38]

Wilde probably would have appreciated being able to send quips from the other side. Conan Doyle's evidence was his assessment of how the alleged writing compared to the real-life writing of Wilde, particularly his use of color. The following sample derived from a text obtained through automatic writing and a Ouija board:

> In clerical twilight I move but I know that in the world there is day and night, seed time and harvest, and red sunset must follow apple-green day. Every year spring throws her green veil over the world and anon the red autumn glory comes to mock the yellow moon. Already the may is creeping like a white mist over land and hedge-row, and year after year the hawthorn bears blood-red fruit after the white death of its may.

Conan Doyle responded enthusiastically: "This is not merely adequate Wilde. It is exquisite Wilde. It is so beautiful that it might be chosen for special inclusion in any anthology of his writings."[39]

Conan Doyle was less convinced about the evidence for Dickens. In discussing a medium who wrote new Dickens, Conan Doyle called it "Dickens gone flat. The fizz, the sparkle, the spontaneity of it is gone. But the trick of thought and of manner remain."[40] He argued that we might well expect that such writing, as interpreted through a medium, would be of lesser quality than the real-life writing of authors, just as his own writing was worse when he used a typewriter rather than a pen. Conan Doyle also noted similarities in the use of tense in this spirit writing and in the actual *Mystery of Edwin Drood*. He further observed that the medium involved was said to not have the ability or education to write such works. Conan Doyle noted, however, that the spirit of Dickens suggested that his London publisher might be willing to pay for the writing, so "a critic might argue therefore that a deception was not entirely without an object." He concluded "that the evidence is on the whole in favor," although it is notable that in the manuscript, he crossed out "strongly" and replaced it with "on the whole."[41]

In Conan Doyle's only known filmed interview, in 1928, he discusses both Sherlock Holmes and spiritualism for more than ten minutes, in an accent that is said to be hard to place.[42] It ends with him slowly walking away from the camera with his dog. This is a poignant scene because we know that within two years he will pass into the great unknown that he spent decades of his life trying to understand. Days before his death, he wrote, "The reader will judge that I have had many adventures. The greatest and most glorious of all awaits me now."[43] We can only hope that he was happy with what he found.

Spring Semester 2018

My thanks to Kathryn Millan, Rick Watson (yes, Watson), and the staff of the Harry Ransom Center at the University of Texas at Austin for their assistance with the research for this paper. Except where otherwise noted, all sources are in the Arthur Conan Doyle archive at the Harry Ransom Center, and the descriptions below are adapted from those of the HRC. All cited works are by Arthur Conan Doyle unless otherwise indicated.

The epigraph comes from Conan Doyle's "The detective of the future," a signed six-page typescript, dated 24 September (no year).

1. Arthur Conan Doyle to "Mam," 11 Nov. 1891.

2. James Douglas, "Is Conan Doyle Mad?," *Sunday Express*, 25 Sept. 1921, available at https://www.arthur-conan-doyle.com/index.php?title=Is_Conan_Doyle_Mad%3F.

3. Andrew Lycett, *The Man Who Created Sherlock Holmes: The Life and Times of Sir Arthur Conan Doyle* (New York, 2007), p. 180.

4. Stephen Fry, preface to *The Hound of the Baskervilles*, audio book, Audible Studios.

5. "Notes on slides to accompany a lecture on psychic photographs."

6. "When I am asked what my system of work is I have . . ."

7. Fry, preface.

8. "The new revelation," handwritten, typed, and carbon copy twenty-two-page manuscript with handwritten deletions and emendations, undated.

9. "The proof of spiritualism," five-page undated mimeograph; article for the National Press Agency Ltd.

10. Ibid.

11. "Lecture re survival and communication after death," sixteen-page handwritten manuscript, notes with revisions, undated.

12. Radio broadcast; "Proof of spiritualism."

13. "Spiritualism: some straight questions and answers," five-page carbon copy typescript with extensive handwritten emendations, undated.

14. "Proof of spiritualism."

15. "Recent psychic research," five-page handwritten manuscript, undated.

16. William Cuthbert Holmes to Arthur Conan Doyle, 8 Apr. 1919.

17. "Broadcast: a chat with Conan Doyle," five-page typescript with handwritten emendations, undated.

18. Ibid.

19. Ibid.

20. Gerald Gardiner, president of the Oxford Union Society, to Arthur Conan Doyle, 28 Apr. 1924.

21. A. Townsend, president of the Oxford Junior Scientific Society, to Arthur Conan Doyle, 12 July 1925.

22. "Lecture re spiritualism," an eighteen-page signed handwritten manuscript, incomplete with a few emendations, undated.

23. "Lecture re spiritualism and Christianity," eight-page handwritten manuscript, undated.

24. Ibid.

25. "Lecture re spiritualism and psychic photographs," seven-page carbon copy typescript, undated.

26. For Conan Doyle's views on Jesus and hell, see "The new revelation"; for the soul's advancement through stages, see "Lecture re spiritualism and psychic photographs."

27. "Note for debate with Bishop Karney."

28. "Lecture re spiritualism and Christianity"; "Recent psychic research."

29. Account books of the Psychic Book Shop, Library and Museum, 29 vols., 1894–1928.

30. Arthur Conan Doyle to G. S. Viereck, 29 May 1929.

31. Richard Jenkyns, "Conan Doyle and Sherlock Holmes," in Wm. Roger Louis ed., *Ultimate Adventures with Britannia* (Austin, 2009), p. 14.

32. "Detective of the future."

33. "The new revelation."

34. "The Adventure of Silver Blaze," *Strand Magazine,* 1892.

35. "Recent psychic research."

36. "Lecture re spiritualism and psychic photographs."

37. "Watchman what of the night?," eight-page handwritten manuscript; handwritten manuscript and notes on six envelopes, undated.

38. "Lecture re spirit communications from dead authors," seventeen-page handwritten manuscript, undated.

39. Ibid.

40. Ibid.

41. "The alleged posthumous writings of great authors," sixteen-page signed handwritten manuscript with emendations, July 1927.

42. "Arthur Conan Doyle Interviewed on Sherlock Holmes and Spirituality." https://www.youtube.com/watch?v=XWjgt9PzYEM&t=3s.

43. Quoted in Algis Valiunas, "The Man Who Hated Sherlock Holmes," *Weekly Standard,* 29 Aug. 1999, https://www.weeklystandard.com/algis-valiunas/the-man -who-hated-sherlock-holmes

P. G. Wodehouse, 1944. Unknown photographer. NPG x137610. © National Portrait Gallery, London.

12

P. G. Wodehouse

JOSEPH EPSTEIN

"The object of all good literature," thinks Sue Brown, a chorus girl and a character in P. G. Wodehouse's novel *Summer Lightning*, "is to purge the soul of its petty troubles." Something to it, quite a bit actually, though Céline, Samuel Beckett, Edward Albee, and a number of other modern writers who pass for serious would strenuously have disagreed. The writing of P. G. Wodehouse—the author of some ninety-five books of fiction and three of memoir, recently republished in a handsome hardbound collection by Everyman's Library in London and the Overlook Press in New York—was not merely unserious but positively anti-serious, and therein lay much of his considerable charm.

As for that anti-seriousness, who other than Wodehouse would describe a figure in one of his novels by saying that "if he had been a character in a Russian novel, he would have gone and hanged himself in a barn"? Who but Wodehouse could mock the moral tradition of the English novel in a single phrase by writing in a novel of his own of "one of those unfortunate misunderstandings that are so apt to sunder hearts, the sort of thing that Thomas Hardy used to write about"? Who but he, through the creation in his novel *Leave it to Psmith* of a poet named Ralston McTodd, would find humor in the hopeless obscurity of much modern poetry? Only Wodehouse would have the always-to-be-trusted Jeeves instruct Bertie Wooster about Nietzsche: "He is fundamentally unsound, sir." Or have Bertie disqualify a young woman because after sixteen sets of tennis and a round of golf she expected one in the evening "to take an intelligent interest in Freud." Who but Wodehouse would say about a character whom he clearly doesn't admire that he "was an earnest young man with political ambitions given, when not slamming [tennis balls] over the net, to reading white papers and studying social conditions"—thus flicking off politics as a time-wasting, even altogether fatuous, preoccupation. At a lower level of anti-seriousness, Wodehouse amusingly mocked crime fiction, crossword puzzles, and antique collecting.

Pelham Grenville Wodehouse (1881–1975) was, like Kipling, Saki, Orwell, and Somerset Maugham, a child of the empire, which meant that while growing up in England he saw very little of his parents, who were off across the sea tending to the British colonies. The third of four sons, Wodehouse grew up in Hong Kong, where his father served as an imperial magistrate. Between the ages of three and fifteen, his biographer Robert McCrum conjectures in *Wodehouse: A Life* (2004), he saw his parents little more than a total of six months. Owing to such circumstances, Wodehouse was naturally never close to his family, and was especially distanced from his mother, a woman said to be cold, imperious, and forbidding. Though cut off from normal family feeling, Wodehouse seems to have made up for it by an ingrained optimism, a sunny disposition, a love of sport, and a powerful imagination for fantasy. From his earliest days, he wanted to be a writer. In his fiction, he created a world that never quite existed but is so amusing as to make one feel it a pity that it didn't.

Wodehouse's public-school days, at a place called Dulwich—C. S. Forester went there, as did Raymond Chandler—were perhaps his happiest. McCrum notes that on the status scale, Dulwich was neither Eton nor Winchester, but "it offered an excellent education for the sons of the imperial servant." The young Wodehouse, an exuberant sportsman, excelled at both rugby and cricket, sports that he followed avidly his life long. As a boy, he was an ardent reader of Dickens, Kipling, J. M. Barrie, and Arthur Conan Doyle, and also adored Gilbert and Sullivan. At Dulwich he studied on the classics side, and his own novels and stories are dotted with references to Queen Boudica, the Midians, Thucydides, Marius among the ruins of Carthage, the Gracchi, and others.

When Wodehouse was nineteen, his father announced that there weren't sufficient funds to send him to Oxford, where his older brothers had gone. He seems to have taken it in stride. He went instead to work at the Hongkong and Shanghai Bank in London, interning in the Bob Cratchit–like role of lowly clerk. In the evenings he wrote stories and articles and supplied comic bits for newspapers and magazines. In fairly short order, he wrote his way out of the bank and into an economically independent freelance life. Writers divide between those who may write well but don't need to do it and those who find life without meaning if they aren't writing. Wodehouse was clearly of the latter camp. Over a long career (he died at ninety-three), along with his novels and stories he wrote plays and musicals (collaborating on occasion with Jerome Kern), supplied lyrics for other people's shows (he wrote the song "Bill" for *Showboat* and worked with Cole Porter on *Anything Goes*), and did his stint in Hollywood. He appears always to have thought himself a professional writer rather than a literary artist, with a wide following more important to him than the praise of critics.

For a writer who never aspired to be other than popular, in later life Wodehouse acquired accolades from many writers who easily cleared the highbrow bar, including T. S. Eliot, W. H. Auden, Evelyn Waugh, Dorothy Parker, Kingsley Amis, Eudora Welty, Lionel Trilling, Bertrand Russell, and Ludwig Wittgenstein. Hilaire Belloc called him "the best writer of English now alive," a handsome tribute seconded by H. L. Mencken. "Temperate admirers of his work," wrote the English drama critic James Agate, "are non-existent."

Wodehouse wrote no faulty sentences, and countless ones that, for people who care about the pleasing ordering of words, give unrivaled delight. In his biography, McCrum offers the following splendid example, one of hundreds, perhaps thousands, that could be adduced: "In the face of the young man who sat on the terrace of the Hotel Magnifique at Cannes there crept a look of furtive shame, the shifty, hangdog look which announces that an Englishman is about to talk French."

The comic touches that bedizen Wodehouse's prose are one of its chief delights. A drunken character is described as "brilliantly illuminated." An overweight baronet "looks forward to a meal that sticks to the ribs and brings beads of perspiration to the forehead." A woman supposed to marry that same stout gentleman has the uneasy feeling that, so large is he, she might be "committing bigamy." A minor character "has a small and revolting mustache"; another "is so crooked he sliced bread with a corkscrew." Wodehouse spun jokes out of clichés. His similes are notably striking. A man known to be unable to keep secrets is likened to "a human collander." Another character is "as broke as the Ten Commandments." The brains of the press departments of the movie studios resemble "soup at a cheap restaurant. It is wiser not to stir them." These similes often arise when least expected: "The drowsy stillness of the afternoon was shattered by what sounded to his strained senses like

G. K. Chesterton falling on a sheet of tin." There is a passing reference to "a politician's trained verbosity," a phrase I find handy whenever watching a contemporary politician interviewed on television. Like Jimmy Durante with jokes, so P. G. Wodehouse with arrestingly amusing phrases—he had a million of 'em.

"I believe there are two ways of writing novels," Wodehouse wrote. "One is mine, making a sort of musical comedy without music and ignoring real life altogether; the other is going right down deep into life, and not giving a damn." No one would accuse P. G. Wodehouse of ever flirting with realism. His fiction is uniformly preposterous. "I don't really know anything about writing except farcical comedy," he wrote to his friend the novelist William Townsend. "A real person in my fiction would stick out like a sore thumb."

Nobody dies in Wodehouse novels or stories. In his fiction there are no wars, economic depression, sex below the neck, little *Sturm* and even less *Drang*, with only satisfyingly happy endings awaiting at the close. English country-house scenes were his favorite milieu. These are populated with aimless young men in spats with names like Stilton Cheesewright, Bingo Little, Tuppy Glossop, and Pongo Twistleton; troublesome young women, terrifying aunts, and eccentric servants; notable props include two-seater roadsters, cigarette holders, monocles, and lots of cocktails.

"Romps" seem to me perhaps the best single word to describe Wodehouse's novels and stories, yet artfully organized romps. The first task of the writer of fiction is to make the unpredictable plausible. Wodehouse's own method, going a step further, was to think of something very bizarre and then make it plausible. But given his outlandish characters, the impossible confusions they encounter, the unlikely coincidences that everywhere arise, plausibility never really comes into play; more accurate to say that he made the improbable delectably palatable.

Wodehouse allowed that he wrote his novels as if they were plays. "In writing a novel I always imagine I'm writing for a cast of actors," he explained to Townsend in one of the letters printed in *Author, Author!* (1962), their collected correspondence. "One of the best tips for writing a play, Guy [Bolton, his chief theatrical collaborator] tells me, is 'Never let them sit down.'" Wodehouse kept his characters in action, and felt that the earlier the introduction of dialogue, the better, the more, and, given his dazzling touch for it, the jollier. "But how about my flesh and blood, my Aunt Julia, you ask," says his character Stanley Ukridge. "No I don't," says the story's narrator. "I'm in the soup," says Gussie Fink-Nottle. "Up to the thorax," replies Bertie Wooster.

To create one imperishable comic character is no small achievement. Robert McCrum holds that Wodehouse created five: Psmith, Lord Emsworth, Aunt Agatha, Bertie Wooster, and Jeeves. I would add as a sixth the irrepressible Galahad Threepwood, the younger brother of Lord Emsworth, an old boy who, during a relentlessly roguish youth, "apparently never went to bed before he was fifty."

Ronald Eustace Psmith is a former Etonian, monocled, appallingly fluent, a master of comic hauteur. Clarence, the ninth Earl of Emsworth, lord of Blandings Castle, is interested only in gardening and in pigs and is two stages beyond absent-minded, described in *Leave It to Psmith* as "that amiable and boneheaded peer," "a fluffy-minded man" who has "a tiring day trying to keep his top hat balanced on his head." Aunt Agatha is female tyranny to the highest power, pure menace, a woman "who eats broken bottles and wears barbed-wire close to the skin." Bertie Wooster and his valet, Jeeves, are the best known of Wodehouse's characters. Bertie, self-described as having "half the amount of brain a normal bloke ought to possess," is a classic instance of the Edwardian knut, one of those upper-class idlers, often second and third sons, with nothing more pressing on their agendas than choosing their dandaical outfit for the day, meeting Algy for lunch at the club, and avoiding those tradesmen foolish enough to have extended them credit.

As for Jeeves, he, undoubtedly, is Wodehouse's greatest creation, a man who does not so much enter as flow into rooms, omniscient in his learning, formally correct in his syntax, infallible in his good sense, ingenious at getting Bertie and Bertie's friends out of misbegotten marriage alliances and entanglements with aunts threatening their inheritances, creating along the way innumerable plots thicker and stickier than carnival taffy. "In the matter of brain and resource," thinks Bertie of Jeeves, "I don't believe I have ever met a chappie so supremely like mother made." Jeeves, who recognizes that his master is "of negligible intelligence," notes that "in an employer brains are not desirable." Not for comedy they certainly aren't.

Wodehouse's fiction does not abound in sympathetic female characters. He was not so much misogynistic, McCrum rightly points out, as gynophobic. Whether bluestockings or ditzy airheads, women in Wodehouse tend to be objects of terror, interfering, dangerous in their potential to undermine the knut way of life. Madeline Bassett—with whom the prospect of a marital connection sends Bertie into shivers—is one of these women. Though of attractive exterior, she is too often on the "point of talking baby talk . . . the sort of girl who puts her hands over a husband's eyes, as he is crawling in to breakfast with a morning head, and says: 'Guess who?'"

Aunts—there are no mothers I have encountered in Wodehouse—
are "all alike": "Sooner or later out comes the cloven hoof." When
Bertie remarks that he had "no idea that small girls were such de-
mons," Jeeves laconically replies: "More deadly than the male, sir."
Galahad Threepwood notes that "the one thing a man with a cold
in his head must avoid is a woman's touch." Stanley Ukridge remarks
that "women have their merits, of course, but if you are to live the
good life, you don't want them around the house." None of Wodehouse's heroes is married.

WODEHOUSE HIMSELF MARRIED, at thirty-three, to Ethel Wayman, an
actress twice widowed with a ten-year-old daughter. The marriage
appears to have been an untroubled one, owing chiefly to each of
its partners allowing the other to go off on his or her own. In Ethel
Wodehouse's case, this seems to have been chiefly to go off shop-
ping, pursue mild forms of social lion hunting, and acquire expensive places for her family to live. In Wodehouse's, it meant being left
alone to write, with time off for lengthy walks with one or another
of the couple's many Pekingese. They had no children together, but
Wodehouse came to love his stepdaughter, Leonora, to whom he
dedicated one of his books: "To Leonora without whose never failing sympathy and encouragement this book would have been finished in half the time." She was the closest he came to having a true
confidant, and her death at forty was a great loss to him.

Life generally, though, was good. Wodehouse's high productivity paid off amply in what Bertie Wooster would call doubloons or
pieces of eight. In London, he and Ethel lived in Mayfair. They had
a butler, cook, maids, footmen, two secretaries, and a chauffeur-
driven Rolls-Royce. He had become, in Robert McCrum's phrase,
"seriously rich." Praise for his writing, meanwhile, flowed in, with
only occasional demurrers. In 1939, Oxford, the university he wasn't
allowed to attend for want of funds, presented him with an honorary degree. Pelham Grenville Wodehouse was on what looked like a
lifelong roll.

And then the roof and the walls, along with the floor, caved in.
The onset of the Second World War found Wodehouse and his family living in Le Tourquet, in northern France near the English Channel, and when the Nazis marched in, Wodehouse, who didn't flee in
time, found himself interned. At first the internment turned out to
be more an inconvenience than anything else, and he was even able
to complete a novel during it. Soon, though, the Nazis learned of
his fame and, gauging the propaganda value of their prisoner, encouraged him through subtle suasion to recount the relative mild-

ness of his detainment in a series of five radio talks, which he gave in the summer of 1941.

The talks were innocuous enough, though it was a grave mistake for the politically naïve Wodehouse to make them. Doing so over Nazi radio put him in company with such genuine traitors as William Joyce, known as Lord Haw-Haw and hanged by the English for treason after the war. He also published in the *Saturday Evening Post* an article, under the title "My War with Germany," in which, in his extreme naïveté, he remarked that he was unable to work up any hostility toward the enemy: "Just when I'm about to feel belligerent about some country I meet a decent sort of chap" from that country, he wrote, causing him to lose "any fighting feelings or thoughts." Wodehouse, in other words, used the occasion of the most murderous events in modern history for light laughs.

The reaction was swift and crushing. Anthony Eden, in Parliament, accused Wodehouse of lending "his services to the German war propaganda machine." Duff Cooper, Churchill's minister of information, held Wodehouse's behavior to be traitorous. A general piling-on was not long in coming. Harold Nicolson refused to believe in Wodehouse's innocence being the cause of his betrayal. A *Daily Mirror* columnist writing as Cassandra, whose real name was William O'Connor, gave a talk over the BBC that began: "I have come to tell you tonight of the story of a rich man [Wodehouse] trying to make his last and greatest sale—that of his own country," and went on to compare him to Judas. The playwright Sean O'Casey called Wodehouse "English Literature's performing flea." Oxford was said to be considering reclaiming his honorary degree. Deep readers began finding evidence of fascism in his books, which were banned from some provincial libraries, and in a few places even burned. Songs to which he had written the lyrics were not allowed over the BBC. There was talk about Wodehouse being hanged as a traitor.

Wodehouse called his own conduct "a loony thing to do"; later he would say it was "insane." Yet it is far from clear that he truly grasped the gravity of his mistake. Malcolm Muggeridge, who later became his friend, thought Wodehouse had a "temperament that unfits him to be a good citizen in the ideological mid-twentieth century." The best defense of Wodehouse, made by George Orwell in 1945, just after the war was over, was that he was not only a political naïf, but gave his talks for the Nazis at precisely the wrong time: the summer of 1941, "at just that moment when the war reached its desperate phase." Orwell ends his defense of Wodehouse by writing "in the desperate circumstances of the time it was excusable to be angry at what Wodehouse did, but to go on denouncing him three or four years later—and more, to let an impression remain that he acted with conscious treachery—is not excusable."

Yet decades passed before Wodehouse was finally forgiven for this contretemps. In 1947 he moved, permanently, to America, and in 1955 took up American citizenship. His friend the humorist Frank Sullivan said his doing so made up "for our loss of T. S. Eliot and Henry James combined," an amusing touch of hyperbole. His wartime broadcasts continued to haunt him, though he claimed to be without self-pity. "I made an ass of myself," he wrote to William Townsend, "and must pay the penalty." Still, he was as productive as ever, producing a book a year. At his eightieth birthday, in a newspaper ad for one of his books, a literary all-star cast that included W. H. Auden, Ivy Compton-Burnett, Graham Greene, Rebecca West, and others signed on to pay tribute to him as "an inimitable international institution and a master humorist." Wodehouse wrote to his old friend Guy Bolton: "I seem to have become the Grand Old Man of English Literature." In 1975 he was knighted by Queen Elizabeth, who was among his most ardent readers, which formally closed the book on his wartime fiasco.

FOR THE BETTER PART OF THE PAST two months I have been reading P. G. Wodehouse early mornings, with tea and toast and unslaked pleasure. Although I haven't made a serious dent in his ninety-five-book oeuvre, before long, I tell myself, I must cease and desist from this happy indulgence, this sweet disease that one of his readers called "P.G.-osis." "You can," says a character in an Isaac Bashevis Singer story, "have too much even of *kreplach*." (Something of a literary puritan, I have followed up each morning's reading of Wodehouse with four or five pages of Aristotle's *Rhetoric* and his *Nicomachean Ethics*—an intellectual antidote, a breath mint of seriousness, you might say.) In a 1961 talk on Wodehouse over the BBC, Evelyn Waugh ended by saying: "Mr. Wodehouse's world can never stale. He will continue to release future generations from captivity that may be more irksome than our own. He has made a world for us to live in and delight in."

The work of humorists is not usually long-lived. Among Americans, two very different examples, James Thurber and S. J. Perelman, seem to have bitten the dust, at least they have for me. Yet Wodehouse remains readable and immensely enjoyable. Perhaps this is owing to his having written about a world that never really existed, so his work, unlike Thurber's and Perelman's, isn't finally time-bound. "I'm all for strewing a little happiness as I go by," Wodehouse wrote to William Townsend, and he did so in ample measure. He would have been pleased to learn that for his readers the gift of that happiness has yet to stop giving.

Spring Semester 2018

A version of this lecture appeared in the *Claremont Review of Books,* 18, 1 (Winter 2018).

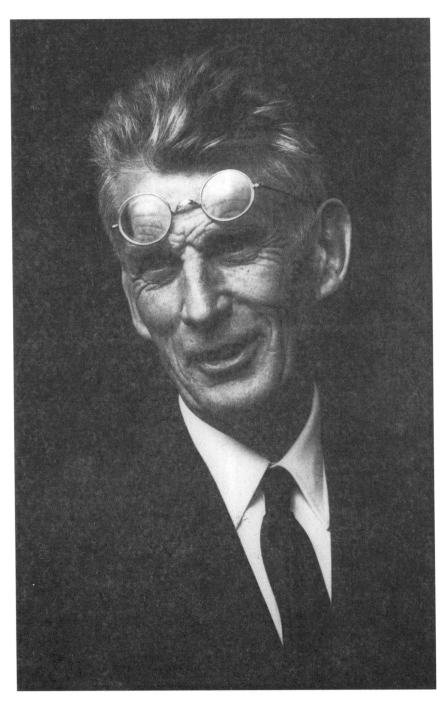

Samuel Beckett, 1979. Photograph by Reg Lancaster.

13

Samuel Beckett and Surrealism

ALAN W. FRIEDMAN

The years 1929–45 have been called Samuel Beckett's "surrealist period." Never much of a joiner, Beckett did not officially belong to the Surrealist group, although he was acquainted with many of its members and with much of their work. He was friends, for example, with Marcel Duchamp, Wassily Kandinsky, Francis Picabia, and Alberto Giacometti. He played chess with several of the Surrealists; he translated numerous Surrealist writings; and he signed one of the Surrealist manifestoes. Beckett also used many of the same images, perspectives, and motifs as the Surrealists, representing and exploring prenatal and dream states, body parts, the unconscious, non sequiturs, implausibility, madness, spontaneity, the marvelous, and something analogous to what André Breton, the leader of the Surrealist movement, called "pure psychic automatism."

Beckett's Surrealist connections were demonstrated in the March 1932 issue of Eugene Jolas's little magazine *transition*, which was subtitled *An International Workshop for Orphic Creation*. It contains "Poetry Is Vertical," Jolas's manifesto on writing, apparently derived from Jung, with its Surrealist call for "the hegemony of the inner life over the outer life, . . . the hallucinatory irruption of images in the dream," the invention of "a hermetic language [and], if necessary, . . . the construction of a new mythological reality."[1] In a rare public expression of group sympathy, Beckett signed the manifesto.

Beckett's debt to Surrealism can be seen in the early story "Echo's Bones" (1933). The prose is allusive, obscure, endlessly restless, and replete with verbally resonant language and "horrible and immediate switches of the focus, and the . . . wild unfathomable energy of the population," as Beckett's editor, Charles Prentice, wrote in rejecting it. These qualities undermine narrative causation, and the text reads like a dream sequence or a series of discrete vignettes. It begins by depicting Belacqua, who is resurrected after his death in a previous story, straddling a "fence, day in day out," a foot in each of two worlds. Locations are dreamlike, shifting from one to another abruptly, whimsically: a "pasture, paved with edible mushrooms," a Parisian room, a graveyard, a seashore. Belacqua encounters a prostitute, the infertile giant Lord Gall of Wormwood, Lady Gall (whom Belacqua is called upon to impregnate and does), a cemetery in which he and a gravedigger dig up his grave so that he can prove it is empty, and "a submarine of souls on the sea," wildly populated by characters who, like Belacqua, died in the collection of stories *More Pricks Than Kicks,* including "little Alba, waving from the conning tower and beckoning in a most unladylike manner."

Although Beckett did not formally endorse Surrealism, the movement influenced his writings from first to last. In turn, he did what he could to further the Surrealists' program. According to the critic Raymond Federman, "[Beckett's] novels and stories of the first period are situated in a still recognizable setting—a city landscape, Dublin, London. Streets are named, houses are described, even nature is described, though ironically. But rather than realistic descriptions . . . these scenes are surreal."[2]

Beckett's monetary needs were great during the early 1930s and the late 1940s. To earn a living, he frequently translated work by others, but affinity may also help explain his being repeatedly asked and drawn to translate the Surrealists, even if he didn't always want that connection widely known. The biographer James Knowlson notes that "Beckett did far more translations than anyone has ever realized, for many of them appeared, at his own request, unsigned." At the time he was writing *Dream of Fair to Middling Women,* Beckett translated at least sixteen pieces (poems and prose poems) for the Surrealist number (September 1932) of Edward Titus's little magazine *This Quarter,* which André Breton, the father of Surrealism, guest-edited. Beckett's translations—of Breton's fictional extracts and poems, three essays by Breton and Paul Éluard for the "Surrealism and Madness" section, an excerpt from René Crevel's *Le Clavecin de Diderot (Diderot's Harpsichord),* and Éluard's poetry—garnered high praise from Titus: "We cannot refrain from singling out Mr. Samuel

Beckett's work for special acknowledgement. His rendering of the Eluard and Breton poems in particular is characterizable only in superlatives"—meaning, presumably, that he had captured the Surrealist quality of the originals.[3] According to the critic Daniel Albright, "Beckett's early translations of the Surrealists were . . . as important to his artistic development as his critical studies of Proust and Joyce."[4] Titus subsequently commissioned Beckett to translate Rimbaud's "Le Bateau ivre," for which the editor happily paid Beckett, even though *This Quarter* folded before it was published. Ironically, the translation was later displaced from its designated slot in *Contemporary Poetry and Prose* (1936) by a letter from Ezra Pound inveighing against what he called "The Coward Surrealists." Beckett's translation, titled "Drunken Boat," was finally published in 1976.

As a major contributor to *This Quarter*'s Surrealist number, Beckett would have been familiar with Breton's statement as guest editor, "Surrealism: Yesterday, To-day and To-morrow." Lois Gordon points out the connection: "Breton's earliest manifestoes emphasized a number of elements that must have been of enormous interest to Beckett: dreams, paradox, chance, and coincidence. . . . These early writings also discussed humor as visible at life's most tragic moments. . . . The intermingling of conscious and unconscious thought functioning would become both subject and technique in the Beckett canon."[5] In addition to Breton's espousal of dreams, several other components of his statement would have been congenial to Beckett: the linking of humor and tragedy (in *Endgame,* Nell comments, "Nothing is funnier than unhappiness, I grant you that");[6] an emphasis on cinematic imagery that resembled Eisenstein's montage; the necessity of "go[ing] onward towards . . . discovery"; automatic writing that manifests itself as "a monologue poured out as rapidly as possible, over which the subject's critical sense claims no share"; and a refusal to rein in the imagination, regardless of "the fear of going mad."[7]

Beckett didn't shy away from representing madness in his writings: it is as commonplace in his fiction as it is in the work of the Surrealists. In the story "Fingal," for example, Belacqua points to the Portrane Lunatic Asylum outside Dublin and says, "My heart's right there," and the narrator of the story "Love and Lethe" concurs: "A mental home was the place for him."[8] Murphy's quest for mental freedom leads him to an institution for the insane, which he finds an agreeable place to work and where he plays chess with the schizophrenic Mr. Endon before dying shortly thereafter. Watt ends up in an asylum with his narrator, Sam, as does Malone, who boasts, "I feel in extraordinary form. Delirium perhaps," along with his fictional character Macmann, and who views the asylum, "the House of Saint John of God," as "a little Paradise."[9]

In *Endgame,* Hamm says he once knew a madman, a painter "who thought the end of the world had come." It was covered in ashes, and "he alone had been spared," which may well be the situation of that play's survivors.[10] And like *Endgame,* much of Beckett's late fiction occurs in what the narrator of *Ill Seen Ill Said* (1981) calls "the madhouse of the skull and nowhere else," a place notably occupied by Lucky in *Waiting for Godot,* by the Unnamable, and by all the characters in *Endgame,* as emphasized by the skull-like set that Roger Blin created with Beckett for its initial performance in 1957.[11] According to the narrator of Beckett's *The Calmative* (1945), "We are needless to say in a skull. . . . All the mortals I saw were alone and as if sunk in themselves."[12] Late Beckett works like "Lessness" (1970) and *Worstward Ho* (1983) can sound at times like mad ramblings or automatic writing or the workings of the unconscious behind the skull. *Worstward Ho,* for example, has the following setting: "In the skull all save the skull gone. The stare. Alone in the dim void. Alone to be seen. Dimly seen. In the skull the skull alone to be seen."[13] The narrator of Beckett's last major work, *Stirrings Still* (1988), ruminates on whether "he was in his right mind . . . he could not but begin to wonder if he was in his right mind."[14] Beckett, ever the scrupulous and self-aware craftsman, consciously produced something akin to what Breton thought an artist could achieve only by turning off his mind.

Though he often made dismissive comments about his translations, Beckett nonetheless seemed pleased with at least some of them and eager for more, and not just for the money they might bring. Shortly after Beckett completed his work for *This Quarter,* his friend the heiress Nancy Cunard asked him to undertake significant translation work for her compendium *Negro: An Anthology* (1934). Beckett translated nineteen pieces, contributing more to the volume than anyone except Cunard and Raymond Michelet, her lover and the "principal contributor."[15] At least six of Beckett's *Negro* translations were of Surrealist works, and his views of them were decidedly mixed. He called Crevel's "The Negress in the Brothel" "miserable rubbish," and took great liberty in translating it despite having been enthusiastic about Crevel's work earlier.[16] Beckett called Jean-Joseph Rabéarivelo's contribution, "A Short Historical Survey of Madagascar," "balls."[17] Another translation, "Murderous Humanitarianism," was an attack on the Catholic Church and what Beckett called its "God of cash." It was signed by eleven members of the "Surrealist

Group in Paris," which Beckett mockingly referred to as "the whole surrealiste guild."[18]

Beckett's friendship with Cunard became lifelong and deep. She had, before the *Negro* project, supported him generously when she had money and he had need; she visited him often when he was recovering from being stabbed in 1938. In the 1950s and 1960s, when she was the one in financial difficulty, Beckett sent her signed copies of *Whoroscope* for her to sell to support herself, and of *Godot*, signed, "with love from Samuel." She thanked him with an elegiac poem, "For Sam: Dec 15, 1963," in which she wrote, "You gave."

Beckett's large contribution to *Negro* suggests a belief in cultural and individual equality and worth. It was a belief that he demonstrated throughout his life in his personal relationships; his wartime participation in the French Resistance; his work in helping resuscitate the Red Cross Hospital at St. Lô, Normandy, after the war; his responding to a request to assist AIDA (L'Association international de défense des victims de la répression dans le monde) by writing the short play *Catastrophe* (1982) and dedicating it to the playwright Vaclav Havel, who had been imprisoned by the Czech government; and his depictions of the downtrodden, infirm, and hapless, which valorized those so depicted without ennobling their suffering. He said, "My people seem to be falling to bits. . . . My characters have nothing"; but remarkably, for the most part they survive, they persist.[19] Given *Negro*'s promulgation of social, racial, cultural, and political justice, Beckett's contribution seems an act of support for both Cunard and her causes, including Surrealism, whose proponents largely shared her racial and political agenda.

SURREALISM WAS MARKED BY NUMEROUS contradictions and paradoxes. Most notable was its advocating violence and madness as principles while also being strongly antipathetic to the destruction and irrationality of the First World War, in which, to their subsequent regret, many Surrealists served. Because the Surrealists accepted Freud's theory that people are born with aggressive instincts that must be both satisfied and contained if civilization is to function, Breton, like the earlier Futurists, made violence, spontaneity, and irrationality central to his movement by espousing them in Surrealism's founding manifesto (1924; revised 1930). The Irish poet and critic Anthony Cronin maintains, "From the beginning a cult of violence which was more than just intellectual had been one of the principal weapons in the surrealist armoury. The first issue of their review had published a photograph of Germaine Berton, who had just murdered a prominent right-wing member of the reactionary Action Française, defiantly surrounded by all the members of the group."[20]

Yet like the Dadaists before them, the Surrealists also denounced what they came to view as the war's mindless devastation, chaos, and absurdity. Max Ernst, a German national who served on both the western and eastern fronts, spoke for many of his generation when he said of his time in the army, "On the first of August 1914 M[ax] E[rnst] died. He was resurrected on the eleventh of November 1918."[21] According to Tristan Tzara, who spent the war in neutral Zurich, "Never has a *casus belli* been more preposterous than that of World War I. The whole European world went to hell because some down-and-out Serb killed a couple of rich and powerful Austrians. These assassinations should have been treated as a simple criminal offense, and that should have been that."[22] Instead, the assassinations became the ultimate absurdist act: a meaningless rationale for the most extravagant slaughter in human history. Guillaume Apollinaire, who gave Surrealism its name in 1917, had initially called war a "beautiful thing." But he came to view the apocalyptic hell of the battlefield, where he was seriously wounded, as the work of a mad humanity "putting out the stars / with shellfire." Just after the war ended, he wrote, "The time has come to light the stars again," but he unfortunately died from his war wound shortly thereafter.

Surrealists came to differ among themselves over whether violence should be expressed literally (as Breton insisted) or metaphorically (as the filmmaker Luis Buñuel maintained). Even Tzara was not a pacifist: he joined both the Republicans in the Spanish Civil War and the French Resistance during the Second World War. Breton's autobiographical novel *Nadja* (1928), whose narrator contemplates such Surrealist principles as violence, spontaneity, and irrationality, ends with the statement: "Beauty will be convulsive or will not be at all." And as if designed to illustrate Breton's misogyny, numerous Surrealist works explicitly represent violence against women: for example, Magritte's *The Menaced Assassin* (1927) and Giacometti's sculpture *Woman with Her Throat Cut* (1932). Magritte's *The Rape* (1934; plate 4) depicts a naked female torso missing a head but with prominent breasts, navel, and vulva that, taken together, suggest a face as much as they do a body, a face eerily and blankly observing the observer and topped with a full head of hair. The clear implication is that men see women solely as bodies in service of men's gratification, not as fully realized people.

Dada and Surrealist art generated an aesthetic and rhetoric of body parts that became common cultural currency after the war, and that greatly influenced Beckett's writings. In Tzara's play *The Gas Heart* (first produced in Paris in 1921), the characters are named for facial features: the Eyebrow, the Eye, the Nose, the Neck, the Mouth, and the Ear. Numerous Surrealist artists took their cues from Tzara's representation of body parts. Jean Arp created detached moustaches that represented the pompous, bourgeois arrogance and stupidity that led to the war, in which he had refused to serve. A precursor of Beckett's *Not I*, which features a bright red mouth emerging from a black curtain eight feet above the floor, Jean Cocteau's film *The Blood of a Poet* (1930) has mouths materialize everywhere, starting with an artist sketching a face whose mouth begins to move. He tries to rub it out, but the mouth attaches itself to the palm of his hand; he then places it on a female statue, which begins to speak, urging him to pass through a mirror into another world.

Born in 1906, Beckett was too young for the First World War, but he experienced its consequences, including the fragmented and disjointed imagery of modernist art, the literature of modernism, and

Figure 13.1. Putting the mobile mouth on a statue in Jean Cocteau's *The Blood of a Poet* (1930).

the rise of fascism in the years leading up to the Second World War. Out of his own wartime experience, he came to write a literature of bodily decrepitude, suffering, and endurance set in bleak, devastated landscapes. Like the Surrealists', Beckett's work is replete with isolated body parts, often limbs represented as independent agents; and while he did not share the Surrealists' crude misogyny, in *Happy Days* he represented an upper-bodied Winnie, who spends her time rummaging in her capacious handbag. Beckett deploys body parts as images of incompleteness or disconnectedness, as if birth or life has become a piecemeal affair when it manages to happen at all. The narrative voice in Beckett's prose work *Company* (1979), for example, depicts an unidentified "you" awaiting an assignation: "Her light step is heard . . . Her face appears at the window. . . . The height or length you have in common is the sum of equal segments. . . . A single leg appears. Seen from above. You separate the segments and lay them side by side."[23]

The voices in the thirteen prose pieces in *Texts for Nothing* struggle in vain to construct or sustain a coherent corporeal identity. The *Text 1* narrator "say[s] to the body, Up with you now, and I can feel it struggling . . . I say to the head, Leave it alone, stay quiet, it stops breathing, then pants on worse than ever . . . I should turn away from it all, away from the body, away from the head, let them work it out between them."[24] In *Text 3*, the voice speculates that he might "sprout a head at last, all my very own, in which to brew poisons worthy of me, and legs to kick my heels with" and perhaps "two legs, or one, in the middle, I'd go hopping. Or just the head, nice and round, nice and smooth, no need of lineaments." *Text 4* offers "a head strewn with arms laid down and corpses fighting fresh, and a body, I nearly forgot." *Text 8*'s narrator wonders, "What's the matter with my head, I must have left it in Ireland, in a saloon, it must be there still, lying on the bar." *Text 10*'s fancies that "the head has fallen behind, all the rest has gone on, the head and its anus the mouth, or else it has gone on alone." *Text 11* reduces the narrator even further: "No arms, no hands, better by far, as old as the world and no less hideous, amputated on all sides, erect on my trusty stumps."[25]

In *Not I,* a play that can be thought of as *Happy Days* act three, Mouth enumerates her minimal condition and remaining parts: "Whole body like gone . . . just the mouth . . . lips . . . cheeks . . . jaws . . . never— . . . what? . . . tongue? . . . yes . . . lips . . . cheeks . . . jaws . . . tongue" (plate 5).[26]

Among the most startling and original images in the theater are Beckett's truncated or partial figures in *Endgame* (1957), *Happy Days*

(1961), *Play* (1963), and *Not I* (1972). Beckett anticipated his depiction of Winnie in *Happy Days,* first stuck up to her breasts and then, in act two, up to her neck in a mound of earth, in the Unnamable's vision of Malone: "I see him from the waist up, he stops at the waist, as far as I am concerned."[27] The absurdity of *Happy Days* results not only from Winnie's extraordinary situation, but also from her blasé attitude about it (plate 6). She apparently accepts her imprisonment as normal even while complaining that "the earth is very tight today, can it be I have put on flesh, I trust not."[28] She recalls that things are no longer "what they were when I was young and . . . foolish and . . . [*faltering, head down*] . . . beautiful . . . possibly . . . I speak of when I was not yet caught—in this way—and had my legs and had the use of my legs." She acknowledges that her circumstances are surreal: "All seems strange. [*Pause.*] Most strange. [*Pause.*] Never any change. [*Pause.*] And more and more strange."[29] Winnie also thinks that her situation might improve as magically as it had worsened. Because she is a creature of the air ("Think of her as a bird with oil on her feathers," Beckett suggested)[30] and because gravity no longer seems to work as it used to, she says, "I fancy . . . that if I were not held—[*gesture*]—in this way, I would simply float up into the blue. [*Pause.*] And that perhaps some day the earth will yield and let me go, the pull is so great, yes, crack all round me and let me out."[31] Or her circumstances could worsen: "One day the earth [might] cover my breasts" and, in so doing, somehow expunge her freer past: "Then I shall never have seen my breasts, no one ever seen my breasts." Stasis and alteration collide as she is constrained to accept her condition: "To have been always what I am—and so changed from what I was."[32]

Winnie recalls a couple who came upon her and Willie, her semi-mobile husband, and failed to make sense of their circumstances. "Standing there gaping at me," Winnie recounts, "What's she doing? he says—What's the idea? he says—stuck up to her diddies in the bleeding ground . . . What does it mean? he says—What's it meant to mean? . . . Why doesn't he dig her out? he says . . . What good is she to him like that?—What good is he to her like that?—and so on—usual tosh." But the wife's mocking response goes some way toward normalizing Winnie's situation: "And you, she says, what's the idea of you, she says, what are you meant to mean?"[33] Yet it's also possible that Winnie imagines the couple as a way of articulating the question that presumably must be uppermost in her mind: why *doesn't* Willie try to dig her out?

Knowlson suggests that images of partial entombment (including those in trash bins in *Endgame* and in urns in *Play*) "may have surfaced from the depths of Beckett's own imagination," but they also came from his experience.[34] For example, Buñuel and Dali's *An Andalusian Dog* (1928), a film that Beckett almost certainly knew, ends with a couple, perhaps representing suppressed human emotions, surreally "sunk in the sand up to their breast-bones."[35]

YET WITH FEW EXCEPTIONS, even Beckett's most forlorn, decrepit creatures, like Winnie and Mouth and the Unnamable, persist. In *Waiting for Godot,* in response to Gogo's "I can't go on like this," Didi says, "That's what you think."[36] In *Endgame,* Hamm half quotes Eliot's *Four Quartets* at Clov ("The end is in the beginning"), but then adds derisively, "and yet you go on." In the play's closing pages Clov and Hamm express their sense of loss and their grim acceptance of the inevitable. First Clov: "I say to myself . . . Clov, you must learn to suffer better than that if you want them to weary of punishing you. . . . It'll never end, I'll never go. [*Pause.*] Then one day, suddenly, it ends, it changes . . . it dies. . . . I say to myself that the earth is extinguished, though I never saw it lit. . . . When I fall I'll weep for happiness." And then Hamm, in his last speech, must also face his end with neither solace nor comfort to ease his going, yet he admires his own endurance and performance: "A little poetry. [*Pause.*] You prayed—[*Pause. He corrects himself.*] You CRIED for night; it comes—[*Pause. He corrects himself.*] It FALLS: now cry in darkness. [*He repeats, chanting.*] You cried for night; it falls: now cry in darkness. [*Pause.*] Nicely put, that."[37] As if the right rhetoric makes everything bearable, even a triumph.

Though reduced to head, torso, and the pot in which he is fixed, the Unnamable nonetheless reiterates to the end that "you must go on, I can't go on, I'll go on," arriving, by enacting what he expresses, at the novel's pseudo-ending: a breathless seven-page sentence that concludes with the phrase "unfinished, unfinishable."[38] Death becomes decreasingly prominent in Beckett's late trio of fictional works, *Company, Ill Seen Ill Said,* and *Worstward Ho,* as well as in *Stirrings Still.* Rather, the emphasis is on keeping going through memory and imagination, dream and narration, loss and unending suffering.

Against all odds, continuity remains Beckett's predominant motif. The Unnamable demands, "Keep going, going on, call that going, call that on" as his tone progresses from mocking to panic to resignation to continuing against all odds.[39] As the narrator of *Text 10* insists, "No, no souls, or bodies, or birth, or life, or death, you've got to go on without any of that junk, that's all dead with words, with excess of words."[40] Commenting on the late play *Catastrophe,* Knowlson sums up what he sees as Beckett's mindset: "Beckett is about going on, persisting; however much you reduce somebody to an object, a victim, there is this resilience and persistence of the human spirit."[41] Despite initial appearances to the contrary, affirmation is strong even in *Catastrophe,* which is often read as prophetic of Vaclav Havel's being freed from prison and becoming president of Czechoslovakia.

As if seeking to reprise the bodily inventory that plays out in *Happy Days* and *Not I,* the autocratic D (director? dictator?) in *Catastrophe* seeks to mold and reduce an immobilized, staged figure, P (prisoner? protagonist?), as an homage to power. D dehumanizes and aestheticizes P by dividing him into a set of discrete body parts that he manipulates and drains of color: hands exposed, joined, whitened; cranium whitened; toes exposed; head down; neck, shins, and knees bared and whitened. At the end of the play, "the dress rehearsal becomes the performance with the surreal intrusion of a play-audience's reaction," a canned burst of applause.[42] But that isn't quite the end: P startlingly challenges and thwarts D's intention when, breaking the frame, he courageously and defiantly raises his head and stares down both the eerily summoned audience whose applause we suddenly hear and the actual audience in the theater. P's gesture may seem hard to read at first, but Beckett was clear in his own mind about it: "'There's no ambiguity there at all. . . . He's saying: You bastards, you haven't finished me yet!"[43] P's action is, among other things, a noble and heroic act of self-assertion, a political and theatrical resistance to the surreal violence that D has sought to impose on him. By so doing, P reclaims his parts, thereby reasserting not only his figural reality and meaning, but also his humanity and wholeness. It is the sort of ultimate maneuver that numerous Beckett characters make: the Unnamable; Winnie when she stares down and sings to Willie as he reaches for a gun at the end of *Happy Days;* the figures in *Play* when they prepare to reprise their narratives interminably; Mouth in *Not I* when she continues her unending narrative even as it becomes unintelligible behind the curtain.

For Beckett, the world is a cruel cosmic joke, and the best one can do is look squarely at reality and courageously defy it. Persistence in suffering may not be much to hang one's hat on, but it seems to have sufficed for Beckett and for many of his characters. For all his Surrealist affinity, Beckett endows his characters with resources sufficient to endure and transcend the limitations imposed upon them by their surreal circumstances.

Spring Semester 2019

1. Eugene Jolas, "Poetry Is Vertical," *transition,* 21 (Mar. 1932), p. 149.
2. Raymond Federman, "The Imaginary Museum of Samuel Beckett," *symplokē,* 10, 1–2 (2002), p. 166.
3. Edward Titus, *This Quarter,* Sept. 1932, p. 6.
4. Daniel Albright, *Beckett and Aesthetics* (Cambridge, 2003), p. 10.
5. Lois Gordon, *The World of Samuel Beckett, 1906–1946* (New Haven, 2012), p. 44.
6. Samuel Beckett, *The Grove Centenary Edition,* ed. Paul Auster (New York, 2006), III, p. 104.
7. André Breton, "Surrealism: Yesterday, To-day and To-morrow," *This Quarter,* Sept. 1932, pp. 11, 15, 19.
8. Beckett, *Grove Centenary Edition,* IV, pp. 91, 114.
9. Ibid., II, pp. 250, 248, 249, 270.
10. Ibid., III, p. 122.
11. Ibid., IV, p. 456.
12. Ibid., IV, p. 269.
13. Ibid., IV, p. 477.
14. Ibid., IV, p. 490.
15. Nancy Cunard, foreword to Raymond Michelet, *African Empires and Civilisation* (London, 1945).
16. Beckett to Thomas MacGreevy, 9 Oct. 1931, Beckett Archive, Trinity College Dublin.
17. Beckett to MacGreevy, 5 Jan. 1933, in *The Letters of Samuel Beckett, Vol. 1, 1929–1940,* ed. Martha Dow Fehsenfeld and Lois More Overbeck (Cambridge, 2009), 149.
18. Ibid.
19. Quoted in Israel Shenker, "Moody Man of Letters," *New York Times,* 5 May 1956.
20. Anthony Cronin, *Samuel Beckett: The Last Modernist* (New York, 1999), p. 83.
21. Quoted in Werner Spies and Sabine Rewald, eds., *Max Ernst: A Retrospective* (New York, 2005), p. xiv.
22. Eric von der Luft, introduction to Tristan Tzara, *The Gas Heart,* trans. Michael Benedikt (Cambridge, 2013), p. 11.
23. Beckett, *Grove Centenary Edition,* IV, p. 441.
24. Ibid., IV, pp. 295–96.
25. Ibid., IV, pp. 305, 307, 322, 328, 332.
26. Ibid., III, pp. 409–10.
27. Ibid., II, p. 286.
28. Ibid., III, p. 149.
29. Ibid., III, pp. 152–54, 158.
30. Quoted in Martha Fehsenfeld, "From the Perspective of an Actress/Critic: Ritual Patterns in Beckett's *Happy Days,*" in Katherine H. Burkman, ed., *Myth and Ritual in the Plays of Samuel Beckett* (Madison, N.J., 1987), p. 50.
31. Beckett, *Grove Centenary Edition,* III, pp. 151–52.
32. Ibid., III, pp. 154, 161.
33. Ibid., III, pp. 156–57.
34. James Knowlson, "A Note on the Visual Imagery of *Happy Days,*" *Young Vic* (blog), 11 Mar. 2015, https://youngviclondon.wordpress.com/2015/03/11/a-note-on-the-visual-imagery-of-happy-days-by-beckett-biographer-jim-knowlson.
35. Luis Buñuel and Salvador Dali, *Un Chien Andalou, This Quarter,* Sept. 1932, p. 157.

36. Beckett, *Grove Centenary Edition*, III, p. 86.

37. Ibid., III, pp. 141, 150–51, 152–53.

38. Ibid., II, p. 407.

39. Ibid., II, p. 285.

40. Ibid., IV, p. 329.

41. Quoted in Jo Glanville, "'Godot Is Here': How Samuel Beckett and Vaclav Havel Changed History," *Guardian,* 15 Sept. 2009.

42. Enoch Brater, *Beyond Minimalism: Beckett's Late Style in the Theater* (Oxford, 1987), p. 150.

43. Quoted in James Knowlson, *Damned to Fame: The Life of Samuel Beckett* (New York, 1996), p. 597.

The book that launched a worldwide craze: *Harry Potter and the Philosopher's Stone*, by J. K. Rowling (1997). Artwork © Thomas Taylor. Bloomsbury Publishing Plc.

14

Harry Potter and Bloomsbury Publishing

NIGEL NEWTON

My subject is the story of one of the greatest wonders of modern publishing. What is most startling, considering the heights of Pottermania today, is quite how ordinary its arrival and reception was as it began its life. I introduced our children's editor, a brilliant man named Barry Cunningham, to the literary agent Christopher Little at the Frankfurt Book Fair. Little, so the legend goes, was picked by Jo Rowling after consulting the *Writers' and Artists' Yearbook*, which is, among other things, a guide to literary agents. She was taken by his name. Christopher sent us the first manuscript when Bloomsbury was on the top floor of the 20th Century Fox Film Building in Soho Square in London. There was just the one typescript, so our colleagues on the children's list handed the pages around to one another while sitting on beanbags on the floor. And they became remarkably excited. They decided to submit it to the next editorial meeting, of which I was chair. That night I gave the typescript to my eight-year-old daughter, Alice. She came down the stairs an hour later on a cloud, saying, "Dad, you've never shown me anything this good before." And she wrote me a reader's report that said: "The excitement in this book made me feel warm inside. I think it is possibly one of the best books an eight- or nine-year-old could read." The next day, I authorized an advance of £1,500 for the rights, saying to my eight equally enthusiastic colleagues at the meeting, "Well, yeah, Alice likes it." Jo's agent played hardball and pushed us up to £2,500. We got the book. What we didn't know at the time was that a dozen or so competitors had turned it down. Perhaps our only claim to real fame is that we were the ones who didn't say no. Thank goodness for that!

This was at the time when e-mail was coming into widespread use, and we all had PCs on our desks for the first time. Our children's marketing manager, Roz Walker, used this newfangled technology to e-mail us every day, saying, "I know you think *Harry Potter* is good, but you don't understand—it's really, really, really good." We thought, "Oh, she does go on!" We did know it was really, really good, though we never imagined the series would sell 500 million copies. One of Britain's leading bookshop chains at the time, Ottakar's, was persuaded by us to make it one of their books of the month. Our initial print run, in June 1997, was 500 hardbacks and 5,150 paperbacks.

That print run had a major error in it, and the books had to be rejected. So we did what the British have always done in such situations: sent them to Australia. Australia was thus the home of the most valuable first-print run in the world, with individual copies from that printing now fetching up to $50,000 a copy.

When the book started to take off, it was not because of anything we did, but because the first children who read it told other children about it—playground marketing, to give it a name—and that was because of the brilliance of the story itself and not the marketing. Nothing can compete with the power of word-of-mouth recommendation. Perhaps 30,000 copies were in print by Christmas 1997.

J. K. Rowling performed in her first literary event in Edinburgh in August 1997 and about twenty children appeared—the early adopters. Thousands would appear at events in later years. Since my daughter Alice was perhaps the first adopter—she was then her school's library assistant—she invited Jo Rowling to speak at Putney High School, in London, which was a big success.

The first big press launch came with the paperback release of *Harry Potter and the Chamber of Secrets*. It is notoriously hard to get press coverage for a paperback launch. We staged an event at Platform 9¾ at King's Cross Station. The children's TV program *Blue Peter* filmed it. There was a Hogwarts steam engine—and pumpkin soup. Dumbledore was there. The King's Cross success led to a nationwide tour, culminating with eight hundred children in Manchester coming to an event, which set a record at the time.

Another event involved *Harry Potter and the Prisoner of Azkaban*, the third volume in the series. Rumors at the time, which proved to be true, purported that children had played truant from school on the day a new Harry Potter came out in order to buy it. We therefore decided to launch the next book at 3:45 p.m. so that children could come after school. Booksellers were intrigued by the time of day, but they cooperated and kept the books under embargo until then. The *Daily Telegraph* ran a front-page photograph of a line of children outside the Lion & Unicorn Bookshop, in Richmond in London. We were suddenly big news. In fact, lines of children waiting to buy the book made the television news on BBC 1, ITV, and Channel 4. It seemed remarkable at the time that we beat the record set by *Hannibal*, the novel by Thomas Harris, published a month previously. *Hannibal* had sold 54,000 copies in its first week, whereas *The Prisoner of Azkaban* sold 64,000 in the first two and a half days. The press loved it—one of the headlines was "Hannibal Eaten for Breakfast by Thirteen-Year-Old."

Harry Potter was such a phenomenon that our trash at Bloomsbury was apparently searched for details of when the next book would come out. Attempts to find out the plot of each book before publication were a real problem with the press, particularly the *Sun*, a Murdoch tabloid, so we tried to maintain strict secrecy. We ceased to produce advance proof copies, and advance advertisements for the books did not give their titles, since those too were secret and would be clues to the stories. Yet on one occasion Jo gave away three details about *Harry Potter and the Goblet of Fire*. This created a feeding frenzy of anticipation. We kept the manuscript in a bank vault, yet we had break-ins at the office. In fact, we allowed only four people in our company to read a Potter manuscript before publication, on a need-to-know basis: the editors Emma Mathewson and Sarah Odedina, the production manager Penny Edwards, and me. (And later, the editor Isabel Ford.)

The next high point came with the Hogwarts Tour. We borrowed a beautiful steam locomotive and then tried to put together a sort of Edwardian train. We were on the road for four or five days. It is quite difficult to take a steam train around the country; you have to schedule the legs of the journey between trips made by the high-speed intercity trains. At each station a thousand children who had won tickets to go on the train and get their books signed by the author were waiting. The carriage for the signings was a library car, a historic one, in fact: it was the train car in which Marshal Foch signed the armistice at the end of the First World War that led to the Versailles Treaty. The train proceeded around the country.

One time when we were in the countryside, about fifty people were standing at the place where we had to stop to put water in the steam engine. We thought, "How did these people know we'd be here, in the middle of nowhere?" The locomotive driver explained, "No, no, they have no idea who you are and don't care. They're trainspotters, and they heard there was a steam train, and so they came to write down the serial number of the engine." We were front-page news for the four days on the train. And on the first day we sold 372,000 books.

I did not know, nor did my colleagues, when each book was going to be finished. We did not want to put any pressure on the author. You never ask writers when their next book will come. Sitting at my desk one day, I got a phone call from Jo's agent, Christopher Little. He said, "Nigel, shall we have a drink at the Pelican Pub?" I responded, "Yes, sure. Did you say the Pelican?" That was where we would meet for the handovers of the manuscripts. I turned to jelly, rushed, got in my car, and drove out to the Pelican in Fulham, near his office. There he was, with two pints at the bar and an innocuous-looking supermarket bag at his feet. We never discussed the bag or the book. We just had our beer and chatted about the weather. But when I left, I was carrying the Sainsbury's bag. It was a classic drop from the world of espionage. We had read our John Le Carré.

Once when the Booksellers Association was holding its annual conference in Brighton, Jo Rowling and Michael Ondaatje came to a lunch for booksellers in my garden. Jo Rowling is perhaps the most talented person I know: brilliant and intense with a great sense of humor and as fun as she was at that lunch.

I WOULD LIKE TO REFLECT ON SOME of the qualities of the series. I think part of why Harry Potter has endured is because of his human qualities: his resourcefulness and intelligence as well as his common sense and self-reliance. Ultimately, it is Harry alone who controls his destiny, who confronts Lord Voldemort. Camaraderie and friendship are nevertheless the qualities that underpin the world of Hogwarts and the close bonds formed there. The psychological foundation of Harry's existence is love, the love that his dead parents hold for him, the love that sustains him through his life and gives him the strength to win his battles against Voldemort. But life at Hogwarts is also about fun; students are imbued with wit and humor as well as practicality. We should all aspire to be Harry, regardless of belief in magic or religion, or of our personal battles of good versus evil. But if we can't be Harry, then we can be his stalwart friends, Ron and Hermione, who are always at his side. Without Ron and Hermione, is Harry fully Harry? We truly can't bear the thought of any of them dying. They are at the heart of the stories.

It is only with the passage of time that we can begin to understand the true scope and breadth of the story. New generations are discovering the books. Some of the kids who are reading Harry Potter today are the children of the early readers. Their mothers and fathers have passed J. K. Rowling's classics on just as parents in the past handed on books by C. S. Lewis or J. R. R. Tolkien or A. A. Milne. Such parents convey to younger generations their enthusiasm for the books that comforted and enthralled them in their own childhoods.

Many of the young people working in the creative industries today are part of Harry Potter's living legacy. It has been a huge part of our destiny at Bloomsbury. We found ourselves with a £100 million in the bank, and we reinvested this money to become a large academic publisher as well as a general one.

We now sell copies of the Harry Potter books, in English, to German eight-year-olds. You can imagine the furor in the Académie Française when *Harry Potter,* in English, went to number one on a French best-seller list, above great works of French culture and literature. Yet there is also an adult dimension. A hilarious moment came when someone from Bloomsbury saw an adult on the London Underground reading *Harry Potter* hidden behind a copy of *The Economist,* which inspired us to publish an edition with adult jackets. Our latest new editions are those illustrated by Jim Kay—they are quite stunning.

I believe we can safely declare Harry Potter a classic for all time.

All of us at Bloomsbury feel very lucky to have played some part in it.

Fall Semester 2018

E. R. Dodds, 1945. Photograph by Walter Stoneman. NPG x167230. © National Portrait Gallery, London.

15

A Battle for the Soul of Classics at Oxford

PAUL WOODRUFF

My story begins with Rosalind, the radical countess of Carlisle. A pillar of the temperance movement, the manager of her husband's vast estates, and a powerful advocate for women's rights and women's education, she was determined that women should marry intelligent men rather than inheritors of titles or money. To that end, she arranged with Benjamin Jowett to hand-pick eligible young Oxford scholars, of a liberal bent, to visit her at Castle Howard or Naworth Castle, there to encounter her four daughters; her seven sons were on their own.

Her eldest daughter, Lady Mary Henrietta, met and married Gilbert Murray, a young scholar from Australia who would be made Regius Professor of Greek at Oxford in 1908 after a brief career at the University of Glasgow and a stint outside academia. I had this story from Murray's niece, Winifred Nicholson (née Roberts) whose father, while an Oxford student, had been sent north by Jowett to mingle with the Howards. There he met and married Lady Cecilia and fathered three children. Winifred, an artist, remembered vividly what her Uncle Gilbert had told her about ancient Greek myths and the tragic plays based on them. I have a fine letter from her telling me what she had learned from her uncle about the *Bacchae,* and I have clear memories of the paintings she made at Mycenae (where I met her) of mythical events in Greek landscapes.

Gilbert Murray was a public intellectual of the best kind. Through his translations of ancient Greek tragedies—which were said to have

Figure 15.1. Gilbert Murray, 1929. Photograph by Lafayette. NPG x47711. © National Portrait Gallery, London.

sold a half-million copies—he made English speakers who were not classically trained acquainted with a rich lode of literature. Once censorship was relaxed, his translations were performed, increasing still further the audience to which he carried the classics. He was, at the same time, active in liberal politics; like many of the Howards, he was a supporter of Irish Home Rule. He backed the League of Nations and other good causes.

In 1936, he stepped aside from the professorship, and the contest to replace him began. Should his successor be a great scholar? A belletrist? An influential teacher? A public intellectual? Murray would be hard to replace.

Murray's translations show him to be a gifted poet in a late-Victorian mode. If you can read Greek tragedy in the original, you know the quality of the choral odes in ancient tragedy. They are often magically lyrical. They do not rhyme; their lyricism shows itself in other ways. But English lyrics rhyme; then as now our ears demand it, and popular lyrics continue to deliver it. Murray had a gift for producing rhyming translations that feel natural. The work of most translators who try to rhyme comes across as stilted and false, stuffed with words that have no proper place in the lines, included merely for the sake of rhyme. Not Murray. Here is an example from a famous ode in Euripides's *Bacchae:*

> Will they ever come to me, ever again,
> The long long dances,
> On through the dark till the dawn-stars wane?
> Shall I feel the dew in my throat, and the stream
> Of wind in my hair? Shall our white feet gleam
> In the dim expanses?
>
> Oh, feet of a fawn to the greenwood fled,
> Alone in the grass and the loveliness;
> Leap of the hunted, no more in dread[1]

Note the lovely half-hidden rhyme of "dances" with "expanses," important words that deserve to rhyme. He has missed one special detail: this ode contains the first use of a transferred epithet to be noticed by ancient Greek critics. Here is William Arrowsmith's version of the last few lines:

> as a running fawn might frisk
> for the green joy of the wide fields,
> free from the fear of the hunt[2]

"Green joy"—that is what had startled Euripides's audience and his readers.

Murray's translations have their detractors, of course. To twentieth-century taste, they seem archaic. And questions about accuracy arise. Murray had the talent to see meanings not explicit in the Greek and to translate lines into English that the Greek poets never wrote, but nevertheless capture their meaning well. Murray was much more than a popularizer of the classics; he was also a fine philological scholar. For much of the nineteenth century, classical scholarship was something done in Germany (or perhaps Glasgow), but not at Cambridge or Oxford. The greatest scholar of midcentury had been George Grote, a banker and reform-minded politician who had nothing to do with Oxbridge. But by the end of the nineteenth century, fine scholars were emerging in Britain. The mark of a great scholar was, and is, the ability to produce a convincing text, on the basis of the manuscripts, and to annotate it in such a way that lesser scholars can write about the text intelligently. A. E. Housman comes to mind for Latin texts; for Greek texts in this period, Richard Jebb was such a fine commentator that his editions of Sophocles remain in use. Gilbert Murray edited Aeschylus and Euripides for Oxford Classical Texts, a definitive series of Greek and Roman works; good enough for their time, both have been re-done by recent scholars on (I believe) sounder principles.

When Murray retired in 1936, what did the study of classics at Ox-ford need most? Three candidates were under discussion. J. D. Den-niston (1887–1949) had an established reputation; his book on Greek particles (1934) has almost biblical standing in the field to this day. (Particles in ancient Greek have no equivalent in English. They are small words that can shade the meaning of a sentence in various ways or show connections among sentences.) Cecil Maurice Bowra (1898–1971), a fellow of Wadham College, was known for his work on Pindar (1928, 1935), and was one of the coeditors, with Murray, of the *Oxford Book of Greek Verse* (1930). Bowra was a scholar, a belletrist, and a poet (or at least he tried to be, until 1929). The Irishman E. R. Dodds (1893–1979) had been professor of Greek at the University of Birmingham since 1924. He had shown his schol-arly proficiency on authors not widely known (mainly Proclus), and was not part of the Oxbridge academic establishment. He too had been a poet in his youth.

The Regius professor was to be chosen by the Prime Minister and appointed by the King, who apparently consulted no one but Mur-ray. Who would the winner be? At Oxford, everyone was betting on Bowra.

BOTH MEN WROTE MEMOIRS. Bowra's covers the years from his birth to 1939; Dodds's memoir, beautifully titled *Missing Persons*, carries him from first memories to his retirement.[3] On Bowra, there is now a thorough biography by Leslie Mitchell, commissioned by Wadham College.[4]

Bowra was born in China two years before the Boxer Rebellion, his first experience of war. His father was in the Chinese Customs Service. He was taken to England when he was five, and when the family returned to China, he stayed on for his education. His public school was Cheltenham. His education was interrupted by military service, after which he went to New College, Oxford, as a more ma-ture student than usual. He began his career as the center of atten-tion in an academic environment—his favorite role in life.

Dodds was born in Ireland. His father, an Ulsterman, died when Dodds was seven, after a brief, brilliant career in teaching that was cut short by alcoholism. His mother was Anglo-Irish, from a vanish-ing class known as squireens. He and his mother were left in poverty. He received good schooling, nevertheless, and nurtured a rebel-lious streak from a young age. He was at Campbell College, in Bel-fast, in 1910 when his class was told the news that King Edward VII

Figure 15.2. Maurice Bowra, 1951. Photograph by Norman Parkinson. NPG x30003, National Portrait Gallery, London. © Norman Parkinson Archive / Iconic Images.

had died—told this by masters who expected the boys to show grief. Dodds believed in always saying what he thought: "But wasn't he a very bad man and not a particularly good king?" This did not go down well with the masters—Ulstermen who were, Dodds wrote, *plus royalistes que le roi*.[5] He was later expelled from this secondary school for writing an insulting letter to his headmaster. But he had already been admitted to Oxford, with a scholarship at University College. At Oxford he would meet and impress Gilbert Murray, experiment with cannabis, do well in *literae humaniores*,[6] and—of course—be rusticated (essentially, expelled) for insulting the Crown by protesting the execution of the leaders of the Easter Rising. He was, however, allowed to sit for his final exams and receive his degree.

First, poetry, then war, and at the end, scholarship.

BOTH DODDS AND BOWRA WERE passionately fond of poets and poetry. For both of them it was poetry first and classical scholarship a distant second. In their day, bright young boys were steered by public schools toward the classics, regardless of their interests. Had they been born in the late twentieth century, I think it unlikely that either would have become a classicist. But the soul of classics was different for their generation. Ancient Greece was the polestar around which intelligent life revolved.

On poetry, however, their tastes differed. Dodds was very close to both W. H. Auden and Louis MacNeice, whose literary executor he was to be. Bowra despised Auden. He viewed Auden as an "impure poet" with no vision, who would "teach the young that poetry was only about rumpled bedclothes."[7] Bowra's favorite ancient poet was Pindar, who made a career of celebrating the aristocratic lineage of victorious athletes whose families could reward a poet for doing so. Pindar, Bowra said, was "more sublime than any poet in the world, sublime by sheer poetry."[8] Bowra saw poets as heroic figures and prophets. He adored, and was adored by, Edith Sitwell, and was friends with W. B. Yeats (as was Dodds). He wrote a great deal about poetry, but his greatest contribution was as what Mitchell calls "an honest broker" of poetry across linguistic boundaries.[9] He read Russian fluently and introduced Russian poetry to English readers. He advocated for Anna Akhmatova and became quite close to the sisters of Boris Pasternak, who lived in exile. Through them, he brought Pasternak's poetry to the attention of English readers and formed a close but long-distance friendship with the great Russian poet.

As for literary criticism, Bowra was a maverick. He detested the fashionable work of F. R. Leavis and Edmund Wilson, proposing that such critics should have "continual prodding with a poisoned dung fork."[10] He was collegial with Enid Starkie, whose work on French poets he admired, but he was often at odds with her over her campaigns on behalf of candidates for the Oxford Professor of Poetry.

He wanted desperately to be a poet, but had recognized by the time he was thirty that he would never achieve distinction as a poet. I suspect that his terrible experiences in the First World War left him with memories on which he would have to draw as a poet, but which he had to keep deeply buried. He spoke lightly about his war experience, when he spoke about it at all, probably to hide the inner wounds. From his youth comes this conventional complaint about war and the interests that it serves:

Gold Dancing in Air (1916)

Parapets stacked with mouldy dead
To keep the wine in the wine glass red

> Boys bayoneted in the night
> To keep official buttons bright.
>
> . . . .
>
> A people lashed to a wheel of fire
> To satisfy a fool's desire.
>
> Fields sliced to shreds and cities sacked
> To keep a mothy creed intact.
>
> Lithe bodies full of sap shot down
> To gild the glory of a crown.

Here is anger and wit enough, but it is not the stuff of poetry—and it anticipates his experience of combat. He was only eighteen when he wrote it, but other young poets, such as Keith Douglas, produced masterpieces from the experience of war.

Love might have brought out the best in Bowra, but he found it a painful subject, one on which, after his adolescence, he was silent. Homosexuality was scandalous during most of his lifetime; acting on it was illegal and deemed immoral. Bowra went out of his way not to be identified as homosexual—to the extent of going out of his way to avoid having any contact with André Gide when he was awarded an honorary degree at Oxford, Gide being known as a defender of pederasty. Bowra did have one affair of the heart, a mysterious one in Petrograd shortly before his active service in the war. There he met a Russian brother-sister pair and evidently fell hard for one or both of them. In this period he wrote the following:

Nocturne

> Dim-shadowed in a silvery mist
> The city lies.
> The moon, as though to swooning kissed
> Upon her lies.
>
> The river from her source
> Is locked in rest.
> And holds a single trembling star
> Within her breast.
>
> Alone in perfect quietness
> I wait for thee,
> And soon shall feel thy loveliness
> Grow one with me.

This is lovely, even if conventional, and creditable work from an adolescent.

Bowra went on to produce many elegant verse translations, especially of Russian poets. Here is an untitled example by Fedor Tyutchev:

> On the horizon rises holy Night,
> And Day, who comforts us, Day, home we love,
> Withdraws her coverlet of golden light
> That covered the abysses from above.
>
> And vision-like the outer world has gone.
> Man, like an orphan in his homelessness,
> Stands naked, all his force and strength fordone,
> Face to face over that obscure abyss.
>
> A dream that long ago passed out of sight
> Seems all that light and living brilliance,
> And in the strange inexplicable night
> He learns the fated legacy of chance.[11]

Bowra believed in translating rhyme and meter. Dodds, by contrast, held to Frost's opinion that poetry could not be translated at all. Dodds was opposed to teaching classics of poetry in translation: "You cannot undress a poet's meaning and re-clothe it in a new suit of words like a tailor's dummy: it has no suit but its birthday suit, and to strip it of that is to destroy it as poetry, or at best to turn it into a different poem on the same subject."[12] Let students read poetry in languages they know, even if it is not so great: "A live dog, he wrote, is better than a dead lion."[13] He loved poetry too much to translate it.

Dodds began writing poetry at a fairly early age. In contrast to Bowra, who thought poets a special heroic caste of prophets and visionaries, Dodds thought anyone could be a poet. He prefaced his small book of poetry with what he called "A Note on Unprofessional Poetry." In it, he wrote, "There is a sense . . . in which every man is original, and therefore *in potentia* a poet. The dullest of us brings to market one new thing—himself."[14] He adds, on the next page: "The self left over from his daily life is but a scanty residue (largest in adolescence, vanishing perhaps completely with accumulated living); and only within the bounds of that self's experience is he a poet at all." Dodds valued honesty in poetry over technique. He never gave up his commitment to telling the truth about his feelings.

In Ireland, through George Russell, known as AE, Dodds met Yeats, who later said he liked the young man's poetry but not the young man. Dodds felt it his duty to contradict Yeats "when the great poet talked nonsense, as it appeared to me he quite often did."[15]

When Yeats said the English were a nation of shopkeepers without imagination, Dodds brought up Shelly and Blake. The great poet was not amused. As a student at Oxford, Dodds ran into a young American at Merton who was writing a thesis on F. H. Bradley. Finding that they had a shared interest in poetry, Dodds invited him to a group they called the Coterie, whose members met "for the purpose of reading our poems to each other and having them torn to pieces critically."[16] This American from Merton read them a poem he had been working on, and for once, the members of the Coterie were silenced. They could not tear apart "The Love Song of J. Alfred Prufrock," which was then presented to an audience for the first time and which simply amazed them. They had heard nothing like it, though they heard in it echoes of French symbolists. The American continued to come to meetings of the Coterie, but said little. Aldous Huxley was apparently also a member, or at least a friend of Dodds.

Dodds was given a professorship at the University of Birmingham in 1924 after teaching briefly at the nascent university-to-be in Reading. He had recently married a scholar of literature, whom he called Bet, who was the love of his life. They had a terrible disappointment when they learned that they could not have children: pregnancy was life-threatening for Bet. She grieved terribly over this, and I believe her grief was the subject of this poem:

Sunt Lacrimae . . .

At sunset from their old Atlantic bases,
Chill from the islands of the western death,
    Strang mists, sea bred,
    Alien, unheralded,
Creep suddenly with salt, benumbing breath
On the safe inland places.

Even so strangely, from the earth-bound years
In that cold purgatory at the root of the mind
    A thin magical rain
    Steals over heart and brain
Of one I love: and suddenly her eyes are blind
With some dead woman's tears.[17]

In 1930, Dodds had an opportunity to hire a junior colleague. A young Mertonian was strongly recommended to him as a scholar who was also a poet. Highly impressed by the young man, Dodds was on tenterhooks till he got the results from the young man's final exams for Greats. He had earned a first-class degree. And so Louis MacNeice came to Birmingham and became one of Dodds's closest friends. He had been isolated as a student at Merton—too much an artist to mingle with the hearties (the athletes) and too hetero-sexual to move with the artistic set. Perhaps also he was too Irish for any in-group at Oxford. In Dodds he found an ideal companion for travel, conversation, and just feeling at home. It was to Dodds that he left his poetry on his untimely death. And it was Dodds who ed-ited the first complete edition of his works.

I have reason to think that MacNeice wrote the gem below about taking tea in Dodds's living room, facing Dodds's beloved garden through a bay window:

Snow

The room was suddenly rich and the great bay-window was
Spawning snow and pink roses against it
Soundlessly collateral and incompatible:
World is suddener than we fancy it.

World is crazier and more of it than we think,
Incorrigibly plural. I peel and portion
A tangerine and spit the pips and feel
The drunkenness of things being various.

And the fire flames with a bubbling sound for world
Is more spiteful and gay than one supposes —
On the tongue on the eyes on the ears in the palms of one's
    hands —
There is more than glass between the snow and the huge
    roses.[18]

In Birmingham, Dodds also became friends with W. H. Auden, whose father was a local doctor. This too was a genuine friendship, lasting over the years. In the 1940s, when Dodds was at Oxford, he continued to have young poets to tea in his salon—but, alas, with-out the beloved garden, which he was not able to re-create in Ox-ford. G. E. L. Owen, who later became a powerful scholar of Greek philosophy, had poetic ambitions, and was part of Dodds's student circle. He told me that he remembered the frisson they all felt on being read "Lay your sleeping head, my love, / Human on my faith-less arm" (which Auden had sent from New York) and on learning that it had been written to a man. There is no finer or more honest love poem (I think) in the English language.

BOWRA SERVED AS A FORWARD OBSERVER in observation posts for the British artillery, 1917–18. He survived death narrowly twice. There was hardly a position more dangerous than that of an artillery observer in the days before satellites. He had to be at the forefront of the line to see the target and call instructions to the guns behind him to raise or lower the fall of shells or to shift them left or right. (I was trained for such duty, and wanted to have it, but was saved from it by my poor eyesight.) An observer served in grave danger, but had one privilege—a telephone line to the artillery behind him. This saved Bowra's life when he was buried in a trench at Cambrai. It was a sturdy, German-made trench, and that helped. But it was the phone that allowed him to call out before he lost consciousness. Luckily, the wire had not been cut. His second close call came during a battle he fought in his pajamas when the bunker where he was sleeping was overrun by the enemy. And no doubt he carried with him the memories of many comrades blown to pieces around him.

Bowra was known to ask Dodds, "What did you do in the war, Doddy?" Dodds had not served. The violent reaction of the King's military to the Easter Rising in Dublin decided the matter for him: he could never wear the King's uniform or ever again raise his glass in a toast to the King. The English military force known as the Black and Tans killed some suspected Irish patriots and arrested many more. The trials of leaders were held in secret and led to executions. Irishmen like Dodds, who had deplored the Rising when it occurred, became so revolted by the English reaction that they fell in line behind Sinn Fein. (I say "English" rather than "British" by design. The Irish were, of course, British. It was the grinding heel of the English that they resented.) At sea on a boat to London, Dodds was seated for dinner with Black and Tans going home on leave. After refusing to toast the King, he was surrounded on deck and threatened with being tossed over the side. He talked the soldiers out of that, so instead they raided his stateroom, stole his pajamas, and threw them overboard. That was Dodds's brush with war. Both men had traumas related to pajamas.

So which of these two deserved to represent the soul of classical studies at Oxford? Murray chose Dodds, to the angry astonishment of Oxford. Today we can easily see that Murray made the right choice. Dodds shifted the course of scholarship in classics in a direction it has taken since. Beyond that, his scholarship covered a wide range of topics and continues to be cited frequently—far more often than Bowra's. As for Denniston, his work on ancient Greek particles continues to be authoritative, but he did little else of note. We may well wonder, however, how Murray came to make the choice he did, based on what he knew at the time. Bowra and Denniston were well known; Dodds's major work lay in the future. Evidently, Murray recognized the limitations of the leading candidates: Bowra was more

belletrist than scholar, and Denniston (while a superb scholar) had
not the talent to move the field forward or to engage the public in
classics, as Murray had done. Dodds had it all—the capacity to be a
field-changing scholar and a public intellectual.

OXFORD SOCIETY TURNED ITS BACK on Dodds and Bet when they
came up to Oxford from Birmingham. They were miserable. The
consensus was that Bowra had been cheated out of what he deserved. Dodds had been virtually a traitor to the Crown. Rumors
of Bowra's eccentric sexuality had queered his chances (they said),
and that was unfair. The pain endured by Dodds and his wife in
their early years at Oxford was almost unbearable. Did he really deserve the Regius Professorship? He must have wondered about this
himself.

In 1936, both Bowra and Dodds had most of their scholarly productivity ahead of them. When you appoint a professor, you look to
the future. Which candidate would be most likely to do the kind of
work that could justify holding the Regius Professorship? The future, as it played out, did not hold the answer, because the appointment itself changed the game. It changed both men's lives. Dodds
produced the more important work after 1936, but he was trying
hard, and somewhat painfully, to live up to his new position. Bowra
did what he liked.

After 1936, Bowra continued to be productive: writing, translating, and holding court at Wadham. He went on to secure a place as
one of Oxford's foremost public intellectuals, did a delightful job as
Warden of his college, and was given a knighthood. His most important work was on the poet Pindar. He edited the Oxford Classical
Text of Pindar's work, translated the poems, and wrote about them.
His book on Sophocles is well regarded. I have read almost everything available about Sophocles, and I have found much that is useful. But I found no useful material in Bowra's book, which is elegant
and conventional, but never probing or adventurous.

Dodds also did work on texts. As a young scholar, he had focused
on Neoplatonism. His first work was an impressive commentary on
Proclus's theology. This connected roughly with the interest he had
in the occult. Fascination with the occult had connected him in
early life with the poet AE and, through him, with Yeats. But after
1936, he felt he should work on texts of more general interest at
Oxford. He produced a magnificent commentary on Plato's *Gorgias,*
for which he traveled to see for himself the manuscripts in various
libraries that had been incorrectly reported to John Burnet (1862–
1928). Burnet, who had lost the Regius Professorship of Greek to

Murray, had edited Plato's text for the Oxford Classical Texts, but unable to travel, he had relied on reports from abroad as to what was in the manuscripts. There is an art to deciphering an ancient or medieval manuscript, which Dodds learned and applied to Plato's dialogue. Dodds also produced a new text of Euripides's *Bacchae*, correcting what he called the faults and fancies of Gilbert Murray's edition.

Outside of Dodds's textual work, he followed Murray's example by giving brilliant lectures on classical topics. (Murray's lectures had so excited Dodds that, as an undergraduate, he had given up his plan to switch to modern English literature and stayed with classics.) The best of these lectures found their way into print in *The Ancient Concept of Progress, and Other Essays on Greek Literature and Belief* (1973). Of these, the most famous is "On Misunderstanding the *Oedipus Rex*," which is required reading for anyone writing on that play. His most famous book was *The Greeks and the Irrational* (1951). Before Nietzsche's influence was felt, scholars had treated the ancient Greeks as models of ordered, rational thought. Dodds changed that.

In retrospect, we can say that Murray's choice was excellent: Dodds became the greatest and most influential classical scholar of his generation, and the one with the broadest range. We cannot say, however, that Bowra would not have been a good choice. Who knows how his career would have developed had he held the famous chair? But I do not think that he had the brilliance or the originality of mind to match Dodds. His work shows him to have been more interested in belles lettres than in game-changing scholarship. His poetic taste shows him to have been stuck in the past, unsuited to appreciating the development of the arts in the twentieth century. Dodds had a mind that was both more adventurous and more meticulous in scholarship.

Bowra's verdict, in the end, was that Dodds was a good choice, though he would have preferred Denniston. In his memoir, he has nothing but good to say about Murray: "It was impossible to know him without loving him."[19] Bowra's friend Cyril Bailey told him that "what seemed like a rebuff could easily turn into a blessing." "He was quite right," Bowra goes on to say: "I was saved from a post to which I was not naturally fitted, and before long my life took a new direction to which I was much more suited."[20]

Fall Semester 2018

1. This is the opening of the second stasimon, lines 862–70; see Gilbert Murray, trans., *Euripides: The Bacchae* (London, 1904).

2. William Arrowsmith, trans., *The Bacchae,* in David Grene and Richmond Lattimore, *Euripides V* (Chicago, 1959).

3. C. M. Bowra, *Memories, 1898–1939* (Cambridge, Mass., 1967); E. R. Dodds, *Missing Persons: An Autobiography* (Oxford, 1977). The missing persons are his former selves, with whom he only partly identifies.

4. Leslie Mitchell, *Maurice Bowra: A Life* (Oxford, 2009).

5. Dodds, *Missing Persons,* p. 17.

6. *Literae humaniores* is the correct name for the degree program known as "Greats," consisting in Dodds's time of ancient history, ancient philosophy, and modern philosophy.

7. Mitchell, *Maurice Bowra,* p. 111.

8. Ibid., p. 96.

9. Ibid., p. 106.

10. Ibid., p. 112.

11. C. M. Bowra, ed., *A Book of Russian Verse* (London, 1943).

12. Dodds, *Missing Persons,* p. 175.

13. Ibid., p. 176.

14. E. R. Dodds, *Thirty-Two Poems with a Note on Unprofessional Poetry.* (London, 1929), p. 9.

15. Dodds, *Missing Persons,* pp. 58–59.

16. Ibid., p. 40.

17. The title alludes to a famous line from Virgil's *Aeneid* (1.462): *"Sunt lacrimae rerum, et mentem mortalia tangunt"* ("These are the tears of things, and mortal matters touch the mind").

18. Louis MacNeice, *Collected Poems,* ed. Peter McDonald (London, 2007), p. 24.

19. Bowra, *Memories,* p. 229.

20. Ibid., p. 270.

Frontispiece to Thomas Hobbes's *Leviathan* (1651). Illustration by Abraham Bosse, incorporating suggestions from Hobbes. Wikimedia Commons.

16

Obedience by the Book

AL MARTINICH

Freedom and authority have been the object of philosophical and political discussion since the seventeenth century, the greatest of English centuries. The first two Stuart kings, James I and his son Charles I, claimed they had absolute authority in their realms. That claim suffered with the beheading of Charles in 1649. The two kings had irritated a large segment of people by their economic and religious policies. People thought—and more importantly, they felt—that the kings had abused their authority and violated English freedom by collecting money in unusual ways, such as via forced loans and levying ship money on inland counties, and by imposing a Roman Catholic–style church on the Protestant nation. Here the concepts of authority and freedom are cheek by jowl. But an understudied third concept is lurking here, obedience.

This lecture looks at five books strongly bound up with the theme of obedience. Civilization requires some hierarchy, some people to command and some to obey. And as the obligation to obey expands, freedom contracts, or so it seems. People who feel they have too little freedom are inclined to rebel, an extreme form of disobedience. Consequently, obedience needs to be discussed explicitly. The story of obedience in Stuart England begins with the Bible, the first book under consideration, because both the Royalists and their opponents began and sometimes ended with it. Royalists liked the Bible because it supported absolute sovereignty. God is the absolute sovereign of the world and the source of all authority. Kings represent the sovereign God on earth. Thomas Hobbes called kings "God's lieutenants" and "mortal gods," but so did Charles's printer John Bil: "The Divine Power . . . infused the life of Authoritie into the King [and] maketh the King in particular the Lieutenant of God . . . with the title of a mortall God."

The coronation ceremony, which takes place in Westminster Abbey because it is a religious ritual, makes explicit the divine appointment of English monarchs. The Archbishop of Canterbury anoints the monarch with chrism. The title "Christ" means "one anointed with oil." The kings become little christs. The beheading of their anointed and consecrated king traumatized a majority of the English. The new Commonwealth government that succeeded Charles knew that its legitimacy was shaky. That is why it required all males over the age of eighteen to take the Engagement, a declaration that they would obey the government. Those who did not take it were legally dead.

The second book is Thomas Hobbes's *Leviathan* (1651), published two years after the execution of the king. His political philosophy is usually called the "social contract." But he distinguished between a contract and a covenant; and governments, he held, were instituted by covenants. By using the word "covenant," he was tying his political theory to the biblical understanding of the relationship between Israel and its sovereign God. More accurate translations of "Old Testament" and "New Testament" are "Old Covenant" and "New Covenant," as he knew. Since the covenant that created the kingdom of England established the Christian king as God's lieutenant, the people of England could not make any additional covenant with God except through the king. So according to Hobbes, the Solemn League and Covenant that the English rebels signed with the Scots in 1643 was a sham: "They that are subjects to a monarch cannot without his leave cast off monarchy and return to the confusion of a disunited multitude nor transfer their person from him that beareth it to another man or other assembly of men."

In 1647, King Charles was in the custody of the army. Ordinary soldiers thought the time was ripe to discuss the political benefits that Parliament should give them for defeating the king. Parliament snubbed them. So they asked their officers to discuss their political future, in hopes that the officers would represent their interests. The desired discussion at Putney Church, outside London, almost immediately turned into a debate. Fortunately, a transcript was made of the speeches. Unfortunately, it was not published until 1891. The debates, which constitute the third book, became easily available in *Puritanism and Liberty* (1951), edited by A. S. P. Woodhouse.

The fourth book to be discussed is *Intellectual Origins of the English Revolution,* by Christopher Hill. It ties in closely with the preceding ones on the English Civil War. The fifth book, *Wild Swans* by Jung Chang, lies far outside Stuart history. But it is so wonderful that I have to include it. A history of China from the perspective of three talented and courageous women, it presents an enormous amount of information about China between 1910 and 1980. In the first two pages, Chang describes the cruel practice of foot binding, informs the reader that adolescent males could be married off to older women, and notes that girls often did not receive proper names. Chang's great-grandmother was "Number Two Girl." (A student of mine told me that her grandmother had no name until 1949, when the new communist government gave her one, probably for bureaucratic reasons.)

THE MOST IMPORTANT THEME in the Bible is obedience. But given human nature, disobedience gets more attention. Soon after God made Adam and Eve, they disobeyed the simple, single command "Don't eat the fruit of that tree." It should have been easy for them to obey. They had plenty of other trees to eat from; they lacked nothing. The moral of the story is that people disobey gratuitously and that, as a consequence, they cause their own worst problems, from birth pains to mortality. The name of the fatal tree, the Tree of the Knowledge of Good and Evil, does not derive from some intrinsic quality of it. The name was prospective. It looked forward to the act of disobedience. In eating its fruit, Adam and Eve acted as if they were better judges of good or evil than God. Some of my students say that the sin of Adam and Eve was God's fault. He should not have given them that pointless command. Thus the universality of the story.

The moral that God punishes disobedience and rewards obedience dominates the history of the Israelites in the Hebrew Bible (the Old Testament). That history, the Deuteronomistic history, told in Joshua, Judges, 1 and 2 Samuel, and 1 and 2 Kings, has a rhythm and a structure. When the Israelites obey God, they prosper; when they do not obey, they suffer. After repenting and returning to obedience, they prosper again, only to relapse and suffer more. Overall, the Israelites do well in the book of Joshua, not so well in the book of Judges, the best under David and Solomon, and so on until both Israel and Judah are destroyed.

The paradigmatic example of the obedient person, the person of faith, is Abraham. At the beginning of Genesis chapter 12, God tells the superannuated Abraham, then known as Abram, to leave his family and country and to go to a land that God will disclose later. He obeys immediately, unquestioningly, and unconditionally: "So Abram went, as the Lord had told him." So obedient was Abraham that he was willing to sacrifice his son because God commanded it: "Take your son, your only son Isaac, whom you love, and . . . offer him as a burnt offering" (Genesis 22:2). This is one of the horrific stories alluded to above.

To return to Adam and Eve, the reader is supposed to generalize from their case and see all authority as Godlike. St. Paul makes the point explicitly: "All authority comes from God." He continues, "Let every person be subject to the governing authorities; for there is no authority except from God, and those authorities that exist have been instituted by God. Therefore, whoever resists authority resists what God has appointed, and those who resist will incur judgment" (Romans 13:2). Royalists loved this passage.

The mission of Jesus also has to be understood in relation to obedience and disobedience. Paul said that just as all human beings disobeyed through Adam, so all human beings are made obedient through Jesus. When Jesus was agonizing in the Garden of Gethsemane the night before he was killed, he begged God to let him live if it was possible, but added "not my will but thy will be done" (Luke 22:42). God's will was Jesus's command because Jesus accepted God's authority. He was "obedient unto death," as Paul says in Philippians 2:8. Christians, as imitators of Christ, are supposed to be willing to die if God wills it. Abraham, of course, was celebrated because he was willing to be "obedient unto" his son's death.

Many of the English rebels took the vocation of imitating Christ seriously. And they were able to find biblical texts to justify their actions. A general argument was that the English were suffering because they were disobeying God in allowing the king to lead a church that was too close in doctrine, governance, and liturgy to Roman Catholicism. Forcing the king to reform the church was a way of obeying God. Rebellion is acceptable in a good cause (see, for example, Judges 3:17). Not too many years after the Restoration, London suffered the Great Plague (1665) and then the Great Fire (1666). Royalists and anti-Royalists agreed that God was punishing England and disagreed only about the sin and the identity of the sinners.

THOMAS HOBBES SUPPORTED KING CHARLES because he thought obedience to government was the first virtue of subjects. When he wrote that human life was "solitary, poor, nasty, brutish, and short," he was referring to life without the protection of government. Because unregulated religion is usually subversive, the sovereign had to be the head of the church. (In the Netflix series *The Crown,* the queen mother lectures Elizabeth II on the weight of her obligations as the head of the church. They supersede love for her sister and even a promise made to her father when he was king.) An important part of Hobbes's proof that God commands people to obey their sovereign unconditionally consists of a comparison of English monarchs to the three most admired rulers in the Bible, Moses, David, and Solomon. Each one was the head of the religion. The high priest served at the pleasure of the king.

On the conditions for salvation, Hobbes wrote, "All that is NECESSARY *to salvation* is contained in two virtues, *faith in Christ,* and *obedience to laws.*" If Adam and Eve had obeyed in the first place, people would not need faith: "Because we're all guilty of disobedience . . . , there is required at our hands now . . . *obedience* for the rest of our time." Hobbes wrote extensively about the Bible because the politics of England was biblical, and the Bible was political. Taking his lead from ancient Israel, Greece, and Rome, he believed that religion was law: "And this law of God, that commandeth obedience to the law civil, commandeth by consequence obedience to all the precepts of the Bible."

AFTER KING CHARLES WAS IN the custody of the army, ordinary soldiers wanted to know what new rights they would have under the new government. They were camped outside London, and neither the city nor Parliament wanted thousands of soldiers near them. Parliament had not paid the army for several months and probably did not intend to pay it. Not needing a large army anymore, Parliament took the attitude of a Hollywood producer, "What've you done for me lately?"

Knowing of the unrest, the General Council of the Army arranged to meet with the representatives of the soldiers at Putney Church. The debates at Putney reveal the aspirations of the ordinary soldiers in straightforward and often eloquent speeches. Just as straightforward are the speeches of the nondemocratic officers, especially Oliver Cromwell's future son-in-law, General Henry Ireton.

The debate began on 28 October 1647, with a reading of the pamphlet *Foundations of Freedom, or An Agreement of the People for a Firm and Present Peace upon Grounds of Common Right,* which was to serve as a written constitution for England. It opens: "Having by our late labours and hazards made it appear to the world at how high a rate we value our just freedom . . ., we declare: That the people of England being . . . very unequally distributed by counties, cities and boroughs for the election of . . . Parliament," and so on. The complaint was about a form of gerrymandering. The *Agreement* lists problems and proposes remedies. Cromwell, who chaired the meeting, was not happy. He thought they would be discussing *The Case of the Army Stated* (1647), not the newly written *Agreement*. He said, "Truly this paper . . . contains in it very great alterations of the . . . government of the kingdom . . . alterations from that government that it's been under . . . since it was a nation."

On the second day, when Ireton had his chance to talk about the substance of the *Agreement of the People*, he said that the phrase, "The people of England" suggested that every inhabitant of England was equal to every other. He denied it. The idea that a person born in England had a birthright to participate in the government was a recipe for "anarchy." Ireton said that he thought that simply being born in England gave a person no political rights. Only those who had "a permanent fixed interest in this kingdom" should have a "share in the disposing of the affairs of the kingdom." He meant property owners.

> Men may justly have by birthright, by their very being born in England, that we should not seclude them out of England, that we should not refuse to give them air and place and ground, and the freedom of the highways and other things, to live amongst us . . . That I think is due to a man by birth. But that by a man's being born here he shall have a share in that power that shall dispose of the lands here, and of all things here, I do not think it a sufficient ground.

He was reacting to the memorable words of Colonel Thomas Rainsborough, the highest-ranking officer to defend the ordinary soldiers. He said that he hoped that the soldiers would have a role in government:

> For really I think that the poorest he that is in England hath [as much] a life to live, as the greatest he; and therefore truly, sir, I think it's clear that every man that is to live under a government ought first by his own consent to put himself under that government; and I do think that the poorest man in England is not at all bound in a strict sense to that government that he hath not had a voice to put himself under; . . . I should doubt whether he was an Englishman or no if he should doubt of these things.

A sticking point concerned property. For those with property, property ownership was required of anyone wanting to participate in the government; for those without property, the franchise was essential. Ireton and other property owners feared that if all adult males could vote, they would deprive owners of their property. As Ireton put it:

> All the main thing that I speak for, is because I would have an eye to property. I hope we . . . do not . . . take away all property. For here is . . . the most important part of the constitution of the kingdom. . . . Now I wish we may consider of what right you will challenge that all people should have right to elections. Is it by the right of nature? If [that is] . . . your ground, then I think you must deny all property too . . . For thus: by that same right of nature . . . he hath the same [equal] right in any goods he sees—meat, drink, clothes—to take and use them for his sustenance. He hath a freedom to the land, [to take] the ground, to exercise it, till it; he hath the same freedom to anything.

One defender of the soldiers' position claimed that when government was established, everyone was free and had property: "I judge every man is naturally free; and I judge the reason why men [chose representatives] when they were in so great numbers that every man could not give his voice [directly], was that they who were chosen might preserve property [for all]." He concluded that to give every man a vote was not to destroy property but to preserve it.

The soldiers were distraught that all their efforts would leave them no better off than when they risked their lives fighting the king. The agitator Edward Sexby said:

> I see that though liberty were our end, there is a degeneration from it. We have . . . ventured our lives, and it was all for this: to recover our birthrights and privileges as Englishmen; and by the arguments urged [by you,] there is none. . . . There are many thousands of us soldiers that have ventured our lives . . . If we had not a right to the kingdom, we were mere mercenary soldiers. . . . Do you [not] think it were a sad and miserable condition, that we have fought [the king] all this time for nothing? All here, both great and small, do think that we fought for something. . . . It had been good in you to have advertised us of it, and believe you would have [had] fewer under your command to have commanded.

Ireton responded to Sexby ("whom I love in my heart") by saying that no one had misled him or others when they joined the army. They should have known that they were fighting for "the liberty of Parliaments." Maximilian Petty attacked Ireton's presupposition that the rich should govern the poor: "The rich would very unwillingly be governed by the poor. And there is as much reason that the rich should govern the poor as the poor the rich—and indeed [that is] no reason. There should be an equal share in both." Ireton took Petty's views to be an attack on property itself. Earlier, Ireton had taken the Hobbesian line:

> The great foundation of justice is that we should keep our covenants one with another. There is no other foundation of right I know of . . . no foundation of that justice . . . this general ground of righteousness, that we should keep covenant one with another. Covenants freely made, freely entered into, must be kept one with another. . . . That which makes it unlawful originally and radically [to take property] is only this: that man is in covenant with me to live together in peace . . . and not to . . . make use of and dispose of, that which by the course of law is in another's possession.

The ordinary soldiers had disobeyed the king so that they could expand their freedom. Neither Parliament nor most of the officers of the army thought they deserved it. Subsequently, parts of the army mutinied, but were smashed by Cromwell's decisive action.

CHRISTOPHER HILL WROTE MANY VALUABLE books about seventeenth-century England, including *Puritanism and Revolution* (1958), *The World Turned Upside Down* (1972), and *The English Bible and the Seventeenth-Century Revolution* (1992), all of which connect religion with justifications for or against revolution. I chose *Intellectual Origins of the English Revolution* (1965) because its major thesis is to prove that revolutionary ideas were a cause of the English Civil War. It was intended to refute the received opinion that the war did not have intellectual causes, unlike the French Revolution, whose leaders had claimed inspiration from the ideas of baron de Montesquieu, Jean-Jacques Rousseau, and others. Hill was at his best when he used short biographies of offbeat characters such as Lodowick Muggleton and Gerard Winstanley to explore some underestimated phenomenon. In this book, his method is similar, except that the chapters focused on major figures such as Sir Walter Raleigh, Francis Bacon, and Edward Coke.

The work of these men, plus the scientists at Gresham College, supposedly constitutes the revolution's intellectual origins. Undoubtedly, the scientific advances in London relating to navigation and technology, Raleigh's efforts to commercialize the colonies, Bacon's emphasis on empirical science and secondary causes, and Coke's promotion of the common law courts are important, but do not seem to me to ground revolution. Not all revolutionary ideas are ideas of revolution; otherwise, Facebook would be one. Hill is on stronger ground in describing Coke's contribution to revolution. Coke "gave Englishmen an historical myth of the English constitution" according to which parliaments preceded kings and judged property rights to have priority over the king's prerogative and courts. Being "the absolute perfection of reason," the common law was superior to the king.

Hill's attempts to make the ideas of Raleigh and Bacon seem to be ideas of revolution are unconvincing, as when he quotes Raleigh: "Whosoever commands the sea, commands the trade; whosoever commands the trade of the world, commands the riches of the world, and consequently the world itself." This interesting idea is not a theory of any political revolution.

Sometimes Hill resorts to strained metaphors:

> Copernicus's theory had "democratized the universe" by shattering the hierarchical structure of the heavens; Harvey "democratized" the human body by dethroning the heart.

> In the social sphere, [Francis] Bacon's method went far to level men's wits, and leaves . . . little to individual excellence.

He sounds desperate when he writes that the innovations of the new science "must have helped the radicals to shake off the dead weight of tradition and precedent which hamstrung early Parliamentarian political thinking." At the end of the book, Hill admits he has not proved his case: "So my conclusion is the banal and eternal one, that history is all very mixed up."

Well, why recommend this book? Because the wealth of information that Hill provides and the unexpected connections he makes are exhilarating, for example, his chapter on Gresham College. Founded by Thomas Gresham for the purpose of educating ordinary people in practical skills, Gresham was decidedly unlike the Oxford and Cambridge colleges that educated future clerics and gentlemen. Because it was in London, Gresham was outside the ecclesiastical and intellectual oversight of the Oxbridge administrators. Its faculty was able to escape notice, too, because it specialized in natural science and mathematics and steered clear of theology. Lectures were free and open to the public. They were given by such distinguished scientists as William Gilbert, who argued in 1600 that the earth is a magnet; Robert Boyle, who is credited with discovering the gas laws; William Harvey, who discovered how blood circulates through veins and arteries; John Napier, who invented logarithms; and John Wallis, whose contributions to mathematics helped lead to Isaac Newton's calculus. Several of these scientists were among the earliest members of the Royal Society of London for Improving Natural Knowledge. All very informative, delightfully told. The parts are greater than the whole.

THE LIVES OF THE THREE MAIN CHARACTERS of *Wild Swans* (1991), a grandmother, a mother, and a daughter, who is the author, Jung Chang, are closely bound up with the major political events of twentieth-century China: the period of the warlords after the fall of the Qing Dynasty; the Second World War; the Chinese Civil War, in which Mao Zedong prevailed over Chiang Kai-shek; the Great Leap Forward; the Cultural Revolution; and China's opening up to the West. "May you live in interesting times" is said to be one of the two harshest curses in Chinese.

Chang's grandmother at the age of fifteen became a concubine of the warlord General Xue Zhi-heng, the chief of police in the warlord government in Peking. After he died, she escaped and married a doctor almost forty years older than she was. They and their one daughter, Chang's mother, survived the Second World War. Chang's mother and father were stalwart communists, faithful to Mao and to communist ideals.

China began drifting into insanity in the late 1950s, the period of the Great Leap Forward. During that time, "uplifting music blared from loudspeakers, and there were banners, posters, and huge slogans painted on the walls proclaiming 'Long Live the Great Leap Forward!' and 'Everybody, Make Steel!,'" a reference to the disastrous plan to have ordinary people make steel by melting their woks and other metal objects in "backyard furnaces," usually little more than large cauldrons. Woks were tossed in because the government made meals communal in 1958. On her way to and from school, Chang used to search "every inch of ground for broken nails" and any other iron that could be tossed into the backyard furnace to help achieve the impossible goal. After food shortages began in 1959, communal meals were abolished because the government could not provide the food. And the people now lacked woks to cook the little food they could gather.

A few years later, Mao launched the Cultural Revolution in order to regain the power that he thought he had lost. Random acts of violence were committed by roving gangs of youths, the Red Guard. Favorite targets were educated people, especially teachers. Chang says that a "hallmark of Maoism . . . was the reign of ignorance." Mao called educated people "spiritual aristocrats." Most universities shut down, or they taught only Maoism. The safest behavior was to do your job and not to think. Once, the path of a broom sweeper was partly blocked by a peasant sitting with her two toddlers and a nursing infant. The sweeper "swept the dust right over them, as though they were not there." But obedience did not guarantee safety. Even though they were completely obedient to Mao and the Communist Party, Chang's parents were persecuted. Her father was imprisoned and tortured. He suffered physically, went insane, and died at an early age. Her mother was sent into the interior to work at hard labor. Except for a few brief moments of doubt, their faith in Mao was absolute. There was always someone else to blame for China's disasters. Chang herself was a loyal Maoist until her early twenties. She embraced these lessons: "Father is close, Mother is close; but Chairman Mao is closer," "Destroy first, and Construction will look after itself," and "The more books you read, the stupider you become."

At the age of eighteen, Chang was ordered to work as a "barefoot doctor," that is, a peasant medical provider with no medical education. She was supposed to learn on the job. Then she became an electrician despite having no electrical education, and soon electrocuted herself. When China became more open in the early 1970s, she attended a university to learn English, taught by teachers who had never heard spoken English.

When Mao died, in 1976, China engaged in "an orgy of weeping." Chang did not join in because she had come to the conclusion that Mao needed or desired "perpetual conflict . . . He understood ugly human instincts such as envy and resentment, and knew how to . . . get people to hate each other." He did not need an agency like the KGB, because he made the people his spies. No book has had a greater emotional impact on me than *Wild Swans*.

Through the poverty, violence, ignorance, cruelty, and oppression shines the strength, perseverance, and decency of three generations of good people. While obedience is not an explicit theme in *Wild Swans*, it does show that even when people scrupulously obey the laws and authorities, if the leader is ignorant, dictatorial, and mercurial, obedience does not ensure security. In short, while obedience is necessary for government to operate, sometimes disobedience is necessary to remove a beast that operates under color of government.

Fall Semester 2017

The British Atlas, or John Bull Supporting the Peace Establishment, 1816. Attributed to Charles Williams. 1868,0808.8321, British Museum.

17

Oxford Dictionary of National Biography

ELIZABETH BAIGENT

"A newly-established state in the late twentieth-century might seek to patent its identity by founding a national airline service," suggests a study of national biographical dictionaries, whereas "its nineteenth-century counterpart was likely to have launched a multi-volume biographical dictionary so as to display historical credentials, to define geographical, linguistic, and cultural boundaries, and to instil a unified sense of pride."[1] Sweden (1835–57) was the perhaps unlikely leader in the race to produce a national biographical dictionary, followed by the Netherlands (1852–78), Austria and Belgium (1860s onward), Germany (from 1875), and Denmark (1887). Many of them had a nationalist agenda: the Belgian dictionary, for example, was initiated in 1845 by royal decree when the nation was only fourteen years old, and many dictionaries were nationally funded and organized.

In Britain, the *Dictionary of National Biography* (*DNB*), known after 2004 as the *Oxford Dictionary of National Biography* (*ODNB*), forms "the national record of men and women who have shaped British history and culture, worldwide."[2] Benedict Anderson famously claimed that nations are "imagined communities," that is, communities shaped primarily by social and cultural criteria. People within a nation-state, Anderson argued, come to see themselves as sharing an identity that is created and sustained by representations and iconography: postage stamps, banknotes, maps, collections in national museums, landscapes dotted with monuments. Printed material is crucial to the imagined community: books standardize the language; banknotes and coins bring national icons into quotidian commerce; schoolroom maps differentiate the home nation from that of others; and national biographical dictionaries reify the nation's past by portraying the lives of its noteworthy members.

Sidney Lee (1859–1926), a literary scholar and the second editor of the *DNB*, suggested in 1911 that the point of biography was to commemorate "those who by character and exploits have distinguished themselves from the mass of mankind."[3] But how can collective national biography work if it simultaneously memorializes those who have distinguished themselves from the unmemorialized mass, following Lee, but represents the collective to whom both the memorialized and the unmemorialized belong, following Anderson? This lecture examines whether the *ODNB* holds a mirror up to its imagined national community and, if so, whether the writing of the nation is largely a hegemonic and elitist project or at least in part a collective one. It asks whether such a dictionary is a "true biography of the nation."[4]

The story starts with the London entrepreneur and publisher George Smith (1824–1901), who resolved to produce a dictionary of national biography. Lee claims that Smith "was attracted by the notion of producing a book which would . . . compete with, or even surpass, works of a similar character which were being produced abroad." Smith "was inspirited by the knowledge that he was in a position to pursue single-handedly an aim in behalf of which Government organisation had elsewhere been enlisted."[5] Smith began work on the *DNB* in 1882 under its first editor, Leslie Stephen (1832–1904), a metropolitan man of letters. The results were published in alphabetical sequence at quarterly intervals between 1885 and 1900. When Stephen retired in 1891, his deputy, Lee, became editor; in 1900 he saw to its end the original *DNB*, which contained biographies of nearly thirty thousand people. There was a tidying-up phase to cover people who had died while the dictionary was being written and to correct errors, and Lee oversaw publication of a corrected reissue of the complete *DNB* in 1908–9.

In 1917 the *DNB*'s publisher, Smith, Elder & Co., gave the *DNB* to the not wholly grateful University of Oxford, which entrusted it to Oxford University Press (OUP). The press extended it with ten fairly slim supplementary volumes, one per decade covering those who had died between 1901 and 1990. By the later twentieth century, the original *DNB* and its supplements were looking fragmented, and the community of the nation that it imagined looked old-fashioned, especially at a time when other nations were beginning to revise their national biographical dictionaries or produce new ones.

In the 1990s, OUP put a toe in the water of revision with *Missing Persons* (1993, edited by Christine Nicholls), a volume covering all historical periods, which brought the *DNB*'s coverage to over 38,000 people. More importantly, it showed what interesting figures from history a revised *DNB* could include—and the fact that the press was deluged with suggestions showed that users felt the existing dictionary to be a deficient mirror of their imagined community, but one worth repolishing to do a better job.

In 1992 the University of Oxford, OUP, and the British Academy undertook to rewrite and extend the *DNB* in the largest British humanities research and publishing project ever pursued. Using the sources and methods available to modern scholars, existing articles were rewritten, and large numbers of new subjects memorialized.

Colin Matthew (1941–1999), a historian of nineteenth-century Britain, was appointed editor of the *Oxford Dictionary of National Biography*. He set its intellectual agenda and made the farsighted decision, by no means self-evident in the early 1990s, that though a print version would be published, the new edition would be primarily electronic. In 2000, following Matthew's untimely death, Brian Harrison (1937–), a historian of modern Britain, was appointed editor, and in 2004 the *ODNB* was published online and in sixty print volumes, with the biographies of 55,000 women and men who had died in or before the year 2000.

Since then, Lawrence Goldman (editor, 2004–14) and David Cannadine (editor, 2014–) have overseen work at OUP to extend the *ODNB*'s coverage online (though not in print), produce spin-off volumes, correct and update existing entries in the light of new research, find innovative ways to bring the dictionary to a wider scholarly and general public, and help readers make the best use of the dictionary's "60,000+ people, 11,000+ portraits, and 72 million words [describing] 2,500 years of British history."

VERY RAPIDLY AND CERTAINLY BEFORE the first alphabetical sequence of volumes was finished, the *DNB* established itself in national intellectual, literary, and establishment life, that is, it began to function as a mirror to an imagined community of the nation. The dictionary's subjects were chosen by the literary and intellectual nation at large: it was via the literary periodical the *Athenaeum* that proposed subjects were announced and others invited. To be in the *DNB* became a mark of distinction, in common literary parlance and in more practical ways that showed how literary, artistic, and historical circles overlapped: a place in the *DNB* helped secure a portrait in the National Portrait Gallery (founded in 1856), a commemorative blue plaque (a scheme begun in 1866) marking a notable person's home, and the acceptance by Oxford's Bodleian Library of one's papers.

Moreover, the dictionary project was widely interpreted early on as a national one. The *Athenaeum* described it as "this important and essentially national undertaking."[6] Lee called it a "patriotic endeavour."[7] A reluctant OUP was urged to taken on the *DNB* "in the national interest"—the same interest that led it to publish the *Oxford English Dictionary* (begun in 1879) as a work of "national significance" and "a dictionary of the English nation."[8]

Although the *DNB* was seen by many as a national institution, it was neither a state-sponsored enterprise nor, Cannadine suggests, an exercise in "national self-regard."[9] Rather, as Matthew pointed out in 1997, "its tone carefully eschewed national triumphality: indeed it was if anything tinged more with cultural pessimism than cultural superiority": "Though prepared in the high-noon of tory imperialism, it avoided to a remarkable extent [a] jingoistic tone and state-worship."[10] The historian Keith Thomas noted in 2005 that "tranquil consciousness of Britain's world superiority made it [the *DNB*] less obviously chauvinistic than its European counterparts, for whom national independence was newer and less secure."[11] Notwithstanding these scholars' later judgments, there was explicitly patriotic rejoicing at the time of publication: "the best dictionary of home biography possessed by any nation" (*Pall Mall Gazette*), "a handsome beating to their most formidable competitor, the Germans" (*Athenaeum*).[12] Lee gloried in the fact that the *DNB*, by not being supported by state funding, was "in truer accord with the self-reliant temperament of the British race."[13] T. B. Strong, accepting the dictionary on behalf of the University of Oxford in 1917, declared that George Smith "had provided a pattern which any great nation would be proud to follow," patriotism clouding the fact that other nations had led rather than followed Britain in this respect.[14] But whether eschewing or embracing patriotic fervor, these authors tacitly agreed that the *DNB* epitomized the nation, that is, it could legitimately be treated as a mirror of the national imagined community.

But which is the nation is question? The *DNB* was mooted as *Biographia Britannica,* but its eventual title claims to be national while declining to reveal the nation in question—a stratagem that Matthew found "brilliant in its open mindedness" and a reflection of

Stephen's concept of nationality as "inclusive, fluid, and pragmatic, and in a sense international"; in fact, the first *DNB* began with the French-born Jacques Abbadie and ended with Wilhelm Zuylestein, who was born near Utrecht.[15] It represented what Matthew called "the nation in effect," covering colonial figures only if they were "known to Whitehall" (home of the British executive).[16]

The *DNB*, like other European dictionaries, reified the ideas of its nineteenth-century founders. Lee thought that the *DNB* should "supply full, accurate, and concise biographies of all the noteworthy inhabitants of the British Islands and the Colonies."[17] The scope of his *national* dictionary thus combines a *geographic* entity (the British Islands) with an *imperial* political entity (the colonies). The first version of the *DNB* is sometimes assumed to be a lexicographical "Temple of British Worthies," a pantheon of the great and the good, and hagiography rather than biography. It is true that Lee thought that it served "the national and beneficial purpose" of allowing future generations access to "their ancestors' collective achievement," but in fact it records not so much collective achievement as collective activity and experience, good and bad.[18] "Dramatically eclectic," it includes "sportspeople, murderers, journalists, actors and actresses, deviant clergymen, transvestites, Agnostics and secularists," as well as fat men, old women, criminals, rogues, and wastrels.[19] Heroes and villains are portrayed not to inspire patriotism or promote virtue, but to add to the dictionary's variety, placing it in a long tradition of recording "eminences" in all fields, including physique.

The *DNB* thus blends the old tradition of cabinets of curiosities with the modern conception of systematic collections, the former reflecting the whole by showing its wondrous extremities, the latter by an orderly application of selection principles. There was some national self-congratulation even for this eclecticism. Keith Thomas noted, "Britain . . . had more 'characters' and 'originals' than other nations because of its tradition of tolerance and freedom," though not everyone thought this a cause for congratulation.[20] In 1917, when OUP was considering whether to take on the *DNB*, William Sanday, theology delegate to the press, advised the use of small type for those involved in "amusements" and for "second-rate articles," evidently considering such persons to dilute the grandeur of the national imagined community.[21]

Quite outside this tendency to include oddities, *DNB* articles could be "pungently disrespectful," as the cultural historian Iain McCalman puts it.[22] J. A. Hamilton on George IV, for example, concludes: "There have been more wicked kings in English history, but none so unredeemed by any signal greatness or virtue. That he was a dissolute and drunken fop, a spendthrift and a gamester, 'a bad son, a bad husband, a bad father, a bad subject, a bad monarch, and a bad friend,' that his word was worthless and his courage doubtful, are facts which cannot be denied."[23] The *DNB* aimed not for hagiography, but to follow the path laid out by the *Oxford English Dictionary:* to describe the nation, not to prescribe what was acceptable in it.

The *DNB*'s much-valued eclecticism did not, however, make it evenhanded. The metropolitan "men of letters" whose culture generated and shaped the *DNB* included entries on people whom they found interesting and whose absence they judged would leave the conception of the nation impoverished. Though catholic, their judgments left systematic gaps that the *ODNB* had to fill.

The *OED* was digitized in 1984, and this set the scene within OUP for Colin Matthew's insistence that the *DNB* follow suit. A digitized and tagged *DNB* allowed Matthew precisely to identify shortcomings and plan how to address them. He appointed specialist consultant editors to expand and change coverage, especially in ill-served areas; hired in-house researchers, including a large number of women, with a broad range of outlooks, scholarly backgrounds, and ages; and consulted via questionnaire a huge variety of interest groups, scholarly and otherwise. In short, Matthew set out to produce a new edition that would reimagine the nation for a new generation.

The *DNB*'s editorial staff had struggled to cover earlier periods of British history and relied more on literary sources than present historians do. The transformation of medieval scholarship, together with a commitment to include as far as possible the kinds of people overlooked in the dictionary generally, transformed the *ODNB*'s coverage. Saxon princesses, abbesses, and women of gentry families are notable additions, and Viking subjects appear in more varied guise than simply as imaginative thugs.

Being metropolitan men, the *DNB*'s editors had "imaginative geographies"[24] defined by the view from the capital and epitomized by frequent use of the phrase "he came to London." Ireland and Scotland were reasonably well covered, industrial parts of northern England and Wales were not, and the "known to Whitehall" principle for the British colonies and dominions meant better coverage of white settler colonies than of Africa or pre-independence America. The *ODNB* editorial team sought to rectify these deficiencies. Colonial Americans (including Native Americans and settlers from outside Britain) were a particular focus, and George Washington, left out of the *DNB* because space was running short by the time the dictionary reached *W,* has his place in *ODNB.*

Moneymaking seemed slightly grubby to the *DNB*'s men of letters, so businesspeople were few in the dictionary, and those were included not because they made money, but because they spent it interestingly as philanthropists, art collectors, or political grandees. Martin Daunton, the consultant editor for business, expanded the coverage to take in businesspeople as varied as large industrialists, department store magnates, and early modern innkeepers.

Ethnicity has for some decades been the most pressing question for many national biographical dictionaries in the New World, but is only just becoming so in Britain as the first generation of migrants to Britain from the Caribbean and Southeast Asia reach the end of their lives. The *ODNB* sought out ethnic minorities from within the British Isles: Gaelic culture was a particular focus, linked perhaps with Colin Matthew's proficiency on the bagpipes. The *ODNB*'s regular updates give the chance to include people such as the Trinidadian calypso musicians Aldwyn Roberts, who performed as Lord Kitchener (1922–2000), and Harold Adolphus Phillips—Lord Woodbine, as he was known (1929–2000)—to enrich the textual and visual portrait of the modern nation.

Although Leslie Stephen wrote of the need to include "the mere rank and file" and thought the *DNB* would be most valuable for its "second rate people," the poor and powerless left only a slight impression in the dictionary. When they did, it was, for example, as sportspeople rather than as trade unionists or in other ways that directly bore on their class position. The use of mass sources such as census, parish, and court records from all periods and spheres of interest helped address this deficiency.

Iain McCalman describes nineteenth-century national biographical dictionaries as resembling "exclusive men's clubs," and the Oxford historian Janet Howarth, an associate editor of the *ODNB*, found in the *DNB* "a relentless focus on women whom men found interesting"—the guests of the male members, as it were.[25] The *ODNB*, under the overarching guidance of Jane Garnett, the consultant editor for women, focused as well on women whom women find interesting. Whole categories of public life—volunteer work, local government, nursing, social and housing work, writing for children, gardening, needlework—were added, along with overlooked individuals in the *DNB*'s traditional areas of interest: national politics, scholarship, writing, exploration. My area of research, travel and exploration, added a host of women, including Kate Marsden, who sledged through Siberia; Annie Taylor, explorer and missionary to China; and Anne Lister, traveler and challenger of norms of gender and sexuality.

The *DNB*'s editors considered biography to be primarily about public life, a distinction applied in gendered way. Much of women's public activity was classified as private: nursing, for example, was

Figure 17.1. Annie Royle Taylor (1855–1922) reading the Bible and drinking tea with her Tibetan friends Pontso (*left*) and Sigu. Taylor, a missionary and explorer, was the first Western woman known to have reached Tibet. Photograph in William Carey, *Adventures in Tibet* (1901), opposite p. 242; National Museums of Scotland.

"private" because its skills were linked with those of domestic management and personal care. The same was true of being a political hostess or running a great estate, because those activities centered on the home. While entries kept men's public and private lives separate, women's private lives were integrated into accounts of their public works, which, it was assumed, they affected. In *ODNB* articles, private and public life are woven together where possible, and the same conventions are applied to men's and women's articles.

The *ODNB,* implicitly accepting Anderson's view of the imagined community, added imaginary characters that say something about the national psyche or the way the nation views itself, acknowledging that "the general memory of the English past is . . . more nurtured by novels, plays, films and television, than by monographs,"[26] and that representations are widely seen as having lives independent of that which they represent. The *ODNB* includes shadowy characters whose existence as a single person is unclear, including Junius, the pseudonymous eighteenth-century defender of liberty;

Jack the Ripper, the serial murderer; and Spring Heeled Jack, the nineteenth-century folklore figure. Real people who became icons include Tommy Atkins, the British equivalent of GI Joe, dating from the Napoleonic Wars, and the Unknown Warrior, who lies in Westminster Abbey, representing all fallen combatants. Those who never existed as real people but symbolize the nation include Britannia, John Bull, and his wife, Joan.

National biographical dictionaries follow the assumption that national life is made largely by individuals. Though the *ODNB* remains dominated by articles on individuals, its group and family articles cover scientific groups, political parties or groupings, family firms, and cultural groups and institutions. Some group entries, such as the one on the Royal Geographical Society, provide a context for articles on affiliated individuals; others groups, like the Arctic Council, turn out to have existed only in popular memory. Articles on gentry families show the structure of home society and culture, whereas ones on foreign industrial spies add detail to Britain's relationship with other countries.

Despite these thoughtfully derived and tirelessly pursued aims, the *ODNB*'s coverage in purely statistical terms was modified, not transformed, because all the *DNB*'s original subjects were retained. For example, the share of women in the dictionary has risen from 4 percent in the *DNB* to 10 per cent in the 2004 edition and to more than 11 percent now.

Change is of course qualitative as well as quantitative. As well as conforming to new standards of historical scholarship, the *ODNB* paid attention to language reflecting changing norms and new sensibilities. "He never married"—the *DNB*'s "economical" code for homosexuality—was replaced with franker treatment, though sensitivity is still needed when the subject is recently dead, and discussion of the sexuality of the long dead has to have a solid evidential base and not impose anachronistic judgments. Local place-names are used in the *ODNB*, so "Beijing" replaced "Pekin" and "Peking." Local, not Anglicized, personal names are similarly used, with care taken to use correct shortened forms, not just to plump for what looks to Anglophones like a surname: this affected Irish, Scottish, and Welsh people as well as those further afield. Names of wars reflect new perspectives, so the Indian Mutiny became an uprising. The view is no longer just from London; other people's imagined communities must be respected.

Gendered judgments and language were challenged. For example, the *DNB*'s biographer of the intrepid explorer and theorist of empire Mary Kingsley (1862–1900) battled valiantly to show her conformity to contemporary gender norms: "Although of daring

and masculine courage . . . Miss Kingsley was full of womanly ten-
derness, sympathy, and modesty, entirely without false shame . . .
Her fine square brow was her chief beauty, and she exercised remarkable personal attraction, heightened by her brilliant conversation and her keen sense of (ever kindly) humour." Her 2004 biographer had no such agenda.

AT LEAST SINCE THE EIGHTEENTH century, Britain has had a tradition of collective portraiture as well as of collective biography: cabinets of miniature portraits and libraries with collections of busts or
portrait friezes serve as "visual exemplars of the British past."[27] The
ODNB's editors decided to include in it some ten thousand images
in a project undertaken with the National Portrait Gallery (NPG).
Peter Funnell, NPG curator and the *ODNB*'s portrait consultant, saw
the chance to produce the largest published and curated collection
of British portraits, "a national iconography."[28] All portraits were
to be "authentic likenesses taken from the life," the visual equivalent of the *ODNB*'s careful collation of reliable facts.[29] This ruled
out doubtful attributions, but also some artistic modes, for example,
highly abstract treatments. For figures alive before 1500, that is, before the tradition of portraiture was established, images from coins,
effigies, stained glass, and manuscripts provide emblems rather
than strict likenesses. Collectively, the images were to reflect the
importance of the subjects and the national community as imagined by the *ODNB*'s editorial priorities; so, for example, portraits of
women were sought out to reduce the dictionary's visual maleness.
The images show readers not only what sitters looked like, but also
what constituted a portrait in each age. Images were to be "visually
rich, not just informative," so the curatorial team chose works by
notable artists and in a variety of media and styles, and no images
were cropped.[30]
The dictionary displays a historiography of scholarship as well as
of portraiture. The project started in a publishing house in a country where university departments of modern history were rare and
scholarly journals and learned societies scarcely existed. The *English
Historical Review*, for example, the first historical periodical in Britain, began publication only after the *DNB* started to appear. The
original *DNB* was written by "in house generalists" (all men), plus
some outside specialists, and its writing helped create British historical research.[31] Thomas Frederick Tout, the distinguished medieval historian; A. F. Pollard, who founded the Institute of Historical
Research in London; and Sir Charles Firth, later Regius Professor
of History in Oxford, all served at the *DNB* and owed much to it.

As Tout remarked, "Like many Oxford men of my generation, I approached historical investigation without the least training or guidance in historical method, and felt very much at a loss how to set to work. The careful and stringent regulations which he [i.e., Stephen] drew up, and the brusque but kindly way in which he enforced obedience to them, constituted for many of us our first training in anything like original investigation."[32] Similarly Pollard thought that at the *DNB* he had "learnt infinitely more . . . than I should have done by staying at Oxford."[33] By contrast, the *ODNB* was more of a clearinghouse for information or a "centre of calculation,"[34] since it was part of a well-established university culture.

The *ODNB* flourishes, but continues to face challenges. The main practical one involves funding. The *ODNB*'s financing model avoids the abrupt changes of policy that have beset some state-supported projects; but reliance on private funding forces the *ODNB* to operate behind a license wall, whereas online access to state-funded dictionaries is often free. The *ODNB*'s staff works valiantly to widen access, for example, by negotiating free access via public libraries in Britain and by making the content suitable for new generations of electronic devices. But the paywall remains, making the *ODNB* a mirror to the nation that not everyone can hold up, a difficulty that will prove ever more challenging to overcome as pressures for open access gain momentum.

Intellectual challenges for the *ODNB* cluster round the conflict between universality and selectivity. It is by nature the selective literary complement to the universal statistical collective that forms the nation. But if selection is inherent to the *ODNB*'s enterprise, then who does it, and how, and with what result? Virginia Woolf, Leslie Stephen's daughter, criticized the exclusivity of her father's *DNB* when she asked, "Is not anyone who has lived a life and left a record of that life worthy of biography—the failures as well as the successes, the humble as well as the illustrious? And what is greatness? And what smallness?"[35] Ironically, small lives stand a better chance of inclusion in the *ODNB* than of being treated in a full-length commercially published biography. Perhaps Stephen, with his "second-" or even "third-rate people," was closer to Woolf's views than she thought.

While in the late twentieth century national biographical dictionaries were criticized for their elitism, by the twenty-first century they found themselves hailed as refuges of reliable, honest, thoughtfully chosen and organized information in an era of fake news, data superabundance, and data misuse, and as vehicles for creating new scholarship and providing well-informed judgments on old. Vaunted alternatives such as Wikipedia depend on the up-to-date scholarship of the *ODNB* and its coequals for individual articles, yet replicate faults of old national biographical dictionaries—Wikipedia's contributors are overwhelmingly male, for example—"rounding up the usual suspects," as it were, rather than relentlessly working to create a new vision. The zeitgeist seems to be turning in favor of the *ODNB* and its peers, with their "*Zertifiziertes Wissen,*" or "guaranteed knowledge," as the German national biographical dictionary has it.[36]

A final aspect of selection goes to the heart of any national biographical dictionary: should nationality be a criterion for selection? "Who can doubt," wrote Colin Matthew in 1995, "that in the course of the next century, as nationality gives way to European Union, so national reference works will do so also."[37] In the time of Donald Trump, Brexit, Viktor Orban, and too many others to list, it is clear that the death of the nationality premise has been greatly exaggerated, and the idea of a universal biography with ever more abundant and ever more linked data begins to look sinister as much as idealistic. In Brexit-era Britain, the elite's confident ability (or even right) to fashion the imagined community of the nation has at least temporarily run into the sands, and perhaps we shall be left with a national portrait whose geographic premise is of declining interest to those who read it, but of increasing import to those who don't. Meanwhile, scholars who would benefit from immersive reading in such a carefully chosen collection of biographies tend instead to focus on pinpoint word searches and miss the whole.

F. W. Maitland declared that the *DNB* "can fairly claim to be national, if only because it reflects the confusion of the national mind."[38] The British national mind of 2019 is no less confused than that of earlier dates, but perhaps the *ODNB* at least helps us see, though not to account for, such confusion, and even to enjoy its lighter side.

Spring Semester 2018

1. Iain McCalman, introduction to Iain McCalman, ed., *National Biographies and National Identity: A Critical Approach to Theory and Editorial Practice,* with Jodi Parvey and Misty Cook (Canberra, 1996), p. i.

2. Robert Faber and B. H. Harrison, "The *Dictionary of National* Biography: A Publishing History," in Robin Myers, Michael Harris, and Giles Mandelbrote, eds., *Lives in Print: Biography and the Book Trade from the Middle Ages to the Twenty-First Century* (New Castle and Boston Spa, 2002).

3. Sidney Lee, *Principles of Biography: The Leslie Stephen Lecture* (Cambridge, 1911), p. 7.

4. Karen Fox, ed., *'True Biographies of Nations?': The Cultural Journeys of Dictionaries of National Biography* (Acton, Australia, 2019).

5. Sidney Lee, "Memoir of George Smith," in *Dictionary of National Biography: 1901 Supplement,* p. xlv.

6. "The Dictionary of National Biography," *Athenæum* 3639 (1897), p. 117.

7. Lee, "Memoir of George Smith," p. xlvi.

8. David Cannadine, "100 Years of Oxford's Dictionary of National Biography," oxfordtoday.ox.ac.uk/news/2017-11-07-100-years-oxfords-dictionary-national-biography

9. Ibid.

10. H. C. G. Matthew, *Leslie Stephen and the New Dictionary of National Biography* (Cambridge, 1997), pp. 16, 12. The "New DNB" was the title of the project that produced the *Oxford DNB.*

11. K. V. Thomas, *Changing Conceptions of National Biography: The Oxford DNB in Historical Perspective* (Cambridge, 2005), p. 26.

12. Ibid., p. 27.

13. Sidney Lee, "The Dictionary of National Biography: A Statistical Account," in Leslie Stephen and Sidney Lee, eds., *Dictionary of National Biography* (63 vols., London, 1885–1900), vol. 63, *Wordsworth–Zuylestein* (1900), p. xxii.

14. Cannadine, "Oxford's Dictionary of National Biography."

15. Matthew, *Leslie Stephen,* pp. 35–36. *Biographia Britannica* referred to an eighteenth-century work of the same name.

16. B. H. Harrison, introduction to H. C. G. Matthew and B. H. Harrison, eds., *Oxford Dictionary of National Biography* (Oxford, 2004), p. viii.

17. Lee, "Statistical Account," p. vi.

18. Ibid., p. xxii.

19. Matthew, *Leslie Stephen,* pp. 12–13.

20. Thomas, *Conceptions of National Biography,* p. 22.

21. Cannadine, "Oxford's Dictionary of National Biography."

22. McCalman, introduction, p. iv.

23. Cited in Matthew, *Leslie Stephen,* pp. 12–13.

24. Edward Said, *Orientalism* (London, 1979), p. 50.

25. McCalman, introduction, p. ii; Howarth, associate editor report for the New DNB, *ODNB* archive.

26. Matthew, *Leslie Stephen,* p. 28.

27. Thomas, *Changing Conceptions of National Biography,* p. 48.

28. Peter Funnell, 1995 consultant editor report for the New DNB, *ODNB* archive.

29. Harrison, introduction to Matthew and Harrison, *Oxford Dictionary of National Biography,* p. v.

30. Funnell, 1995 report.

31. Matthew, *Leslie Stephen,* p. 19.

32. Henry Summerson, "T. F. Tout and the Dictionary of National Biography," in Joel Rosenthal and Caroline Barron, eds., *Thomas Frederick Tout (1855–1920): Repositioning History for the Twentieth Century* (London, in press). My thanks to Dr. Summerson for allowing me to quote from this essay.

33. Cited in Brian Harrison, "Buried Treasure in Oxford's Modern History Faculty,"   https://www.history.ox.ac.uk/buried-treasure-oxfords-modern-history -faculty.

34. Bruno Latour, *Science in Action: How to Follow Scientists and Engineers through Society* (Milton Keynes, 1987), p. 215.

35. Virginia Woolf, "The Art of Biography" (1939), in *Selected Essays*, ed. David Bradshaw (Oxford, 2009), p. 121.

36. Deutsche Biographie, https://www.deutsche-biographie.de/?language=de.

37. Matthew, *Leslie Stephen*, p. 35.

38. Cited in Thomas, *Conceptions of National Biography*, p. 36.

Codrington Library, All Souls College, Oxford, with a statue of Christopher
Codrington III by Sir Henry Cheere (1732–34).

18

The Problem with Monuments
A View from All Souls

EDWARD MORTIMER

Given the fierce arguments in the United States about what one might call contested historical legacies in public spaces, it might be interesting to examine some of the similar arguments that have been raging almost as ferociously in Britain. In America, the bitterest arguments seem to concern the memorialization of people or events connected with slavery and the Civil War, although there are also many about the way North America was colonized by Europeans and about the fate of the Native American peoples. It is also slavery that comes back to haunt the British, along with the broader history of their empire.

In Britain, disputes about slavery do not concern any large number of people held as slaves there. That seems to have been quite rare in modern times, though whether Lord Mansfield's famous judgment of 1772 actually ended slavery in England remains unclear. What is incontestable, however, is that British companies and individuals played a leading, often dominant role in the Atlantic slave trade from the seventeenth to the early nineteenth century, and that many British people owned large numbers of slaves working on plantations in the Caribbean, and derived great profit from them. Some of these men (they were mainly, though not exclusively, men) used their wealth for philanthropic and educational purposes in Britain, and they are commemorated by statues and in the names of buildings or institutions. Beyond that, it has been argued that capital derived from slavery and the slave trade played an important part in the Industrial Revolution and, thereby, in the rise of Britain as a world power. But just how important remains a matter of dispute among historians.

When Britain abolished slavery, in 1833, an enormous compensation was paid out to slave owners, 40 percent of the treasury's budget that year. The loan taken out to cover this was huge—a freedom-of-information request recently revealed that it was finally paid off only in 2015—but still considered insufficient, and the freed slaves were taxed to make up the shortfall.

Around the world—notably in India and, later, Africa—British power expanded from the late eighteenth century until, by the early twentieth century, much of Earth's land surface was painted red, at least on British maps. And even beyond the formal empire, Britain exercised great influence in countries that remained nominally independent, such as China and Iran, and derived great profit from it. While much of this expansion was ratified by treaties between Britain and local rulers, superior military and naval force played a key role in the expansion and retention of empire. Attempts to resist British rule or influence were often ruthlessly crushed, and much wealth was extracted from colonies and other subject territories for the benefit of the British population, particularly its ruling elite.

By the late nineteenth century, many British writers and statesmen were identifying British interests with those of the empire. Soldiers and entrepreneurs who played a part in its conquest or preservation were celebrated, and in due course commemorated, as heroes; and—as with slavery and the slave trade—wealth derived from the empire was devoted to philanthropic causes in Britain. The word "imperialist" may have acquired a pejorative connotation today, but a hundred years ago many British people were happy to be so described. Indeed, it was in defense of the empire that Britain fought the world wars of the twentieth century, and imperial troops, that is, soldiers recruited from British colonies, fought and died in large numbers in those wars, often thousands of miles from their homes.

So it is not surprising that Britain's cities, universities, and even churches are full of statues and other monuments commemorating people who played a significant part in building and preserving the British Empire. What is surprising, perhaps, is that these facts have only quite recently become the subject of major public controversy.

For many at Oxford, the wake-up call came in 2015, with the arrival of the "Rhodes Must Fall" movement. It had started in South Africa, where it sought, and rapidly achieved, the removal of a statue at the University of Cape Town commemorating Cecil Rhodes.

Figure 18.1. A "Rhodes Must Fall" demonstration in Oxford. *Daily Telegraph*. Photograph by © Chris J. Ratcliffe.

Rhodes, a remarkably successful British commercial and political entrepreneur, in the late nineteenth century made a great deal of money from diamond mining in South Africa and opened up large areas farther north, whose white settlers named them "Rhodesia" in his honor, to British control and exploitation. He served as Prime Minister of the Cape Colony from 1890 to 1896 and played a leading role in the events that led to the war of 1899, in which Britain defeated the Boers (descendants of Dutch settlers) and brought the whole of South Africa into the British Empire.

Rhodes had been educated at Oriel College, Oxford, and in his will he left the college what was then the very large sum of £100,000. Forty thousand of this was to finance the construction of a new building on Oxford's High Street; the rest was to support the endowment of Fellowships and other college expenses. The building, completed in 1911, was decorated with a number of statues, including one of Rhodes.

No notice on the outside of that building tells you what it is or who it belongs to. I must have passed by it quite a few hundred times, often wondering what it was and who was the grandiose figure, well above eye level, that forms the centerpiece of its façade. (I could easily have found out, but my curiosity was too weak. I always forgot to ask.) Such is the Rhodes whose fall, or removal, the movement in Oxford has been demanding.

The bulk of Rhodes's fortune was willed to the establishment of the Rhodes Trust and its program of scholarships for students from Germany, the United States, and the then British colonies. Rhodes expected the trustees to adapt his plans to respond effectively to changing circumstances, and over the decades they have done so. Soon after his death, they created several more scholarships for Canada. Later changes included twice abolishing, and twice re-creating, the German scholarships, and opening up the scholarships to women.

In 2003, to mark the centenary of the Rhodes Scholarships and to continue the Rhodes Trust's historic commitment to leadership development for Africa, it joined in creating the Mandela Rhodes Foundation, which Nelson Mandela described as "a chance to close the circle of history."

Yet, ironically, it was a black South African Rhodes scholar, Ntokozo Qwabe, who brought the Rhodes Must Fall movement to Oxford. When reproached with hypocrisy and urged to give his scholarship back, he replied, "I'm no beneficiary of Rhodes. I'm a beneficiary of the resources and labour of my people which Rhodes pillaged and slaved."

At first, Oriel College, caught on the back foot, announced that it was embarking on a six-month consultation exercise on what to do with the statue. But that was brought to a swift end by the new Vice-Chancellor of the university, Louise Richardson, who acted decisively in her first days in office in January 2016—and by the reaction of Oriel's alumni. It was widely reported that many of the latter were threatening to stop supporting the college financially if Rhodes was removed—not because they endorsed Rhodes's behavior or views, but from concern that if the college could dishonor one benefactor in this manner, their own donations might be similarly treated at some future date.

In Oxford, then, the Rhodes Must Fall movement did not achieve its immediate objective. And it is perhaps worth mentioning that even in South Africa, its impact outside university campuses seems so far to be limited. One of the main thoroughfares in Cape Town is still called Rhodes Drive; the monumental statue of Rhodes, pointing north with the words "your hinterland is there," still towers over the Company's Garden, alongside the South African parliament;

and the cottage where he lived and died, in the seaside suburb of Muizenberg, still houses a museum devoted to his life and work.

But the attempt to remove the statue from Oxford High Street certainly had an impact on the university, and on Britain more widely. Oxford's Chancellor, Chris Patten, perhaps unwisely equated the movement with efforts to abridge freedom of expression on British and American campuses, suggesting that "if people at a university are not prepared to demonstrate the sort of generosity of spirit which Nelson Mandela showed towards Rhodes and towards history, if they are not prepared to embrace all those values which are contained in the most important book for any undergraduate, Karl Popper's *Open Society,* if they are not prepared to embrace those issues then maybe they should think about being educated elsewhere."

This remark served to inflame the debate more than it calmed it, even though Lord Patten went on to express the hope that the students "will embrace those issues and engage in debate"—which, broadly speaking, is what has happened. Rhodes remains on his plinth in the High Street, and I recently heard one of the Rhodes Must Fall movement's sympathizers acknowledge that the group had effectively "collapsed." (He later amended this to "imploded.")

THE RHODES MUST FALL MOVEMENT received extensive coverage in the national press, much of it in the form of scathing denunciation. One journalist, Harry Mount, began his article in the *Evening Standard* by recalling that when a student at Oxford, he had studied for his finals in the magnificent Codrington Library at All Souls, watched over by the statue (in Roman costume) of its eponymous founder, Christopher Codrington III, member of a leading slave-owning family that made its fortune from Caribbean sugar plantations.

"My delightful surroundings," Mount wrote, "were paid for with slave money. Still, no self-important Oxford undergraduates have yet demanded that Codrington's statue and his peerless library be torn down." Codrington, he thought, unlike Rhodes, was "just too far back in history"—he died in 1710—"to make the fashionable list of modern hate figures".

It is true that Codrington's statue and library have not, as yet, become major targets of student or public hostility. But that probably has less to do with Codrington being "far back in time" than with the fact that All Souls has no students of its own (it is essentially an institute of advanced study and research), and that the statue is not on a public street but inside the library, access to which is fairly strictly controlled. In March 2016 when the Rhodes Must Fall campaign staged a march from Oriel College to Rhodes House (headquarters of the Rhodes Trust), passing through Radcliffe Square, onto which the library abuts, All Souls firmly bolted its gate on that side for the whole day. Fellows were asked to refer any media inquiries to the university press office, for which the Warden supplied a standard response: "The Codrington Library is for students and researchers. Its name and its statues record and reflect facts of history which—as with the history of slavery itself—cannot be changed."

Three months later, one member of Rhodes Must Fall staged a solo demonstration, standing shirtless outside the front gate of All Souls with a chain round his neck and the words "All Slaves College" painted in red on his chest (plate 7). Beyond that, nothing untoward has so far occurred. But the Common Ground movement, which came into existence in 2017, has called for the library to be renamed and for Codrington's statue to be moved to a museum, to avoid "glorifying" him.

Meanwhile, All Souls has taken a number of measures that could be considered preventive, while others are still under consideration. In October 2016, on the initiative of two of its younger Fellows—one a lawyer and former Rhodes scholar, the other a historian of French colonialism—the college held an excellent one-day conference, "Addressing the History of Slavery: The Case of Christopher Codrington," whose concluding panel, entitled "What Is to Be Done?," included memorable contributions from a representative of the Rhodes Must Fall movement and from Michelle Codrington, a black teacher based in Oxford whose name almost certainly indicates that her forebears worked as slaves on the Codrington estates.

Since then, All Souls has agreed to launch an annual scholarship scheme, funding graduates from Caribbean countries to study at other Oxford colleges, as well as making a gift of £100,000, spread over five years, to Codrington College, a theological college in Barbados founded by the same Christopher Codrington, and therefore in some sense a sister institution to All Souls. (Its current principal, Dr. Michael Clarke, attended the 2016 conference and spoke on the panel "The World of Christopher Codrington.")

Also, a cardboard notice leaning against the back of the statue in the library gives a rather fuller and more balanced account of Codrington's career and opinions than the triumphalist Latin epitaph penned by Joseph Addison and carved into the pedestal. And in March 2018 a stone memorial tablet was erected by the entrance to the library—accessible and visible from the square during working hours—with the inscription "In memory of those who worked in slavery on the Codrington Plantations in the West Indies."

Few Fellows of the college share Common Ground's desire to re-name the library, or its view that the statue could be "understood in its colonial context" only if relocated "to somewhere like a museum." But many of them, myself included, feel that they owe something to the people of the Caribbean or to those of Afro-Caribbean descent, and are looking for a way to pay that debt that would be more than symbolic—something that would bring the life of the Caribbean into the college's core activities and academic community. One suggestion is an annual visiting professorship; another, a more permanent research fellowship in Caribbean studies.

Meanwhile, Oxford has become embroiled in a new historical storm.

AT THE CENTER OF IT IS NIGEL BIGGAR, Regius Professor of Moral and Pastoral Theology and canon of Christ Church Cathedral. He drew attention to himself in December 2015 with an article in *The Times* at the height of the Rhodes Must Fall row, defending Cecil Rhodes's reputation, and followed it up with a longer version in the magazine *Standpoint*. The articles, especially the second one, gave a reasonably balanced and careful analysis of the posthumous accusations brought against Rhodes and the extent to which they are supported by the facts.

At the end of 2017, however, Biggar returned to the charge, and on a much broader front. On November 30, he published an article in *The Times* entitled "Don't Feel Guilty about Our Colonial History," picking up on a controversy already raging in American academia about a pro-colonial article in the *Third World Quarterly* by Bruce Gilley, a political scientist at Portland State University, an article that was withdrawn, most regrettably, after the editor "received serious and credible threats of personal violence." Biggar concluded that "Bruce Gilley's case for colonialism calls for us British to moderate our post-imperial guilt."

Not mentioned in Biggar's article was the McDonald Centre for Theology, Ethics, and Public Life, of which he is the director; nor its "five-year interdisciplinary project," "Ethics and Empire." This project, according to the announcement on the center's website, aims to "gather colleagues from Classics, Oriental Studies, History, Political Thought, and Theology in a series of workshops to measure apologias and critiques of empire against historical data from antiquity to modernity across the globe." While this might seem an unexceptionable, indeed laudable objective, the announcement goes on to adopt a distinctly polemical tone, saying that the project "begs to differ" with an alleged consensus, stretching across "most reaches of contemporary academic discourse," according to which, "by definition, 'empire' is imperialist, imperialism is wicked, and empire is therefore unethical." It lists three purposes of the project: "to trawl the history of ethical critiques of 'empire'"; "to test the critiques against the historical facts of empire"; and thereby "to garner possible ethical resources for contemporary deployment."

What exactly is meant by "ethical resources" or, indeed, "deployment" is not clear, but the announcement mentions three sets of "ethical questions of urgent public importance" that "the history of empire can illuminate." First there would be debates about "the moral responsibility of global powers to defend and promote 'humane' values and to maintain or impose peace in faraway parts of the world"—about which, it is suggested, "contemporary discussion is shaped, and sometimes distorted, by assumptions about 'empire' and 'imperialism.'" Next would come discussions of the "social, legal and political tensions generated by the co-existence in a single polity of significantly different cultures"—for the handling of which, it is suggested, reflection on the experience of multinational and multicultural empires may be a source of wisdom. Finally, the project would examine claims by "the descendants of the subjects of empire" for "restitution or compensation for alleged imperial crimes." And the announcement adds that Biggar intends to use the project's results "to develop a nuanced and historically intelligent Christian ethic of empire" and thereby "to enable a morally sophisticated negotiation of contemporary issues such as military intervention for humanitarian purposes in culturally foreign states, the cohesion of multicultural societies, and settling imperial pasts."

The project, according to the announcement, "will run for five years from 1 June 2017 to 31 August 2022." Its first colloquium, "Ethics and Empire: The Ancient Period," took place on 6–7 July 2017. The announcement is undated and, despite its use of the future tense, seems to have been posted shortly after the appearance of Biggar's article in *The Times* in November 2017. Certainly, it was only then that the announcement attracted wide attention, and during December a veritable storm of academic opprobrium broke over Biggar's head.

On the 19th of that month, an open letter appeared, signed by fifty-eight Oxford academics describing themselves as "scholars who work on histories of empire and colonialism and their after-effects, broadly understood." Only about half the signatories identified themselves as historians, but they included some well-known and respected ones—the prime instigator being, apparently, Professor James McDougall, author of widely praised books on Algerian history.

After proclaiming that "we teach our students to think seriously and critically about those histories and their contemporary legacies," the signatories stated that they were writing "to express [their] opposition to the public stance recently taken on these questions by Nigel Biggar . . . and the agenda pursued in his recently announced project entitled 'Ethics and Empire.'" Their professed concern was that Biggar's views "risk being misconstrued as representative of Oxford scholarship," and that they tended to reinforce, particularly among students, "a pervasive sense that contemporary inequalities in access to and experience at our university are underpinned by a complacent, even celebratory, attitude towards its imperial past." The signatories therefore felt obliged "to express [their] firm rejection" of these views.

The scholars went on to make some valid points about the contradictions and fallacies inherent in Biggar's approach, but fell into the trap of emulating his polemical tone. They concluded, rather grandly, by announcing, "Neither we, nor Oxford's students in modern history will be engaging with the 'Ethics and Empire' programme, since it consists of closed, invitation-only seminars. Instead, we want students and the wider public to know that the ideas and aims of that project are not those of most scholars working on these subjects in Oxford, whether in the history faculty or elsewhere." It was not clear whether this was a complaint that they had not (yet) been invited to the seminars or—more probably—a declaration of intent to boycott them even if invited. Similarly, the statement that students would follow suit could be simply a prediction, but sounded unpleasantly as though these teachers intended to forbid their students to attend.

Altogether, the position of the letter's authors is almost as opaque and confused as that of Biggar. Their statement that "there is no sense in which neutral 'historical data', from any historical context, can simply be used to 'measure' the ethical appropriateness of either critiques of or apologia for empire" seems very sweeping and amounts almost to an abdication of the right of historians to make ethical judgments of any sort—a self-denying ordinance that, it seems fairly clear, none of the signatories themselves could really live up to.

The authors prefaced their remarks with the statement that "Professor Biggar has every right to hold and to express whatever views he chooses or finds compelling, and to conduct whatever research he chooses in the way he feels appropriate." But their intervention was nonetheless predictably denounced, in many quarters, as a threat to academic freedom. Indeed, Trevor Phillips, one of Britain's leading black commentators and a former head of the Council for Racial Equality, accused them of using "an attack line of which Joseph Stalin would have been proud."

Even so, their lead was followed two days later by 193 self-styled "scholars of empire" from other universities, many of them in America, who issued a "collective statement" registering their "surprise and concern at the recently-announced 'Ethics and Empire' project" and calling on Oxford "to clarify the nature of its support for the project, the source of its funding, the research protocols that will be put in place to ensure that its outputs are subject to due peer scrutiny, and what measures will be taken to safeguard principles of equality, inclusivity and diversity".

To the question about the funding for the project, there has not been a direct answer, but the McDonald Centre "is generously supported by the McDonald Agape Foundation," founded and chaired by Alonzo L. McDonald, an American businessman, and based in Birmingham, Michigan. The purpose of this foundation (advertised in block capitals at the top of its website) is "ENCOURAGING DISTINGUISHED SCHOLARS FOR CHRIST." One of its directors, and also a member of the McDonald Centre's advisory council, is the British politician Jonathan Aitken, a former Conservative Member of Parliament—and Cabinet minister—who was convicted of perjury in 1999 and became a born-again Christian while in prison. (McDonald himself, according to his foundation's website, "converted to Catholicism aged 79.")

Part of the problem, clearly, is that Professor Biggar, a theologian and ethicist, waded into the historians' territory. In fact, when his project was first announced, it had a co-leader, Professor John Darwin, who is indeed a respected historian of empire, based at Nuffield College. But Darwin did not make any public statement in the project's defense. Instead, soon after the controversy erupted, he resigned for "personal reasons," which Biggar claimed had nothing to do with the project—but again, Darwin has not confirmed this.

Similarly, the project includes, according to its website, "a core group of researchers" who "will attend each workshop." In the original announcement, three of these were ethicists—two from Princeton, one from the University of Virginia—and the fourth was a colleague of Biggar's at Christ Church who specializes in early modern intellectual history, Professor Sarah Mortimer—no relation of mine, as far as I know. But her name disappeared from the website, leaving the three American ethicists on their own. It is hard to resist the conclusion that while many Oxford historians would not wish to associate themselves with the public attacks on Biggar, even those initially predisposed to join his project were gravely embarrassed by the polemical way he presented it, and the more or less political agenda he intends it to serve.

On the specific question of empire, it seems incontrovertible that all historical empires involved plenty of pretty hideous exploitation and extreme brutality, extending in many cases to genocide, even if eventually they also did some good; and that attempts to categorize this or that empire as "good" or "bad" belong not to serious history but to the school of *1066 and All That.*

But that surely doesn't absolve us from making moral judgments, albeit sometimes nuanced ones, about the actions of individuals. And we still need to think about what messages we convey about our-selves when great institutions or buildings carry either the names of those individuals or statues apparently perpetuating their status as heroes. In most cases, I favor providing more context rather than removing or renaming, but we need only think of such examples as Hitler, Stalin, or Saddam Hussein to realize that there is no simple, one-size-fits-all answer to these questions. They need to be consid-ered carefully on their merits, as coolly and rationally as possible.

There is also a broader point to be made about our relationship with the past.

"The past is a foreign country," L. P. Hartley famously wrote. "They do things differently there." And obviously it is true that dif-ferent norms and ethical standards of behavior prevailed in past so-cieties, just as they do in different cultures in the world today. But whereas "cultural relativism" is generally frowned on in the spatial dimension—we recoil, for instance, from any suggestion that female genital mutilation should be tolerated wherever it forms part of a local culture—we tend to embrace it in the temporal dimension, dismissing with equal vigor any suggestion that people in the past, or their actions, should be judged by "today's standards."

To understand this apparent paradox, one must look at the con-text. In the spatial dimension, we are asserting the universal validity of our own values. In the temporal one, we are defending our own culture and tradition against what we see as attempts to besmirch or demolish it.

Hence, one of the most frequent responses when someone pro-poses to remove a statue or rename a building that commemorates a historic figure is to say, "You can't change the past" or "You can't rewrite history." But historians quickly point out that those two state-ments are not identical. It is true that you cannot change the past, but you can rewrite history: that is precisely what historians do, all the time. History is not the past; it is the account of the past that we learn, and teach, in the present.

Historians strive for objectivity and, I hope, are honest in presenting the past as they know and understand it, rather than deliberately twisting it to serve present purposes. As far as possible, they seek to clear away fiction and discover genuine facts. But there are an infinite number of such facts, and the historian's task is not to try to list them all. Rather, she must select those that appear to her significant, worth drawing attention to.

Whose attention? That of her contemporaries, of course. So history is constantly being rewritten as each succeeding age seeks to understand and evaluate the past in the light of its own beliefs, values, and preoccupations. That process is inevitably subjective, and inevitably involves constant change, constant rewriting. Most of the controversial statues were erected, and buildings named, not in the lifetimes of those they commemorate, but at a later date, by people who wished to make a political point for their own time. By making a statement about history, they were also making one about themselves—their values and their priorities. And we, today, have to decide whether we wish to associate ourselves with that statement or to say something different, something that will be better understood by, and less hurtful to, some of our contemporaries.

Having tried to be a historian, I am not in favor of obscuring the past or of destroying the evidence of what people in past generations said and thought. But in the way we arrange our public spaces today, and the names by which we designate our great buildings and institutions, I think we owe it to ourselves, to our contemporaries, and perhaps even to future generations to make it clear where we stand.

Spring Semester 2018

Plate 1. William Powell Frith, *A Private View at the Royal Academy, 1881* (1883). Detail showing Oscar Wilde (see chapter 8). Royal Academy of Arts, London. Wikimedia Commons.

Plate 2. *Daisy* wallpaper pattern, designed by William Morris, 1862 (see chapter 9). E. 442-1919, Victoria and Albert Museum.

Plate 3. *Compton* wallpaper pattern, designed by William Morris, 1896 (see chapter 9). E. 607-1919, Victoria and Albert Museum.

Plate 4. Rene Magritte, *Le Viol* (*The Rape*), 1934 (see chapter 13). 1976-06 DJ, Menil Collection, Houston. © 2019 C. Herscovici / Artists Rights Society (ARS), New York.

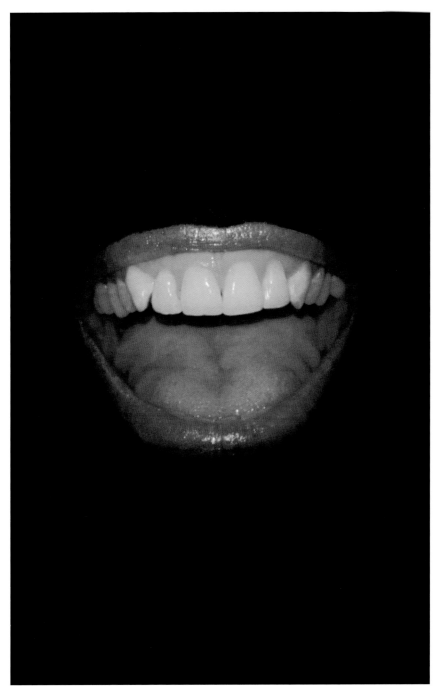

Plate 5. Lisa Dwan as Mouth in Samuel Beckett's *Not I* (see chapter 13).

Plate 6. Dianne Wiest as Winnie in Samuel Beckett's *Happy Days*, 2019 (see chapter 13). Center Theatre Group, Mark Taper Forum, Los Angeles. Photograph by © Craig Schwartz.

Plate 7. Oluwafemi Nylander with "All Slaves College" painted on his chest, protesting outside the Codrington Library, All Souls College, Oxford (see chapter 18). *Cherwell*, 20 June 2016.

Plate 8. Jacob Rees-Mogg, MP, at the funeral of Margaret Thatcher, 17 April 2013 (see chapter 24). © Colin McPherson. Corbis Historical, Getty Images.

Viceroy Curzon in procession to Sanchi Tope, Madya Pradesh, during his first tour
of India, November 1899. Photograph by Lala Deen Dayal.

19

The Social History of the Raj

MAX HASTINGS

In *The Lion and the Eagle* (2018), Kathleen Burk's recent book comparing the British and U.S. imperial experiences, she notes that few American public servants chose to make their lives in their nation's overseas possessions or client states. Most preferred to serve out their appointed terms in faraway places and then return thankfully home. Their British counterparts, by contrast, often remained for decades or even lifetimes in the colonies, and above all in India, "the jewel in the crown."

In 1971, I made a film for BBC TV in Simla, the summer capital of the Raj, about a cluster of elderly English ladies who had "stayed on." Their houses were full of chintz armchairs and faded sepia images of a long-vanished Albion, together with reverential portraits of our dear Queen. They knew that their mustily remembered pasts and illusions would face shipwreck if they encountered the reality of late-twentieth-century Britain. Thus, they lingered in the Himalayan foothills until death did them part.

The grandest of them, Mrs. Hermione Montague, who lived with an English companion and twenty-three dogs, spurned social contact with two sisters who occupied a modest house less than a mile away. Their father had been in trade, owning a store at the foot of the hills. He was thus classed, in Raj vernacular, as a "boxwallah"; he was not a "pukka sahib," a proper gentleman.

Encounters with such people in various corners of the world imbued me with pity for the melancholy of the circumstances of many

Figure 19.1. A British man getting a pedicure from an Indian servant, with other servants in attendance.

imperialists abroad, rather than envy of the grandeur that permitted William Hickey, for instance, an early-nineteenth-century lawyer in India, to boast a household of sixty-three servants, including eight men who waited at table, eight who worked in the stables, a coachman, three mowers, and four grooms. To us of the twenty-first century, there is a preposterousness about the manner in which a few tens of thousands of British soldiers and civilians lorded for three centuries over an ever-expanding mass of the subcontinent and its inhabitants.

In *The British in India: A Social History of the Raj* (2019), David Gilmour seems of the same opinion as he examines the processes and processions of our forefathers and their families in India through the eras of the East India Company and the high Victorian Raj, followed by slow descent toward the messy mid-twentieth-century departure. Gilmour is the author of distinguished books that include a biography of Lord Curzon, a controversial viceroy, and *The Ruling Caste,* a study of India's administrators during the Raj. *The British in India* is a companion volume of sorts, an exhaustive social history of the daily lives, manners, and mores of the men, women, and children who lived under the Union Flag in what we might characterize as Kipling country. He has studied their marriages, servants, eating and drinking habits, education, adulteries, recreations, houses, and gardens. He assembles a fascinating record that includes some happiness, much that was stoically endured, and more than a few wretched experiences and relationships.

Horace Walpole wrote in 1783, "No man ever went to the East Indies with good intentions." Many of Walpole's contemporaries sailed to the far shores, in Gilmour's words, "with the intention of either making a fortune or retrieving one they had squandered or lost in some other way. 'Shaking the pagoda tree' was a phrase much used—a pagoda in this sense denoting a gold or silver coin." If a man escaped premature death by violence or disease, which felled many, wealth seemed extraordinarily easy to attain. Thackeray's imbecilic Jos Sedley in *Vanity Fair* flourished mightily in the post of collector of Boggley Wollah.

The 1760s were deemed the most corrupt decade in the history of British India, when even the East India Company's army officers on meager salaries enriched themselves by exploiting campaign subsistence allowances. Many dreamed not of rising to field commands but of securing a paymastership, both a literal and figurative key to a treasure chest. Prize money was pretty good, too. Arthur Wellesley was granted £4,000 for his 1799 capture of Seringapatam. Lord Combermere was a military bungler who nonetheless earned £60,000 for the 1826 siege of Bharatpur. Such numbers indicate the scale of plunder swilling around India in those days, to be scooped up by greedy white hands.

Lord Cornwallis, governor-general and commander in chief from 1786 to 1793, adopted two policies with radical consequences, one malign and one benign: he decreed the exclusion of Indians from eligibility for all senior military and civil posts, thus institutionalizing a racial divide. And he insisted that officials should live on their salaries, forswearing private trading, which eventually gave the members of the Indian Civil Service (ICS) an extraordinary reputation for probity. To this was added high competence when, in 1855, entry into the ICS by competitive examination was substituted for the earlier system of patronage. For most of the last century of empire, only officials of the Sudan Political Service commanded greater prestige than those of the ICS.

Young men who went east were variously motivated. Henry White King joined the Indian Medical Service in the 1850s to escape a "harsh stepmother." Some of his contemporaries forged dynasties.

Rudyard Kipling wrote, "Certain families serve India generation after generation as dolphins follow in line across the open sea." When Alexander Wynch became governor of Madras in 1773, his five sons joined the local civil service or the Madras Army. Others sought adventure, not least through the pursuit of exotic animals. Charles Kincaid joined the ICS in 1891, fired by his father's tales of hunting orangutans in Borneo and aspiring to match his sporting exploits.

Educational and professional qualifications for appointments were arbitrary and perverse: a persistent legend held that in the midst of a 1758 voyage, a butcher aboard an East India Company ship was summarily promoted to ship's surgeon. As late as 1913, a knowledge of Latin was mandatory for entrants to the Imperial School of Forestry. The most important qualifications for success were physical and emotional hardiness and a capacity for sustained hard work, together with indifference to the plight of the subject Indian peoples and the filth and poverty of their country, conspicuous everywhere except in the palaces of maharajahs and the residences of superior Britons.

In 1901 there were just 155,000 British soldiers and civilians of all ages and both sexes in India. Many were stationed in areas so remote that they struggled to muster four for bridge or tennis. Consider the plight of an Englishwoman who met a district officer on home leave who was desperate to secure a wife before his return, to assuage the loneliness of his existence in some remote station. Acceptance of a hasty proposal of marriage meant almost instant separation from family and friends, a brief honeymoon, and a long sea voyage. The traveling continued by stifling train and perhaps bumping bullock carts. A memsahib eventually started a new life, in Gilmour's words, in "a barely furnished bungalow with many insects and little sanitation, a place where she would have found life very limited and boring had she not been shortly to give birth to her first child in extremely primitive conditions."

He describes the shortcomings of hearth and home in most parts of India. Beds, tables, and wardrobes fared best if their legs were wrapped in strips of cloth that had been wrung out in paraffin and then set in old tins containing an inch of water, to fend off ants. Gallant attempts to create English lookalike gardens usually foundered in the heat. The coziness of interiors was not enhanced by many husbands' insistence on adorning the walls of the family bungalow with the heads of animals they had slaughtered.

It was a struggle to keep a legion of servants up to the mark, especially the "punkah wallah," who was supposed to pull a string

Figure 19.2. A British woman being carried in a sedan chair, c. 1890s.

all night to move the punkah—a strip of cloth on a wooden frame suspended from the ceiling—and sustain a breeze over the sahib's bed. H. M. Kisch wrote testily home in the 1860s: "You can have no idea of the irritation caused in a tropical climate by a sleepy punkah wallah at night . . . you become food for mosquitoes on your face and sandflies on your feet, while the heat of the climate and wrath at the punkah wallah irritate you beyond endurance."

Yet if some servants failed to satisfy their masters and mistresses, others became beloved members of the family, the ayah, or children's nanny, being often foremost among these. In Kipling's boyhood, after an outing his ayah had to remind him to resume speaking English back at home. In countless families in which emotional deprivation was etched into the experience of the young, Gilmour notes, many in adulthood remembered their ayah "as a second mother, perhaps more loveable than their real mother, an always reassuring figure who had represented warmth and security."

He describes the diet on which officials subsisted, a parody of that back home, with horrid little eggs from scrawny chickens and bacon that bore scant resemblance to any side cut from a Black Berkshire. Most sahibs persisted in training Indian cooks to produce the nearest they could contrive to the daily bill of fare in Bournemouth or Billericay, in places where the mercury passed 100 degrees Fahrenheit. Having myself eaten stodgy bread-and-butter pudding at Clarke's Hotel in Simla, I can testify to the sublime inappropriateness of such dishes, yet the British clung to them as doggedly as to the passes of the North-West Frontier.

Social life was grimly formal, guided by rules of precedence and a conviction that not to dress for dinner was to commit that worst of crimes: lower British prestige in the eyes of the Indians. In a philistine society lacking access to art galleries, opera, or ballet, and enjoying only amateur theater, relatively few people read books. Dinner parties were dominated by "diary conversation"—what we did yesterday, what we would do tomorrow, prospects for promotion. Herbert Gee, a newcomer to India—a "griffin," as such men were known—lamented, "We almost entirely lose sight of the aesthetic and fine arts side of existence." Boredom and the chronic weariness brought on by hard work in a merciless climate caused tempers to run short.

"The club," such as almost every "station" boasted, was the focus of social life, with its whist, "burra pegs"—large drinks—and occasional dances. British India was overwhelmingly administered by members of the middle class, with aristocrats venturing east only to fill the highest offices, yet snobberies were sustained with morbid punctiliousness. Many women from modest suburban backgrounds at home put on airs, treating perceived British inferiors almost as ungenerously as the large domestic staff to which they were ill accustomed. A political officer resigned from his club when he heard that it proposed to admit such lowlifes as engineers and forest officers. A member of the Bengal Pilot Service was blackballed for undisclosed reasons following his marriage: it was assumed that his new wife had been categorized as either Anglo-Indian—"country-bred"—or merely common.

For India-born children, England—though always spoken of as "home"—was a dim, mysterious place until they saw it for the first time, perhaps at age six or seven. Then there was a culture shock. The actor Spike Milligan's first impression of a British dock on a winter morning was of "terrible noise, and everything so cold and grey": he yearned to return to Rangoon, even though his family life there had been relatively humble. Most children for years retained a stronger sense of belonging to India than to England, where the only merit of multistory houses—in contrast to India's bungalow culture—was that they could slide down the banisters.

THE LOVE AND SEX LIVES OF Gilmour's subjects fill many pages, partly because these loomed large in their enthusiasms and frustrations, and also because the anecdotage makes irresistible reading. Richard Wellesley, brother of the future Duke of Wellington and in 1798 governor-general in Calcutta, wrote despairing letters to his wife, Hyacinthe, describing his unfulfilled needs, to which even tiger hunting and pig sticking did not seem adequate alternatives: "This climate excites one sexually most terribly." She, who declined to join him, responded by figuratively urging him to take a cold bath and restrain his beastly urges. Each round of their unhappy correspondence took ten months to sail to England and back, and before many exchanges had taken place, Wellesley resorted to the inevitable local mistress.

More than a few women who accepted marriage to British officials lived to regret it. Edyth Gubbins loved Mughal architecture and the music of Wagner but found herself living with an army captain who regarded the Taj Mahal with contempt and cared only for massacring wildlife. Alexandra Campbell, daughter of an army officer, had five children by a railway engineer whom she had married in 1890, before tiring of his enthusiasm for trains. She abandoned him without notice or explanation, retiring to live with her parents in Darjeeling until he drank himself to death and she was free to remarry.

John Hewett was long separated from his wife, but when he was appointed lieutenant-governor of the North-Western Provinces in 1907, she abruptly returned to enjoy the glories of being hailed as "her ladyship." The couple occupied separate wings of Government House in Nainital, a town in the Himalayan foothills, and seldom addressed each other.

Especially at the lower end of the social scale, wives whose husbands died young frequently remarried as swiftly as opportunity occurred, to secure a means of subsistence. When a gunner died of fever in the 1830s, an officer's wife recorded that the widow was importuned by three suitors before the body was cold, and remarried within a week, a process subsequently repeated twice more.

Perhaps the most exotic record of multiple alliances was set by Frances Croke, born in India in 1728. The daughter of a civil servant, she first married at fifteen and then did so again at twenty following her husband's death. This bridegroom survived the wedding

only by twelve days, freeing her to return to England with William
Watts, by whom she had four children. When he expired, in 1764,
she returned to India and married a chaplain sixteen years younger
than her, of whom she swiftly tired. He was persuaded to sail for
England by the award of a generous pension, conditional on his absence. Thereafter she lived as a popular Calcutta hostess until her
death in 1812, the year that her grandson Lord Liverpool became
Britain's Prime Minister.

Many British settlers married or cohabited with Indian women,
defying the disapproval of the memsahibs. In 1937 a visitor to the
Himalayan foothills found that most of the area's white planters had
wed local women. The manager of a Darjeeling tea garden tied the
knot with Jeti, one of his pickers, though she was forbidden to set
foot in the local planters' club. The anthropologist Verrier Elwin
was said to have "married his fieldwork," wedding successively two
tribal women and becoming recognized as an academic expert on
the region's sexual habits.

Priapic British men grumbled that the lack of privacy imposed by
the constant presence of servants was an impediment to adultery.
The rules of the Raj and indeed of the entire empire sustained an
obsession with keeping up appearances in front of the "natives," so
when Miles Smeeton in 1936 fell in love with the wife of his commanding officer, he was obliged to leave the regiment. The woman
in the case was "an adventurous lady called Beryl, who had once
walked across China to Burma," dismissing warnings of the threat
of rape and bandits: "Oh, I shan't worry about that. I'd far prefer
dishonour to death."

Amid the desperation of the junior ranks of the ruling caste for
sexual relationships, in the first eighteen years of the nineteenth
century 380 girls from a Calcutta orphan school, mostly Eurasian
(Anglo-Indian), married British men. The offspring of such alliances were much mocked for their supposed "chee-chee" accents
and dusky hue, causing many to seek to disguise their mixed heritage. The Gurkha officer John Masters, a splendid mid-twentieth-
century author of many novels about India, discovered only late in
life that he had an Indian forebear—a family concubine.

Teenage classmates refused to dance with the pretty Anglo-
Indian girl "Queenie" Thompson, whose professions of Tasmanian
origins fooled no one. Especially bitchy contemporaries asserted
that she "used to whitewash herself from the waist up." All this
ceased to matter, however, when she emerged into a new life across
the world with the name Merle Oberon. So did another Eurasian,
Vivien Hartley, whose mother was said to be partly Parsi. She too

enjoyed triumphant reinvention: as Vivien Leigh, belle of the big-screen Confederacy.

IN GILMOUR'S CONCLUDING CHAPTER, he asserts his view of his own role as a chronicler in the spirit of Christopher Isherwood exploring 1930s Berlin: "a camera with its shutter open." He declines to offer "a balance sheet to weigh indigo planters who tyrannized Indian peasants against doctors who saved Indian lives," or famine workers and canal builders against brutal soldiery. He acknowledges that imperialism usually means the conquest and exploitation of one people by another, involves deaths and injustices, but that does not mean that it did nothing positive during its 3,000-year history. Nor does it mean that all imperialists were bad people. Complexity of motive is a theme permeating this book.

Gilmour has been traveling and researching in India for decades. He offers an observation about its people that often impresses modern British visitors: most educated Indians are astonishingly indulgent toward the imperial heritage, acknowledging the rule of law, the professional civil service, the universities, and an impartial judiciary as contributions to be set in the balance against the Raj's indisputable racism, cultural condescension, exploitation, and dreadful periodic cruelties.

It is refreshing to see Gilmour reassert truths that should be obvious, but are no longer held to be so, about the mixed legacy of empire in general and the Raj in particular. British officials in India were often insensitive to local customs and susceptibilities, as well as contemptuous of local religions, but, Gilmour asks, "Was it really wrong of them to aspire to change some of those customs—to campaign against female infanticide, to abolish the burning alive of widows, to prevent Naga tribesmen from scalping the women and children of other tribes?"

Gilmour's three important works on India make manifest his deep affection for, as well as knowledge of, the subcontinent. If his latest book has any flaw, it is that it paints so grisly a portrait of the social lives of servants of the Raj that it perhaps underplays the romance many discovered during long careers in India—the grip that that stupendous country exercised upon them. On the whole, it probably suited men better than women because their work enabled them to engage and commit, as few wives could, though until recent times the same might be said of women's lives in Britain. But everyone who has read British memoirs of India composed between the eighteenth and late twentieth centuries knows how many are dominated by passionate memories of their writers' experiences there.

Most people's lives in most places and at most periods of history are damnably dull. This is especially true for the provincial middle class, who provided a large majority of the people who ran the Raj. In India, unless their marriages were loveless or their professional circumstances unusually sterile, the British ruling caste encountered people and places a thousand times more memorable than their counterparts at home, who spent lifetimes commuting from terraced villas to dreary offices.

Fall Semester 2018

A version of this lecture appeared in the *New York Review of Books,* 4 April 2019.

David Lloyd George, Georges Clemenceau, and Woodrow Wilson, Paris, January 1919. Bettmann Archive / Getty Images.

20

Warnings from Versailles, 1919

MARGARET MACMILLAN

We often recall the First World War and the two decades that followed as a grim chapter of history, the prelude to an even costlier and more destructive war from 1939 to 1945. We remember terrible losses—the nine million or more dead in battle, the civilians who died of preventable disease or starvation, the ghastly influenza epidemic that, in the dying days of the war and the shaky first moments of peace, may have carried off as many as fifty million around the world. We think of a Europe that once led the world in wealth, innovation, and political power, only to emerge from the war diminished, its Russian and Austro-Hungarian empires in tatters, Bolshevism and ethnic nationalism threatening more upheaval and misery.

Yet when the Allies gathered at the Paris Peace Conference in Versailles one hundred years ago, from January to June 1919, the time was also one of hope. The Allied leaders promised their own peoples a better world in recompense for all they had suffered, and President Woodrow Wilson made of those promises a crusade for humankind: a war to end all wars, a world safe for democracy. Wilson's League of Nations was meant to create an international community of democratic nations. By providing collective security for one another, they would not only end aggression but also build a fairer and more prosperous world. These ideas drew support around the globe—from Europe, where Wilson was greeted as a savior, to the West's colonies, and even in struggling nations such as China.

But the world was to discover that making peace endure was a matter not just of hopes and ideas but also of will, determination, and persistence. Leaders need to negotiate as well as to inspire; to be capable of seeing past short-term political gains; and to balance the interests of their nations against those of the international community. For want of such leadership, among other things, the promise of 1918 soon turned into the disillusionment, division, and aggression of the 1930s.

This outcome was not foreordained at Versailles. Although some of the decisions made there certainly fueled populist demagoguery and inspired dreams of revenge, the calamity of the Second World War owed as much to the failure of the democracies' leaders in the interwar decades to deal with rule-breaking dictators such as Mussolini, Hitler, and the Japanese militarists. A century later, similar forces—ethnic nationalism, eroding international norms and cooperation, and vindictive chauvinism—and authoritarian leaders willing to use them are again appearing. The past is an imperfect teacher, its messages often obscure or ambiguous, but it offers both guidance and warning.

"Making peace is harder than waging war," Prime Minister Georges Clemenceau reflected in 1919 as the victorious powers drew up peace terms, finalized the shape of the new League of Nations, and tried to rebuild Europe and the global order.

For Clemenceau and his colleagues, among them Wilson and David Lloyd George, the British Prime Minister, the prospect was particularly daunting. Europe was not tired of war and revolution, as it had been in 1815, when negotiators met in Vienna to wind up the Napoleonic Wars. Nor had aggressor nations been utterly defeated and occupied, as they would be in 1945. Rather, leaders in 1919 confronted a world in turmoil. Fighting continued throughout much of eastern Europe, the Caucasus, and the Middle East. Russia's Bolshevik Revolution of 1917 had apparently set off a series of unstoppable revolutionary waves that threatened to overwhelm even the victors' societies.

The war had damaged or destroyed old political and social structures, particularly in Central Europe, leaving formerly stable and prosperous peoples adrift, desperate for someone or something to restore their status and a form of order. Ethnic nationalists seized the opportunity to build new countries, but these states were often hostile to one another and oppressive to their own minorities. Inevitably, too, old and new rivalries came to the surface as leaders in Paris maneuvered to promote the interests of their nations.

Wilson and company also had to deal with a phenomenon that their forerunners at the Congress of Vienna had never had to consider: public opinion. The publics in Allied countries took an intense interest in what was happening in Paris, but what they wanted was contradictory: a better world matching the Wilsonian vision, on the one hand, and retribution on the other.

Many Europeans felt that someone must be made to pay for the war. In France and Belgium, which Germany had invaded on the flimsiest of pretexts, the countryside lay in ruins, with towns, mines, railways, and factories destroyed. Across the border, Germany was unscathed because little of the war had been fought there. The British had lent vast sums to their allies (their Russian debts were beyond hope of recovery), had borrowed heavily from the Americans, and wanted recompense.

John Maynard Keynes, not yet the world-renowned economist he was to become, suggested that the Americans write off the money the British owed them so as to reduce the need to extract reparations from the defeated, and then concentrate on getting Europe's economy going again. The Americans, Wilson included, rejected the proposal with self-righteous horror. And so the Allied statesmen drew up a reparations bill that they knew was more than the defeated could ever pay. Austria and Hungary were impoverished remnants of the once vast Habsburg Empire, Bulgaria was broke, and the Ottoman Empire was on the verge of disintegrating. That left only Germany capable of meeting the reparations bill.

The circumstances of Germany's defeat had left its citizens in no mood to pay. That feeling would grow stronger over the decade to follow. And its outcome contains a warning for our era: the feelings and expectations of both the winners and the losers, however unrealistic, matter and require careful management.

Toward the end of the war, the German High Command under Generals Erich Ludendorff and Paul von Hindenburg had effectively established a military dictatorship that kept all news from the front under wraps. The civilian government in Berlin knew as little as the public about the string of defeats the country's military suffered in the late spring and summer of 1918. When the High Command suddenly demanded that the government immediately sue for an armistice, the announcement came like a thunderbolt.

The German chancellor appealed to Wilson in a series of open letters, and the U.S. president, somewhat to the annoyance of the European Allies, took on the role of arbiter between the warring sides. In doing so, Wilson made two mistakes. First, he negotiated with Germany's civilian government rather than the High Command, allowing the generals to avoid responsibility for the war and its outcome. As time went by, the High Command and its right-wing supporters put out the false story that Germany had never lost on the battlefield: the German military could have fought on, perhaps even to victory, if the cowardly civilians had not let it down. Out of this grew the poisonous myth that Germany had been stabbed in the back by an assortment of traitors, including liberals, socialists, and Jews.

Second, Wilson's public statements that he would not support punitive indemnities or a peace of vengeance reinforced German hopes that the United States would ensure Germany's light treatment. The U.S. president's support for the revolution that overthrew Germany's old monarchy and paved the way for the parliamentary democracy of the Weimar Republic compounded this misplaced optimism. Weimar, its supporters argued, represented a new and better Germany that should not pay for the sins of the old.

The French and the other Allies, however, were less concerned with Germany's domestic politics than with its ability to resume fighting. The armistice signed in the famous railway carriage at Compiègne on 11 November 1918 reads like a surrender, not a cessation of hostilities. Germany would have to evacuate all occupied territory and hand over its heavy armaments as well as the entirety of its navy.

Even so, the extent of the military defeat was not immediately clear to the German public. Troops returning from the front marched into Berlin in December 1918, and the new socialist chancellor hailed them with the words "No enemy has overcome you." Apart from those living in the Rhineland, on the western edge of the country, Germans did not experience firsthand the shame of military occupation. As a result, many Germans, living in what a distinguished German scholar called the dreamland of the winter of 1918–19, expected the Allies' peace terms to be mild—milder, certainly, than those Germany had imposed on revolutionary Russia with the Treaty of Brest-Litovsk in March 1918. The country might even expand if Austria, newly formed out of the German-speaking territories of the vanished Austro-Hungarian Empire, decided to join its fate to Germany's.

The actual Treaty of Versailles, published in the spring of 1919, came as a shock. Public opinion from right to left was dismayed to learn that Germany would have to disarm, lose territory, and pay reparations for war damage. Resentment focused in particular on Article 231 of the treaty, in which Germany accepted responsibility for starting the war and which a young American lawyer, John Foster Dulles, had written to provide a legal basis for claiming reparations. Germans loathed the "war guilt" clause, as it came to be known, and there was little will to pay reparations.

Weimar Germany—much like Russia after the collapse of the Soviet Union—nursed a powerful and lasting sense of national humiliation. For many years, the German Foreign Office and its right-wing
supporters did their best to further undermine the legitimacy of the
Treaty of Versailles. With the help of selectively released documents,
they argued that Germany and its allies were innocent of starting
the war. Instead, Europe had somehow stumbled into disaster, so
either everyone or no one was responsible. The Allies could have
done more to challenge German views about the origins of the war
and the unfairness of the treaty. Instead, at least in the case of the
English-speaking peoples, they eventually came rather to agree with
the German narrative, and this fed into the appeasement policies of
the 1930s.

Peace would take a very different form in 1945. With memories
of the previous two decades fresh in their minds, the Allies forced
the Axis powers into unconditional surrender. Germany and Japan
were to be utterly defeated and occupied. Selected leaders would be
tried for war crimes and their societies reshaped into liberal democracies. Invasive and coercive though it was, the post–Second World
War peace generated far less resentment about unfair treatment
than did the arrangements that ended the First World War.

The terms of Versailles were not the only obstacle to a lasting
resolution of European conflicts in 1919. London and Washington
undermined the chances for peace by quickly turning their backs
on Germany and the rest of the continent.

Although never as isolationist as some have claimed, the United
States turned inward soon after the Paris Peace Conference. Congress rejected the Treaty of Versailles and, by extension, the League
of Nations. It also failed to ratify the guarantee given to France that
the United Kingdom and the United States would come to its defense if Germany attacked. Americans became all the more insular
as the calamitous Great Depression hit and their attention focused
on their domestic troubles.

America's withdrawal encouraged the British—already distracted
by troubles brewing in the empire—to renege on their commitment
to the guarantee. France, left to itself, attempted to form the new
and quarreling states in Central Europe into an anti-German alliance, but its attempts turned out to be as ill fated as the Maginot
Line in the west. One wonders how history might have unfolded
if London and Washington, instead of turning away, had built a
transatlantic alliance with a strong security commitment to France
and pushed back against Adolf Hitler's first aggressive moves, while
there was still time to stop him.

Again, the post-1945 world was different from the one that emerged in 1919. The United States, then the world's leading power, joined the United Nations and the economic institutions set up at Bretton Woods. It also committed itself to the security and reconstruction of western Europe and Japan. Congress approved these initiatives in part because President Franklin Delano Roosevelt made building the postwar order a bipartisan enterprise—unlike Wilson, who had doomed the League of Nations by alienating Republicans. Wilson's failure encouraged the isolationist strain in U.S. foreign policy; Roosevelt, followed by Harry S. Truman and Dwight D. Eisenhower, countered and contained that impulse. The specter of communism did its part by alarming even the isolationists. The establishment of the Soviet empire in eastern Europe, and Soviet rhetoric about the coming struggle against capitalism, persuaded many Americans that they faced a pressing danger that required continued engagement with allies in Europe and Asia.

Today's world is not wholly comparable to the worlds that emerged from the rubble of the two world wars. Yet as the United States once again turns inward and tends only to its immediate interests, it risks ignoring or underestimating the rise of populist dictators and aggressive powers until the hour is dangerously late. President Vladimir Putin of Russia has already violated international rules and norms, most notably in Crimea, and others—such as President Recep Tayyip Erdogan of Turkey and Chinese President Xi Jinping—seem willing to do the same. And as Washington and other democratic powers abdicate their responsibility for the world, smaller powers may abandon their hopes for a peaceful international order and instead submit to the bullies in their neighborhoods. A hundred years on, 1919 and the years that followed still stand as a somber warning.

Spring Semester 2019

A version of this lecture appeared online in *Foreign Affairs*, 8 January 2019.

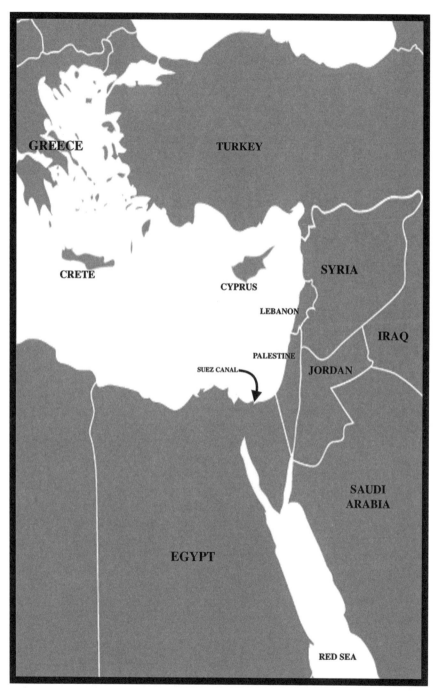

Cyprus and the eastern Mediterranean. Map by Holly McCarthy.

21

The British Defense of Cyprus, 1941

GEORGE KELLING

Unfulfilled plans for military operations can be the driest dust that blows. In reading memoirs and narratives of the buildup to the 1944 invasion of France, I have to admit that my eyes glaze over at analysis of the early but never consummated Operations Roundup, Sledgehammer, Roundhammer, and I tend to just turn the pages. These plans lying on the shelf, though they contribute little to the unfolding of events, can give insight into the state of thinking at the time they were devised. The plan for the defense of Cyprus in 1941 is such an example. It is also arguable that the plan marked a change in the tempo of the war.

In the early days of the Second World War, the situation of Cyprus was secure, tied in geopolitically with the protection of the Levant. Britain and France had a joint defense agreement for the area, with French forces predominating. Cyprus was garrisoned by a French colonial regiment under the French command in Lebanon and Syria, and the French fleet patrolled the nearby waters. So long as the British-French alliance was healthy, an invasion of Cyprus was hard to imagine.

By the spring of 1940, however, the situation had begun to deteriorate dramatically. The collapse of Norway and Denmark was prelude to the rapid fall of France and the Low Countries, with France accepting an armistice in June. The security of Cyprus was turned on its head as France and the French Levant were transformed from allies into unfriendly neutrals. The hostility and naval danger was enhanced by the British attack on the French fleet at Mers-el-Kebir, in northwestern Algeria, on 3 July 1940. The French garrison on Cyprus was withdrawn; a few of the soldiers joined the nascent Free French Forces of de Gaulle. The peril increased with the German invasion of mainland Greece, followed by a dramatic airborne assault on Crete, both marked by Luftwaffe superiority and rather ignominious British evacuations.

Thus, in a few months the island went from being a comfortable base surrounded by friendly territory to an endangered outpost surrounded by hostile powers and unfriendly neutrals. Nearby Syria and France were in at least informal cooperation with the Germans, while after the stunning success of the *Fallshirmjaeger* (German paratroopers) in Crete and Corinth, it seemed obvious that Cyprus would be the next item on Hitler's menu. At the same time, the jackals were beginning to circle the camp. Fascist Italy was notorious for its habit of picking up pieces of other campaigns, having carved out zones in Yugoslavia and Greece while attacking France on 10 June 1940, some two weeks before the capitulation. Since Italy had territories in the nearby Dodecanese, Mussolini considered himself heir to an eastern Mediterranean domain, and even supposedly neutral France was not uninvolved. The first air raid on the island was conducted by the Italian Air Force. Though it did little harm, it inaugurated a series of raids that continued for several years. On one occasion the island received attacks by German, Italian, and Vichy French aircraft.

The more dangerous threats to British sovereignty came from friends and allies. Even in abject defeat, Greece still had ambitions for the island. The Greek state had been wrested from the Turks by sheer determination through years of struggle and the death of countless patriots. What by 1940 came to be called the *Megali Idea,* or great idea, was the dream of uniting all Greek-speaking peoples under the Greek flag. The idea had added Crete and Thrace, and the dream included *enosis,* or union, with northern Epirus or southern Albania, the Dodecanese, and Cyprus. In other words, Greek policy had turned its thoughts to Cyprus even before the fall of Greece.

On 14 April, ten days before the evacuation of the Greek mainland, but when the end of the campaign was obvious, the American ambassador in Athens reported that the King had told him that he would prefer to evacuate his court to Cyprus rather than Crete. He suggested that Britain might cede an enclave in Cyprus to Greece so that he could continue to reign from Greek soil. On 3 May, the president of the Greek Council wrote to the British ambassador to Greece (who was by that time in Crete), suggesting that to encourage the Greeks in their time of crisis, the British might grant Cyprus to Greece as a personal present. According to the proposal, during the war the British would continue to administer the island under the aegis of the Greek crown, and full administration would be taken over by Greece after the peace.

Although he is rightly remembered as an unreconstructed Victorian imperialist, Winston Churchill did not reject such ideas out of hand. Even before the King's approach to the American ambassador, Churchill, perhaps wrongly considering that Greece would be subservient to British influence, cabled the British Middle East commander: "If, however, [the King] or any part of the Greek Army is forced to leave Greece every facility will be afforded to them in Cyprus."[1] The governor immediately cabled the Colonial Office that such an act would make Cyprus ungovernable and in effect mark the end of British rule on the island.

Doubts about the future of the island were not confined to the Hellenic world. The Australian Prime Minister, Robert Menzies, had been extremely critical of Churchill's conduct of the war and in particular of what he viewed as Churchill's cavalier willingness to sacrifice Australian troops in his adventures, a legacy reaching back at least as far as the Gallipoli debacle in the First World War. With the dispatch of an Australian light armored regiment to Cyprus, Menzies saw it all happening again: "It appears that intention is to hold Cyprus *at least for the time being* . . . [but] . . . no further troops can be made available for Cyprus" (emphasis added). The forecast was clear: "You will of course appreciate what this means. Another forced evacuation will . . . have serious effect on public opinion in America and elsewhere while in Australia there are certain to be serious reactions." His conclusions were logical, given his knowledge of the situation: "Cyprus should be held—and to that end should be garrisoned by a sufficiently strong force—or, if such a force is not available then the enterprise should be abandoned."[2]

The British governor of the island, William Denis Battershill, echoed Curtin's gloomy prognostication. His insights came from being the man on the spot: "Morale of the majority of Cypriots is at its lowest ebb, having sunk rapidly after Crete . . . There are many mutterings. In event of invasion we can expect little help from [the population] and some might even turn against us." He deplored the cost to those under his administration of a potential operation that he perceived as having no military benefit: "[A battle would] involve *inter alia* destruction of main towns and villages with much of life . . . We shall gain nothing in prestige, but we shall cause untold suffering to the civilian Cypriots."[3]

While Churchill maintained a stiff upper lip concerning plans for the island, there were stirrings up and down Whitehall. Opinions differed in the Foreign Office, but the trend was toward a *real-politiker* view of possession of Cyprus as part of the overall postwar strategy for defense of the Mediterranean. One example of the dozens of Foreign Office memos on the topic is perhaps typical of this view: "It is most unlikely that we shall in practice be able to maintain our sovereignty over Cyprus in the political conditions likely to succeed after the war."[4] Perhaps the minute that best revealed the Foreign Office official mind was by Reginald Bowker on 28 May 1941, as the Allies were evacuating Crete: "It is . . . possible that, *on taking Cyprus,* the Germans will declare it to be a part of Greater Greece" (emphasis added).[5]

The Colonial Office was left out of the speculation, ostensibly because of an oversight, but its objections were not decisive. The final word was in the hands of the Prime Minister. On 6 June 1941, he sent a note to the Foreign Secretary bringing the discussion to a close: "It is much better to leave all questions of territorial readjustment until after the war . . . I do not think we should cede an inch of British territory during the war." Even at this dark hour, Churchill's innate optimism shone through, though it was tempered by a healthy realism: "It does not follow that Cyprus will be immediately taken. If it is the Germans will be able . . .to give it nominally to the Greek Quisling Government while using it . . . This will not make much difference to what happens."[6]

With that decision the discussion ended, but not the crisis. The ball passed into the court of the military command, which had to plan for what was seen as an imminent assault on the island. When considering the plan for defense of Cyprus with the earlier one for the defense of England, the contrast is notable. For the latter, Churchill envisioned a defense by the entire population to contest every block and field; his "Finest Hour" speech, delivered almost exactly a year earlier, is rightly remembered as evocative of the spirit of the times. The raising of the Home Guard and stay-behind parties to wreak havoc behind German lines made it clear that a people's war was envisioned and would probably have been put into effect in case the Germans invaded.

In Cyprus, Governor Battershill and the colonial authorities realized that the Cypriots could not be relied on to assist in defense of the island. And images of French roads clogged with refugees in 1940, making military deployments all but impossible, were still vivid in the military official mind. On 23 May, the colonial administration's guidance to the population in case of invasion repeated three times "*stay where you are*" (emphasis in the original), pointing out that the enemy would machine-gun refugees from the air and that streams of those in flight would clog the roadways needed by the defense forces.[7] It made no mention of resisting the invader on the beaches or in the interior. The governor and his staff were well aware of the situation on the island and the Cypriots' outlook, as well as the experience of civilian resistance in mainland Greece and on Crete.

Some voices noted the tepid call to arms. G. O. Toit, an English resident of the colony, wrote to one of its English-language newspapers on 23 May, during the Battle of Crete: "I searched your pages for some inspiring official message to be of good cheer . . . and what do I find? Two notices . . . one promises shilling currency notes in the near future . . . the other . . . the publication of the Fifth Report of the Cyprus Commission for the Preservation of Official Monuments." His frustration was clear: "Ye Gods! When will someone arise and inspire us with the will for the preservation of Cyprus, the Empire, and our heritage of freedom? . . . Never once a flesh-and-blood personal appeal in the direct and impassioned language which Cypriots in particular expect and understand?"[8] It is hard not to sympathize with Toit, but he did not seem to light a fire under the authorities.

As Churchill reassured, the Foreign and Colonial Offices sparred, Australia carped, the governor expected an invasion, and G. O. Toit fulminated, the understaffed garrison of the island had a battle to prepare for. The German juggernaut appeared all but invincible, given what observers at the time saw as easy German victories over Denmark, Norway, the Low Countries, and France, and in recent weeks successful assaults on continental Greece and Crete, the last three engagements resulting in ignominious and costly British evacuations. It appeared that the German airborne assault on Crete could be easily replicated on Cyprus.

I have found nothing in the records to indicate that there was a conscious decision not to evacuate, but the defense plan called for a defense of the interior, which would have precluded evacuation even if the British had had the air and naval power to make another such retreat possible. Coastal defense was not totally neglected; for example, the remains of a machine-gun post still overlook the rocks near Paphos, where Aphrodite is supposed to have come out of the sea. It was well understood that in case of an invasion, the situation would have been grave.

As NOTED, IT WAS TO BE A DEFENSE by British forces, not a people's war. The garrison included an infantry battalion of the Cyprus

Regiment and some part-timers from the Cyprus Volunteer Force, but local units were not prominent in the defense scheme. The records contain a number of comments on the suitability of Cypriots for military life. For example, a pre-war War Office study noted, in a section titled "Climate, Effect on Natives": "Though probably in great measure responsible for the constitutional laziness and thriftless nature of the aboriginal Cypriot, the climate cannot be said to have any marked effect on the native population."[9] The war diary of a member of a pack transport group explained: "It may prove of interest the peculiarity of Cypriot Troops. Their grandfathers were all, probably, brigands living in mountain villages . . . Murder is unfortunately not unheard of. Men will knife each other over a gambling debt at cards; men will shoot at the regtl [regimental] police and kill them . . . Gambling is popular and very difficult to control and with the fortnightly . . . pay a man may lose all his money and that leads to selling kit."[10] It is impossible to say how accurate these dismal views of the Cypriot were, but it is obvious that the British command did not expect to raise any reliable units from the villages.

In a somewhat halfhearted attempt to use Cypriots for the island's defense, the Cyprus Commando was formed in Nicosia on 26 June 1941. Despite the view of the Cypriots as brigands—who would, presumably, possess traits that could be exploited for irregular warfare—the command saw its first task as making proper soldiers out of the approximately sixty commandos. The commander gave them basic military training, with an early emphasis on teaching them to shave. The record notes that the recruits lacked coordination and suppleness. It is hard to read between the lines of the bare-bones war diary, but it appears that the intent was to train soldiers rather than a band of guerrillas. The unit was issued the prestigious Commando green beret, but their armaments consisted of captured 6.5 mm Italian rifles; no mention is made of automatic weapons, grenades, or demolition materials. The unit made reconnaissances of likely hideouts and established ammunition and fuel depots in a forest, but the project seems to have generated little enthusiasm, or reflected much realism. The Cyprus Commando was disbanded about six months after it stood up.

The defense scheme relied on eleven inland strongpoints. Perhaps influenced by the heady air of the Cyprus of Aphrodite, the Crusaders, and Richard the Lionheart, the strongpoints were given the evocative name "keeps." The plan called for twelve keeps, most of them on high ground, to be garrisoned by one or more companies supported by mobile and armored units. A large central reserve of two brigade groups would be available to go to the aid of keeps under attack, and some fighter airfields would be defended and used to support the keeps.

Rather than static fortresses, the keeps were to be bases for mobile columns roaming outside their perimeters. The columns would screen the keeps and keep the roads open for the central reserve. The plan, which made evacuation all but impossible, in effect assumed the enemy could land from the sea at will; it therefore prohibited supply dumps and installations near the coast. It is easy to pick holes in the plan. There is a certain unreality about medieval keeps, out of range of one another for mutual fire support and open to defeat in detail. The keeps would have been an invader's dream. Such speculation shows only the accuracy of seventy-five years' hindsight. Full understanding of the effect of airpower and the vulnerability of airfields to ground attack, as well as of underground and guerrilla warfare, was yet to come.

As it turned out, the crisis, if it ever existed, was fleeting. The British invasion of Syria began on 10 July, the date of the Australian

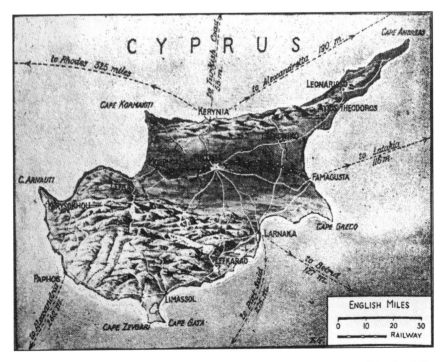

Figure 21.1. Cyprus, with distances to major Mediterranean ports. Map by Felix Gordon. *War Illustrated*, 20 June 1941.

Prime Minister's despairing letter. With the Syrian and Palestinian airfields in Allied hands, British air support against any Axis invasion of Cyprus was ensured. This island's defenses remained weak, and a German-Italian invasion was not impossible, but it would have served no obvious strategic purpose. Not all the omens were unfavorable. By mid-1941, the British ULTRA program for breaking German codes was becoming reliable. Although well aware of the danger of overreliance on ULTRA, Britain's strategists knew that decoded German signals traffic made almost no reference to an attack on Cyprus. Perhaps more significant, the British were aware of the upcoming German invasion of the Soviet Union. This highly classified information was available only to the London command post and the highest levels of the Middle East command. The beleaguered planners in Cyprus were unaware of these impending events.

In addition, it now seems clear that the Nazi authorities never envisioned a German invasion of Cyprus. In the aftermath of the successful invasion of Crete, the German juggernaut appeared invincible. The commander of the airborne assault on Crete was ready to continue. Kurt Student, commander of the Luftwaffe's XI Air Corps, which had conducted the assault, was raring to go and proposed an early assault on Cyprus to follow up the dramatic victory in Crete. He did not speak for the Nazi power structure. The Cretan campaign had been a pyrrhic victory: German casualties were so heavy that Hitler, opportunist that he was, never attempted another airborne coup. The Germans did not totally discard the idea of an attack on Cyprus, and such an assault would have been at least theoretically possible through 1943.

THE FOG OF WAR WAS THICK. While we now know that the threat of a German invasion of the island never really existed, it was less clear at that time in London and overseas. Most British officials assumed the island would be lost. Even Winston Churchill, for all his optimistic pronouncements, appears to have felt the Germans would attack and conquer. It is difficult to criticize their analyses. No responsible official could realistically have ruled out a German attack.

The British defense plan is more difficult to evaluate. Since the invasion did not take place, it is impossible to say how the plan and its keeps would have worked in practice. It is hard to banish the idea of the "keep" as a crusader castle from which armored vehicles, like the knights of old, would sally forth over the drawbridge to smite the foe. Apart from the nomenclature, the idea is not particularly unusual. In fact, it is quite similar to the "boxes" used against the

Japanese offenses in India in 1944 and even more like the strongholds in the second Chindit operation in Burma. A close reading is more interesting for what it leaves out than what it says. The *Cyprus Defence Scheme* more or less assumes German air superiority, and the appendix dealing with the concept of the keep does not mention friendly or enemy airpower. Logistics are not discussed, nor is stocking the keeps in advance of the battle. It is notable that the seven or so keeps appear to have been out of range to give one another mutual fire support. Also not commented on is that the dispersion of the keeps across the island appears to assume that the Germans would have been able to land by sea or air at will. After the German takeovers of France and Crete, these types of attack were clearly possible and, when put into operation, effective. Since the troops available for defense of the island were in any case insufficient, the plan appears to be one of despair, an attempt to make the best of an impossible situation.

A German invasion backed by sea- and airpower would likely have become a series of last stands, with the German forces wiping out the keeps one by one. The inland location of the keeps all but precluded evacuation. After the ignominious evacuations of Norway, Dunkirk, Greece, and Crete, the Cyprus commander may have been told that there would be no more evacuations. (I have found no document stating this.) The goal was to do or die. Whether that supposition is correct or not, mid-1941 saw the end of the nosedive that British fortunes had taken since the spring of 1940. Norway, Dunkirk, Greece, Crete, and losses in the North African desert represented a string of disasters that was at least given a temporary pause. Successes in Syria and Iraq went far to stabilize the eastern Mediterranean, and the German invasion of Russia made an invasion of Britain unlikely. Mid-941 was not a turning point, but perhaps can be seen as a milestone.

The invasion threat came and went and the war moved on. Although the British established Cyprus as a strategic base to help safeguard the security of the Suez Canal and Britain's other interests in the Middle East, and although it filled that role in the years before the war and does so today, British possession of the island was a strategic deficit in 1939–45. The incident is forgotten, but it perhaps took on a new life in the 1950s, since the sites partially prepared for the keeps could well have seen later service as hideouts for the EOKA Greek nationalist movement.

Spring Semester 2018

1. Churchill to General Wilson, Athens, 13 Apr. 1941, quoted in Churchill, *The Grand Alliance,* vol. III of *The Second World War* (New York, 1950), p. 225.

2. Menzies to Churchill, 8 June 1941, WM (41) 58/1, CAB 65/18.

3. Message Cyprus to CO No. 228, 5 June 1941, CO 968/6/9.

4. Minute, E. Warner, 25 Apr. 1941, R4176, FO 371/23776.

5. Minute, Reginald Bowker, 28 May 1941, R4176, FO 371, 23776.

6. Churchill to Foreign Secretary, 6 June 1941, CAB 66/16, FO 371/23726, FO 371/29846, CO 67/316/13, PREM 3/113.

7. Military Situation Report for the Week Ending 16 June 1941, CO 968/27/1.

8. *Cyprus Post,* 23 May 1941.

9. General Staff War Office, "Military Report on Cyprus," c. 1938, p. 60.

10. War Diary of No. 1 Pack Transport Group, Royal Army Service Corps, 1941, WO169/11558.

The destruction of the King David Hotel, Jerusalem, by Irgun terrorists, 22 July 1946. The attack on the hotel, which housed offices of the British civil and military authorities, helped confirm the British view of Palestine as a "troublesome, expensive, and useless burden."

22

How the British Left Palestine

BERNARD WASSERSTEIN

Nothing in his life became him like the leaving it. The death of the Thane of Cawdor is thus reported by Malcolm to Duncan in act one, scene four of *Macbeth*. The poor thane, who never even gets to appear in person in the play, enters literary memory solely via this brief posthumous encomium.

The British Empire is sometimes eulogized in like manner. No doubt, empires after 1945 were pernicious and doomed; nevertheless, we are told, nothing became the British like the way they left theirs. The relatively nonviolent British end of empire (so this line of thinking goes) was a model of imperial abnegation almost without parallel, contrasting with other imperial endings, such as those of the Dutch in the East Indies, the French in Algeria, or the Portuguese in Angola and Mozambique. Of course, the reality was different—as the cases of Kenya, Cyprus, and Aden, among many others, testify. Nevertheless, those of us who grew up in Britain in the post-war decades recall the newsreel footage of the British flag being lowered and a new one raised in peaceful transfers of sovereignty in one after another colony, from the Gold Coast in 1957 right through to those epic scenes in Hong Kong in 1997.

The British mandate in Palestine was unique in many ways, in particular in the manner of its ending on 15 May 1948. As has often been noted, this was the only dependent territory from which Britain ever withdrew without handing over authority to any successor government. Refusing to commit to implement the United Nations partition resolution of 29 November 1947, the British government embraced an apparent policy toward Palestine of *après nous le déluge*. This accusation is voiced in several accounts of the end of the mandate. Arthur Koestler dubbed the British withdrawal "Operation Deluge."[1] Zeev Sharef, secretary of the Provisional Government of Israel at its inception and the official chiefly responsible for construction of the state's administrative machine in 1947–48, wrote: "Chaos was implicit in the British Government's decision . . . The British departure plan ruled out any transfer of government institutions and public services to the trustworthy charge of the successor authority and this inimical official attitude could not but have a provocative effect on the individuals carrying out the plan."[2] The Palestinian historian Issa Khalaf agrees, complaining that the withdrawal was "confused and disorderly, having taken place under conditions of almost complete anarchy."[3]

I recall an interview in 1970 with one of the mandatory governmental officials involved, John Sheringham. Even twenty-two years after the event, he felt the shame of this policy of scuttle. So far as he was concerned, nothing *less* became the mandate than Britain's manner of leaving it. Was he right?

There can be little argument that at the level of high policy making in London, the end of the mandate was marked by a despairing anxiety on the part of the British government to be rid of Palestine, seen as a troublesome, expensive, and useless burden. Britain was unwilling to be seen by the Arab states, on which its strategic and economic dominance in the Middle East depended, as aiding and abetting the establishment of a Jewish state. It therefore abstained in the UN vote on partition and forbade the UN Palestine Commission even to set foot in the country until 1 May 1948. In fact, apart from a small advance party in March, the commission never arrived in Palestine and on 14 May was formally disbanded.

If we turn our attention from London to Jerusalem, does a different picture emerge? In an article published in 1988, Wm. Roger Louis analyzed the role of the head of the government of Palestine, the High Commissioner, Sir Alan Cunningham. On the basis of a scrutiny of his papers, Louis to some extent salvaged Cunningham's reputation, concluding that, whatever his other failings, he "presided over a well-organized and carefully planned withdrawal that took place entirely according to plan."[4]

Cunningham, Louis concluded, was primarily concerned with trying to preserve some semblance of peace and to minimize bloodshed. "He saw his job," Louis noted, "principally as holding the ring while the civil administration closed down and British troops evacuated." From the Olympian heights of Government House, he largely delegated handling of the withdrawal to his officials.

Let us descend to those lower levels and survey what happened in the government offices and in the towns and villages of Palestine between November 1947 and May 1948 as the struggle for the succession to the mandate intensified. Three contextual points should be borne in mind. First, in spite of its long experience of imperial acquisition, Britain in the spring of 1948 had relatively little of imperial de-accession. Among the few notable instances were Iraq in 1932 and the more recent end of the Raj in India. Both were followed by terrible bloodshed. Neither offered a promising model for emulation. Secondly, the withdrawal was a colossal logistic exercise. It involved the transshipment of 55,000 military personnel (as of 1 December 1947), 6,000 British policemen and officials, the disposal of huge quantities of governmental assets of all kinds, and the removal or destruction of 250,000 tons of military stores. Thirdly, the withdrawal took place against the background of civil war between the Arabs and Jews, and of Jewish attacks against British military targets. The carnage was horrific, and the British were powerless to contain it. By early 1948, the government of Palestine was clearly, as the American consul in Jerusalem reported on 9 February, "in a state of disintegration."[5]

The managing director of the mandatory administration's withdrawal was Eric Mills, an official who had served continuously in Palestine since the start of British rule in December 1917. As "Commissioner on Special Duty," Mills was charged with advising on and, in effect, overseeing the liquidation of the mandatory government. Isaiah Berlin, who had met him in 1934 on his first visit to Palestine, called him "a clever, disillusioned, cynical person"—but like some of Berlin's snap judgments, this was perhaps unfair.[6] Mills, who had been controller of the 1931 census of Palestine and director of manpower during the Second World War, was an able and conscientious administrator. Whatever degree of success the operation enjoyed must be attributed in large measure to him.

Immediately upon the UN partition vote, Mills issued a draft "general scheme" for withdrawal. This provided for the transfer of governmental fixed assets such as post offices, schools, telephone exchanges, and hospitals, as well as vehicles, machinery, records, and stores, as far as possible to local authorities, pending the emergence of successor governments.[7]

Mills went into detail on every conceivable aspect of the withdrawal. For example, special care was to be taken in regard to the security of the "large quantities of dangerous cultures and vaccines in the bacteriological laboratories." It would be "very serious," Mills pointed out, if looting took place" in those places.[8] In accordance with his guidance, the Public Works Department prepared voluminous "handing over notes" on public utilities and infrastructure such as water and sewage works, roads and bridges, machinery, and surveying instruments.

A crucial aspect of the scheme was the future of governmental records. In early 1948, instructions were issued for the selective destruction of records. The guiding principle was "to destroy as much as possible that does not involve frustration of a successor administration."[9] Fortunately for historians, there was a raft of exceptions. Among records designated to be spared were those concerning births, marriages, and deaths, nationality and citizenship. Although most "Secret Registry" files were to be destroyed, a critical exception was made for papers "whose destruction would frustrate a successor government, provided that their publication would not embarrass HMG [His Majesty's Government] or injure an individual." And the instruction to officials added: "In doubtful cases the degrees of frustration or embarrassment must be weighed against each other." All files in the "top secret" registry were to be destroyed or downgraded before "Z-Day" (the last day of British rule). Others were to be stored and then handed over to the UN Commission. Mills suggested that "plans and field records" of the Surveys Department, which alone weighed six tons, might be shipped to England.[10]

The process of destruction and preservation, however, turned out to be haphazard. Many papers scheduled for destruction were preserved. None appear to have been transferred to the UN. Some were shipped to Cyprus. Others were sent to England and opened to researchers at points after 1966, some as late as 2013. Those remaining in Palestine for the most part ended in archives in Israel (or under Israeli control after 1967), and much of what I report here is drawn from them. Many documents bearing on security that were supposed to be destroyed in fact survived. Bank vaults in Jerusalem with a capacity of 135 cubic meters were set aside for the secure storage of governmental files. But the fighting in Jerusalem was particularly severe around Barclay's Bank (the government of Palestine's banker), which ended up just on the Israeli side of the final demarcation line in the city. Any files stored there were probably among those captured by a "SWAT" team of Israeli archivists specially commissioned to locate and scoop up such files while the war was still raging. Overall, a surprising amount of important documentation survived.

One British bureaucratic legacy that proved to be of critical importance to both Jews and Arabs was the accumulation of land rec-

ords, particularly thousands of maps, deeds, and registers of ownership, which British officials made considerable efforts to preserve.
Some had been destroyed in a Jewish bombing of the Land Registry
office in Jerusalem in 1944. The incident heightened British concern about the security of the rest. Mills emphasized that the land
registers were "of vital importance to the whole country."[11] He ordered microfilm copies to be made, and records were assembled for
photography.

What was to be done with prisoners? In the absence of assured
continuity of service by prison guards, they could hardly be left behind under lock and key. Serious British offenders could be moved
to England. But what of Palestinians? A partial amnesty was granted
in less serious cases, reducing the prison population. This had already been substantially diminished by the escape of 251 prisoners
from the Acre jail in May 1947 and of a further 18 in December. As
of 17 March 1948, 2,177 prisoners remained in custody, including
407 political detainees and 110 criminal lunatics. It was decided to
release nearly all the detainees. Further releases of ordinary prisoners over the next few weeks reduced the total to 1,200. The remaining Jewish and Arab convicts were redistributed to prisons within
the territory of their respective proposed states, and confidential
contacts were established with the Jewish Agency and the Arab
Higher Committee; each agreed to take responsibility for prisoners
of their nationality after 15 May.

Then there was the problem of the railways. Even had the British
been ready to hand them over to successor states, they could not
be partitioned, since there was a unified system for the country as
a whole. So what would be done with the buildings, rolling stock,
and personnel? In a memo dated 12 April 1948, the general manager despaired of any easy solution. Noting that the system had already suffered severely from looting and destruction, he feared that
the entire organization would soon disintegrate. By the end of the
mandate, hardly any trains were running. Nevertheless, on 13 May
the last chief accountant of the Palestine Railways transferred to
his Jewish successor in Haifa the keys to the head office and safes
there, as well as "two spare motors for the accounting machines, several sporting trophies . . . also an automatic pistol my own personal
property which please hand over to the proper authorities." He
concluded, almost as if he were speaking at a retirement party and
handing over a gold watch, "I take this opportunity of thanking you
most sincerely for your long and valuable service with the Palestine
railways and wishing you a happy and prosperous future."[12]

While men and goods could be withdrawn, the same did not apply
so easily to beasts. What about the 257 horses and 27 camels of the

Palestine Police? Mills noted that the animals represented an asset
that should, strictly speaking, be transferred to the United Nations
at the end of the mandate. But he expressed concern that "there is
every reason for supposing that the animals cannot be tended and
fed after the administration ends."[13] The inspector-general of police declared himself "most anxious that no horses should be left
ownerless on the termination of the Mandate."[14] He proposed, "as a
humane measure," that horses above the age of twelve years be destroyed.[15] Some were sent to the knacker's yard—though given food
taboos, there was probably little market for horsemeat in Palestine.
The remaining horses were offered for sale at £P30 each. It was a
bargain price, but there were few takers. In the end, it was decided
to reduce the price to P£15 per horse and to divide them, as it were,
by nationality: those in Jewish areas might be sold to Jewish buyers,
those in Arab areas to Arabs. As for the police camels, they were to
be offered to Bedouin sheikhs in Beersheba.

IN MANY RESPECTS THE WITHDRAWAL did not proceed as smoothly
in real life as in Mills's scheme. Not all local authorities were able or
willing to take responsibility for institutions that were to be transferred to them. In Nablus, for example, the municipality declared itself unable to afford the expense of maintaining the governmental
hospital after 15 May. The government rejected an appeal for transition funding, and the district commissioner advised the mayor to
"take up the matter with whatever Arab authority or body he thinks
fit in order to obtain assistance."[16]

Here we reach a critical point: the government's superficially
nonpolitical policy of handing over to local authorities obscured
an underlying reality of acquiescence in the partition of Palestine.
That is because nearly all local authorities in Palestine were controlled either by Jews or by Arabs. In the later stages of the mandate,
indeed, local authority boundaries had been deliberately delineated
so as to be mainly Jewish or Arab—in effect, a form of proto-par-
tition. Moreover, Arab and Jewish district officers were appointed
largely in accordance with the ethnic composition of each district.
In the case of the municipalities, most were wholly or largely mono-
ethnic: Tel Aviv and Netanya, for example, were Jewish; Nablus and
Hebron, Arab. The two most important exceptions were Jerusalem
and Haifa.

In Jerusalem, owing to the inability of Arabs and Jews to agree on
the choice of a mayor, the municipality had been controlled since
1945 by an unelected commission. Its head in the final months of
the mandate was a retired Palestine government official, Richard

Figure 22.1. British soldiers enforcing a curfew in Tel Aviv, July 1946. Photograph by Haim Fain. National Library of Israel.

Graves (brother of the poet Robert Graves). A bomb attack in December 1947 led all Jewish officials to leave the municipality building and move to a separate office in a Jewish district. Graves tried unavailingly to persuade them to return. On 25 April, he recorded: "Government have instructed me to recognize—unofficially so to speak—the new Jewish municipal committee appointed to look after the Jewish area." In the very last days of the mandate, the remaining municipal funds were split: a check for £30,000 was issued to the head of the Jewish municipal committee, and one for £27,500 was handed to a representative of the Arab section.[17]

As for Haifa, uniquely in Palestine, it was designated a reserved enclave where the British military occupation would persist for several weeks after 15 May while the army completed its withdrawal through Palestine's most important port. But by 21 April, the Haganah (the Jewish underground army) had won control of the city except for the British-controlled harbor area, the main road, and the airport. Over the next few days, most of Haifa's Arab population fled in British army and navy convoys. Here the British not only acquiesced in partition; they colluded in what we would now call ethnic cleansing. At any rate, that is one way of looking at their actions.

The government and the Haifa municipality agreed that as of 15 May, the municipality would take over "control and management" of the Port Authority, with the proviso that it would provide full facilities for completion of the withdrawal of British forces. At a meeting on 12 May, most of the authority's files and accounts were transferred to representatives of the municipality "in the capacity of a trustee pending the establishment of a settled form of government in Palestine."[18]

In some cases, the government machine was not so much bequeathed to successors as disemboweled from within. By the end of March, the thirty thousand Palestinian civil servants were being supervised by not more than two hundred remaining British officials. In these circumstances, Jewish and Arab officials of the mandatory government, who, of course, had little to look forward to from the British, scrambled to seize control of what remained of the administrative apparatus. The fate of the government-run Palestine Broadcasting Service illustrates this process.

The PBS, founded in 1936, broadcast in English, Arabic, and Hebrew from its transmitter in Ramallah, ten miles north of Jerusalem. Its director from 1945 to 1948 was Edwin Samuel, a British Jew and long-serving government official who was the eldest son of the first High Commissioner under the mandate, Sir Herbert Samuel. In his scheme for withdrawal, Mills proposed that the PBS should continue to transmit a news service "up to the last." He recommended that when that was no longer possible, consideration should be given to "removing vital parts to immobilize [the] transmitter to prevent mischief makers misusing it."[19] By late 1947, the broadcasting studios in Jerusalem had perforce been split: the Hebrew service employees, fearful of attacks, had moved with their files, records, and equipment to studios in Rehavia, a Jewish district, while the Arabic service remained in Broadcasting House in Musrara, an Arab district. In January 1948, PBS program planning was decentralized, so the Arabic and Hebrew services became completely separate, except that all broadcasts went out through the Ramallah transmitter. Each service operated with a separate bank account.

By the time Samuel was evacuated from the country on 20 April, Jerusalem was in a state of siege. The division of the service was almost complete, though broadcasting continued until the last day of the mandate. (The High Commissioner's farewell address was its swan song.) When the Ramallah transmitter was damaged in the fighting, transmissions were divided, too: Arabic ones went out from reserve equipment in Ramallah, Hebrew ones on a low-powered emergency transmitter in the General Post Office in west Jerusalem.

The war left the Ramallah transmitter station in Jordanian hands and the Jerusalem headquarters building under Israeli control. But the broadcasting service had already been partitioned. As the assistant director, Rex Keating, later recalled: "The PBS example was quickly followed by other Departments, despite all the efforts of Government to stop them. The split became total. In effect, the incipient Israeli government was being realized."[20]

Much of the rest of the administration was bifurcated in like manner. But this worked overwhelmingly to the advantage of the Jews, even leaving aside their military victory. The Zionists, with their pre-existing institutional apparatus, a state in the making, succeeded in establishing a far-reaching organization in the last months of British rule with the objective of taking over as smoothly as possible key functions of government upon the conclusion of the mandate. They co-opted most of the Jewish mandatory officials as civil servants of the new state—though not Samuel, who, somewhat to his chagrin, was not offered a job by the Israeli government.

Meanwhile, the Arab Higher Committee, headed from exile by the former Mufti of Jerusalem, proved itself toothless and internally divided. It had no significant institutional foundations. Palestinian Arab society, unlike Jewish, depended heavily on governmental services in such matters as education, health, and social welfare. Unlike the Zionists, the Palestinian Arabs had no effective military organization, merely scattered bands of volunteers, barely trained and poorly armed. By early May, all but one of the members of the Arab Higher Committee had fled the country. The committee requested that Arab officials take charge of governmental departments. Where they could, they did so. But the irruption from across the Jordan of forces loyal to King Abdullah led them to see him and not the committee as their most likely future employer. Quite apart from his military power, which rested on the British-officered Arab Legion, Abdullah had other advantages: he ruled an existing state that had close links with sections of the Palestinian notable elite, and he enjoyed continuing British military, diplomatic, and economic support. An attempt by the Mufti, in September 1948, to set up an "All-Palestine Government" in Egyptian-occupied Gaza soon collapsed. Abdullah swept aside any ambitions of the Palestinian Arabs to a separatist nationalism and, with the private blessing of both the British and the Israelis, united the two banks of the Jordan under his autocratic rule.

Mills's scheme did not, of course, make provision for the armed
forces, which operated under a separate withdrawal plan. Both Jews
and Arabs protested bitterly that British military actions in Palestine in 1948 favored the other side. The military withdrawal plan
required the army to abstain from involvement in fighting between
Jews and Arabs. It was to concentrate on holding open the lines of
communication for withdrawal. But as Benny Morris writes, "The
guideline of impartiality . . . translated . . . into a policy of quietly
assisting each side in the takeover of areas in which that side was
dominant."[21] At the same time there was large-scale looting of
arms and military stores and a flourishing black market in military
equipment.

A FASCINATING PICTURE OF THE UNDERSIDE of the British withdrawal
is provided in a source that has hardly been noticed by historians of
Palestine: the memoir and diary of Ivor Wilks, who in 1948 was a
twenty-year-old second lieutenant in the British Army in Palestine.
As a satire of army life, Wilks's narrative bears comparison with
Evelyn Waugh's *Sword of Honour* trilogy. Wilks was not only a gifted
writer, but also a socialist and an intellectual who later became a
professional historian, ending his career as a professor of African
history at Northwestern University. His faux-naïf memoir is an extraordinary literary, historical, and human document.

From 23 December 1947, Wilks was stationed at an army base
near Haifa where petroleum was stored for the army. The base was
situated between two villages, Nesher (Jewish) and Balad al-Shaykh
(Arab). One of Wilks's responsibilities was to measure each night
the amount of petrol in storage tanks on the base. After a time, he
noticed discrepancies in the reported and actual amounts of petrol.
He discovered that a diversionary pipe had been opened and large
amounts of fuel were being siphoned off for use by foreign Arab
forces that had infiltrated Balad al-Shaykh. He also learned that
his commanding officer, Captain Webster, was illicitly permitting a
Haganah unit in Nesher to steal empty jerry cans.

Webster was a closet homosexual with a batman as flamboyant
in his sexual orientation as his master was secretive in his. One day
Wilks learned that Webster was supplying the Haganah not only
with old cans from the camp but also with arms that were "surplus
to requirements." Wilks protested:

> I decided to press him on the nature of his arrangement with
> Nesher's Haganah unit. His answer took me completely by sur-
> prise. "Praff [Webster's Haganah contact]," he said, "talked the

matter over and suggested that a handgun should be valued at £(Palestinian) 15 and ammunition at around P£1 for 10,000 rounds." I was taken aback. I had been brought up to think of arms trading as reprehensible. I said something to that effect to Webster. His reply took me by surprise and I can recollect only the gist of it. "I am," he said, or words to that effect, "a businessman by profession and I was doing business with Praff. I was giving him a good deal because they would rather get a bargain from a businessman than receive a free gift from a do-gooder." I was more than a little impressed by this gem of capitalistic wisdom.[22]

Webster was undoubtedly an outlier in his political outlook, as he was in his sexuality. There is ample evidence that some British troops, prompted by anti-Semitism that was stoked by Jewish terrorism and profiteering, transferred large quantities of military equipment to Arabs. But for the most part, the actions of British soldiers were dictated neither mainly by political partisanship nor by greed. Wilks makes clear that Webster had one passionate desire that he shared with nearly all his fellow soldiers in Palestine and that in large measure dictated his—and their—actions: to get home as soon as possible. These mixed motives sometimes led to apparently contradictory behavior. Wilks, although drawn to socialist Zionism, participated, almost without realizing what was going on, in a delivery of British arms from Haifa to the Egyptian army at the border south of Gaza.

Wilks was attracted to the Zionists by more than ideology. A sexual innocent, he was suborned by "Valentina," a young Jewish woman in Haifa who introduced him to "friends" who turned out to be Haganah agents. He relates how, at the request of one of Valentina's "friends," Dan Laner, later an Israeli major general, he helped spirit a consignment of Czechoslovak arms through Haifa's port for the Palmach (the Haganah's elite strike force).

In the last days of the mandate, Wilks was ordered by Webster to mediate between the *mukhtar* (village head) of Balad al-Shaykh and the Haganah unit in Nesher. The latter demanded the surrender of arms left behind by the infiltrators. Little was produced, and the Haganah announced that it would conduct a search of Balad al-Shaykh. The villagers could recall a massacre by the Haganah in the village and another one nearby on the previous New Year's Eve: seventy people, including women and children, had been killed. (That was the latest episode in a cycle of tit-for-tat violence by Jews and Arabs in the Haifa district over the previous few months.) The villagers were no doubt also mindful of the slaughter two weeks earlier of over a hundred Arab civilians by Jewish terrorists in the village of Deir Yassin near Jerusalem. They did not wait to see how such a Haganah search would turn out. At midnight on 24 April, Wilks recorded in his diary:

> The Arabs have gone, carrying what they could with them. The rest has been looted, the few belongings they had to leave, and the horses, goats and fowl. I don't know what would have happened had the Arabs allowed an immediate search of the town. . . . I believe that even the Haganah commander would have left them in the town once sure that it was neutralized. But the Arabs, by and large, believed that their lives were in danger, and fled.[23]

Wilks was troubled about his role in this miserable affair. His mind was not eased when, at their last meeting, Laner gave him a Swiss watch as a gift for his help in "avoiding a heavy loss of life in Balad esh-Sheikh."[24]

In his tedious, lonely life on the army base, Wilks fantasized about taking Valentina back to England as his bride. Only at the end, in a bitter disclosure scene, did he find out that she was a Haganah agent who had bedded him, as she had other British soldiers, as a matter more of duty than love.

On 14 May the High Commissioner departed, the State of Israel was declared, and the Palestinian Arab *nakba* (catastrophe) took shape. Although the mandate terminated at midnight, some British forces remained in the Haifa enclave, which was gradually reduced in size until 30 June. Wilks was among those who left on the very last day.

WHAT EMERGES FROM ALL THIS? Recent historians have shattered the picture of the end of the British Empire as a process of peaceful and consensual retraction. Pankaj Mishra, for example, has written of "the British Empire's ruinous exit strategy." He denounces the "masters of disaster from Cyprus to Malaysia, Palestine to South Africa."[25] The end of the Raj, he reminds us, condemned up to a million people to death and created the world's largest refugee population. By including Palestine in his philippic, he insists that Britain could not shirk its share of responsibility for what occurred in the wake of the British departure.

At the time, most British commentators tended to adopt a view that mingled self-pity with self-congratulation. They complained bitterly that the rest of the world refused to offer anything other than advice in Palestine and had left Britain holding the baby. At the same time, Cunningham asserted that "we left with dignity, using all our efforts to the last for the good of Palestine."[26]

Neither post-imperial polemics nor self-interested apologetics provide a satisfactory framework for understanding what happened in Palestine in 1948. But one conclusion, at any rate, emerges clearly from the evidence: the proposition that the British simply washed their hands of Palestine can no longer be sustained, at any rate as regards the men on the spot. Jon and David Kimche (echoed by others cited earlier) were far from accurate in their claim of unadulterated scuttle: "There had been no attempt to transfer Government and administrative matters to the Jews and the Arabs. The British officials burnt their files, destroyed their records and departed."[27] Notwithstanding the British government's ostensible stance of noninvolvement, the mandatory administration did not pursue a scorched-earth policy. Nor did the British limit themselves to seeking an even balance between the warring parties. It would be more correct to conclude that in the final weeks of the mandate, the mandatory government participated directly in the implementation of partition—though not in the form envisaged by the UN. In doing so, the British helped pave the way for the establishment of Israel and for Abdullah's takeover of the West Bank.

The last word, fittingly, goes to Eric Mills, who, writing with some foresight as early as 1936, penned this "epitaph," which he appended to a letter to Edwin Samuel:

Epitaph

Here lies Palestine Aleph Yod!
Have mercy on her soul, Lord God!
Unwanted child of Arab and Jew
She needs no love
So let your tears be few.[28]

Spring Semester 2018

1. Arthur Koestler, *Promise and Fulfilment: Palestine, 1947–1949* (London, 1949), p. 162.

2. Zeev Sharef, *Three Days* (London, 1962), p. 22.

3. Issa Khalaf, *Politics in Palestine: Arab Factionalism and Social Disintegration, 1939–1948* (Albany, N.Y., 1991), p. 202.

4. Wm. Roger Louis, "Sir Alan Cunningham and the End of British Rule in Palestine," *Journal of Imperial and Commonwealth History*, 16, 3 (1988), pp. 128–47.

5. Robert B. Macatee (Jerusalem) to State Dept., 9 Feb. 1948, *Foreign Relations of the United States, 1948*, vol. V, pt. 2 (Washington, 1976), p. 606.

6. Isaiah Berlin to Mendel and Marie Berlin, [24 Sept. 1934], in Isaiah Berlin, *Letters*, vol. 1, *1928–1946* (New York, 2004), p. 101.

7. Mills to all heads of departments and district commissioners, "Secret and Personal," 2 Dec. 1947, Israel State Archives (henceforth ISA) 401/34 - מ.

8. Ibid.

9. Office Order No. 1, Chief Secretary's Office, 23 Jan. 1948, ISA 401/34 - מ.

10. Mills to all heads of departments and district commissioners, "Secret and Personal," 2 Dec. 1947.

11. Ibid.

12. W. D. Charlton to J. Beliavsky, 11 May 1948, quoted in A. J. Sherman, *Mandate Days: British Lives in Palestine, 1918–1948* (London, 1997), p. 240.

13. Mills to Financial Secretary, 2 Feb. 1948, ISA 401/35 - מ.

14. H. R. F. Butterfield for Inspector-General, Palestine Police, to Chief Secretary, 16 Mar. 1948, ibid.

15. Butterfield for Inspector-General to Chief Secretary, 1 Jan. 1948, ibid.

16. Director of Medical Services to District Commissioner, Samaria District, 3 Apr. 1948, ISA 6616/20 - מ.

17. For more details, see my *Divided Jerusalem: The Struggle for the Holy City* (3rd ed., New Haven, 2008), pp. 143–44.

18. General Manager, Palestine Railways & Ports Authority, to Mayor of Haifa, 6 May 1948, ISA 929/12 - פ, and related documents in this file.

19. Mills to all heads of departments and district commissioners, "Secret and Personal," 2 Dec. 1947.

20. R. Keating, quoted in Andrea L. Stanton, *This Is Jerusalem Calling: State Radio in Mandate Palestine* (Austin, Tex., 2013), pp. 193–94.

21. Benny Morris, *1948: A History of the First Arab-Israeli War* (New Haven, 2008), p. 80.

22. Ivor Wilks, *A Once and Past Love: Palestine 1947, Israel 1948: A Memoir*, Program of African Studies, Special Papers Series, ISSN 1949-0283 (Evanston, Ill., 2011), p. 73.

23. Ibid., p. 99.

24. Ibid., p. 101.

25. Pankaj Mishra, "The Malign Incompetence of the British Ruling Class," *New York Times* (intl. ed.), 19–20 Jan. 2019.

26. Address by Cunningham at Chatham House, 22 July 1948, *International Affairs*, 24, 4 (1948), pp. 481–90.

27. Jon and David Kimche, *Both Sides of the Hill: Britain and the Palestine War* (London, 1960), p. 145.

28. Mills to Samuel, 17 Aug. 1936, ISA 655/63 - פ.

Clockwise from top left: Winston Churchill, c. 1940s, NYP 45063, Imperial War Museums; Clement Atlee, 1938, photograph by Bassano Ltd., NPG x16588 © National Portrait Gallery, London; Harry Truman, 1945, photograph by Frank Gatteri, U.S. Army Signal Corps, Harry S. Truman Library and Museum; Dwight Eisenhower, November 1947, official U.S. Army photograph, USA P-16071, Naval History and Heritage Command.

23

America Confronts the British Superpower, 1945–1957

DEREK LEEBAERT

The 2003 U.S.-British invasion of Iraq got me interested in how history is misused when trying to understand Anglo-American relations since 1945. In the run-up to the Iraq War, policy makers on both sides of the Atlantic were influenced by calls to action from well-credentialed enthusiasts whose simplified analogies ignored the basics of inquiry. A week before the invasion, for example, one eminent academic, who had made himself a mobilizing voice for war, drew positive lessons from the 1956 Suez Crisis to make his case. "[Prime Minister Anthony] Eden," he wrote a week before the invasion, "was quite right to want to punish Egypt for her piracy, which—had it come off successfully—would have proved 'no end of a lesson' to the Middle East in its dealings with the West."[1] It is a big if, and other supposed insights from the past were equally bizarre.

These problems of foreign policy artistry brought me to the twentieth-century myth that seems most relevant to the world today. It is this: at the end of the Second World War, the British Empire was too weak and too dispirited to continue as a global imperial power; thus, a confidently prosperous, well-armed America assumed leadership of the West—and did so while creating a U.S.-led international order that has continued ever since.

On the face of it, the tale is strange. Britain, heart of a historic and militarily adroit empire covering a quarter of the world's land surface, was unlikely to "hand on the baton of democracy," "liquidate" its realms, or "retreat" from a singular global presence—especially not in an alleged "thousand days" after it had played a pivotal role in winning the bloodiest conflict in history.[2] Equally unconvincing is the notion that the United States, a self-contained continental island-state, traditionally fenced off by oceans and high tariffs, suddenly dropped its insularity and transformed itself into a global political-military force.

This myth rests on some lesser ones that are laid out below. To believe any of them makes it hard to explain why, by the beginning of 1957, the just-reelected administration of Dwight Eisenhower issued a "declaration of independence" from British authority, and why it was only then that the United States explicitly took over, in the words of its vice president, Richard Nixon, "the foreign policy leadership of the free world."[3]

Today, it is difficult to exercise such leadership if one doesn't know the roots of world turmoil, much of which springs from the dozen years after the Second World War. Another reason for clearing away the myths is to avoid succumbing to the notion that America is an "empire," even the heir of the British Empire. To believe that "we're an empire now," as is heard frequently in government and academia, makes it easy to conclude that America can fine-tune the planet. Only by the loosest of definitions is America an empire. In fact, there are few places on the map where America can lay down the law, and to believe that the United States exercised any sort of imperial control after the Second World War makes one wonder what Eisenhower, Nixon, and Secretary of State John Foster Dulles were talking about sixty years ago when they finally proclaimed their "declaration of independence."

The term "superpower" was coined in 1944 by Professor William T. R. Fox at Columbia University to categorize nations that possessed "great power *plus* great mobility of power." For a country to function as a superpower, it had to be able to project force almost anywhere it pleased, among other factors. Fox identified the "Super Powers" of that moment as the United States, the Soviet Union, and the British Empire. But after the war ended, neither the Soviet Union nor the United States fully met those requirements. The Soviet Union was the most massive unitary land power ever, yet it lacked overseas reach except through spying and subversion. The United States possessed an atomic monopoly of unknown extent as well as unparalleled industrial heft. But the country had no intention of continuing to entangle itself abroad: it took years to accept the need to garrison

GIs in Europe and Asia, to develop a naval presence in the Persian Gulf, and to build an intelligence capability that offered more than amateurish adventuring.

In contrast, the British Empire and Commonwealth was planetary, with deep relationships nearly everywhere, including those of secret intelligence. Britain drew upon statecraft and experience that—as many U.S. officials, businesspeople, and military men believed—outweighed any other nation's. For most of the dozen years after the war, the American press wrote of Britain deploying a million fighting men across a thousand ports and garrisons. Those reports weren't far off.

During these years, Britain led the world in jet aviation, life sciences, and civil atomic power, and it became the third nuclear-armed state in 1952. By 1954, its Army of the Rhine was the strongest military presence in western Europe. The pre-war system of international trade had collapsed, and during most of this period no substitute took its place. London was still banker to much of the world and equally the heart of its largest trading area.

Yet today's conventional wisdom insists that the British Empire in 1945—or by the latest in 1947—"wanted out" and that the United States "willy-nilly" became a superpower.[4] In addition, one renowned historian states that America possessed the unique ability "to affect the course of events in the developing world," which, of course, remained a largely colonial one.[5] Britain's economy was damaged grievously by the war—but not to the extent imagined today. "It's common to read accounts of how the war bankrupted Britain," says one observer.[6] Except Britain never went bankrupt. "Bankruptcy" is a hard word. It doesn't lend itself to shorthand, and it didn't occur for Britain.

Through the years ahead, Britain endured a roller-coaster ride of ghastly balance-of-payments crises while, paradoxically, its productivity soared. Labour and Conservative party leaders alike kept insisting that recovery was right around the corner. U.S. decision makers tended to agree. Almost everyone expected the huge U.S. loan that Clement Attlee's Labour government received in 1946 to be a onetime bridge to recovery, although what "recovery" meant—whether it referred to the country's the relative strength in 1900, 1914, or 1939—was never defined.

Sensible observers on either side of the Atlantic insisted that Britain's renewal depended on the colonies. That was one reason why neither the Labour government nor its Conservative opponents would accept a retreat from global power. These men had no sense of the empire being lost and no intention of seeing tycoons from Chicago or Houston slice up the Asian subcontinent or the Middle East.

In turn, Americans wanted to keep a politically messy world at arm's length, no matter what was being said in the better drawing rooms of the Northeast about U.S. "responsibilities." They weren't confident in their wealth and strength, as it is claimed today, and exhibit A was their ongoing dread of a revived Depression. Meanwhile, the Labour government's daunting foreign secretary, Ernest Bevin, who dominated Attlee's cabinet, told anyone who would listen that he had to set an example of resolve for the Americans. If he didn't, "all Europe should fall" to Stalin.[7] Germany barely existed as a state, and France was a broken reed.

By February 1947, Bevin was taking steps to "shock" (his term) the Americans into deeper political-military involvements. Evidence shows that he was bluffing about withdrawing all British troops from Greece. Yet that was the critical shock that led to President Truman's overwrought speech to Congress in March about the need to confront "terrorists" and "terrorist activities" almost anywhere.

Dollars soon flooded into Greece, and the myth of the British Empire having "liquidated" itself took hold, especially because London also acceded during those weeks to India's independence and announced an end to Britain's mandate in Palestine. But no matter how one looks at these events, it is a myth that Britain "terminate[d] assistance to Greece" in 1947, let alone that "financial exigencies" compelled Britain "to withdraw from the eastern Mediterranean."[8] Nor was the United States ever "hand-delivered the job of world policeman."[9] What were the Americans to police? China? The Indian subcontinent? Southeast Asia? Africa? And with what?

Later in 1947, Britain suffered the first of its post-war financial crises, and Washington, after high-profile negotiations, changed the terms of its loan. Otherwise, Foreign Secretary Bevin largely did as he pleased. The British didn't lower their Imperial Preference trade barriers, nor did they take any further steps to make the pound sterling convertible to dollars, as had also been pledged both at Bretton Woods in 1944 and in obtaining the 1945–46 loan. Instead, they began to undermine efforts at a West European federation, which Congress was laying down as a condition of receiving money from the Marshall Plan, introduced that June.

Despite a chilling balance-of-payments dilemma, the British looked militarily formidable: they were the slowest of the Big Three to demobilize; they retained conscription, unlike the Americans; and the RAF's lead in jet fighters appeared unassailable.

Americans might have had doubts about whether Britain was a land of socialist slackers or of commercial predators, an empire of colonial exploiters or of global peacekeepers. But they welcomed having the West's second-strongest military, as well as its second-strongest economy, on their side. That was because in 1948 a clear path to a third world war suddenly appeared. Bevin and Truman saw no difference between Nazism and Stalinism. The Soviet-backed coup in Czechoslovakia that February confirmed it for them. Stalin's attempt to oust his former allies from Berlin followed that summer. If he succeeded, the British and Americans would begin a general retreat from Germany. Such was his reasoning. Then the Continent's fearful, demoralized democracies would fall to communist subversion.

The response to Stalin's blockade was the Berlin airlift. U.S. generals expected the RAF to carry half the freight. After all, the famed RAF had quite recently been vital to winning the war, and the RAF could now draw on the royal air forces of Australia, New Zealand, and Canada, and that of South Africa.

During this showdown, two points illustrate U.S. hesitancy and, in contrast, Britain's determination to act as a superpower. One observation is forgotten; the other is unknown. First, it is doubtful that the Americans would have remained in Berlin if not for Bevin. It was "Bevin in London who rallied the Western cause," concludes one of the best analyses of this moment of decision, and he did so by demanding that the four thousand GIs in Berlin stay put.[10] Second, had the Red Army nonetheless decided to push through to the Channel—which would have meant cutting through the British occupation zone—American forces were under White House orders not to respond. They were only to fire if attacked directly. Not until December would those orders be changed, and in secret so as not to appear provocative.

Being a superpower means being capable of projecting power anywhere in the world. In 1948, and for years afterward, the British had such mobility. The Americans didn't. To this end, the Labour government allowed the U.S. Air Force to deploy nuclear-armed bombers on airfields in England. That would have been the only way for the Americans to strike into Russia if worse came to worst over Berlin.

As a superpower, Britain naturally had far-flung political-military commitments beyond Europe: in Southeast Asia, the subcontinent, Africa, Latin America, North America (i.e., Canada), and the Middle East, which, Foreign Office mandarins explained patiently to the Americans, was the crossroads of empire. In the Middle East, to be sure, Britain gave up the Palestine mandate, but that was hardly giving up much. Britain dominated much else in the region, such as the enormous assembly point of imperial forces at Suez. Iraq was a fiefdom, and the Persian Gulf's sheikdoms were well policed. Nor did Britain hesitate to threaten force when crossed. Once the new State of Israel pushed into Egyptian territory during its first war with its Arab neighbors in 1948–49, the British delivered, on New Year's Eve, an ultimatum to Prime Minister David Ben-Gurion that he read as a "declaration of war." And he received Britain's threat from the hands of the U.S. ambassador to Israel, as Harry Truman had ordered. Contrary to legend, Truman's support for Israel turned on a dime once he was safely elected in November. The Americans wouldn't play a military role in the Middle East for years.

On a happier note, the Attlee government's *Economic Survey for 1949* was exuberant. The industrial machine was humming, it reported, and output kept increasing. By April of that year, Bevin had succeeded in his effort to commit the Americans to the defense of western Europe, although little in the way of an "organization" stood behind the North Atlantic Treaty, and the U.S. Army had but twelve tanks on the Continent capable of combat. Troublingly, the United States slid into recession that spring, and hypochondriac Americans convinced themselves that the Depression was about to return. They could only do so much overseas, or so they supposed.

Then, over the summer, Britain plunged into a financial crisis far worse than any before. In early September, Bevin arrived in Washington to negotiate, saying that he was "probably on one of the most important missions in history," and no one among the Americans disagreed.[11] Yet an episode that came close to being the worst global economic catastrophe of the century can't be found in the literature. Ruin was barely averted, largely because of British devaluation.

But much else in the world looked terribly wrong. Stalin had detonated an atomic bomb in August, and Mao Zedong was on the verge of proclaiming his People's Republic of China. This sequence of disasters prompted a top-secret National Security Council study on the future of the British Empire. Senior officials at State, Defense, Treasury, and the CIA scrutinized which "global commitments"— including treaties, other overseas agreements and obligations, and military deployments—might, in extremis, be abandoned by London. If such abandonments occurred, how might they affect America? By the time NSC 75, with its anodyne title "British Military Commitments," was delivered to Truman ten months later, the United States was at war.

THE CONSENSUS CONCLUSION BEHIND NSC 75 was this: the British Empire and Commonwealth would stay much as it had been, covering the globe with its nearly one million men under arms and who knew how many in reserve. No "retreat" was discernible, in contrast to "adjustment," and "replacement" was not expected to be needed. Specifically, India's independence in 1947 had made the entire entity stronger: the world's largest democracy (India) and its largest Muslim nation (Pakistan) were now woven into Britain's global political-economic-military alliance structure.

NSC 75 drew an imposing picture. American energy and goodwill couldn't substitute for the empire's global presence. The United States did not need to vastly expand its forces overseas to face the combined threat from Moscow and Beijing. Instead, it should support this formidable ally in Europe, the Middle East, Africa, and Southeast Asia. That included backing its reserve currency. All this was an effective, efficient way to leverage U.S. strength and to achieve stability in parts of the world that had little to do with the American experience.

By the summer of 1950, a worsening guerrilla war in Malaya posed economic dangers to Britain. Malaya was a federation under British authority, and its hard-currency exports of rubber and tin were vital to Britain's recovery and therefore to the empire's role in the world. The value of these exports, from a peninsula about the size of Maine, were roughly equivalent to one-seventh of all U.S. exports.

The only way to defend Malaya against communist revolution, British officials told Washington, was by enabling France to hold the line to the northeast against Sino-Soviet expansion in Indochina (i.e., against Viet Minh nationalists, who were supposedly a cat's-paw for Stalin). Britain's High Commissioner for South East Asia, Malcolm MacDonald, proved uniquely convincing at pushing this line of reasoning. To the British and then to the Americans, he soon became known as one of the two "Macs" in Asia, the other being General Douglas MacArthur, supreme commander in Japan. Myths abound about how the United States got into Vietnam. In the end, no French politician or general, no American congressman or admiral, came close to having MacDonald's impact on the decisions in Washington that led America step-by-step into Vietnam. Known to the Americans as "the wise man of Asia," he maintained his advocacy for U.S. commitment even after France's defeat in 1954. Yet MacDonald's influence goes unnoticed by historians of this tragedy. To write of the making of America's Vietnam War without knowing of him is like writing of America's war in the Pacific without knowing of MacArthur.

The British described their counterinsurgency operations in Malaya as one of three Asian "fronts" in the war against communist expansion, for which, insisted MacDonald, the ultimate stakes were India and then the Middle East. But the one authentic battlefront was in Korea, where, in June 1950, Stalin had timed, equipped, and instigated a full-blown invasion across the thirty-eighth parallel. To be sure, GIs and Tommies fought side by side. But it is another myth that the British Empire rallied to the blue flag of the United Nations. British forces participated in Korea only after Secretary of State Dean Acheson threatened that summer to essentially terminate relations with London. (Acheson's ferocity undermines the fantasy that he was an "anglophile" in "Bond Street tailoring.")[12] Nor did Congress have any patience with British arguments that other, greater worldwide imperial responsibilities had to be upheld.

Among those "other responsibilities" was the British position in Iran. Until recently, Iran had been a quasi colony. Foreign Office mandarins insisted that it was only Britain that deterred Soviet meddling across the eight-hundred-mile border. But patriotic Iranians despised Britain's presence. The Anglo Iranian Oil Company basically ran the country, at least until those patriots nationalized oil production in March 1951. Negotiations over the AIOC's future proved fruitless, and by the summer of 1951, the British, according to the State Department, were set to "revert to their traditional tactics" of using or threatening violence.

President Truman urged restraint, as did every editorial page in America. Attlee had the good sense that July to stand down despite being ridiculed by Churchill for his "kicked spaniel diplomacy." Instead, Attlee's government put sanctions in place to try starving Iran into submission. In mid- October, he authorized the largest airlift of troops anywhere since the Second World War—and it was against Egypt, which was governed, if that is the word, by the tottering monarchy of Farouk I. Six thousand British soldiers swooped into the Suez Canal Zone to secure docks and ordnance depots from outraged nationalists who were sick of having their land occupied by what was then a foreign command of some 160,000.

SUCH MUSCULAR FOREIGN POLICIES didn't prevent Labour's defeat on 25 October in the 1951 general election. Churchill, who was nearly seventy-seven, returned to Downing Street in his only peacetime stint as Prime Minister. One of the bigger myths of this era is that Churchill's second premiership was inconsequential and that he was infirm for most of it, notably after a severe stroke in June 1953, from which he in fact rebounded fast. Yet these were among the most dramatic and effective years of his long life. His best prose heard or read was still to come, as the future prime minister Harold Macmillan chronicled, adding that "Churchill's mastery of the House of Commons remained as great as ever" through much of this period.[13] And this second premiership witnessed Churchill's most forceful handling of the Americans by far.

Even though Britain descended once more into financial disaster at the start of 1952, Churchill began threatening the Americans in ways that he would never have dared when he was beholden to them during the war. They needed to stifle their backseat driving in the Middle East; further pressures to federate with western Europe had to stop; and Britain would henceforth deal directly with Soviet Russia as it thought best. The "or else" included pulling the Commonwealth Division from Korean combat and reconsidering U.S. rights to those vital airfields. Once Truman announced in March that he wouldn't seek another term, it became clear that Churchill was contending for leadership of the West.

Eisenhower's election in November hardly quelled Churchill's ambition. Besides, by year's end Britain's economy was bouncing back (because of austerity and huge U.S. commodity purchases for the Korean War). Malaya seemed secure, thanks to a ruthless crackdown that included deploying an armada of bombers, fighters, air transports, and ten helicopters that the Americans threw in. Stalin's death in March 1953 offered new opportunities in London. Churchill told Eisenhower he would take the initiative to negotiate with Stalin's successors no matter what the Americans did. In the Middle East, he took an even firmer line. In May, when John Foster Dulles became the first U.S. secretary of state to visit the region, Churchill took visibly public steps to undercut his negotiations with Egypt's new military regime. But Churchill was happy to use the Americans as needed, such as allowing them in August "to become Britain's accomplice and trigger-man" in returning the Shah of Iran to power.[14]

Churchill's ties with Franklin Roosevelt had never been the "friendship" that Churchill perceived or that writers today mythologize. His personal relations with Eisenhower were only marginally better. As the Americans slid further into Vietnam—where they were paying for some 80 percent of France's war effort—the British began to back away from any prospect of joint military involvement. After all, Malaya was now secure, as Churchill told his cabinet, while he let the Americans know that "Great Britain will in no circumstances intervene in Vietnam" to avert France's defeat.[15] In the summer of 1954, Eisenhower concluded that the British had a "veto" over U.S. policy in Southeast Asia, as they did in the Middle East, where, for instance, they forbade American aid to Egypt.

THE UNITED STATES BY THIS STAGE was looking ever more like a superpower, if less so acting like one. Immense new naval and jet aviation capacities were at hand; the CIA had expanded enormously, dwarfing Britain's MI6, though not equaling its quality; and apparently, Eisenhower's administration would be keeping GIs in Europe, despite what Congress had been promised when ratifying the North Atlantic Treaty in 1949. Moreover, the Americans were entering other alliance arrangements, such as the Southeast Asia Treaty Organization in September 1954, although everyone in Washington concerned with this issue emphasized that it was up to the British Empire and Commonwealth to enforce SEATO's accords.

As for Soviet Russia, the summit that Churchill had urged didn't occur. His own cabinet as well as the Americans compelled him to cease acting unilaterally toward Russia. In the Middle East, Britain had finally reached a Suez Canal Base Agreement in 1954 with Egypt's strongman, Colonel Gamal Abdel Nasser. Washington had much less to do with achieving this deal than is believed, but in any event, guerrilla skirmishing in the Canal Zone ended. Henceforth, the supposedly indispensable crossroads of empire was meant to be quiet and safe. Yet the Americans got caught in the blowback from Israel.

The Israelis activated what they called a "terror unit" that was secretly embedded in Cairo.[16] The purpose was to foment a bloody upheaval in Egypt, which included planting evidence to incriminate the Muslim Brotherhood. Such violence, believed top officials in Tel Aviv, might induce British forces to remain in Suez and to serve as a buffer between Egypt and Israel. Moreover, anticipated the Israelis, ties between Cairo and the United States would be ruined once Egypt spun out of control, with Nasser's leadership discredited. Therefore, U.S. consulate libraries in Alexandria and Cairo were bombed in addition to British-owned cinemas.

Yet Israel's terror unit couldn't derail the Base Agreement. British forces withdrew as planned, and London then allowed the Americans to deliver aid to Cairo. But nearly everything else went terribly wrong. On 31 January 1955, the Egyptians executed two of the terrorists. In retaliation, Israeli paratroopers killed thirty-eight Egyptian soldiers in Gaza—all of which occurred in a climate of intensifying border clashes between Israel and its four adjoining neighbors along a six-hundred-mile armistice line. The Eisenhower administration moved quickly to have Israel censured in the United

Nations for the attack. Churchill's government provided diplomatic backing. Yet sabotage and murder kept being followed by expanded reprisals and revenge.

Anthony Eden, upon finally becoming Prime Minister in April, tried to mediate. He attempted to use American good offices as well. Nothing worked to mitigate the violence. Egypt and (less so) Syria received large, unprecedented arms shipments from the Soviet bloc that fall as terror and counterterror mounted with Israel. The Americans, however, grew skeptical of Israel's cries of self-defense.

Before long, Eisenhower said that he was spending most of his working hours on the Middle East. Then came another step toward all-out war. On the night of 11 December, in response to what Israel claimed was Syrian aggression, the Israeli Defense Forces launched a brigade-sized assault on positions along the northeastern shore of the Sea of Galilee, killing fifty-four and capturing thirty while losing six of their own. Again with British support, Eisenhower once more had Israel censured at the UN, and he privately threatened Tel Aviv with economic sanctions. On Eisenhower's instructions, his ambassador to the UN charged that "previous representations by the Council and the United States government had failed to halt the mass of Israeli attacks on its Arab neighbors and that the whole Palestine situation had deteriorated as a result."[17]

In this case, the myths being encountered are of an enduringly harmonious U.S.-Israeli relationship and of shared strategic interests. Eisenhower's censures and his threats of sanctions are strangely absent from nearly all recent studies of these fraught years at the intersection of U.S., British, Israeli, and Arab relations. When Britain and France conspired with Israel to attack Egypt in October and November 1956, Eisenhower quickly attributed Israel's involvement to its desire for "expansion."

"Those British are still my right arm," he huffed to a speechwriter as the debacle at Suez got under way.[18] Ten years earlier, it would have been inconceivable to speak of the original superpower in such patronizing terms; ten years later, it would have been overblown to consider Britain anything that significant. This was also the juncture where the Americans (echoed by Canada) made their "declaration of independence" as Britain, in the words of Geoffrey Crowther, longtime editor of *The Economist*, recognized itself as "no longer a Super-power."[19] But there may be elements of myth as well in regarding Suez as the final, dramatic break point in thinking of the British Empire and Commonwealth as one of the Big Three.

Arguably, that came in October 1957 when the Americans were shaken by the Soviet success with *Sputnik*—and with ICBM launch vehicles—as their own rockets kept blowing up on the launch pads, live on TV. *Sputnik* set the United States apart from its friends, foreclosing any willingness at State, the White House, or the Pentagon to keep up facades of unity in their dealings with troublesome allies—Britain and its empire being the most consequential of these. Whatever the moment, America's place in the world was shown to be irretrievably altered when, on the eve of his election to the presidency in 1960, Senator John F. Kennedy decreed that "American frontiers are on the Rhine and the Mekong and the Tigris and the Euphrates."[20] Truman, Eisenhower, Marshall, Acheson, or Dulles could ever have imagined this. But it is a vision of Britain and of the British Empire that Ernest Bevin and Winston Churchill wouldn't have thought twice about expressing during their years in power.

Spring Semester 2019

1. Andrew Roberts, "How Eden Was Sunk by Suez," *Telegraph*, 16 Mar. 2003.

2. Andrew Roberts says, "An exhausted Great Britain handed on the baton to the United States"; see "Becoming the World's Policeman," *Wall Street Journal*, 18 Apr. 2014. "Liquidation" is what Peter Clarke believes occurred; see *The Last Thousand Days of the British Empire: Churchill, Roosevelt, and the Birth of the Pax Americana* (New York, 2008), p. xxiv.

3. "Eisenhower's Declaration of Independence on Foreign Policy," *Time*, 12 Nov. 1956; Richard Nixon, *RN: The Memoirs of Richard Nixon* (New York, 1978), p. 178.

4. Bret Stephens, *America in Retreat: The New Isolationism and the Coming Global Disorder* (New York, 2014), p. 26; Clarke, *Last Thousand Days*, p. xiv.

5. Fredrik Logevall, *Embers of War: The Fall of an Empire and the Making of America's Vietnam* (New York, 2013), p. 98.

6. Neal Acherson, "As the Toffs Began to Retreat," *London Review of Books*, 22 Nov. 2018.

7. Oct. 16, 1946, CAB 131/1 DO (46) 27.

8. Hal Brands, *What Good Is Grand Strategy? Power and Purpose in American Statecraft from Harry S. Truman to George W. Bush* (Ithaca, N.Y., 2014), p. 23; Melvyn Leffler, *For the Soul of Mankind: The United States, the Soviet Union, and the Cold War* (New York, 2008), p. 61.

9. Stephens, *America in Retreat*, p. 24.

10. Jean Edward Smith, *Lucius D. Clay: An American Life* (New York, 1992), p. 495.

11. "U.S. Will Sidestep Pound's Devaluing," *New York Times*, 1 Sept. 1949.

12. Logevall calls Acheson an "Anglophile of the first order" (*Embers of War*, p. 218). As for "Bond Street tailoring," Henry Kissinger concocts that detail in "Cold Warrior," *New York Times Book Review*, 15 Oct. 2006.

13. Harold Macmillan, *Tides of Fortune, 1945–1955* (New York, 1969), p. 493.

14. Christopher de Bellaigue, *Patriot of Persia: Muhammad Mossadegh and a Tragic Anglo-American Coup* (New York, 2012), p. 6.

15. Quoted in David Watry, *Diplomacy at the Brink* (Baton Rouge, La., 2014), p. 70.

16. "IDF Declassifies Docs," *Haaretz*, 11 May 2015, quoting documents from Nehemiah Argov, Ben-Gurion's military secretary.

17. "50 Years Ago: 1956: Censure of Israel," *International Herald Tribune*, 13 Jan. 2006.

18. Emmet John Hughes, *The Ordeal of Power: A Political Memoir of the Eisenhower Years* (New York, 1963), p. 220.

19. Geoffrey Crowther, "Reconstruction of an Alliance," *Foreign Affairs*, Winter 1956–57.

20. John F. Kennedy, "Remarks of Senator John F. Kennedy, University of Kentucky, Lexington, KY, October 8, 1960," American Presidency Project.

Boris Johnson, Prime Minister and leading proponent of Brexit, July 2018. Photograph by Andrew Parsons.

24

Brexit
An Historical Romance

GEOFFREY WHEATCROFT

In 1962, the United Kingdom made its first application to join the European Economy Community, or Common Market, as everyone then called it. One English politician decided to oppose this bid, and that October he did so in a rousing speech that conjured up memories of the First World War battles at Gallipoli and Vimy Ridge. More than that, to join the EEC would mean "the end of Britain as an independent European state," he said. "I make no apology for repeating it. It means the end of a thousand years of history." There were echoes there of earlier phrases, some happier than others. In 1940, Winston Churchill had famously told his people to "brace ourselves to our duties, and so bear ourselves, that if the British Empire and its Commonwealth last for a thousand years, men will still say, 'This was their finest hour,'" but then he was facing an antagonist who spoke of "the thousand-year Reich."

And yet there was something more striking about those particular "thousand years of history." For a long time now, since well before the referendum in June 2016 in which a majority of the British people voted to leave what is now the European Union, and much more often since then, those who call themselves Euroskeptics but who might more accurately be called Europhobes, right-wing Conservatives who passionately favor Brexit, or British departure from the European Union, have again and again invoked history, or their versions of it. But that speaker in 1962 wasn't a Tory at all; he was Hugh Gaitskell, the leader of the opposition, a moderate social democrat leading the Labour Party, who would doubtless have liked to consider himself an internationalist and to repudiate any charge of jingoism or nativism.

History is a very potent drug, above all national history. The nineteenth-century French writer Ernst Renan said that to be a nationalist required two things: hatred of your neighbors and ignorance of your own history, the second of which may ostensibly be less nasty but even more dangerous. Certainly much of modern history is explained by another phrase. Giovanni Giolitti, the Italian prime minister one hundred years ago, said that countries were nourished by "beautiful national legends." The context was interesting. Giolitti was explaining why he didn't want the Italian archives opened to prying scholars, whose investigations might tend to undermine those legends—and to be sure, the official version of the so-called Risorgimento was legendary enough.

Much of earlier history has been variously understood and misunderstood, written and rewritten, appropriated and misappropriated, used and abused. One could say that nearly every nationalist movement—and Brexit is very much an English nationalist movement— has partaken of rewritten history, intellectual dishonesty, and invented tradition. All across nineteenth-century Europe, enthusiasts reconstructed what had been dialects as national languages, rediscovered (or sometimes simply made up) ancient national epics and antique documents on which could be based historic claims for independence, traditional frontiers, irredenta, or whatever.

But even those earlier Slovene or Slovak enthusiasts might have been impressed by the appetite for dubious history-mongering among our Brexiteers. Members of the coyly named European Research Group, of whom Jacob Rees-Mogg (plate 8) is only the most egregious, have tried to wring our withers and make our flesh creep by citing the Corn Laws, King Henry VIII, and King John. Some of these dollops of potted history are quaint or contradictory or plain wrong, but they are all invoked for one purpose. And there is one date more intoxicating than any other.

In the British Isles—to use a phrase that is now frowned on by some—our Celtic fringes have long been prolific in this regard, eagerly using the past for the purposes of the present, albeit often an imaginary past. The classic case is the invented tradition of the Highlands, about which first Lord Macaulay and then Hugh Trevor-Roper wrote most amusingly. This was a confection in any case, but it became quite absurd when it was turned into the purported culture not only of the Highlands and Islands but of the whole country, where everyone from Fife to Galloway was supposed to wear a kilt and play the bagpipes. In 1821, King George IV became the first Hanoverian monarch to visit Scotland, where he held court at Holyrood and donned a kilt, worn over pink tights. Or as Macaulay put it, the king "thought that he could not give a more striking proof of his respect for the usages which had prevailed in Scotland before the Union, than by disguising himself in what, before the Union, was considered by nine Scotchmen out of ten as the dress of a thief."

That hasn't stopped modern Scottish nationalists from conjuring up yet more inventions, from the office of "Makar," vaguely like Poet Laureate, to the dreadful dirge "Flower of Scotland," which celebrates the Battle of Bannockburn in 1314 and has become a kind of national anthem sung by rugby fans. In one foolish line, Robert the Bruce's men fought for "Your wee bit Hill and Glen," although most Scots live and always have lived in the Lowlands, away from hills and glens.

One might argue, as Trevor-Roper did on one occasion, for all his derision, that this misunderstanding of their history, and oblivion of their real long-standing intestine differences, was less harmful to the Scots than a much more accurate awareness of ancient conflicts has been to the peoples of Ireland. All modern Irish nationalism, notably the strain called republicanism, has tried to wish those conflicts away while always exploiting them. Wolf Tone's saying that "Protestant, Catholic and Dissenter" should discard those identities for "the common name of Irishman" is intoned by those who have often enough most energetically killed Protestants.

For most of the last century, the Dublin government made an irredentist claim on Northern Ireland, while for most of those years it was governed by the party called the Soldiers of Destiny, or Fianna Fáil. The Irish national anthem is the sanguinary "Soldier's Song"— "Mid cannons' roar and rifles' peal, / We'll chant a soldier's song"— which begins, in Irish Gaelic, "Sinne Fianna Fáil," and this was, I think, the only country where the ruling party's name was sung in the first line of the anthem. Fianna Fáil and its rival Fine Gael, or the Band of Gaels, like *Dáil* for the parliament and *Taoiseach* for the Prime Minster, are all fine pieces of invented tradition, conjured up from the mists of the Middle Ages. It would be unkind to say that Ireland is the one country where leaders and parties are given names in a dead language, but *Taoiseach* might certainly seem an unfortunate name today. Chosen or invented in the 1930s, it doesn't actually mean "prime minister"; it means "leader," like "Duce" or "Fuhrer," a fashionable type of name at the time.

That was part of a larger invention, seen in the name of "republicanism" and its claim to the whole "island of Ireland." This republicanism has been continually inspired by dreams of an only partly imaginary past, from the incursion of Strongbow and his Anglo-Norman knights in the twelfth century to Poynings' Law to the savage Tudor wars in Ireland to "the curse of Cromwell" and the Battle of the Boyne, the Penal Laws, and the Famine. The implication is that some distant polity lost to English oppression would be restored, although no Irish republic, indeed no Irish state, ever existed before the twentieth century. The late Fred Halliday, a great scholar of Iran and the Arab world, and an Irishman himself, once suggested that if his compatriots wanted a great national hero, they should choose him who first created a united Ireland, King Henry VIII.

On the other hand, Orangemen had their own invigorating dreams of the past as they sang about "the old cause / That gave us our freedom religion and laws," and their father's sash "worn at Derry, Aughrim, Enniskillen and the Boyne." One hears less of that nowadays, and in any case Ulster Protestants don't seem very popular in America. Here is another case of historical amnesia. The figure of twenty million (or more) Irish Americans is sometimes cited. But most of them are actually what old-fashioned Americans call Scotch-Irish, descended not from "green" famine Irish who emigrated from the 1840s on, but from Ulster Presbyterians who had emigrated a century earlier. One might add that for all the tragic martyrdom of Catholic Ireland in the century that followed William of Orange's victory at the Battle of the Boyne in 1690, without King Billy's victory, the United States of America could not possibly exist.

And there is something else. Writing about nationalism and national history, and who can and can't write it, the late E. J. Hobsbawm said that while a proud attachment to either the Irish Catholic or Ulster Protestant tradition might be compatible with the serious study of Irish history, "to be a Fenian or Orangeman, I would judge, is not so compatible, any more than being a Zionist is compatible with writing serious history of the Jews." The line about Zionists might be debatable, and there aren't many Orangemen writing history nowadays, but there are plenty of books written by self-proclaimed Fenians or republicans, and these books are without exception worthless.

ALL THAT MIGHT SOUND A LITTLE HARSH coming from an Englishman, and might seem a digression. But my subject is my own country, which needs no lessons in national mythmaking. Although it was Gaitskell the Labour leader who spoke of a thousand years of history, it is the Brexiteers who have latterly played endless variations on his theme. This knot of fewer than eighty Europhobic Tory MPs in a House of Commons of 650 Members has dictated the political narrative for some time past. Eight years ago they bullied David Cameron, then newly installed as Prime Minister in coalition with the strongly pro-European Liberal Democrats, into promising such a referendum if the Tories won an outright parliamentary majority in the next election.

There have been very few referendums in the United Kingdom. The first was in 1975 when Harold Wilson, despite a strong earlier reluctance, called a referendum on whether Britain should remain as a member of the EEC, which it had joined at last two years earlier under Edward Heath's Tory government. This was a tactical maneuver to brush over divisions within Wilson's Labour Party, and both the larger parties were divided during the referendum, in which the British voted to remain by a wide margin. Thirty years later, in the summer of 2004, Tony Blair astonished and horrified his closest allies, Europhiles all, by promising out of the blue that a referendum would be held on whether to endorse the newly promulgated European Constitution. This was the result of a private deal between Blair and Rupert Murdoch, who promised in return the support of his tabloid the *Sun* at the British general election that was to follow the next spring.

In the event, that election coincided with referendums in which the Dutch and, more importantly, the French rejected the Constitution. A month after the election, in which he was returned to office (after a fashion, gaining a parliamentary majority with only 35 percent of the popular vote), Blair told the Commons that following the French and Dutch votes, "there is no point in having a referendum, because of the uncertainty it would produce." At that point, Angela Browning, a Tory backbencher, reminded Blair of what he had told the *Sun* four weeks earlier: "Even if the French voted No, we would have a referendum. That is a government promise." When Cameron gave his own promise, he half hoped that he wouldn't have to honor it, or that if he did, Remain would win.

Had Cameron known a little more history, he might have refused to hold a referendum in the first place, by way of citing the two outstanding Prime Ministers since the war. When Churchill wanted to hold a referendum for the first time, in 1945, Clement Attlee, the Labour leader, replied, "I could not consent to the introduction into our national life of a device so alien to all our traditions as the referendum, which has only too often been the instrument of Nazism and Fascism." Thirty years later, Margaret Thatcher, the new

Conservative leader of the opposition, said, "The late Lord Attlee was right when he said that the referendum was a device of dictators and demagogues." As yet we don't have fascism in England, or a dictator, but we have plenty of demagogues, and the Brexit referendum was an exercise in naked demagogy. As it was, Cameron lacked Wilson's guile or Blair's shamelessness. And so to the referendum, the victory of Leave, and Cameron's abrupt departure

That demagogy is something the Brexiteers are, not surprisingly, reluctant to admit, but then there are other problems that seem to elude them. A number of prominent figures in their ranks are Roman Catholics, by upbringing or conversion. The former Conservative leader Iain Duncan-Smith and the MPs Sir William Cash and Rees-Mogg were born Catholics, and Charles Moore, sometime editor of the *Spectator* and the *Daily Telegraph,* for both of which he still writes, left the Church of England for Rome in protest at the ordination of women. Brexit apart, they are all what Keynes would have called laissez-fairies, favoring the untrammeled free-enterprise and free-market principles of the Manchester school. Which means that their grasp of moral and pastoral theology is as shaky as that of history. They seem unaware that this "Manchester" economic liberalism is one of the few such doctrines to have been specifically and repeatedly condemned by the Vatican at least since 1891 and Pope Leo XIII's great encyclical *Rerum Novarum.*

That is only a small part of their curious—and curiously Whiggish and Protestant—reading of history. One word that has become important to the Brexiteers is "vassal" or "vassalage." It had long disappeared from common currency, although it speaks to sentimental yearning, sometimes harmlessly enough. Every summer the BBC Promenade Concerts at the Albert Hall gives one of the greatest of all music festivals, ending in September with the Last Night of the Proms, a frolicsome event when the audience joins in singing patriotic songs, with a cheerful lack of irony. They still sing "Land of Hope and Glory" and the lines "Wider yet and further shall thy bounds be set," generations after those bounds stopped being set further and contracted to where they began. Then the Prommers sing the eighteenth-century tub-thumper "Rule Britannia, Britannia rules the waves / Britons never never never shall be slaves," whose words, by James Thomson, didn't show much irony even at the time, when, however they might have "been," Britons certainly owned and traded plenty of slaves.

For the Brexiteers, Britons never never never shall be vassals. Once again, Rees-Mogg was to the fore, although for a man who greatly enjoys invoking history, he recently made a serious mistake by publishing a purported work of history, a collection of biographical essays called *The Victorians*. Other books of late may have received more savage reviews, but they don't immediately come to mind. "Staggeringly silly," "mind-bogglingly banal," "cliche-ridden," "abysmal," and "soul-destroying" were some of the choicer epithets. Although Andrew Roberts, the self-proclaimed "extremely right-wing" polemicist and biographer of Churchill, managed to deliver the generous, indeed unique, verdict that Rees-Mogg's book was "clear-sighted, well-researched and extremely well written," even Simon Heffer, another ardent Brexiteer, was obliged to dismiss the book as "a turkey." This is mentioned not out of malice. One of the redeeming merits of conservatives used to be that they did know some history. No longer, it seems: another purported work of history by a Brexiteer, *The Churchill Factor* by Boris Johnson, was likewise described by one learned critic as a "self-aggrandising pot-boiler."

One of Rees-Mogg's Victorian "titans" is Sir Robert Peel, who is praised for adopting free trade when he repealed the Corn Laws in 1846. But Rees-Mogg has also condemned Peel for doing so with the support of opposition MPs in the House of Commons despite the defection of a large number of his own Tories, which is what Theresa May had forlornly hoped to do at one point with her Brexit deal. That was indeed so with Peel, one of three such cases in the nineteenth century, which may have been what Bismarck had in mind with his rule of English politics, that progressive governments take office to pass reactionary measures, while reactionary governments take office to pass progressive measures. The third case was the Second Reform Act in 1867, expanding the franchise, but the first was the passage of Catholic emancipation in 1829 by the Duke of Wellington's ministry. If Rees-Mogg deplores such scissions, he ought logically to sympathize with the High Tory Ultras who fought to the end against Catholic emancipation, and to regret the schism and temporary alliance that has allowed him and his co-religionists to practice their faith freely. Rees-Mogg is also a devotee of the cult of Charles the Martyr, on the whole nowadays confined to eccentrics from the extreme High, or "ritualist," end of the Church of England. It is likewise hard to see how someone who would have once been regarded as a proponent of "Popish tyranny and arbitrary power," as the Book of Common Prayer used to say, can join in these ceremonies peculiarly associated with another church, not that logic seems to have much to do with the Brexit debate much of the time.

And yet the 1840s is less a favorite of the Brexiteers than the 1530s. Sir John Redwood has been a Tory MP for more than thirty years. He is a man of some academic standing, an Oxford history graduate and DPhil, a Fellow of All Souls, and the author of *Reason, Ridicule, and Religion: The Age of Enlightenment in England, 1660–1750.* He does know some history, and he doesn't let us forget it.

There has been a long tradition of history-mongering, through the sixteenth, seventeenth, and eighteenth centuries, which evolved into what Herbert Butterfield denounced as the Whig interpretation of history. Earlier history-mongers invoked an ancient constitution dating from Anglo-Saxon times, which is to say before the Conquest and the "Norman yoke," under which monarchy had been contractual, in a form guarded by common law and Parliament. This version held that kings who broke the contract had been rightly brought down from their seats: Edward II in 1327, Richard II in 1399, Charles I in still more dramatic fashion in 1649, and James II in 1688. The great Elizabethan jurist Sir Edward Coke went even further when he managed to trace this constitution beyond the Anglo-Saxons to the ancient Britons.

If not quite so chronologically ambitious, Rees-Mogg takes us back to the turn of the thirteenth century when he anathematizes the government White Paper on the terms for departing the EU by calling it "the greatest vassalage since King John paid homage to Philip II at Le Goulet in 1200." Here is one more selective use of history. King John lost Normandy to the French, it is true, but he also stood up for a time to the papacy, which is to say to Innocent III, that most imperious of medieval popes, a Jew- and Muslim-hating crusader.

Then we come forward a century to find another Brexiteer whispering the last enchantments of the Middle Ages. Boris Johnson is the journalist turned politician who served briefly as Foreign Secretary and succeeded Theresa May as Prime Minister. The journalist and historian Sir Max Hastings, once Johnson's editor at the *Daily Telegraph,* dismisses his erstwhile colleague as a "sexual adventurer and charlatan," although a glance at the White House suggests that those may not be absolute disqualifications for high office in these strange times. Johnson made another pick out of the historical lucky dip, suggesting that "the authors of the Chequers proposal risk prosecution under the fourteenth-century statute of praemunire, which says that 'no foreign court or government shall have jurisdiction in this country,'" and never mind that the statute was long ago repealed. These invocations of medieval history remind some of us of a certain age of Tony Hancock, the English comedian, with his patriotic peroration "And what of Magna Carta? Did she die in vain?"

Then the Brexiteers move on to the sixteenth century. Redwood was the first of the Brexiteers to cite the 1533 Act in Restraint of Appeals, which claimed "by divers sundry old authentic histories and chronicles it is manifestly declared and expressed that this realm of England is an empire, and so hath been accepted in the world." When Charles Moore denounced the Archbishop of Canterbury for saying something or other insufficiently patriotic, he added, "The archbishop, when looking at Brexit, should remember the Act in Restraint of Appeals. After all, if it had not been passed, his Church would not exist and he would not be living in Lambeth Palace and making speeches in the Lords." That act was part of the process by which England broke with Rome and became a Protestant country. If he follows his own argument, shouldn't Moore lament the fact that Jesuits and Roman Catholic country gentlemen are no longer disemboweled at Tyburn? And in any case, for these history-mongering dreamers, "it matters not, apparently," as Ferdinand Mount observed, "that the various statutes of praemunire, like the Act in Restraint of Appeals, were repealed fifty years ago and more."

In 1559 the Act in Restraint of Appeals was toughened up by the Act of Supremacy, which has, needless to say, also been cited by Brexiteers, and which held that "no foreign prince, person, prelate, state or potentate hath or ought to have any jurisdiction, power, superiority, pre-eminence or authority ecclesiastical or spiritual within this realm." That was the first year of Queen Elizabeth's reign, a reign that was woven into the very tapestry of beautiful national legend. In some ways it may have been a misfortune that the greatest of English writers lived during that reign. Michael Billington of the *Guardian,* the outstanding theater critic of our time, has plausibly suggested that the history plays rather than the tragedies are the pinnacle of Shakespeare's genius. And yet those grand plays are, among other things, what Hollywood calls flagwavers, agitprop on behalf of the Tudor dynasty, giving a grossly tendentious version of the fourteenth and fifteenth centuries.

Later and lesser writers extolled the sea dogs of Good Queen Bess's reign. In Victorian days, Tennyson wrote "The Revenge," a tale of Sir Richard Greville's heroism: "Sink me the ship, Master Gunner—sink her, split her in twain! / Fall into the hands of God, not into the hands of Spain!" If Theresa May knows that bombastic poem, she might, when meeting European leaders, have thought of the line "And they praised him to his face with their courtly foreign grace," not that they have been praising her much lately.

But none touched the heights of Shakespeare in *Henry V:* "Cry God for Harry, England and St George!" Patriotic legend has often enough been conjured up before now and in better causes. It was not by accident that Laurence Olivier's film version of *Henry V* was made in 1944, just as another English army was fighting in Normandy, and on 6 June 1944 there were infantry subalterns who steeled themselves as their landing craft approached Gold Beach with the thought "And gentlemen in England now abed shall think themselves accursed they were not here."

An inconvenient truth is that Greville and those other sea dogs were in fact pirates, and that King Henry was a war criminal whose slaughter of the French prisoners at Agincourt horrified Christian Europe at the time. Even in our time, so potent are memories of Shakespeare's age that when our present queen acceded to the throne in 1952, there was much excited chatter in the press about a new Elizabethan age. And as the great historian Sir Michael Howard said, this was truer than those who used the phrase knew, "for once again we were, as we had been then, a power of the second rank, teetering on the edge of bankruptcy and punching far beyond our weight in international affairs."

Any study of "beautiful national legends," rewritten history, and invented tradition would find plenty of material in the way that different countries have dealt with the legacy of the world war that ended in 1945. The most remarkable case was Charles de Gaulle's legend that the French people, apart from a handful of cowards and traitors, had been united in their determination to resist the German conqueror and the German occupation. In more somber truth, for most of the war, most French people may have been subjective resisters in wishing to be rid of the Germans, but many were objective collaborators in the sense of accepting the occupation. French men and women actively collaborated with Germans in their most terrible crimes, a truth it took the French Republic generations to acknowledge, and military historians have pointed out the striking fact that between 1939 and 1945, more French soldiers fought for the Axis than for the Allies.

In the course of creating a new democratic German Federal Republic, it was not so much convenient as almost essential to exaggerate the importance of the so-called German resistance and to overlook the fact, which has more recently been dissected by much German scholarship, that many of those who served the Federal Republic had formerly served the Third Reich, some of them in senior positions and with shameful records. The Russians had no need to create a myth of military valor, since it is a matter of historical fact that the Wehrmacht was defeated by the Red Army. But Stalin added his own legend when he insisted that "after this war no one dared any more to deny that vitality of the Soviet state system," and that victory had validated his economic system—five year plans, slave labor, and all.

Much less widely recognized has been the American version, the slow, subtle process of turning it into "the good war." If you visit the remarkable National World War II Museum in New Orleans, for example, with its matchless collection of aircraft, tanks, and landing craft, you might easily leave under the impression that the war was simply a contest between the United States and the Third Reich. This connects with the extravagant American cult of Winston Churchill, now well-nigh seen as the man who inspired the Americans people to resist Hitler and then led them to victory against him.

What has been erased from national memory is the fact that for most of the American people for most of the years from Pearl Harbor to Tokyo Bay, "the war" meant the war in the Pacific. Dwight Macdonald said at the time, "Not the least ironical aspect of this most ironical of wars" was that "the war in the Pacific has always been more popular with all classes of Americans than the war in Europe." Since it was, as he said, hard to portray the conflict with Japan as a "good war" rather than a straightforward imperial contest for mastery, a steady, subtle revision was necessary over many years.

And yet none quite surpass our own English beautiful national legend—while one date and one name overshadow any others in the great romance of Brexit. "His life stopped in 1940," says Hester, the heroine of Terence Rattigan's play *Flight Path,* about her faithless, sodden lover, a former fighter pilot. "He loved 1940, you know. There were some like that." Winston Churchill was surely like that, and so are his implausible epigones of the European Research Group, UK Independence Party (UKIP), and now Nigel Farage's Brexit Party. But then one may sometimes feel that our life as a nation stopped in 1940 and that we have never come to terms with that heroic moment.

"Iconic" has become an annoying vogue word, as the great H. W. Fowler would have said, but it can be apt enough, and an iconography of Sir Winston Churchill could well be compiled. By now it is hard to keep count of the times that his visage has appeared urging Brexit on the front page of the *Sun* and the *Daily Mail,* our two most popular tabloids. One favorite is the—yes, iconic—photograph of Churchill taken by Karsh of Ottawa in 1941, scowling defiantly, and another is the statue by Ivor Roberts-Jones, which broods over Parliament Square. Not long ago a man was sitting in front of that statue draped in a Union Jack across which were the words "Leave Means Leave."

Much of the blame lies with Churchill himself. He said in that summer of 1940 that "we are fighting by ourselves alone but not for ourselves alone," and later about "the time when we were alone." Not a few people have been reminded lately of David Low's famous cartoon after Dunkirk, a Tommy on the cliffs of Dover, rifle to his side, punching the air with the defiant words "Very well alone." It was a coincidence that the movies *Dunkirk* and *Darkest Hour,* both set in 1940, came out not long after the referendum. Both are pretty good travesties of history, *Darkest Hour* preposterously so, and they have had an effect far from what their makers intended, with Charles Moore acclaiming *Darkest Hour* as "a splendid Brexit film."

In truth, of course, we weren't "alone" even in 1940, and heroic as that hour may have been, "we" didn't win the war. "Face it, General," said the writer Antoine de Saint-Exupery, deflating de Gaulle's self-promoted national legend, "France was defeated and our Allies won." Something of the same might have been said to Churchill if anyone had been brave enough. Instead there was an intense mixture of pride and relief when victory came, followed by a very slow realization that the fruits of victory for the British were by no means all sweet, since imperial retreat was followed by comparative economic decline and, finally, national paralysis. After 1918, the Italian nationalist Gabriele D'Annunzio coined the wretched phrase *vittoria mutilata:* Italy had won the war but lost the peace, he said, quite wrongly in both cases, as it happens. Behind the rage of the Brexiteers lies a sense that we too had suffered a mutilated victory. Now cutting ourselves off from Europe as we did at Dunkirk (in a rather different way) means that we can somehow redeem that humiliation.

One of the true heroes of 1940 was Sir Henry Tizard, a physicist, President of Magdalen College, Oxford, and a great patriotic Englishman who may be said without exaggeration to have helped save his country. He was a go-between for the scientists of academe and the officials of Whitehall, and without his work in ensuring that radar was installed around the coastline, the Battle of Britain might have been lost. Nine years later, he wrote a minute that the Brexiteers, with all their dreams of past glories, from "this realm of England is an empire" to "Very well alone," might have heeded.

"We persist in regarding ourselves as a Great Power," Tizard wrote in 1949, "capable of everything and only temporarily handicapped by economic difficulties. We are not a Great Power and never will be again. We are a great nation, but if we continue to behave like a Great Power we shall soon cease to be a great nation." That could have been an epigraph—or epitaph?—for my country's story during my lifetime, culminating in our latest national nervous breakdown. "At times of crisis, myths have their historical importance," Churchill said in 1940, and maybe he was right—then. But at other times of crisis, myths can be dangerous, or even disastrous.

Spring Semester 2019

Isaiah Berlin reading in the Codrington Library, All Souls College, Oxford, 1988.
Photograph by Deborah Elliott.

25

Light Reading for Intellectual Heavyweights

PHILIP WALLER

Imagine a mid-Victorian bearded bloke looking like an Old Testament prophet, who, after his morning's intellectual exertions and a spot of lunch, likes nothing better than to stretch out on the chaise longue, cigarette in hand, eyes half closed, while his wife reads to him from Dinah Mulock Craik's *Agatha's Husband* (1853), a triple-decker he ordered from Mudie's library in which the eponymous heroine is an orphan—and heiress. The first volume recounts her courtship; in the second, the plot thickens when husband Nathaniel learns that his brother, a characteristically villainous major, has misappropriated Agatha's inheritance. He determines to hide the dastardly brother's misdeeds from Agatha while he sorts things out. His secretiveness and further misunderstandings cause husband and wife to suspect each other of infidelity, whereupon Nathaniel starts acting unfeelingly and Agatha concludes volume two by sobbing uncontrollably. In volume three, after rightness is restored, they fall into each other's arms, this time amid tears of joy.

So who was the bearded bloke? Until September 2017, his name was quite literally common currency, the face of the British £10 note, because he was Charles Darwin. As for the moral of this, it may be stretching the evidence to rank *Agatha's Husband* alongside Alexander von Humboldt's *Personal Narrative of Travels* (1818–29) as a seminal influence on Darwin's ideas; still, it doesn't seem to have harmed the great man, and, who knows, it may have provided affirmation of his philosophy of life, of progress and harmony not in spite of but because of apparent setbacks and conflicts. Darwin's favorite relaxation was reading romantic sagas. His son George took a dim view of the quantity of trash his dad gobbled up; but Darwin, unrepentant, avoided stories that didn't contain a pretty face and a happy ending.

George Darwin's discomposure ultimately leads to "Pseuds Corner," the hallowed burial ground of pretentiousness that recently celebrated its golden jubilee in *Private Eye*. Intellectual affectation is inseparable from the reading habit. One question is purpose built to incite it: what book most inspired you? When Vincent McDonnell was asked this, he immediately initiated a rummage around his mental attic to come up with a suitable immortal from the Irish literary pantheon that would most flatter him as a fellow Irish scribe. Was it to be Joyce's *Portrait of the Artist* or that tougher nut *Ulysses*? Tricky, this; but at least McDonnell recognized he couldn't get away with *Finnegans Wake*, because no one would believe him. "Even the words were gibberish," A. J. P. Taylor once pronounced; and he execrated modernist writers for exploding the English literary tradition like artillery blasting the landscape in the First World War.[1] Poets, of course, have always been allowed to drift off into dreamy unintelligibility. That is how we expect such unworldly creatures to behave—namely, not to make sense and to starve accordingly—but the whole point of prose is that it must be understood. During the early twentieth century, the standard of living for ordinary British people rose higher than throughout their history. It was unforgivable, therefore, that they were let down by a literary elite producing unappetizing stuff, just when books had never been cheaper. It wasn't a matter of waiting for folk to catch up with literary fashion. Most never got there because, holding firm values, they didn't want to get there. Anyway, why should the common reader take to modernist authors who showed clear contempt for them?

Back to Vincent McDonnell. When he thought again about the question, he realized he had been a humbug. It wasn't an esoteric classic but "a cheap, dog-eared paperback" by Tex Burns that had most influenced him. "Tex Burns" was the pseudonym of Louis L'Amour, whom John Wayne extolled as the world's most interesting man. Can you get any finer praise than that? Actually, yes; but Louis L'Amour might be judged so perfect a name for fiction writing that it was beyond improvement. He nonetheless twice gave himself a makeover. A North Dakota vet's son, Louis started out with the surname LaMoore. He then Frenchified it, the better to weave his magic. By the 1950s, Louis was churning out not bodice-rippers but westerns—sales of which eventually topped 250 million copies worldwide—and when you are hitching up your chaps and buckling on your Colt 45, hard-bitten Tex Burns rather than heart-rending Louis L'Amour was the partner you handpicked to ride the range. Vincent McDonnell was age seven when he chanced on *The Rustlers of West Fork* (1951). He had never beheld a library, but forty years on, his memory of the novel remained vivid: "[I] still recall the thrill, the excitement and the suspense of the story. One scene, in which Hopalong Cassidy . . . escaped over the mountains with a crippled man and his daughter during a blizzard, is still vivid today."[2] It made him want to be a writer.

The craze for asking what books most influenced people is likely as old as reading itself. That it once had religious implications is obvious, because leisure eaten up by entertainment was suspect, the devil having plenty of work for idle minds as well as idle hands. "Recreation" in its purest sense represents "re-creation": a rebirth of the spirit, by God's grace purged of iniquity. The modern age goes in for secular religions, of which the foremost cult is socialism; hence, the interest roused in 1906 when the twenty-nine MPs who constituted the first parliamentary Labour Party were asked what books had most influenced them. Socialists having their own sacred texts, it might be assumed that Marx's Gothic thriller *Das Kapital* or his *Reader's Digest* version, the *Communist Manifesto,* would top their list. They didn't. Marx got two mentions; even devotees such as Tommy Jackson, a Clerkenwell compositor and founding member of Britain's Communist Party, reckoned fewer than fifty people in the country had read *Das Kapital* all the way through. George Bernard Shaw boasted of being one, calling it "the only book that ever turned me upside down." He stayed in this position, according to Max Beerbohm, for the rest of his life. Rather than Marx, the decisive influences on the Labour MPs were Ruskin, with 17 nominations; Dickens, 16; Carlyle, 13, Walter Scott, 11; Shakespeare, 9; Robbie Burns, 8; Tennyson, 6; Charles Kingsley, 5; Thackeray, 4; and so on. The basis of British socialism was ethical, not economic. This was confirmed by 14 nominations for the Bible, 8 for Bunyan's *Pilgrim's Progress,* and 4 for the Free Church minister Henry Drummond, whose *Natural Law in the Spiritual World* (1883) is now effectively forgotten. That Methodism more than Marx shaped the emerging Labour Party is a familiar thesis.

It can be objected that the first Labour MPs—indeed, politicians nigh on universally—hardly qualify as intellectual heavyweights; but this would be too disdainful. Although most pioneering Labour

MPs lacked formal education beyond board school, they personified a working-class autodidactic culture. Then it was that countless ordinary people exhibited an unquenchable appetite for knowledge. Importantly, autodidacts were—and are—unconfined by specialism and voraciously read classics of all kinds.

It is a short step from asking what books most influenced people to telling them what books should most influence them. The Victorians did not hold back in the homiletic department. Its faculty chair was Sir John Lubbock, a polymathic brain box and versatile man of action who promoted bank holidays, protected ancient monuments, and played his violin to bees to prove their deafness. As president of the Working Men's College, he lectured in 1885 on the "Hundred Best Books." This he reissued in various guises, selling half a million copies at home by 1914 and innumerable elsewhere in over thirty foreign editions. Lubbock's Best Hundred covered every category—religion, science, philosophy, ethics, logic, history, political economy, natural history, biography, the epic, poetry, drama, the novel, and so forth. It was a tall order by any measure, and Lubbock shunned insularity. While British writers predominated and the availability of translations was problematic, he took in not just all of Europe but headed east, incorporating a large slice of the Qur'an and Persian and Hindu epics before reaching Confucius. *She-king* and *Analects* he did not particularly rate, but included them because they were "held in the most profound veneration by the Chinese race, containing 400,000,000 of our fellow men." Moreover, he added considerately, "both works are quite short."[3]

Lubbock did not otherwise attain today's standards. He was emphatic that books "must be read for improvement rather than for amusement." He conceded that "light and entertaining books are valuable, just as sugar is an important article of food, especially for children, but we cannot live upon it." Furthermore, "there are books which are no books, and to read which is mere waste of time; while there are others so bad, that we cannot read them without pollution; if they were men we should kick them into the street." His Hundred comprised only books that "no one can read without being the better for them." Lubbock was not Gradgrind. Literature that made better workers was "useful, no doubt, but by no means the highest use of books." His aim was more like a Platonic ideal: "The best books elevate us into a region of disinterested thought where . . . the trouble and anxieties of the world are almost forgotten."[4]

Lubbock had many an imitator; indeed, pretty well every busybody and bore in the land discharged rival Best Hundreds. Lord Acton, limbering up to become Regius Professor of History at Cambridge, released one even more strenuous than Lubbock's. But to presume that every Victorian was fitted with a humor bypass is preposterous. On the contrary, solemn allocution inspired iconoclastic comedy. "The Hundred Best Soporifics" was hailed as a truer depiction of the exercise; and Jerome K. Jerome's *The Idle Thoughts of an Idle Fellow* (1886), dedicated to his pipe, was customized for all "tired of reading 'the best hundred books.'"

Did Lubbock's plan have no takers? It might seem a vanity, except that Routledge's brought out all the titles in a series and people like Police Sergeant Hewitt, who considered himself superior, could be found brooding over Lubbock's list. His son noted drily that it "included nearly all the books one didn't want to read, or gave up if one tried," books you would "expect to find in every intelligent gentleman's private library; with . . . their leaves uncut."[5] He then disclosed the reading his father most relished. These were the best sellers Marie Corelli, Rider Haggard, Anthony Hope, Stanley Weyman, and the up-and-coming Edgar Wallace.

Such pharisaism was right up J. M. Barrie's Quality Street. Barrie himself wasn't so different, except for being the most aware of authors. In *What Every Woman Knows* (1908), he divulged, "There are few more impressive sights in the world than a Scotsman on the make"; but it was in *Alice Sit-By-The-Fire* (1905) that he took aim at literary name-dropping:

> ALICE. Are you very studious, Cosmo?
> COSMO. My favourite authors are William Shakespeare and William Milton. They are grand, don't you think?
> ALICE. I'm only a woman . . . and I'm afraid they sometimes bore me, especially William Milton.
> COSMO [*with relief*]. Do they? Me, too.

This returns us to our Labour MPs. It does not impugn the truthfulness of their declarations about which books most influenced them to suppose they read other things too and enjoyed them more. Knowing their answers would be published, and striving to make a profound impression, they put on the equivalent of their Sunday suit. Yet it would transgress the bounds of credulity if they were never entranced by the best sellers of their day, such as Hall Caine, who penned the first million-selling novel in Britain, or Nat Gould, who at his death in 1919 had turned out 130 horse-racing novels and clocked up sales of 24 million. Or Charles Garvice: Arnold Bennett identified him as "the most successful novelist in England," and in 1912–13 alone he sold 1,750,000 copies to add to the 6 million already snapped up. His literary agent, Eveleigh Nash, said of the sixpenny Garvices that they were as plentiful as the leaves of Vallom-brosa—a delightful simile deployed in *Paradise Lost* about the vast number of fallen angels, although whether its author was William or John Milton, I can never quite remember.

IT IS OBLIGATORY THAT EVERY TALE must have a twist, so here are two quite similar scenes. The first was an at-home in the early 1870s at the swanky Regent's Park address of a celebrity literary couple who were living in sin, as liberal intellectuals are still (I believe) com-pelled by law to do. The male host confidentially disclosed to their rapt guests, "Celia is going to have a baby!" The second occurred fifty years later, just after the First World War, when, at a packed meeting in Paisley containing newly enfranchised women, a note was handed up to the platform speaker. This read: "Will Mrs Bur-nett Smith tell us whether Captain Hannay is going to marry Jean Adair?"

Here the game has been given away—or perhaps not, because who now knows Mrs. Burnett Smith's prolific output of romances under the pen name Annie S. Swan? What her audience was avid to find out was the denouement of her story running in the *People's Friend*. This still leaves unidentified the Regent's Park residents. He was George Henry Lewes, the positivist critic, biographer of Goethe, and paramour of Mary Ann Evans, immortal as George Eliot; and the Celia who was having a baby was the sister of Dorothea Brooke, the heroine of *Middlemarch,* which was then being serialized.

No one will want to argue that George Eliot and Annie S. Swan are co-equals, yet there is need to acknowledge that a gripping story could seize both a literary salon and a newsagent's clientele. United with these were fuddy-duddy dons: legend had it that the Dean of King's College London and the Cambridge University registrary cut chapel to be the first to learn how *The Hound of the Baskervilles* (1902) ended. We should, therefore, guard against literary snobbery and resist a temptation to divide works into highbrow and lowbrow, as if phrenology was an exact science. To assume that only the best peo-ple read the best books is a fallacy; similarly, it should be granted that best sellers were read by all.

Reading is an altogether baffling business. No two people read the same book in the same way; likewise, no one person reads the same book for a second time in the same way. When evaluating the impact of books, for too long literary scholars poured over the text and ignored the audience. Reception history aims to reverse that imbalance; still, it remains true that we can't easily know how books are read, what holds or loses readers' attention, and what sensations

Figure 25.1. Annie S. Swan (1859–1943), best-selling Scottish author of more than two hundred works of romantic fiction. Besides publishing under her maiden name, she wrote as Mrs. Burnett Smith and David Lyall. Photograph by Edward Drummond Young. PGP 347, Scottish National Portrait Gallery, Edinburgh.

they experience. Readers of George Eliot may have hopped over her ruminations about religion and evolution, deeming them tiresome. Many a classic resembled the best seller in having a well-crafted tale, populated by characters whose fortunes readers could relate to. Both convention and choice dictate for us, as for the Victorians, that a rattling good read must involve emotional turmoil and moral quandaries before, ideally, right is triumphant and wrong vanquished.

Also to be weighed is how stories come to readers in different forms, including abridgment and serialization. The journalist who quizzed the first Labour MPs about the books that influenced them was W. T. Stead, who learned his trade as a publicist during Gladstone's Bulgarian atrocities campaign in 1876. Ten years later, he courted imprisonment for exposing child prostitution and white slavery; in 1912, he sank with the *Titanic*. His belief that the dead communicate with the living means that we cannot rule out him one day sensationally reporting on his own drowning. Until then, arresting among Stead's feats was his exploitation of new printing technology and the expiration of copyright protection for myriad dead authors. In May 1895, he launched Penny Poets, followed in January 1896 by Penny Novels. By October 1897, his sixty volumes of Penny Poets had cleared 5 million, and ninety Penny Novels 9 million. These last were condensations of classics, cut to 30,000–40,000 words, ditching a huge amount of verbiage and, in the process, bringing the George Eliots of literature closer to the Annie S. Swans. As we reel in horror at the philistinism and brutality involved, let's remember that the same and worse are perpetrated in adaptations for radio, television, and cinema, and that theater reputations are regularly made by amputating Shakespeare and dressing what is left in a snazzy modern wardrobe. Also remember that many a classic author wrote hurriedly. The notion that readers should dwell on their every word is a superstition. Sir Walter Scott, scribbling to pay off debts, endorsed "the laudable practice of skipping."

Exceptional people in practically every respect behave like unexceptional people. David Lloyd George liked to unwind with what he dubbed "shilling shockers": cliff-hanging thrillers and pulsating romances. His predecessor as Premier, Herbert Asquith, consumed thrillers too; alternatively, he sat up in bed translating Kipling into Greek. "Surely that was an effort," queried his wife. "Not at all; it was a relaxation," he purred, with the effortless superiority of a Balliol Greats man.[6] The following evening, their last in Downing Street, he read the Bible. And what part? Naturally, the Crucifixion. There was no political resurrection for Asquith three days later or any other time; yet at whatever point he retired to bed and in whatever condition—his nickname was Perrier Jouet—he never broke the habit of reading for two hours. There isn't space to pursue all off-duty prime ministerial reading, although it would be unpardonable to disregard Harold Macmillan, who was always keen to go to bed with a Trollope.

Recent Prime Ministers appear more interested in photo-ops as they set off on holiday with the title of some improving reading accidentally peeping out from under their arm. In this they are allies of the chattering classes, who are mortified if not seen with the book of the moment. How else to explain Stephen Hawking's *A Brief History of Time* occupying the best-seller list for a record-busting 237 weeks after publication in 1988? Similarly, to take this quest abroad, consider the impact of Hugo Chavez when in 2006 he denounced George W. Bush as the devil and waved in the air Noam Chomsky's *Hegemony or Survival*. Chavez nominated Chomsky's polemic against America's unsleeping "Quest for Global Dominance" as essential reading for the Venezuelan Assembly and for all Americans. Originally published in 2003 and languishing at #160,772 on Amazon on the Wednesday Chavez gave his speech, by Thursday afternoon it had been catapulted into the top ten. Doubtless, the coffee tables of Islington and Notting Hill as well as of Manhattan and Brentwood–Bel Air groaned under the weight of its radical chic.

HERE WE HAVE STRAYED FROM THE THEME of light reading for intellectual heavyweights into heavy reading for—well, the point shouldn't be pressed. Instead, it is an opportunity to commend an obiter dictum of Oliver Edwards, a Wiltshire gentleman's son who was at Oxford with Samuel Johnson. When they met some fifty years later at St. Clement Danes, Edwards remarked at the conclusion of their chat: "You are a philosopher, Dr Johnson. I have tried in my time to be a philosopher but, I don't know how, cheerfulness was always breaking through." It must be hoped the same befell Hilary Benn, who at Christmas 1976 was given by his mother, wife of Tony the Labour minister who grandly renounced an inherited peerage, Isaac Deutscher's three-volume biography of Trotsky along with— a nice maternal touch—the *Communist Manifesto* in his stocking. Should that not be completely stunning, the knockout blow can be administered by contemplating Tony Blair's carefully calibrated admission in 2006 that Deutscher's trilogy "made a very deep impression" on him. In 2017, he embellished this, revealing that when he was an undergraduate, it transformed him into a bit of a Trot: "I picked it up . . . and I literally didn't stop reading it all night . . . I suddenly thought the world's full of these extraordinary causes and injustices and here's this guy, Trotsky, who was so inspired by all this that he went out to create a Russian revolution and change the world. It was like a light going on."[7] Blair being a singular marvel, beyond caricature, it is not at all contradictory that in 1996, when he was only leader of the opposition and didn't want to spook Middle England, he suppressed any memory of his one-night stand with Trotsky and instead selected Scott's *Ivanhoe* to take to his desert island.

That is more like it, and it brings us back to Lloyd George, who admitted to Gladstone's daughter that he couldn't read novels that ended badly. This is paramount: at the finish of a story, readers shouldn't be left downcast but uplifted, their fiber boosted so that they can return revitalized to the serious cares of life. If there is to be a shoot-out between realist misery and gossamer romance, the smart money will be on the love-struck winning almost every time.

Space should also be reserved for mystery and adventure. The Nobel laureate W. B. Yeats used to lap up Dorothy L. Sayers detec-

Figure 25.2. William Butler Yeats reading a volume of William Blake, c. 1920. Photograph by Bain News Service. Prints and Photographs Division, Library of Congress.

tive stories and Zane Grey westerns: "One can read them while the mind sleeps," he said with apparent nonchalance. This was Willie being lordly, after Sean O'Casey espied the books on his mantelpiece. Flustered that he should be discovered devouring that sort of thing rather than, say, toying with an eight-hundred-page philosophical novel by Dostoevsky or some other depressed and depressing Russian, he decided to brazen it out. But instead of his mind being switched off, it is more believable to suppose it was wide-awake with excitement.

Last, there is the peculiar case of Isaiah Berlin and Jules Verne. Once encountered, never forgotten, with his booming, imperative voice and torrential talk, timed at almost four hundred words a minute, the historian of ideas Isaiah Berlin was a stenographer's nightmare made flesh. It is almost unimaginable now, yet once upon a time an Oxford don was a prize catch for fashionable social gatherings in the capital. Not just any performing don; rather, Isaiah Berlin in particular. He sported all the right credentials: an exotic provenance from a Russian-Latvian émigré family, schooled at St Paul's, followed by a double First at Oxford, All Souls Fellowship, then onward and upward to the presidency of the British Academy, a knighthood and Order of Merit, the last being the summit of distinction because the number of honorees alive at any one time was severely rationed. Berlin had grabbed Churchill's attention by sending brilliant dispatches from wartime Washington. On the strength of this, Churchill in 1944 instructed his secretary to invite Berlin to luncheon. He swiftly grew disenchanted as Berlin gave dim-witted answers to his probing questions about how long the war would last and FDR's chances of reelection. Churchill fumed to an aide that Berlin was only another civil servant after all, proficient on paper but useless face-to-face. It turned out he had been cross-examining the petrified songsmith Irving Berlin, composer of "A White Christmas." Isaiah, by contrast, was always dependably scintillating. It isn't difficult to imagine a hostess entrancing a friend with the prospect of a supper that included Berlin because, while frightfully intellectual of course, he could recite the plots of over fifty Jules Verne novels.

This being true, a question naturally arises: was his accomplishment simply a show-off party piece, or did Jules Verne mean more to him? Undoubtedly, Berlin had a prodigiously retentive brain, but to rattle off over fifty Jules Verne titles, let alone their plots, would seem to be overdoing things and to put him in the train-spotter collector-maniac class. And yet, and yet . . . Michael Ignatieff's biography records that Berlin first read *Twenty Thousand Leagues under the Sea* in Russian translation, and later in life, when asked what he had wanted to be as a boy, he replied that "he used to dream of being a scientist in a Jules Verne novel, undersea, watching the world of nature through a porthole." Ignatieff explains this as a philosophical fantasy, "exploring the depths, yet remaining immune from their dangers"; but there is another interpretation, Berlin's own, to be gleaned from an essay on education.[8] Highlighting the importance of popularizers, however imperfect their rendering, he instanced Voltaire's *Elements of the Philosophy of Newton* (1738) and how, a century and a half later, "those other great *vulgarisateurs,* Jules Verne and H. G. Wells, in their own highly imaginative way," had had "an immensely liberating effect." A "gifted expositor," he maintained, "can put life into virtually any topic."[9]

One oddity to note is that while in the English-speaking world an admiration for Verne will at best be thought an amiable eccentricity, in Continental Europe it is otherwise. Across most of the globe, intellectuals are an endangered species, but not in Verne's native France, which remains their natural habitat—Paris especially, where they can sound off and procreate with joyous abandon. There Verne is esteemed for his enduring imprint on avant-gardism and surrealism. In 2017, shortly after President Macron assumed office and became Jupiter, the Élysée Palace let it be known that Macron was a Jules Verne fan and that the First Dog, the presidential pet, was named Nemo.[10]

In that same essay on education, Berlin roundly berated academic abstruseness, jargon, and windy theorizing—"Pretentious rhetoric, deliberate or compulsive obscurity or vagueness, metaphysical patter studded with irrelevant or misleading allusions to (at best) half understood scientific or philosophical theories or to famous names, is an old, but at present particularly prevalent, device for concealing poverty of thought or muddle, and sometimes perilously near a confidence trick."[11] This was in 1975. In the intervening forty-plus years, the climate has deteriorated rather than improved; but that is another story. Jane Austen, who replaced Charles Darwin as the face of the £10 banknote, anticipated the approaching fog with her usual percipience. She has Catherine Morland confess in chapter 16 of *Northanger Abbey* (1803), "I cannot speak well enough to be unintelligible."

To conclude: great men and women do not inhabit a separate planet from the rest of us, and there is no embarrassment in putting your feet up. Particularly if you have to slog through impossibly dreary academic tomes and articles. Hard labor of that kind is character-building above whatever the Victorians endured; still, it is seldom you must read each word, and it is part of the intelligent person's armory to be adept at gutting, to establish what is significant and what isn't. The literary scholar George Saintsbury, who was a wine connoisseur as well as omnivorous reader, designated it "the art of . . . skimming-cum-skipping."[12]

Everyone benefits from time off. It is no paradox that after struggling with academic heavy lifting, you may well read every word of light literature; but the lighter stuff is not by virtue of that to be belittled. Any reading can trigger adventitious associations and spark serendipitous ideas that help in tackling other problems. Cross-pollination is inherent in the exercise. No need, therefore, to scold yourself or apologize for indulging in fun. Every sermon should finish with a benediction, and mine is this: go forth and enjoy your soaps. The main thing is to be intellectually honest. And to keep fresh. To put that another way: shun clichés like the plague.

Fall Semester 2018

1. A. J. P. Taylor, *English History, 1914–1945* (Oxford, 1965), p. 179.

2. Frank Shovlin, "From Tucson to Television," in Clare Hutton and Patrick Walsh, eds., *The Irish Book in English, 1891–2000* (Oxford, 2011), p. 151.

3. Lord Avebury [Sir John Lubbock], *The Pleasures of Life,* 20th ed. (London, 1890), preface.

4. Quoted in Philip Waller, *Writers, Readers, and Reputations: Literary Life in Britain, 1870–1918* (Oxford, 2008), pp. 69–71.

5. C. H. Rolph [C. R. Hewitt], *London Particulars* (Oxford, 1980), pp. 83–84.

6. Countess of Oxford and Asquith, *Off the Record* (London, 1943), pp. 32–33.

7. *The Times,* 11 Aug. 2017.

8. Michael Ignatieff, *Isaiah Berlin: A Life* (London, 1998), p. 22.

9. Isaiah Berlin, "General Education," *Oxford Review of Education,* 1, 3, 1975.

10. *The Times,* 29 Aug. 2017, p. 31. Verne died in Amiens in 1905; Macron was born there in 1977.

11. Berlin, "General Education."

12. Quoted in Frank Swinnerton, *Background with Chorus: A Footnote to Changes in English Literary Fashion between 1901 and 1917* (London, 1956), p. 70.

British Studies at
the University of Texas, 1975–2019

Fall Semester 1975

Paul Scott (Novelist, London), 'The *Raj Quartet*'
Ian Donaldson (Australian National University), 'Humanistic Studies in Australia'
Fritz Fellner (Salzburg University), 'Britain and the Origins of the First World War'
Wm. Roger Louis (History), 'Churchill, Roosevelt, and the Future of Dependent Peoples during the Second World War'
Michael Holroyd (Biographer, Dublin), 'Two Biographies: Lytton Strachey and Augustus John'
Max Beloff (Buckingham College), 'Imperial Sunset'
Robin Winks (Yale University), 'British Empire-Commonwealth Studies'
Warren Roberts (HRHRC) and David Farmer (HRHRC), 'The D. H. Lawrence Editorial Project'
Harvey C. Webster (University of Louisville), 'C. P. Snow as Novelist and Philosopher'
Anthony Kirk-Greene (Oxford University), 'The Origins and Aftermath of the Nigerian Civil War'

Spring Semester 1976

Joseph Jones (English), 'World English'
William S. Livingston (Government), 'The British Legacy in Contemporary Indian Politics'
John Higley (Sociology), 'The Recent Political Crisis in Australia'
Round Table Discussion, 'Reassessments of Evelyn Waugh': Elspeth Rostow (Dean, General and Comparative Studies), Standish Meacham (History), and Alain Blayac (University of Paris)
Jo Grimond (former Leader of the Liberal Party), 'Liberal Democracy in Britain'
Round Table Discussion, 'The Impact of Hitler on British Politics': Gaines Post

(History), Malcolm Macdonald (Government), and Wm. Roger Louis (History)

Round Table Discussion, 'Kipling and India': Robert Hardgrave (Government), Gail Minault (History), and Chihiro Hosoya (University of Tokyo)

Kenneth Kirkwood (Oxford University), 'The Future of Southern Africa'

C. P. Snow, 'Elite Education in England'

Hans-Peter Schwarz (Cologne University), 'The Impact of Britain on German Politics and Society since the Second World War'

B. K. Nehru (Indian High Commissioner, London), 'The Political Crisis in India'

Round Table Discussion, 'Declassification of Secret Documents: The British and American Experiences Compared': Robert A. Divine (History), Harry J. Middleton (LBJ Library), and Wm. Roger Louis (History)

Fall Semester 1976

John Farrell (English), 'Revolution and Tragedy in Victorian England'

Anthony Honoré (Oxford University), 'British Attitudes to Legal Regulation of Sex'

Alan Hill (English), 'Wordsworth and America'

Ian Nish (London School of Economics), 'Anglo-American Naval Rivalry and the End of the Anglo-Japanese Alliance'

Norman Sherry (University of Lancaster), 'Joseph Conrad and the British Empire'

Peter Edwards (Australian National University), 'Australia through American Eyes: The Second World War and the Rise of Australia as a Regional Power'

Round Table Discussion, 'Britain and the Future of Europe': David Edwards (Government), Steven Baker (Government), Malcolm Macdonald (Government), William S. Livingston (Government), and Wm. Roger Louis (History)

Michael Hurst (Oxford University), 'The British Empire in Historical Perspective: The Case of Joseph Chamberlain'

Ronald Grierson (English Banker and former Public Official), 'The Evolution of the British Economy since 1945'

Marian Kent (University of New South Wales), 'British Oil Policy between the World Wars'

Constance Babington-Smith (Cambridge University), 'The World of Rose Macaulay'

Round Table Discussion, 'Adam Smith after 200 Years': William Todd (History), Walt Rostow (History and Economics), and James McKie (Dean, Social and Behavioral Sciences)

Spring Semester 1977

Carin Green (Novelist) and Elspeth Rostow (American Studies), 'The Achievement of Virginia Woolf'

Samuel H. Beer (Professor of Government, Harvard University), 'Reflections on British Politics'

David Fieldhouse (Oxford University), 'Decolonization and the Multinational Corporations'

Gordon Craig (Stanford University), 'England and Europe on the Eve of the Second World War'

John Lehmann (British Publisher and Writer), 'Publishing under the Bombs— The Hogarth Press during World War II'

Round Table Discussion, 'The Author, His Editor, and Publisher': Philip Jones (University of Texas Press), William S. Livingston (Government), Michael Mewshaw (English), David Farmer (HRC), Roger Louis (History), and William Todd (History)

Dick Taverne (former Member of Parliament), 'The Mood of Britain: Misplaced Gloom or Blind Complacency?'

Round Table Discussion, 'The Origins of World War II in the Pacific': James B. Crowley (Yale University), Lloyd C. Gardner (Rutgers University), Akira Iriye (University of Chicago), and Wm. Roger Louis (History)

Rosemary Murray (Cambridge University), 'Higher Education in England'

Burke Judd (Zoology) and Robert Wagner (Zoology), 'Sir Cyril Burt and the Controversy over the Heritability of IQ'

Round Table Discussion, 'The Wartime Reputations of Churchill and Roosevelt: Overrated or Underrated?': Alessandra Lippucci (Government), Roger Louis (History), William S. Livingston (Government), and Walt Rostow (Economics)

Fall Semester 1977

Donald L. Weismann (Art and Art History), 'British Art in the Nineteenth Century: Turner and Constable—Precursors of French Impressionism'

Standish Meacham (History), 'Social Reform in England'

Joseph Jones, 'Recent Commonwealth Literature'

Lewis Hoffacker (former US Ambassador), 'The Katanga Crisis: British and Other Connections'

Round Table Discussion, 'The Copyright Law of 1976': James M. Treece (Law), Wm. Roger Louis (History), Warren Roberts, and Bill Todd (History)

Round Table Discussion, 'Freedom at Midnight: A Reassessment of Britain and the Partition of India Thirty Years After': Charles Heimsath (Visiting Professor of Indian History), Bob Hardgrave (Government), Thomasson Jannuzi, (Center for Asian Studies), C. P. Andrade (Comparative Studies), and William S. Livingston (Government),

Lord Fraser of Kilmorack (Conservative Party Organization), 'The Tory Tradition of British Politics'

Bernth Lindfors (English), 'Charles Dickens and the Hottentots and Zulus'

Albert Hourani (Oxford University), 'The Myth of T. E. Lawrence'

Mark Kinkead-Weekes (University of Kent) and Mara Kalnins (British Writer), 'D. H. Lawrence: Censorship and the Expression of Ideas'

J. D. B. Miller (Australian National University), 'The Collapse of the British Empire'

Round Table Discussion, 'The Best and Worst Books of 1977': Peter Green (Classics), Robert King (Dean, Social and Behavioral Sciences), William S. Livingston (Government), Bob Hardgrave (Government), Wm. Roger Louis (History), and Warren Roberts (HRHRC)

Spring Semester 1978

Round Table Discussion, 'British Decadence in the Interwar Years': Peter Green (Classics), Malcolm Macdonald (Government), and Robert Crunden (American Studies),

Round Table Discussion, 'R. Emmet Tyrrell's *Social Democracy's Failure in Britain*': Terry Quist (UT Undergraduate), Steve Baker (Government), and Wm. Roger Louis (History),

Stephen Koss (Columbia University), 'The British Press: Press Lords, Politicians, and Principles'
John House (Oxford University), 'The Rhodesian Crisis'
T. S. Dorsch (Durham University), 'Oxford in the 1930s'
Stephen Spender (English Poet and Writer), 'Britain and the Spanish Civil War'
Okot p'Bitek (Ugandan Poet), 'Idi Amin's Uganda'
David C. Goss (Australian Consul General), 'Wombats and Wivveroos'
Leon Epstein (University of Wisconsin), 'Britain and the Suez Crisis of 1956'
David Schoonover (Library Science), 'British and American Expatriates in Paris in the 1920s'
Peter Stansky (Stanford University), 'George Orwell and the Spanish Civil War'
Alexander Parker (Spanish and Portuguese), 'Reflections on the Spanish Civil War'
Norman Sherry (Lancaster University), 'Graham Greene and Latin America'
Martin Blumenson (Department of the Army), 'The Ultra Secret'

Fall Semester 1978

W. H. Morris-Jones (University of London), 'Power and Inequality in Southeast Asia'
Round Table Discussion, 'The British and the Shaping of the American Critical Mind: Edmund Wilson's *Letters on Literature and Politics*': Hartley Grattan (History), Gilbert Chase (American Studies), Bob Crunden (American Studies), and Wm. Roger Louis (History)
James Roach (Government), 'The Indian Emergency and its Aftermath'
Bill Todd (History), 'The Lives of Samuel Johnson'
Lord Hatch (British Labour Politician), 'The Labour Party and Africa'
John Kirkpatrick (HRHRC), 'Max Beerbohm'
Brian Levack (History), 'Witchcraft in England and Scotland'
M. R. Masani (Indian Writer), 'Gandhi and Gandhism'
A. W. Coates (Economics), 'The Professionalization of the British Civil Service'
John Clive (Harvard University), 'Great Historians of the Nineteenth Century'
Geoffrey Best (University of Sussex), 'Flight Path to Dresden: British Strategic Bombing in the Second World War'
Kurth Sprague (English), 'T. H. White's *Once and Future King*'
Gilbert Chase (American Studies), 'The British Musical Invasion of America'

Spring Semester 1979

Round Table Discussion, 'P. N. Furbanks's Biography of E. M. Forster': Peter Green (Classics), Alessandra Lippucci (Government), and Elspeth Rostow (LBJ School)
Round Table Discussion, 'E. M. Forster and India': Wm. Roger Louis (History), Bob Hardgrave (Government), Gail Minault (Professor of History), Peter Gran (History), and Bob King (Dean of Liberal Arts)
Paul M. Kennedy (University of East Anglia), 'The Contradiction between British Strategic Policy and Economic Policy in the Twentieth Century'
Richard Rive (Visiting Fulbright Research Fellow from South Africa), 'Olive Schreiner and the South African Nation'
Charles P. Kindleberger (Massachusetts Institute of Technology), 'Lord Zuckerman and the Second World War'
John Press (English Poet), 'English Poets and Postwar Society'

Richard Ellmann (Oxford University), 'Writing a Biography of Joyce'
Michael Finlayson (Scottish Dramatist), 'Contemporary British Theater'
Lawrence Stone (Institute for Advanced Study, Princeton), 'Family, Sex, and Marriage in England'
C. P. Snow, 'Reflections on the Two Cultures'
Theodore Zeldin (Oxford University), 'Are the British More or Less European than the French?'
David Edwards (Government), 'How United the Kingdom: Greater or Lesser Britain?'
Michael Holroyd (British Biographer), 'George Bernard Shaw'
John Wickman (Eisenhower Library), 'Eisenhower and the British'

Fall Semester 1979

Robert Palter (Philosophy), 'Reflections on British Philosophers: Locke, Hume, and the Utilitarians'
Alfred Gollin (University of California, Santa Barbara), 'Political Biography as Political History: Garvin, Milner, and Balfour'
Edward Steinhart (History), 'The Consequences of British Rule in Uganda'
Paul Sturges (Loughborough University, UK), and Dolores Donnelly (Toronto University), 'History of the National Library of Canada'
Sir Michael Tippett (British Composer), 'Moving into Aquarius'
Steven Baker (Government), 'Britain and United Nations Emergency Operations'
Maria Okila Dias (University of São Paulo), 'Intellectual Roots of Informal Imperialism: Britain and Brazil'
Alexander Parker (Spanish and Portuguese), 'Reflections on *Brideshead Revisited*'
Barry C. Higman (University of the West Indies), 'West Indian Emigrés and the British Empire'
Gaines Post (History), 'Britain and the Outbreak of the Second World War'
Karen Gould (Art and Art History), 'Medieval Manuscript Fragments and English Seventeenth-Century Collections: New Perspectives from *Fragmenta Manuscripta*'
Round Table Discussion, 'Jeanne MacKenzie's *Dickens: A Life*': John Farrell (English), Eric Poole (HRHRC) and James Bieri (English):
Joseph O. Baylen (Georgia State University), 'British Journalism in the Late Victorian and Edwardian Eras'
Peter T. Flawn (President, University of Texas), 'An Appreciation of Charles Dickens'

Spring Semester 1980

Annette Weiner (Anthropology), 'Anthropologists in New Guinea: British Interpretations and Cultural Relativism'
Bernard Richards (Oxford University), 'Conservation in the Nineteenth Century'
Thomas McGann (History), 'Britain and Argentina: An Informal Dominion?'
Mohammad Ali Jazayery (Center for Middle Eastern Studies), 'The Persian Tradition in English Literature'
C. Hartley Grattan (History) 'Twentieth-Century British Novels and the American Critical Mind'
Katherine Whitehorn (London *Observer*), 'An Insider's View of the *Observer*'
Guy Lytle (History), 'The Oxford University Press's *History of Oxford*'
C. P. Snow, 'Reflections on *The Masters*'

Harvey Webster, '*The Masters* and the Two Cultures'

Brian Blakeley (Texas Tech University), 'Women and the British Empire'

Stephen Koss (Columbia University), 'Asquith, Balfour, Milner, and the First World War'

Tony Smith (Tufts University), 'The Expansion of England: New Ideas on Controversial Themes in British Imperialism'

Stanley Ross (History), 'Britain and the Mexican Revolution'

Rowland Smith (Dalhousie University), 'The British Intellectual Left and the War, 1939–1945'

Richard Ellmann (Oxford University), 'Oscar Wilde: A Reconsideration and Problems of the Literary Biographer'

James Bill (Government), 'The United States, Britain, and the Iranian Crisis of 1953'

Fall Semester 1980

Decherd Turner (HRHRC), 'The First 1000 Days'

Wm. Roger Louis (History), 'Britain and Egypt after the Second World War'

Alistair Horne (Woodrow Wilson Center), 'Britain and the Fall of France'

Round Table Discussion, 'Literary Fraud: H. R. Trevor-Roper and the Hermit of Peking': Edward Rhodes (History), Peter Green (Classics), William Todd (History), and Wm. Roger Louis (History),

Mark Kinkead-Weekes (Kent University), 'D. H. Lawrence's *Rainbow:* Its Sense of History'

Sir John Crawford (Australian National University), 'Hartley Grattan: In Memoriam'

John Stubbs (University of Waterloo), 'The Tory View of Politics and Journalism in the Interwar Years'

Donald L. Weismann (Art and Art History), 'British Art in the Nineteenth Century'

Fran Hill (Government), 'The Legacy of British Colonialism in Tanzania'

R. W. B. Lewis (Yale University), 'What's Wrong with the Teaching of English?'

Charlene Gerry (British Publisher), 'The Revival of Fine Printing in Britain'

Peter Gran (History), 'The Islamic Response to British Capitalism'

Tina Poole (HRHRC) 'Gilbert and Sullivan's Christmas'

Spring Semester 1981

Bernard N. Darbyshire (Visiting Professor of Government and Economics), 'North Sea Oil and the British Future'

Christopher Hill (Oxford University), 'The English Civil War'

Elizabeth Heine (UT San Antonio), and Wm. Roger Louis (History), 'A Reassessment of Leonard Woolf'

Bernard Richards (Oxford University), 'D. H. Lawrence and Painting'

Miguel Gonzalez-Gerth (Spanish and Portuguese), 'Poetry Once Removed: The Resonance of English as a Second Language'

John Putnam Chalmers (HRHRC), 'English Bookbinding from Caedmon to Le Carré'

Peter Coltman (Architecture), 'The Cultural Landscapes of Britain: 2,000 Years of Blood, Sweat, Toil & Tears to Wrest a Living from this Bloody Mud'

Thomas H. Law (former Regent, University of Texas), 'The Gold Coins of the English Sovereigns'

Round Table Discussion, 'Canadian-American Economic Relations': Sidney Weintraub (LBJ School), James W. McKie (Economics), and Mary Williams (Canadian Consulate, Dallas)

Amedée Turner (European Parliament), 'Integrating Britain into the European Community'

Muriel C. Bradbrook (Cambridge University), 'Two Poets: Kathleen Raine and Seamus Heaney'

Ronald Sampson (Industrial Development Department, Aberdeen), 'Scotland— Somewhat of a British Texas?'

Fall Semester 1981

Jerome Bump (English), 'From Texas to England: The Ancestry of Our Victorian Architecture'

Lord Fraser of Kilmorack, 'Leadership Styles of Tory Prime Ministers since the Second World War'

William Carr (University of Sheffield), 'A British Interpretation of American, German, and Japanese Foreign Policy 1936–1941'

Iqbal Narain (Rajasthan University, Jaipur), 'The Ups and Downs of Indian Academic Life'

Don Etherington (HRHRC), 'The Florence Flood, 1966: The British Effort—or: Up to our Necks in Mud and Books'

E. V. K. Fitzgerald (Visiting Professor of Economics), 'The British University: Crisis, Confusion, and Stagnation'

Robert Crunden (American Studies), 'A Joshua for Historians: Mordecai Richter and Canadian Cultural Identity'

Bernth Lindfors (English), 'The Hottentot Venus and Other African Attractions in Nineteenth-Century England'

Chris Brookeman (London Polytechnic), 'The British Arts and Society'

Nicholas Pickwoad (Freelance Book Conservator), 'The Libraries of the National Trust'

Kurth Sprague (English), 'John Steinbeck, Chase Horton, and the Matter of Britain'

Martin J. Wiener (Rice University), 'Cultural Values and Socio-Economic Behavior in Britain'

Werner Habicht (University of Würzburg), 'Shakespeare in Nineteenth-Century Germany'

Spring Semester 1982

Stevie Bezencenet (London College of Printing), 'Contemporary Photography in Britain'

Jane Marcus (English), 'Shakespeare's Sister, Beethoven's Brother: Dame Ethel Smyth and Virginia Woolf'

Wilson Harris (English) and Raja Rao (Philosophy), 'The Quest for Form: Britain and Commonwealth Perspectives'

Al Crosby (American Studies), 'The British Empire as a Product of Continental Drift'

Lord St. Brides (Visiting Scholar), 'The White House and Whitehall: Washington and Westminster'

Elizabeth Fernea (English and Middle East Studies), 'British Colonial Literature of the Middle East'

Maurice Evans (Actor and Producer), 'My Early Years in the Theater'

Joan Bassin (Kansas City Art Institute), 'Art and Industry in Nineteenth-Century England'

Eugene N. Borza (Pennsylvania State University), 'Sentimental British Philhellenism: Images of Greece'

Ralph Willett (University of Hull), 'The Style and Structure of British Television News'

Wm. Roger Louis (History), 'Britain and the Creation of the State of Israel'

Peter Russell (Oxford University), 'A British Historian Looks at Portuguese Historiography of the Fifteenth Century'

Rory Coker (Physics), 'Frauds, Hoaxes and Blunders in Science—a British Tradition?'

Ellen DuBois (State University of New York, Buffalo), 'Anglo-American Perspectives on the Suffragette Movement'

Donald G. Davis, Jr. (Library Science), 'Great Expectations—and a Few Illusions: Reflections on an Exchange Teaching Year in England'

Anthony Rota (Bertram Rota Ltd.), 'The Changing World of the Bookdealer'

Eisig Silberschlag (Visiting Professor of Judaic Studies), 'The Bible as the Most Popular Book in English'

Fall Semester 1982

Woodruff Smith (UT San Antonio), 'British Overseas Expansion'

The Rt. Hon. George Thomas (Speaker of the House of Commons), 'Parliamentary Democracy'

Nigel Nicolson (English Historian and Biographer), 'The English Country House as an Historical Document'

Lord St. Brides (Visiting Scholar), 'A Late Leaf of Laurel for Evelyn Waugh'

Lt. Col. Jack McNamara, USMC (Ret.), 'The Libel of Evelyn Waugh by the *Daily Express*'

James Wimsatt (English), 'Chaucer and Medieval French Manuscripts'

Christopher Whelan (Visiting Professor, UT Law School), 'Recent Developments in British Labour Law'

Brian Wearing (University of Canterbury, Christchurch), 'New Zealand: In the Pacific, but of It?'

Robert Hardgrave (Government), 'The United States and India'

James McBath (University of Southern California), 'The Evolution of *Hansard*'

Paul Fromm (University of Toronto), 'Canadian–United States Relations: Two Solitudes'

John Velz (English), 'When in Disgrace: Ganzel's Attempt to Exculpate John Payne Collier'

Wm. Roger Louis (History), 'British Origins of the Iranian Revolution'

Spring Semester 1983

Sir Ellis Waterhouse (Oxford University), 'A Comparison of British and French Painting in the Late Eighteenth Century'

E. J. L. Ride (Australian Consul General), 'Australia's Place in the World and Her Relationship with the United States'

Edward Bell (Royal Botanic Gardens, Kew), 'Kew Gardens in World History'

The Very Rev. Oliver Fiennes (Dean of Lincoln), 'The Care and Feeding of Magna Carta'

C. V. Narasimhan (former Under-Secretary of the United Nations), 'Last Days of the British Raj: A Civil Servant's View'

Warren G. Osmond, 'Sir Frederic Eggleston and the Development of Pacific Consciousness'

Richard Ellmann (Oxford University), 'Henry James among the Aesthetes'

Janet Caulkins (University of Wisconsin–Madison), 'The Poor Reputation of Cornish Knights in Medieval Literature'

Werner Habicht (University of Würzburg), 'Shakespeare and the Third Reich'

Gillian Peele (Oxford University), 'The Changing British Party System'

John Farrell (English), 'Scarlet Ribbons: Memories of Youth and Childhood in Victorian Authors'

Peter Russell (Oxford University), 'A Not So Bashful Stranger: *Don Quixote* in England, 1612–1781'

Sir Zelman Cowen (Oxford University), 'Contemporary Problems in Medicine, Law, and Ethics'

Dennis V. Lindley (Visiting Professor of Mathematics), 'Scientific Thinking in an Unscientific World'

Martin Blumenson (Department of the Army), 'General Mark Clark and the British in the Italian Campaign of World War II'

Fall Semester 1983

Anthony King (University of Essex), 'Margaret Thatcher and the Future of British Politics'

Alistair Gillespie (Canadian Minister of Energy, Mines, and Resources), 'Canadian-British Relations: Best and Worst'

Charles A. Owen, Jr. (University of Connecticut), 'The Pre-1400 Manuscripts of the *Canterbury Tales*'

Major-General (Ret.) Richard Clutterbuck (University of Exeter), 'Terrorism in Malaya'

Wayne A. Wiegand (University of Kentucky), 'British Propaganda in American Public Libraries during World War I'

Stuart Macintyre (Australian National University, Canberra), 'Australian Trade Unionism between the Wars'

Ram Joshi (Visiting Professor of History), 'Is Gandhi Relevant Today?'

Sir Denis Wright (former British Ambassador to Iran), 'Britain and the Iranian Revolution'

Andrew Horn (University of Lesotho), 'Theater and Politics in South Africa'

Philip Davies (University of Manchester), 'British Reaction to American Politics: Overt Rejection, Covert Assimilation'

H. K. Singh (Embassy of India), 'United States-Indian Relations'

Round Table Discussion, 'Two Cheers for Mountbatten: A Reassessment of Lord and Lady Mountbatten and the Partition of India': Wm. Roger Louis (History), Ram Joshi (Visiting Professor of History), and J. S. Mehta (LBJ School)

Spring Semester 1984

M. S. Venkataramani (Jawaharlal Nehru University), 'Winston Churchill and Indian Freedom'

Sir John Thompson (British Ambassador to the United Nations), 'The Falklands and Grenada in the United Nations'

Robert Farrell (Cornell University), 'Medieval Archaeology'

Allon White (University of Sussex), 'The Fiction of Early Modernism'
Round Table Discussion, 'Orwell's *Nineteen Eighty-Four*': Peter Green (Classics), Wm. Roger Louis (History), Miguel Gonzalez-Gerth (Spanish and Portuguese), Standish Meacham (History), and Sid Monas (Slavic Languages and History)
Uriel Dann (University of Tel Aviv), 'Hanover and Britain in the Time of George II'
José Ferrater-Mora (Bryn Mawr College), 'A. M. Turing and his "Universal Turing Machine"'
Rüdiger Ahrens (University of Würzburg), 'Teaching Shakespeare in German Universities'
Michael Brock (Oxford University), 'H. H. Asquith and Venetia Stanley'
Herbert Spiro (Free University of Berlin), 'What Makes the British and Americans Different from Everybody Else: The Adversary Process of the Common Law'
Nigel Bowles (University of Edinburgh), 'Reflections on Recent Developments in British Politics'
Harold Perkin (Rice University), 'The Evolution of Citizenship in Modern Britain'
Christopher Heywood (Sheffield University), '*Jane Eyre* and *Wuthering Heights*'
Dave Powers (Kennedy Library), 'JFK's Trip to Ireland, 1963'
R. W. Coats (Visiting Professor of Economics), 'John Maynard Keynes: The Man and the Economist'
David Evans (Astronomy), 'Astronomy as a British Cultural Export'

Fall Semester 1984

John Henry Faulk, 'Reflections on My Sojourns in the British Middle East'
Lord Fraser of Kilmorack, 'The Thatcher Years—and Beyond'
Michael Phillips (University of Edinburgh), 'William Blake and the Rise of the Hot Air Balloon'
Erik Stocker (HRHRC), 'A Bibliographical Detective Story: Reconstructing James Joyce's Library'
Amedée Turner (European Parliament), 'Recent Developments in the European Parliament'
Michael Hurst (Oxford University), 'Scholars versus Journalists on the English Social Classes'
Charles Alan Wright (Law), 'Reflections on Cambridge'
J. M. Winter (Cambridge University), 'Fear of Decline in Population in Britain after World War I'
Henk Wesseling (University of Leiden), 'Dutch Colonialism and the Impact on British Imperialism'
Celia Morris Eckhardt (Biographer and author of *Fannie Wright*), 'Frances Wright and *England as the Civilizer*'
Sir Oliver Wright (British Ambassador to the United States), 'British Foreign Policy—1984'
Leonard Thompson (Yale University), 'Political Mythology and the Racial Order in South Africa'
Flora Nwapa (Nigerian Novelist), 'Women in Civilian and Military Rule in Nigeria'
Richard Rose (University of Strathclyde), 'The Capacity of the Presidency in Comparative Perspective'

Spring Semester 1985

Bernard Hickey (University of Venice), 'Australian Literary Culture: Short Stories, Novels, and "Literary Journalism"'

Kenneth Hafertepe (American Studies), 'The British Foundations of the Smithsonian Castle: The Gothic Revival in Britain and America'

Rajeev Dhavan (Visiting Professor, LBJ School and Center for Asian Studies), 'Race Relations in England: Trapped Minorities and their Future'

Sir John Thompson (British Ambassador to the United Nations), 'British Techniques of Statecraft'

Philip Bobbitt (Law), 'Britain, the United States, and Reduction in Strategic Arms'

David Bevington (Drama Critic and Theater Historian), 'Maimed Rites: Interrupted Ceremony in *Hamlet*'

Standish Meacham (History), 'The Impact of the New Left History on British and American Historiography'

Iris Murdoch (Novelist and Philosopher), and John O. Bayley (Oxford University), 'Themes in English Literature and Philosophy'

John P. Chalmers (HRHRC), 'Malory Illustrated'

Thomas Metcalf (University of California, Berkeley), 'The Architecture of Empire: The British Raj in India'

Robert H. Wilson (English), 'Malory and His Readers'

Lord St. Brides, '*A Passage to India:* Better Film than Novel?'

Derek Pearsall (York University), 'Fire, Flood, and Slaughter: The Tribulations of the Medieval City of York'

E. S. Atieno Odhiambo (University of Nairobi), 'Britain and Kenya: The Mau Mau, the "Colonial State," and Dependency'

Francis Robinson (University of London), 'Indian Muslim Religious Leadership and Colonial Rule'

Charles B. MacDonald (U.S. Army), 'The British in the Battle of the Bulge'

Brian Levack (History), 'The Battle of Bosworth Field'

Kurth Sprague (English), 'The Mirrors of Malory'

Fall Semester 1985

A. P. Thornton (University of Toronto), 'Whatever Happened to the British Commonwealth?'

Michael Garibaldi Hall (History), and Elizabeth Hall (LBJ School), 'Views of Pakistan'

Ronald Steel (Visiting Professor of History), 'Walter Lippmann and the British'

Douglas H. M. Branion (Canadian Consul General), 'Political Controversy and Economic Development in Canada'

Decherd Turner and Dave Oliphant (HRHRC), 'The History of the Publications of the HRHRC'

Robert Fernea (Anthropology), 'The Controversy over Sex and Orientalism: Charles Doughty's *Arabia Deserta*'

Desley Deacon (Government), 'Her Brilliant Career: The Context of Nineteenth-Century Australian Feminism'

John Lamphear (History), 'The British Colonial "Pacification" of Kenya: A View from the Other Side'

Kingsley de Silva (University of Peradeniya, Sri Lanka), 'British Colonialism and Sri Lankan Independence'

Thomas Hatfield (Continuing Education), 'Colorado on the Cam, 1986: From "Ultra" to Archaeology, from Mr. Micawber to Mrs. Thatcher'
Carol Hanbery MacKay (English), 'The Dickens Theater'
Round Table Discussion, 'The Art of Biography: Philip Ziegler's *Mountbatten*': Ronald Brown, Jo Anne Christian, Wm. Roger Louis (History), Harry Middleton (LBJ Library), and Ronald Steel

Spring Semester 1986

Round Table Discussion, '*Out of Africa:* The Book, the Biography, and the Movie': B. J. Fernea (English and Middle Eastern Studies), Bernth Lindfors (English), and Wm. Roger Louis (History)
Robert Litwak (Woodrow Wilson Center), 'The Great Game: Russian, British, and American Strategies in Asia'
Gillian Adams Barnes (English), and Jane Manaster (Geography), 'Humphrey Carpenter's *Secret Gardens* and the Golden Age of Children's Literature'
Laurie Hergenhan (University of Queensland), 'A Yankee in Australia: The Literary and Historical Adventures of C. Hartley Grattan'
Brian Matthews (Flinders University, Adelaide), 'Australian Utopianism of the 1880s'
Richard Langhorne (Cambridge University), 'Apostles and Spies: The Generation of Treason at Cambridge between the Wars'
Ronald Robinson (Oxford University), 'The Decline and Fall of the British Empire'
William Rodgers (Social Democratic Party), 'Britain's New Three-Party System: A Permanent or Passing Phenomenon?'
John Coetzee (University of Cape Town), 'The Farm Novel in South Africa'
Ayesha Jalal, (Cambridge University), 'Jinnah and the Partition of India'
Andrew Blane (City College of New York), 'Amnesty International: From a British to an International Movement'
Anthony Rota (Antiquarian Bookseller and Publisher), 'London Pride: 1986'
Elspeth Rostow (LBJ School), 'The Withering Away of Whose State? Colonel Qaddafi's? Reflections on Nationalism at Home and Abroad, in Britain and in the Middle East'
Ray Daum (HRHRC), 'Broadway—Piccadilly!'

Fall Semester 1986

Round Table Discussion: Dean Robert King and Members of the '"Unrequired Reading List" Committee—The British Component'
Paul Sturges (Loughborough University, UK), 'Popular Libraries in Eighteenth-Century Britain'
Ian Bickerton (University of Missouri), 'Eisenhower's Middle East Policy and the End of the British Empire'
Marc Ferro (Visiting Professor of History), 'Churchill and Pétain'
David Fitzpatrick (Visiting Professor of History, Queen's University, Ontario), 'Religion and Politics in Ireland'
Adam Watson (University of Virginia), 'Our Man in Havana—or: Britain, Cuba, and the Caribbean'
Norman Rose (Hebrew University), 'Chaim Weizmann, the British, and the Creation of the State of Israel'
Elaine Thompson (American University), 'Legislatures in Canberra and Washington'

Wm. Roger Louis (History), 'Suez Thirty Years After'

Antonia Gransden (University of Nottingham), 'The Writing of Chronicles in Medieval England'

Hilary Spurling (British Biographer and Critic), 'Paul Scott's *Raj Quartet:* The Novelist as Historian'

J. D. B. Miller (Australian National University), 'A Special and Puzzling Relationship: Australia and the United States'

Janet Meisel (History), 'The Domesday Book'

Spring Semester 1987

Round Table Discussion, 'Contemporary Perspectives on Evolution': Miguel Gonzalez-Gerth (Spanish and Portuguese), Robert Fernea (Anthropology), Joe Horn (Psychology), Bruce Hunt (History), and Delbert Thiessen (Psychology)

Alistair Campbell-Dick (Strategic Technology), 'Scottish Nationalism'

Anthony Mockler (British Freelance Historian and Biographer), 'Graham Greene: The Interweaving of His Life and Fiction'

Michael Crowder (Visiting Professor of African History, Amherst College), 'The Legacy of British Colonialism in Africa'

Carin Green (Classics), 'Lovers and Defectors: Autobiography and *The Perfect Spy*'

Lord St. Brides, 'The Modern British Monarchy'

Victor Szebehely (Aerospace Engineering), 'Sir Isaac Newton'

Patrick McCaughey (National Gallery of Victoria, Melbourne), 'The Persistence of Landscape in Australian Art'

Adolf Wood (*Times Literary Supplement*), 'An Informal History of the *TLS*'

Nissan Oren (Hebrew University), 'Churchill, Truman, and Stalin: The End of the Second World War'

Sir Michael Howard (Oxford University), 'Britain and the First World War'

Sir John Graham (former British Ambassador to NATO), 'NATO: British Origins, American Security, and the Future Outlook'

Daniel Mosser (Virginia Polytechnic Institute and State University), 'The Chaucer Cardigan Manuscript'

Sir Raymond Carr (Oxford University), 'British Intellectuals and the Spanish Civil War'

Michael Wilding (University of Sydney), 'The Fatal Shore? The Convict Period in Australian Literature'

Fall Semester 1987

Round Table Discussion, 'Anthony Burgess: The Autobiography': Peter Green (Classics), Winfred Lehmann (Linguistics), Wm. Roger Louis (History), and Paul Woodruff (Philosophy)

Robert Crunden (History and American Studies), 'Ezra Pound in London'

Carol MacKay (English), and John Henry Faulk (Austin), 'J. Frank Dobie and Thackeray's Great-Granddaughter: Another Side of *A Texan in England*'

Sarvepalli Gopal (Jawaharlal Nehru University and Oxford University), 'Nehru and the British'

Robert D. King (Dean of Liberal Arts), 'T. S. Eliot'

Lord Blake (Visiting Professor of English History and Literature), 'Disraeli: Problems of the Biographer'

Alain Blayac (University of Montpellier), 'Art as Revelation: Gerard Manley Hopkins's Poetry and James Joyce's *Portrait of the Artist*'

Mary Bull (Oxford University), 'Margery Perham and Africa'

R. J. Moore (Flinders University, Adelaide), 'Paul Scott: The Novelist as Historian, and the *Raj Quartet* as History'

Ian Willison (British Library), 'New Trends in Humanities Research: The *History of the Book in Britain* Project'

The Duke of Norfolk, 'The Lion and the Unicorn: Ceremonial and the Crown'

Hans Mark (Chancellor, UT System), 'The Royal Society, the Royal Observatory, and the Development of Modern Research Laboratories'

Henry Dietz (Government), 'Sherlock Holmes: A Centennial Celebration'

Spring Semester 1988

Lord Jenkins (Oxford University), 'Changing Patterns of British Government from Asquith via Baldwin and Attlee to Mrs. Thatcher'

Lord Thomas (author of *The Spanish Civil War* and *Cuba, or the Pursuit of Freedom*), 'Britain, Spain, and Latin America'

Round Table Discussion, 'Chinua Achebe: The Man and His Works': Barbara Harlow (English), Bernth Lindfors (English), Wahneema Lubiano (English), and Robert Wren (University of Houston)

Charles Townshend (Keele University, UK), 'Britain, Ireland, and Palestine, 1918–1947'

Richard Morse (Woodrow Wilson Center), 'T. S. Eliot and Latin America'

Chinua Achebe (Nigerian Novelist), 'Anthills of the Savannah'

Tapan Raychaudhuri (Oxford University), 'The English in Bengali Eyes in the Nineteenth Century'

Lord Chitnis (Rowntree Trust and the British Refugee Council), 'British Perceptions of U.S. Policy in Central America'

Kurth Sprague (English), 'Constance White: Sex, Womanhood, and Marriage in British India'

George McGhee (former US Ambassador to Turkey and Germany), 'The Turning Point in the Cold War: Britain, the United States, and Turkey's Entry into NATO'

Robert Palter (Trinity College), 'New Light on Newton's Natural Philosophy'

J. Kenneth McDonald (CIA), 'The Decline of British Naval Power, 1918–1922'

Yvonne Cripps (Visiting Professor of Law), '"Peter and the Boys Who Cry Wolf": *Spycatcher*'

Emmanuel Ngara (University of Zimbabwe), 'African Poetry: Nationalism and Cultural Domination'

Kate Frost (English), 'Frat Rats of the Invisible College: The Wizard Earl of Northumberland and His Pre-Rosicrucian Pals'

B. Ramesh Babu (Visiting Professor of Government), 'American Foreign Policy: An Indian Dissent'

Sir Antony Ackland (British Ambassador to the United States), 'From Dubai to Madrid: Adventures in the British Foreign Service'

In the Spring Semester 1988, British Studies helped sponsor four lectures by Sir Brian Urquhart (former Under-Secretary of the United Nations) under the general title 'World Order in the Era of Decolonization.'

Fall Semester 1988

Round Table Discussion, 'Richard Ellman's *Oscar Wilde*': Peter Green (Classics), Diana Hobby (Rice University), Wm. Roger Louis (History), and Elspeth Rostow (American Studies),

Hugh Cecil (University of Leeds), 'The British First World War Novel of Experience'

Alan Knight (History), 'Britain and the Mexican Revolution'

Prosser Gifford (Former Deputy Director, Woodrow Wilson Center, Washington, DC), and Robert Frykenberg (University of Wisconsin–Madison), 'Stability in Post-Colonial British Africa: The Indian Perspective'

Joseph Dobrinski (Université Paul-Valéry), 'The Symbolism of the Artist Theme in *Lord Jim*'

Martin Stannard (University of Leicester), 'Evelyn Waugh and North America'

Lawrence Cranberg (Fellow, American Physical Society), 'The Engels-Marx Relationship and the Origins of Marxism'

N. G. L. Hammond (Bristol University), 'The British Military Mission to Greece, 1943–1944'

Barbara Harlow (English), 'A Legacy of the British Era in Egypt: Women, Writing, and Political Detention'

Sidney Monas (Slavic Languages and History), 'Thanks for the Mummery: *Finnegans Wake*, Rabelais, Bakhtin, and Verbal Carnival'

Robert Bowie (Central Intelligence Agency), 'Britain's Decision to Join the European Community'

Shirley Williams (Social Democratic Party), 'Labour Weakness and Tory Strength—or, The Strange Death of Labour England'

Bernard Richards (Oxford University), 'Ruskin's View of Turner'

John R. Clarke (Art History), 'Australian Art of the 1960s'

Round Table Discussion, 'Paul Kennedy's *The Rise and Fall of the Great Powers*': Alessandra Lipucci (Government), Wm. Roger Louis (History), Jagat Mehta (LBJ School), Sidney Monas (Slavic Languages and History), and Walt Rostow (Economics and History)

Spring Semester 1989

Brian Levack (History), 'The English Bill of Rights, 1689'

Hilary Spurling (Critic and Biographer), 'Paul Scott as Novelist: His Sense of History and the British Era in India'

Larry Carver (Humanities Program), 'Lord Rochester: The Profane Wit and the Restoration's Major Minor Poet'

Atieno Odhiambo (Rice University), 'Re-Interpreting Mau Mau'

Trevor Hartley (London School of Economics), 'The British Constitution and the European Community'

Archie Brown (Oxford University), 'Political Leadership in Britain, the Soviet Union, and the United States'

Lord Blake (Editor, *Dictionary of National Biography*), 'Churchill as Historian'

Weirui Hou (Shanghai University), 'British Literature in China'

Norman Daniel (British Council), 'Britain and the Iraqi Revolution of 1958'

Alistair Horne (Oxford University), 'The Writing of the Biography of Harold Macmillan'

M. R. D. Foot (Editor, *Gladstone Diaries*), 'The Open and Secret War, 1939–1945'

Ian Willison (former Head of the Rare Books Division, British Library), 'Editorial Theory and Practice in The History of the Book'

Neville Meaney (University of Sydney), 'The "Yellow Peril": Invasion, Scare Novels, and Australian Political Culture'

Round Table Discussion, '*The Satanic Verses*': Kurth Sprague (American Studies), Peter Green (Classics), Robert A. Fernea (Anthropology), Wm. Roger Louis (History), and Gail Minault (History and Asian Studies)

Kate Frost (English), 'John Donne, Sunspots, and the British Empire'

Lee Patterson (Duke University), 'Chaucerian Commerce'
Edmund Weiner and John Simpson (Editors of the new *OED*), 'Return to the Web of Words'
Ray Daum (HRHRC), 'Noel Coward and Cole Porter'
William B. Todd (History), 'Edmund Burke on the French Revolution'

Fall Semester 1989

D. Cameron Watt (London School of Economics), 'Britain and the Origins of the Second World War: Personalities and Politics of Appeasement'
Gary Freeman (Government), 'On the Awfulness of the English: The View from Comparative Studies'
Hans Mark (Chancellor, UT System), 'British Naval Tactics in the Second World War: The Japanese Lessons'
T. B. Millar (Menzies Centre for Australian Studies, London), 'Australia, Britain, and the United States in Historical Perspective'
Dudley Fishburn (Member of Parliament and former Editor of *The Economist*), '*The Economist*'
Lord Franks (former Ambassador in Washington), 'The "Special Relationship"'
Herbert L. Jacobson (Drama Critic and friend of Orson Welles), 'Three Score Years of Transatlantic Acting and Staging of Shakespeare'
Roy Macleod (University of Sydney) 'The "Practical Man": Myth and Metaphor in Anglo-Australian Science'
David Murray (Open University), 'Hong Kong: The Historical Context for the Transfer of Power'
Susan Napier (UT Assistant Professor of Japanese Language and Literature), 'Japanese Intellectuals Discover the British'
Dr. Karan Singh (Ambassador of India to the United States), 'Four Decades of Indian Democracy'
Paul Woodruff (Philosophy), 'George Grote and the Radical Tradition in British Scholarship'
Herbert J. Spiro (Government), 'Britain, the United States, and the Future of Germany'
Robert Lowe (*Austin American-Statesman*), '"God Rest You Merry, Gentlemen": The Curious British Cult of Sherry'

Spring Semester 1990

Thomas F. Staley (HRHRC), 'Harry Ransom, the Humanities Research Center, and the Development of Twentieth-Century Literary Research Collections'
Thomas Cable (English), 'The Rise and Decline of the English Language'
D. J. Wenden (Oxford University), 'Sir Alexander Korda and the British Film Industry'
Roger Owen (Oxford University), 'Reflections on the First Ten Years of Thatcherism'
Robert Hardgrave (Government), 'Celebrating Calcutta: The Solvyns Portraits'
Donatus Nwoga (University of Nigeria, Nsukka), 'The Intellectual Legacy of British Decolonization in Africa'
Francis Sitwell (Etonian, Seaman, and Literary Executor), 'Edith Sitwell: A Reappraisal'
Robert Vitalis (Government), 'The "New Deal" in Egypt: Britain, the United States, and the Egyptian Economy during World War II'

James Coote (Architecture), 'Prince Charles and Architecture'
Harry Eckstein (University of California, Irvine), 'British Politics and the National Health Service'
Alfred David (Indiana University), 'Chaucer and King Arthur'
Ola Rotimi (African Playwright and Theater Director), 'African Literature and the British Tongue'
Derek Brewer (Cambridge University), 'An Anthropological Study of Literature'
Neil MacCormick (University of Edinburgh), 'Stands Scotland Where She Should?'
Janice Rossen (Senior Research Fellow, HRHRC), 'Toads and Melancholy: The Poetry of Philip Larkin'
Ronald Robinson (Oxford University), 'The Decolonization of British Imperialism'

Fall Semester 1990

Round Table Discussion, 'The Crisis in the Persian Gulf': Hafez Farmayan (History), Robert Fernea (Anthropology), Wm. Roger Louis (History), and Robert Stookey (Center for Middle Eastern Studies)
John Velz (English), 'Shakespeare and Some Surrogates: An Account of the Anti-Stratfordian Heresy'
Michael H. Codd (Department of the Prime Minister and Cabinet, Government of Australia), 'The Future of the Commonwealth: An Australian View'
John Dawick (Massey University, New Zealand), 'The Perils of Paula: Young Women and Older Men in Pinero's Plays'
Gloria Fromm (University of Illinios, Chicago), 'New Windows on Modernism: The Letters of Dorothy Richardson'
David Braybrooke (Government), 'The Canadian Constitutional Crisis'
Sidney Monas (Slavic Languages and History), 'Paul Fussell and World War II'
James Fishkin (Government), 'Thought Experiments in Recent Oxford Philosophy'
Joseph Hamburger (Yale University), 'How Liberal Was John Stuart Mill?'
Richard W. Clement (University of Kansas), 'Thomas James and the Bodleian Library: The Foundations of Scholarship'
Michael Yeats (Former Chairman of the Irish Senate and only son of the poet William Butler Yeats), 'Ireland and Europe'
Round Table Discussion, 'William H. McNeill's *Arnold J. Toynbee: A Life*': Standish Meacham (Dean, Liberal Arts), Peter Green (Classics), Wm. Roger Louis (History), and Sidney Monas (Slavic Languages and History)
Jeffrey Meyers (Biographer and Professor of English, University of Colorado), 'Conrad and Jane Anderson'
Alan Frost (La Trobe University, Melbourne), 'The Explorations of Captain Cook'
Sarvepalli Gopal (Jawaharlal Nehru University), 'The First Ten Years of Indian Independence'
Round Table Discussion, 'The Best and Worst Books of 1990': Alessandra Lippucci (Government), Wm. Roger Louis (History), Tom Staley (HRHRC), Steve Weinberg (Physics), and Paul Woodruff (Philosophy)

Spring Semester 1991

David Hollway (Prime Minister's Office, Government of Australia), 'Australia and the Gulf Crisis'
Diane Kunz (Yale University), 'British Post-War Sterling Crises'

Miguel Gonzalez-Gerth (Spanish Literature and the HRHRC), 'T. E. Lawrence, Richard Aldington, and the Death of Heroes'

Robert Twombly (English), 'Religious Encounters with the Flesh in English Literature'

Alan Ryan (Princeton University), 'Bertrand Russell's Politics'

Hugh Kenner (Johns Hopkins University), 'The State of English Poetry'

Patricia Burnham (American Studies), 'Anglo-American Art and the Struggle for Artistic Independence'

Round Table Discussion, 'The Churchill Tradition': Lord Blake (former Provost of Queen's College, Oxford), Lord Jenkins (Chancellor, Oxford University), Field Marshal Lord Carver (former Chief of the Defence Staff), Sir Michael Howard (former Regius Professor, Oxford, present Lovett Professor of Military and Naval History, Yale University), with a concluding comment by Winston S. Churchill, M.P.

Woodruff Smith (UT San Antonio), 'Why Do the British Put Sugar in Their Tea?'

Peter Firchow (University of Minnesota), 'Aldous Huxley: The Poet as Centaur'

Irene Gendzier (Boston University), 'British and American Middle Eastern Policies in the 1950s: Lebanon and Kuwait; Reflections on Past Experience and the Post-War Crisis in the Gulf'

John Train (*Harvard* Magazine and *Wall Street Journal*), 'Remarkable Catchwords in the City of London and on Wall Street'

Adam Sisman (Independent Writer, London), 'A. J. P. Taylor'

Wm. Roger Louis (History), 'The Young Winston'

Adrian Mitchell (Melbourne University), 'Claiming a Voice: Recent Non-Fiction Writing in Australia'

Bruce Hevly (University of Washington), 'Stretching Things Out versus Letting Them Slide: The Natural Philosophy of Ice in Edinburgh and Cambridge in the Nineteenth Century'

Henry Dietz (Government), 'Foibles and Follies in Sherlock's Great Game: Some Excesses of Holmesian Research'

Summer 1991

Wm. Roger Louis (History), and Ronald Robinson (Oxford University), 'Harold Macmillan and the Dissolution of the British Empire'

Robert Treu (University of Wisconsin–Lacrosse), 'D. H. Lawrence and Graham Greene in Mexico'

Thomas Pinney (Pomona College), 'Kipling, India, and Imperialism'

Ronald Heiferman (Quinnipiac College), 'The Odd Couple: Winston Churchill and Chiang Kai-shek'

John Harty (Alice Lloyd College, Kentucky), 'The Movie and the Book: J. G. Ballard's *Empire of the Sun*'

A. B. Assensoh (Southern University, Baton Rouge), 'Nkrumah'

Victoria Carchidi (Emory and Henry College), 'Lawrence of Arabia on a Camel, Thank God!'

James Gump (University of California, San Diego), 'The Zulu and the Sioux: The British and American Comparative Experience with the "Noble Savage"'

Fall Semester 1991

Round Table Discussion, 'Noel Annan's *Our Age*': Peter Green (Classics), Robert D. King (Dean, Liberal Arts), Wm. Roger Louis (History), and Thomas F. Staley (HRHRC)

Christopher Heywood (Okayama University), 'Slavery, Imagination, and the Brontës'

Harold L. Smith (University of Houston, Victoria), 'Winston Churchill and Women'

Krystyna Kujawinska-Courtney (University of Lodz), 'Shakespeare and Poland'

Ewell E. Murphy, Jr. (Baker Botts, Houston), 'Cecil Rhodes and the Rhodes Scholarships'

I. N. Kimambo (University of Dar es Salaam), 'The District Officer in Tanganyika'

Hans Mark (Chancellor, UT System), 'The Pax Britannica and the Inevitable Comparison: Is There a Pax Americana? Conclusions from the Gulf War'

Richard Clutterbuck (Major-General, British Army, Ret.), 'British and American Hostages in the Middle East: Negotiating with Terrorists'

Elizabeth Hedrick (English), 'Samuel Johnson and Linguistic Propriety'

The Hon. Denis McLean (New Zealand Ambassador to the United States), 'Australia and New Zealand: The Nuisance of Nationalism'

Elizabeth Richmond (English), 'Submitting a Trifle for a Degree: Dramatic Productions at Oxford and Cambridge in the Age of Shakespeare'

Kenneth Warren, M.D. (Director for Science, Maxwell Macmillan), 'Tropical Medicine: A British Invention'

Adolf Wood (*Times Literary Supplement*), 'The Golden Age of the *Times Literary Supplement*'

Eugene Walter (Poet and Novelist), 'Unofficial Poetry: Literary London in the 1940s and 1950s'

Sidney Monas (Slavic Languages and History), 'Images of Britain in the Poetry of World War II'

St. Stephen's Madrigal Choir, 'Celebrating an English Christmas'

Spring Semester 1992

Jeremy Treglown (Critic and Author), 'Wartime Censorship and the Novel'

Toyin Falola (History), 'Nigerian Independence, 1960'

Donald S. Lamm (W.W. Norton and Company), 'Publishing English History in America'

Colin Franklin (Publisher and Historian of the Book), 'The Pleasures of Eighteenth-Century Shakespeare'

Thomas F. Staley (HRHRC), '*Fin de Siècle* Joyce: A Perspective on One Hundred Years'

Sarvepalli Gopal (Jawaharlal Nehru University), '"Drinking Tea with Treason": Halifax and Gandhi'

Michael Winship (English), 'The History of the Book: Britain's Foreign Trade in Books in the Nineteenth Century'

Richard Lariviere (Sanskrit and Asian Studies), 'British Law and Lawyers in India'

Round Table Discussion, 'A. S. Byatt's *Possession*': Janice Rossen (Visiting Scholar, HRHRC), John P. Farrell (English), and Wm. Roger Louis (History)

William H. McNeill (University of Chicago), 'Arnold Toynbee's Vision of World History'

Derek Brewer (Cambridge University), 'The Interpretation of Fairy Tales: The Implications for English Literature, Anthropology, and History'

David Bradshaw (Oxford University), 'Aldous Huxley: Eugenics and the Rational State'

Steven Weinberg (Physics), 'The British Style in Physics'

Sir David Williams (Cambridge University), 'Northern Ireland'

Summer 1992

R. A. C. Parker (Oxford University), 'Neville Chamberlain and Appeasement'

Adrian Wooldridge (Oxford University and *The Economist*), 'Reforming British Education: How It Happened and What America Can Learn'

Chris Wrigley (Nottingham University), 'A. J. P. Taylor: An English Radical and Modern Europe'

Fall Semester 1992

Round Table Discussion, 'E. M. Forster's *Howards End:* The Movie and the Book': Robert D. King (Linguistics), Wm. Roger Louis (History), Alessandra Lippucci (Government), and Thomas F. Staley (HRHRC)

Lord Skidelsky (Warwick University), 'Keynes and the Origins of the "Special Relationship"'

Sir Samuel Falle (former British Ambassador), 'Britain and the Middle East in the 1950s'

Ian MacKillop (University of Sheffield), 'We Were That Cambridge: F. R. Leavis and *Scrutiny*'

Walter Dean Burnham (Government), 'The 1992 British Elections: Four-or-Five-More Tory Years?'

Don Graham (English), 'Modern Australian Literature and the Image of America'

Richard Woolcott (former Secretary of the Australian Department of Foreign Affairs), 'Australia and the Question of Cooperation or Contention in the Pacific'

Ian Willison (1992 Wiggins Lecturer, American Antiquarian Society), 'The History of the Book in Twentieth-Century Britain and America'

Iain Sproat, (Member of Parliament), 'P. G. Wodehouse and the War'

Standish Meacham (History), 'The Crystal Palace'

Field Marshal Lord Carver (former Chief of the British Defence Staff), 'Wavell: A Reassessment'

Lesley Hall (Wellcome Institute for the History of Medicine, London), 'For Fear of Frightening the Horses: Sexology in Britain since William Acton'

Michael Fry (University of Southern California), 'Britain, the United Nations, and the Lebanon Crisis of 1958'

Brian Holden Reid (King's College, London), 'J. F. C. Fuller and the Revolution in British Military Thought'

Neil Parsons (University of London), '"Clicko," or Franz Taaibosch: A Bushman Entertainer in Britain, Jamaica, and the United States *c.* 1919–40'

John Hargreaves (Aberdeen University), 'God's Advocate: Lewis Namier and the History of Modern Europe'

Round Table Discussion, 'Robert Harris's *Fatherland*': Henry Dietz (Government), Robert D. King (Linguistics), Wm. Roger Louis (History), and Walter Wetzels (Germanic Languages)

Kevin Tierney (University of California), 'Robert Graves: An Outsider Looking In, or An Insider Who Escaped?'

Spring Semester 1993

Round Table Discussion, 'The Trollope Mystique': Janice Rossen (author of *Philip Larkin* and *The University in Modern Fiction*), Louise Weinberg (Law School), and Paul Woodruff (Plan II Honors Program and Philosophy)

Bruce Hunt (History), 'To Rule the Waves: Cable Telegraphy and British Physics in the Nineteenth Century'

Martin Wiener (Rice University), 'The Unloved State: Contemporary Political Attitudes in the Writing of Modern British History'

Elizabeth Dunn (HRHRC), 'Ralph Waldo Emerson and Ireland'

Jason Thompson (Western Kentucky University), 'Edward William Lane's "Description of Egypt"'

Sir Michael Howard (Yale University), 'Strategic Deception in the Second World War'

Gordon A. Craig (Stanford University), 'Churchill'

Round Table Discussion, 'The Indian Mathematician Ramanujan': Robert D. King (Linguistics), James W. Vick (Mathematics), and Steven Weinberg (Physics)

Martha Merritt (Government), 'From Commonwealth to Commonwealth, and from Vauxhall to *Vokzal:* Russian Borrowing from Britain'

Sidney Monas (Slavic Languages and History), 'James Joyce and Russia'

Peter Marshall (King's College, London), 'Imperial Britain and the Question of National Identity'

Michael Wheeler (Lancaster University), 'Ruskin and Gladstone'

Anthony Low (Cambridge University), 'Britain and India in the Early 1930s: The British, American, French, and Dutch Empires Compared'

Summer 1993

Alexander Pettit (University of North Texas), 'Lord Bolingbroke's *Remarks on the History of England*'

Rose Marie Burwell (Northern Illinois University), 'The British Novel and Ernest Hemingway'

Richard Patteson (Mississippi State University), 'New Writing in the West Indies'

Richard Greene (Memorial University, Newfoundland), 'The Moral Authority of Edith Sitwell'

Fall Semester 1993

Round Table Discussion, 'The British and the Shaping of the American Critical Mind—Edmund Wilson, Part II': Wm. Roger Louis (History), Elspeth Rostow (American Studies), Tom Staley (HRHRC), and Robert Crunden (History and American Studies)

Roseanne Camacho (University of Rhode Island), 'Evelyn Scott: Towards an Intellectual Biography'

Christopher Heywood (Okayama University), 'The Brontës and Slavery'

Peter Gay (Yale University), 'The Cultivation of Hatred in England'

Linda Ferreira-Buckley (English) 'England's First English Department: Rhetoric and More Rhetoric'

Janice Rossen (HRHRC), 'British University Novels'

Ian Hancock (O Yanko Le Redzosko) (Linguistics and English), 'The Gypsy Image in British Literature'

James Davies (University College of Swansea), 'Dylan Thomas'

Jeremy Lewis (London Writer and Editor), 'Who Cares about Cyril Connolly?'

Sam Jamot Brown (British Studies) and Robert D. King (Linguistics), 'Scott and the Antarctic'

Martin Trump (University of South Africa), 'Nadine Gordimer's Social and Political Vision'

Richard Clogg (University of London), 'Britain and the Origins of the Greek Civil War'

Herbert J. Spiro (United States Ambassador, Ret.), 'The Warburgs: Anglo-American and German-Jewish Bankers'

Colin Franklin (Publisher and Antiquarian Bookseller), 'Lord Chesterfield: Stylist, Connoisseur of Manners, and Specialist in Worldly Advice'

Jeffrey Segall (Charles University, Prague), 'The Making of James Joyce's Reputation'

Rhodri Jeffreys-Jones (University of Edinburgh), 'The Myth of the Iron Lady: Margaret Thatcher and World Stateswomen'

John Rumrich (English), 'Milton and Science: Gravity and the Fall'

J. D. Alsop (McMaster University), 'British Propaganda, Espionage, and Political Intrigue'

Round Table Discussion, 'The Best and the Worst Books of 1993': David Edwards (Government), Creekmore Fath (Liberal Arts Foundation), Betty Sue Flowers (English), and Sidney Monas (Slavic Languages and History)

Spring Semester 1994

Thomas F. Staley (HRHRC), 'John Rodker: Poet and Publisher of Modernism'

Martha Fehsenfeld, and Lois More Overbeck (Emory University), 'The Correspondence of Samuel Beckett'

M. R. D. Foot (Historian and Editor), 'Lessons of War on War: The Influence of 1914–1918 on 1939–1945'

Round Table Discussion, 'Requiem for Canada?': David Braybrooke (Government), Walter Dean Burnham (Government), and Robert Crunden (American Studies)

Ross Terrill (Harvard University), 'Australia and Asia in Historical Perspective'

Sir Samuel Falle (British Ambassador and High Commissioner), 'The Morning after Independence: The Legacy of the British Empire'

Deborah Lavin (University of Durham), 'Lionel Curtis: Prophet of the British Empire'

Robin W. Doughty (Geography), 'Eucalyptus: And Not a Koala in Sight'

Al Crosby (American Studies and History), 'Captain Cook and the Biological Impact on the Hawaiian Islands'

Gillian Adams (Editor, *Children's Literature Association Quarterly*), 'Beatrix Potter and Her Recent Critics'

Lord Amery, 'Churchill's Legacy'

Christa Jansohn (University of Bonn), and Peter Green (Classics), '*Lady Chatterley's Lover*'

R. A. C. Parker (Oxford University), 'Neville Chamberlain and the Coming of the Second World War'

John Velz (English), 'King Lear in Iowa: Jane Smiley's *A Thousand Acres*'

Jan Schall (University of Florida), 'British Spirit Photography'

Daniel Woolf (Dalhousie University), 'The Revolution in Historical Consciousness in England'

Fall Semester 1994

Kenneth O. Morgan (University of Wales), 'Welsh Nationalism'

Round Table Discussion, 'Michael Shelden's *Graham Greene: The Man Within*': Peter Green (Classics), Wm. Roger Louis (History), and Thomas F. Staley (HRHRC)

Robert D. King (Linguistics), 'The Secret War, 1939–1945'

Brian Boyd (University of Auckland), 'The Evolution of Shakespearean Dramatic Structure'

Lord Weatherill (former Speaker of the House of Commons), 'Thirty Years in Parliament'

Hans Mark (Aerospace Engineering), 'Churchill's Scientists'

Steven Weinberg (Physics), 'The Test of War: British Strengths and Weaknesses in World War II'

Dennis Welland (University of East Anglia), 'Wilfred Owen and the Poetry of War'

Alan Frost (La Trobe University), 'The *Bounty* Mutiny and the British Romantic Poets'

W. O. S. Sutherland (English), 'Sir Walter Scott'

Hazel Rowley (Deakin University, Melbourne), 'Christina Stead's "Other Country"'

Herman Bakvis (Dalhousie University), 'The Future of Democracy in Canada and Australia'

Peter Stansky (Stanford University), 'George Orwell and the Writing of *Nineteen Eighty-Four*'

Henry Dietz (Government), 'Sherlock Homes and Jack the Ripper'

James Coote (Architecture), 'Techniques of Illusion in British Architecture'

Round Table Discussion, 'The Best and Worst Books of 1994': Dean Burnham (Government), Alessandra Lippucci (Government), Roger Louis (History), Sidney Monas (Slavic Languages and History), and Janice Rossen (HRHRC)

Spring Semester 1995

Elizabeth Butler Cullingford (English), 'Anti-Colonial Metaphors in Contemporary Irish Literature'

Thomas M. Hatfield (Continuing Education), 'British and American Deception of the Germans in Normandy'

Gary P. Freeman (Government), 'The Politics of Race and Immigration in Britain'

Donald G. Davis, Jr. (Library and Information Science), 'The Printed Word in Sunday Schools in Nineteenth-Century England and the United States'

Brian Bremen (English), "Healing Words: The Literature of Medicine and the Medicine of Literature'

Frances Karttunen (Linguistic Research Center), and Alfred W. Crosby (American Studies and History), 'British Imperialism and Creole Languages'

Paul Lovejoy (York University, Canada), 'British Rule in Africa: A Reassessment of Nineteenth-Century Colonialism'

Carol MacKay (English), 'Creative Negativity in the Life and Work of Elizabeth Robins'

John Brokaw (Theatre and Dance), 'The Changing Stage in London, 1790–1832'

Linda Colley (Yale University), 'The Frontier in British History'

Iwan Morus (University of California, San Diego), 'Manufacturing Nature: Science, Technology, and Victorian Consumer Culture'

Brian Parker (University of Toronto), 'Jacobean Law: The Dueling Code and "A Faire Quarrel" (1617)'

Kate Frost (English), '"Jack Donne the Rake": Fooling around in the 1590s'

Mark Kinkead-Weekes (University of Kent), 'Beyond Gossip: D. H. Lawrence's Writing Life'

Summer 1995

S. P. Rosenbaum (University of Toronto), 'Leonard and Virginia Woolf at the Hogarth Press'

Maria X. Wells (HRHRC), 'A Delicate Balance: Trieste, 1945'

Kevin Tierney (University of California, Berkeley), 'Personae in Twentieth Century British Autobiography'

Fall Semester 1995

Brian Levack (History), 'Witchcraft, Possession, and the Law in Jacobean England'

Janice Rossen (HRHRC), 'The Home Front: Anglo-American Women Novelists and World War II'

Dorothy Driver (University of Cape Town), 'Olive Schreiner's Novel *From Man to Man*'

Philip Ziegler (London), 'Mountbatten Revisited'

Joanna Hitchcock (Director, University of Texas Press), 'British and American University Presses'

Samuel H. Beer (Harvard University), 'The Rise and Fall of Party Government in Britain and the United States, 1945–1995'

Richard Broinowski (Australian Ambassador to Mexico and Central America), 'Australia and Latin America'

John Grigg (London), 'Myths about the Approach to Indian Independence'

Round Table Discussion, '*Measuring the Mind* by Adrian Wooldridge and *The Bell Curve* by Richard J. Herrnstein and Charles Murray': David Edwards (Government), Sheldon Ekland-Olson (Dean of Liberal Arts), Joseph Horn (Psychology), and Robert D. King (Linguistics)

Paul Addison (University of Edinburgh), 'British Politics in the Second World War'

John Sibley Butler (Sociology), 'Emigrants of the British Empire'

Round Table Discussion, '*Carrington*': Peter Green (Classics), Robin Kilson (History), Wm. Roger Louis (History), Sidney Monas (Slavic Languages and History), and Elizabeth Richmond-Garza (English)

Spring Semester 1996

Kevin Kenny (History), 'Making Sense of the Molly Maguires'

Brigadier Michael Harbottle (British Army), 'British and American Security in the Post-Cold War'

Carol MacKay (English), 'The Singular Double Vision of Photographer Julia Margaret Cameron'

John Ramsden (University of London), '"That Will Depend on Who Writes the History": Winston Churchill as His Own Historian'

Jack P. Greene (Johns Hopkins University), 'The *British* Revolution in America'

Walter D. Wetzels (German), 'The Ideological Fallout in Germany of Two British Expeditions to Test Einstein's General Theory of Relativity'

Thomas Pinney (Pomona College), 'In Praise of Kipling'

Michael Charlesworth (Art History), 'The English Landscape Garden'

Stephen Gray (South African Novelist), 'The Dilemma of Colonial Writers with Dual Identities'

Jeremy Black (University of Durham), 'Could the British Have Won the War of American Independence?'

Dagmar Hamilton (LBJ School), 'Justice William O. Douglas and British Colonialism'

Gordon Peacock and Laura Worthen (Theatre and Dance), 'Not Always a Green and Pleasant Land: Tom Stoppard's *Arcadia*'

Bernard Crick (University of London), 'Orwell and the Business of Biography'

Geoffrey Hartman (Yale University), 'The Sympathy Paradox: Poetry, Feeling, and Modern Cultural Morality'

Dave Oliphant (HRHRC), 'Jazz and Its British Acolytes'

R. W. B. Lewis (Yale University), 'Henry James: The Victorian Scene'

Alan Spencer (Ford Motor Company), 'Balliol, Big Business, and Mad Cows'

Peter Quinn: A Discussion of His Novel, *Banished Children of Eve*

Summer1996

Martin Stannard (Leicester University), 'Biography and Textual Criticism'

Diane Kunz (Yale University), 'British Withdrawal East of Suez'

John Cell (Duke University), 'Who Ran the British Empire?'

Mark Jacobsen (U.S. Marine Corps Command and Staff College), 'The North-West Frontier'

Theodore Vestal (Oklahoma State University), 'Britain and Ethiopia'

Warren F. Kimball (Rutgers University), 'A Victorian Tory: Churchill, the Americans, and Self-Determination'

Louise B. Williams (Lehman College, City University of New York), 'British Modernism and Fascism'

Fall Semester 1996

Elizabeth Richmond-Garza (English and Comparative Literature), 'The New Gothic: Decadents for the 1990s'

Robin Kilson (History), 'The Politics of Captivity: The British State and Prisoners of War in World War I'

Sir Brian Fall (Oxford University), 'What Does Britain Expect from the European Community, the United States, and the Commonwealth?'

Wm. Roger Louis (History), 'Harold Macmillan and the Middle East Crisis of 1958'

Ian Willison (Editor, *The Cambridge History of the Book in Britain*), 'The History of the Book and the Cultural and Literary History of the English-Speaking World'

Walter L. Arnstein (University of Illinois), 'Queen Victoria's Other Island'

Noel Annan (London), '*Our Age* Revisited'

Michael Cohen (Bar-Ilan University, Tel Aviv), 'The Middle East and the Cold War: Britain, the United States, and the Soviet Union'

Reba Soffer (California State University, Northridge), 'Catholicism in England: Was it Possible to Be a Good Catholic, a Good Englishman, and a Good Historian?'

Wilson Harris (Poet and Novelist), 'The Mystery of Consciousness: Cross-Cultural Influences in the Caribbean, Britain, and the United States'

H. S. Barlow (Singapore), 'British Malaya in the late Nineteenth Century'

Donald G. Davis, Jr. (Library and Information Science), 'British Destruction of Chinese Books in the Peking Siege of 1900'

Round Table Discussion, '*Michael Collins*': Elizabeth Cullingford (English), Kevin Kenny (History), Robin Kilson (History), and Wm. Roger Louis (History)

A. G. Hopkins (Cambridge University), 'From Africa to Empire'
Austin Chapter of the Society for the Preservation and Encouragement of Barber Shop Quartet Singing in America

Spring Semester 1997

Round Table Discussion, 'T. S. Eliot and Anti-Semitism': Robert D. King (Jewish Studies), Sidney Monas (Slavic Languages and History), and Thomas F. Staley (HRHRC)
Phillip Herring (University of Wisconsin–Madison), 'Djuna Barnes and T. S. Eliot: The Story of a Friendship'
Bryan Roberts (Sociology), 'British Sociology and British Society'
Andrew Roberts (London), 'The Captains and the Kings Depart: Lord Salisbury's Skeptical Imperialism'
Colin Franklin (London), 'In a Golden Age of Publishing, 1950–1970'
Susan Pedersen (Harvard University), 'Virginia Woolf, Eleanor Rathbone, and the Problem of Appeasement'
Andrew Seaman (Saint Mary's University, Halifax, Nova Scotia), 'Thomas Raddall: A Novelist's View of Nova Scotia during the American Revolution'
Gordon Peacock (Theatre and Dance), 'Noel Coward: A Master Playwright, a Talented Actor, a Novelist and Diarist: Or a Peter Pan for the Twentieth Century?'
Roland Oliver (University of London), 'The Battle for African History, 1947–1966'
Alistair Horne (Oxford University), 'Harold Macmillan's Fading Reputation'
Richard Begam (University of Wisconsin–Madison), 'Samuel Beckett and the Debate on Humanism'
Christopher Waters (Williams College), 'Delinquents, Perverts, and the State: Psychiatry and the Homosexual Desire in the 1930s'
Sami Zubaida (University of London), 'Ernest Gellner and Islam'
Walter Dean Burnham (Government), 'Britain Votes: The 1997 General Election and Its Implications'

Fall Semester 1997

Judith Brown (Oxford University), 'Gandhi: A Victorian Gentleman'
Thomas Cable (English), 'Hearing and Revising the History of the English Language'
Round Table Discussion, 'The Death of Princess Diana': Judith Brown (Oxford), David Edwards (Government), Elizabeth Richmond-Garza (English), Anne Baade (British Studies), Alessandra Lippucci (Government), and Kevin Kenny (History)
David Hunter (Music Librarian, Fine Arts Library), 'Handel and His Patrons'
Anne Kane (Sociology), 'The Current Situation in Ireland'
James S. Fishkin (Government), 'Power and the People: The Televised Deliberative Poll in the 1997 British General Election'
Howard D. Weinbrot (University of Wisconsin–Madison), 'Jacobitism in Eighteenth-Century Britain'
J. C. Baldwin, M.D. (Houston), 'The Abdication of King Edward VIII'
Kenneth E. Carpenter (Harvard University), 'Library Revolutions Past and Present'
Akira Iriye (Harvard University), 'Britain, Japan, and the International Order after World War I'

Anthony Hobson (London), 'Reminiscences of British Authors and the Collecting of Contemporary Manuscripts'

David Killingray (University of London), 'The British in the West Indies'

Alan Knight (Oxford University), 'British Imperialism in Latin America'

Round Table Discussion, 'King Lear in Iowa: The Film *A Thousand Acres*': Linda Ferreira-Buckley (English), Elizabeth Richmond-Garza (English), Helena Woodard (English), and John Velz (English)

Timothy Lovelace (Music) and the Talisman Trio

Spring Semester 1998

Richard Ollard (Biographer and Publisher), 'A. L. Rowse: Epitome of the Twentieth Century'

Round Table Discussion, 'Arundhati Roy's *The God of Small Things*': Phillip Herring (HRHRC), Brian Trinque (Economics), Kamala Visweswaran (Anthropology), and Robert Hardgrave (Government)

Jonathan Schneer (Georgia Institute of Technology), 'London in 1900: The Imperial Metropolis'

Trevor Burnard (University of Canterbury, New Zealand), 'Rioting in Goatish Embraces: Marriage and the Failure of White Settlement in British Jamaica'

Felipe Fernández-Armesto (Oxford University), 'British Traditions in Comparative Perspective'

Michael Mann (University of California, Los Angeles), 'The Broader Significance of Labour's Landslide Victory of 1997'

Dane Kennedy (University of Nebraska), 'White Settlers in Colonial Kenya and Rhodesia'

Round Table Discussion, 'Noel Annan, Keynes, and Bloomsbury': Jamie Galbraith (LBJ School), Elspeth Rostow (LBJ School), and Walt Rostow (Economics and History)

Lisa Moore (English), 'British Studies—Lesbian Studies: A Dangerous Intimacy?'

James Gibbs (University of the West of England), 'Wole Soyinka: The Making of a Playwright'

Marilyn Butler (Oxford University), 'About the House: Jane Austen's Anthropological Eye'

R. J. Q. Adams (Texas A&M University), 'Britain and Ireland, 1912–1922'

John M. Carroll (Asian Studies), 'Nationalism and Identity in pre-1949 Hong Kong'

Round Table Discussion, 'The Irish Referendum': Anne Kane (Sociology), Kevin Kenny (History), Wm. Roger Louis (History), and Jennifer O'Conner (History)

Fall Semester 1998

Louise Hodgden Thompson (Government), 'Origins of the First World War: The Anglo-German Naval Armaments Race'

John P. Farrell (English), 'Thomas Hardy in Love'

Carol MacKay (English), 'The Multiple Conversions of Annie Besant'

Roy Foster (Oxford University), 'Yeats and Politics, 1898–1921'

Robert Olwell (History), 'British Magic Kingdoms: Imagination, Speculation, and Empire in Florida'

Sara H. Sohmer (Texas Christian University), 'The British in the South Seas: Exploitation and Trusteeship in Fiji'

Helena Woodard (English), 'Politics of Race in the Eighteenth Century: Pope and the Humanism of the Enlightenment'

D. A. Smith (Grinnell College), 'Impeachment? Parliamentary Government in Britain and France in the Nineteenth Century'

Round Table Discussion, 'The Irish Insurrection of 1798': Robert Olwell (History), Lisa Moore (English), and Kevin Kenny (History)

Robert D. King (Jewish Studies), 'The Accomplishments of Raja Rao: The Triumph of the English Language in India'

Donald G. Davis, Jr. (Library and Information Science and History), 'Religion and Empire'

A. D. Roberts (University of London), 'The Awkward Squad: African Students in American Universities before 1940'

Chaganti Vijayasree (Osmania University, Hyderabad), 'The Empire and Victorian Poetry'

Martha Deatherage (Music), 'Christmas Celebration: Vauxhall Gardens'

Spring Semester 1999

Round Table Discussion, '*Regeneration:* Pat Barker's Trilogy on the First World War': Betty Sue Flowers (English), Wm. Roger Louis (History), and Paul Woodruff (Humanities)

Alistair Campbell-Dick (Cybertime Corporation), 'The Immortal Memory of Robert Burns'

Hugh Macrae Richmond (University of California, Berkeley), 'Why Rebuild Shakespeare's Globe Theatre?'

Ralph Austen (University of Chicago), 'Britain and the Global Economy: A Post-Colonial Perspective'

Jerome Meckier (University of Kentucky), 'Aldous Huxley's American Experience'

Peter Marsh (Syracuse University), 'Joseph Chamberlain as an Entrepreneur in Politics: Writing the Life of a Businessman Turned Statesman'

Roger Adelson (Arizona State University), 'Winston Churchill and the Middle East'

Margot Finn (Emory University), 'Law, Debt, and Empire: The Calcutta Court of Conscience'

Fred M. Leventhal (Boston University), 'The Projection of Britain in America before the Second World War'

Larry Siedentop (Oxford University), 'Reassessing the Life of Isaiah Berlin'

Ross Terrill (Harvard University), 'R. H. Tawney's Vision of Fellowship'

Juliet Fleming (Cambridge University), 'The Ladies' Shakespeare'

Elizabeth Fernea (English and Middle Eastern Studies), 'The Victorian Lady Abroad: In Egypt with Sophia Poole and in Texas with Mrs. E. M. Houstoun'

Richard Schoch (University of London), 'The Respectable and the Vulgar: British Theater in the Mid-Nineteenth Century'

Ferdinand Mount (Editor, *TLS*), 'Politics and the *Times Literary Supplement*'

Fall Semester 1999

Round Table Discussion, 'The Boer War, 1899–1902': Barbara Harlow (English), John Lamphear (History), and Wm. Roger Louis (History)

Sharon Arnoult (Southwest Texas State University), 'Charles I: His Life after Death'

Kenneth O. Morgan (Oxford University), 'Lloyd George, Keir Hardie, and the Importance of the "Pro-Boers"'

Richard Cleary (Architecture), 'Walking the Walk to Talk the Talk: The Promenade in Eighteenth-Century France and England'

Keith Kyle (Journalist and Historian), 'From Suez to Kenya as Journalist and as Historian'

Malcolm Hacksley (National English Literary Museum, Grahamstown, South Africa), 'Planting a Museum, Cultivating a Literature'

Ben Pimlott (University of London), 'The Art of Writing Political Biography'

Geraldine Heng (English), 'Cannibalism, the First Crusade, and the Genesis of Medieval Romance'

A. P. Martinich (Philosophy), 'Thomas Hobbes: Lifelong and Enduring Controversies'

Round Table Discussion, 'Lyndall Gordon's *T. S. Eliot: An Imperfect Life*': Brian Bremen (English), Thomas Cable (English), Elizabeth Richmond-Garza (Comparative Literature), and Thomas F. Staley (HRHRC)

Shula Marks (University of London), 'Smuts, Race, and the Boer War'

Round Table Discussion, 'The Library of the British Museum': William B. Todd (English), Irene Owens (Library and Information Science), and Don Davis (Library and Information Science and Department of History)

Henry Dietz (Government), '*The Hound of the Baskervilles*'

Spring Semester 2000

Susan Napier (Asian Studies), 'The Cultural Phenomenon of the Harry Potter Fantasy Novels'

Round Table Discussion, '*Dutch: A Memoir of Ronald Reagan:* A Chapter in the "Special Relationship"?': Wm. Roger Louis (History), Harry Middleton (LBJ Library), and Elspeth Rostow (LBJ School)

Norman Rose (Hebrew University, Jerusalem), 'Harold Nicolson: A Curious and Colorful Life'

Charlotte Canning (Theatre and Dance), 'Feminists Perform Their Past'

John Ripley (McGill University), 'The Sound of Sociology: H. B. Tree's *Merchant of Venice*'

Sergei Horuji (Russian Academy of Sciences), 'James Joyce in Russia'

Janice Rossen (Biographer and Independent Scholar), 'Philip Toynbee'

Max Egremont (Novelist and Biographer), 'Siegfried Sassoon's War'

Paul Taylor (London School of Economics and Political Science), 'Britain and Europe'

Lord Selborne (Royal Geographical Society), 'The Royal Geographical Society: Exploration since 1830'

Craig MacKenzie (Rand Afrikaans University, Johannesburg), 'The Mythology of the Boer War: Herman Charles Bosman and the Challenge to Afrikaner Romanticism'

Peter Catterall (Institute of Contemporary British History, London), 'Reform of the House of Lords'

Bernard Porter (University of Newcastle), 'Pompous and Circumstantial: Sir Edward Elgar and the British Empire'

Craufurd D. Goodwin (Duke University), 'Roger Fry and the Debate on "Myth" in the Bloomsbury Group'

Jamie Belich (University of Auckland), 'Neo-Britains? The "West" in Nineteenth-Century Australia, New Zealand, and America'

Round Table Discussion, 'Norman Davies's *The Isles*': Sharon Arnoult (Midwestern State University, Wichita Falls), Raymond Douglas (Colgate University),

Walter Johnson (Northwestern Oklahoma State University), David Leaver (Raymond Walters College, Cincinnati), and John Cell (Duke University)

Fall Semester 2000

Round Table Discussion, 'Paul Scott, the Raj Quartet, and the Beginning of British Studies at UT': Peter Green (Classics), Robert Hardgrave (Government and Asian Studies), and Wm. Roger Louis (History)

Suman Gupta (Open University), 'T. S. Eliot as Publisher'

Jeffrey Cox (University of Iowa), 'Going Native: Missionaries in India'

Kevin Kenny (Boston College), 'Irish Nationalism: The American Dimension'

Joseph Kestner (University of Tulsa), 'Victorian Battle Art'

James E. Cronin (Boston College), 'From Old to New Labour: Politics and Society in the Forging of the "Third" Way'

Gerald Moore (Mellon Visiting Research Fellow, HRHRC), 'When Caliban Crossed the Atlantic'

Richard Howard (Shakespearean Actor, London), '"Health and Long Life to You": A Program of Irish Poetry and Prose Presented by an Englishman, with Anecdotes'

Stephen Foster (Northern Illinois University), 'Prognosis Guarded: The Probable Decolonization of the British Era in American History'

Frank Prochaska (University of London), 'Of Crowned and Uncrowned Republics: George V and the Socialists'

Robert H. Abzug (History and American Studies), 'Britain, South Africa, and the American Civil Rights Movement'

Paula Bartley (Visiting Research Fellow, HRHRC), 'Emmeline Pankhurst'

Thomas Jesus Garza (Slavic Languages), 'A British Vampire's Christmas'

Spring Semester 2001

Betty Sue Flowers (UT Distinguished Teaching Professor), 'From Robert Browning to James Bond'

Larry Carver (English), 'Feliks Topolski at the Ransom Center'

Oscar Brockett (Theatre and Dance), 'Lilian Baylis and England's National Theatres'

Linda Levy Peck (George Washington University), 'Luxury and War'

R. James Coote (Architecture), 'Architectural Revival in Britain'

Adam Roberts (Oxford University), 'Britain and the Creation of the United Nations'

Mark Southern (Germanic Studies), 'Words over Swords: Language and Tradition in Celtic Civilization'

Round Table Discussion, 'Ben Rogers's *A Life of A. J. Ayer*': David Braybrooke (Government and Philosophy), Al Martinich (History and Philosophy), David Sosa (Philosophy), and Paul Woodruff (Plan II and Philosophy)

Bartholomew Sparrow (Government), 'British and American Expansion: The Political Foundations'

Jose Harris (Oxford University), 'Writing History during the Second World War'

Charles Loft (Westminster College), 'Off the Rails? The Historic Junctions in Britain's Railway Problem'

Dan Jacobson (University of London), 'David Irving and Holocaust Denial'—Special Lecture

Dan Jacobson (University of London), 'Self-Redemption in the Victorian Novel'

George S. Christian (British Studies), 'The Comic Basis of the Victorian Novel'
Paul Taylor (London *Independent*), 'Rediscovering a Master Dramatist: J. B. Priestley'

Fall Semester 2001

Round Table Discussion, 'Ray Monk's Biography of Bertrand Russell, *The Ghost of Madness*': Al Martinich (History and Philosophy), David Sosa (Philosophy and British Studies), and Paul Woodruff (Plan II and Philosophy)
Alex Danchev (Keele University), 'The Alanbrooke Diaries'
Robert M. Worcester (LSE and Market Opinion Research International), 'Britain and the European Union'
Martha Ann Selby (Asian Studies), 'The Cultural Legacy of British Clubs: Manners, Memory, and Identity among the New Club-Wallahs in Madras'
Roger Owen (Harvard University), 'Lord Cromer and Wilfrid Blunt in Egypt'
James Loehlin (English), 'A Midsummer Night's Dream'
Jeffrey Meyers (Biographer), 'Somerset Maugham'
Elspeth Rostow (LBJ School), 'From American Studies to British Studies—And Beyond'
Nicholas Westcott (British Embassy), 'The Groundnut Scheme: Socialist Imperialism at Work in Africa'
Round Table Discussion, 'The Anglo-American Special Relationship': Gary Freeman (Government), Wm. Roger Louis (History), Elspeth Rostow (American Studies), and Michael Stoff (History)
Christopher Heywood (Sheffield University), 'The Brontës: A Personal History of Discovery and Interpretation'
James Bolger (New Zealand Ambassador and former Prime Minister), 'Whither New Zealand? Constitutional, Political, and International Quandaries'
R. J. Q. Adams (Texas A&M), 'Arthur James Balfour and Andrew Bonar Law: A Study in Contrasts'
Ferdinand Mount (Editor, *Times Literary Supplement*), 'British Culture since the Eighteenth Century: An Open Society?'
James Loehlin (English), 'A Child's Christmas in Wales'

Spring Semester 2002

Round Table Discussion, 'Adam Sisman's *Boswell's Presumptuous Task*': Samuel Baker (English), Linda Ferreira-Buckley (English), Julie Hardwick (History), and Helena Woodward (English)
A. G. Hopkins (History), 'Globalization: The British Case'
Susan Napier (Asian Studies), 'J. R. R. Tolkein and *The Lord of the Rings:* Fantasy as Retreat or Fantasy as Engagement?'
Wilfrid Prest (Adelaide University), 'South Australia's Paradise of Dissent'
Tom Palaima (Classics), 'Terence Rattigan's *Browning Version*'
Alan H. Nelson (University of California, Berkeley), 'Thoughts on Elizabethan Authorship'
Penelope Lively (London), 'Changing Perceptions of British and English Identity'
Hans Mark (Aerospace Engineering), 'The Falklands War'
David Butler (Oxford University), 'Psephology—or, the Study of British Elections'
Robert L. Hardgrave (Government), 'From West Texas to South India and British Studies'
Geoffrey Wheatcroft (London), 'The Englishness of English Sport'

Eileen Cleere (Southwestern University), 'Dirty Pictures: John Ruskin and the Victorian Sanitation of Fine Art'

Jamie Belich (Auckland University), 'A Comparison of Empire Cities: New York and London, Chicago and Melbourne'

Churchill Conference: Geoffrey Best (Oxford University), Sir Michael Howard (Oxford University), Warren Kimball (Rutgers University), Philip Ziegler (London), Wm. Roger Louis (History)

Catherine Maxwell (University of London), 'Swinburne's Poetry and Criticism'

Round Table Discussion, 'Churchill and the Churchill Conference': Rodrigo Gutierrez (History), Adrian Howkins (History), Heidi Juel (English), David McCoy (Government), Joe Moser (English), Jeff Rutherford (History), William S. Livingston (UT Senior Vice President), and Wm. Roger Louis (History)

Fall Semester 2002

James K. Galbraith (LBJ School of Public Affairs), 'The Enduring Importance of John Maynard Keynes'

Michael Green (University of Natal), 'Agatha Christie in South Africa'

Sumit Ganguly (Asian Studies), 'Kashmir: Origins and Consequences of Conflict'

Margaret MacMillan (University of Toronto), 'At the Height of His Power: Lloyd George in 1919'

Douglas Bruster (English), 'Why We Fight: *Much Ado About Nothing* and the West'

John Darwin (Oxford University), 'The Decline and Rise of the British Empire: John Gallagher as an Historian of Imperialism'

Kevin Kenny (Boston College), 'The Irish in the British Empire'

David Wallace (University of Pennsylvania), 'A Chaucerian's Tale of Surinam'

Peter Bowler (Queen's University, Belfast), 'Scientists and the Popularization of Science in Early Twentieth-Century Britain'

Bernardine Evaristo (London), 'A Feisty, Funky Girl in Roman England'

Frank Moorhouse (Australia), 'Dark Places and Grand Days'

David Cannadine (University of London), 'C. P. Snow and the Two Cultures'

Round Table Discussion, 'Edmund S. Morgan's Biography of Benjamin Franklin': Carolyn Eastman (History), Bruce Hunt (History), Wm. Roger Louis (History), Alan Tully (History)

Mark Lawrence (History), 'The Strange Silence of Cold War England: Britain and the Vietnam War'

Tom Cable (English), 'The Pleasures of Remembering Poetry'

Spring Semester 2003

Round Table Discussion, 'W. G. Sebald's *Rings of Saturn*': Brigitte Bauer (French and Italian), Sidney Monas (History and Slavic Languages), Elizabeth Richmond-Garza (English and Comparative Literature), Walter Wetzels (Germanic Studies)

Diana Davis (Geography), 'Brutes, Beasts, and Empire: A Comparative Study of the British and French Experience'

Colin Franklin (Publisher), 'Rosalind Franklin—Variously Described as "The Dark Lady of DNA" and "The Sylvia Plath of Molecular Biology"'

Sidney Monas (History and Slavic Languages), 'A Life of Irish Literature and Russian Poetry, Soviet Politics and International History'

Neville Hoad (English), 'Oscar Wilde in America'

Selina Hastings (London), 'Rosamond Lehman: Eternal Exile'
Bernard Wasserstein (Glasgow University), 'The British in Palestine: Reconsiderations'
Anne Chisholm (London), 'Frances Partridge: Last of the Bloomsberries'
Philip Morgan (Johns Hopkins University), 'The Black Experience and the British Empire'
Jeremy duQuesnay Adams (Southern Methodist University), 'Joan of Arc and the English'
Didier Lancien (University of Toulouse), 'Churchill and de Gaulle'
Avi Shlaim (Oxford University), 'The Balfour Declaration and Its Consequences'
Martin J. Wiener (Rice University), 'Murder and the Modern British Historian'
Winthrop Wetherbee (Cornell University), 'The Jewish Impact on Medieval Literature: Chaucer, Boccaccio, and Dante'
Philippa Levine (University of Southern California), 'Sex and the British Empire'

Summer 2003

Donald G. Davis, Jr. (History and the School of Information), 'Life without British Studies Is Like . . .'
Kurth Sprague (English and American Studies), 'Literature, Horses, and Scandal at UT'
David Evans (Astronomy), 'An Astronomer's Life in South Africa and Texas'
Tom Hatfield (Continuing Education), 'Not Long Enough! Half a Century at UT'

Fall Semester 2003

Richard Oram (HRHRC), 'Evelyn Waugh: Collector and Annotator'
Round Table Discussion, 'Booker Prize Winner James Kelman: Adapting a Glasgow Novel for the Texas Stage': James Kelman (Glasgow), Mia Carter (English), Kirk Lynn, and Dikran Utidjian
Simon Green (All Souls College, Oxford University), 'The Strange Death of Puritan England, 1914–1945'
Elizabeth Richmond-Garza (English and Comparative Literature), '*Measure for Measure*'
Lewis Hoffacker (U.S. Ambassador), 'From the Congo to British Studies'
A. P. Thornton (University of Toronto), 'Wars Remembered, Revisited, and Reinvented'
Deryck Schreuder (University of Western Australia), 'The Burden of the British Past in Australia'
Robert Mettlen (Finance), 'From Birmingham to British Studies'
Paul Schroeder (University of Illinois), 'The Pax Britannica and the Pax Americana: Empire, Hegemony, and the International System'
Ferdinand Mount (London), 'A Time to Dance: Anthony Powell's *Dance to the Music of Time* and the Twentieth Century in Britain'
Brian Bond (University of London), '*Oh! What a Lovely War:* History and Popular Myth in Late-Twentieth Century Britain'
Wendy Frith (Bradford College, England), 'The Speckled Monster: Lady Mary Wortley Montagu and the Battle against Smallpox'
Harry Middleton (LBJ Library), 'The Road to the White House'
Jeremy Lewis (London), 'Tobias Smollett'
Christian Smith (Austin, Texas), 'Christmas Readings'

Spring Semester 2004

Round Table Discussion, 'The Pleasures of Reading Thackeray': Carol Mackay (English), Judith Fisher (Trinity University), George Christian (British Studies)

Thomas F. Staley (HRHRC), '"Corso e Recorso:" A Journey through Academe'

Patrick O'Brien (London School of Economics), 'The Pax Britannica, American Hegemony, and the International Order, 1793–2004'

Michael Wheeler (former Director of Chawton House Library), 'England Drawn and Quartered: Cultural Crisis in the Mid-Nineteenth Century'

Walter Wetzels (Germanic Studies), 'Growing Up in Nazi Germany, and later American Adventures'

Kathleen Wilson (State University of New York, Stony Brook), 'The Colonial State and Governance in the Eighteenth Century'

Elizabeth Fernea (English and Middle Eastern Studies), 'Encounters with Imperialism'

Chris Dunton (National University of Lesotho), 'Newspapers and Colonial Rule in Africa'

Miguel Gonzalez-Gerth (Spanish and Portuguese), 'Crossing Geographical and Cultural Borders—and Finally Arriving at British Studies'

Peter Stansky (Stanford University), 'Bloomsbury in Ceylon'

Round Table Discussion, '*The Crimson Petal and the White*': John Farrell (English), Betty Sue Flowers (LBJ Library), Wm. Roger Louis (History), Paul Neimann (English)

Ann Curthoys (Australian National University), 'The Australian History Wars'

Martha Ann Selby (Asian Studies), 'Against the Grain: On Finding My Voice in India'

Steven Isenberg (UT Visiting Professor of Humanities), 'A Life in Our Times'

Summer 2004

Carol Mackay (English), 'My Own Velvet Revolution'

Erez Manela (Harvard University), 'The "Wilsonian Moment" in India and the Crisis of Empire in 1919'

Scott Lucas (Birmingham University), '"A Bright Shining Mecca": British Culture and Political Warfare in the Cold War and Beyond'

Monica Belmonte (U.S. Department of State), 'Before Things Fell Apart: The British Design for the Nigerian State'

Dan Jacobson (London), 'Philip Larkin's "Elements"'

Bernard Porter (University of Newcastle), '"Oo Let 'Em In? Asylum Seekers and Terrorists in Britain, 1850–1914'

Fall Semester 2004

Richard Drayton (Cambridge University), 'Anglo-American "Liberal" Imperialism, British Guiana, 1953–64, and the World Since September 11'

David Washbrook (Oxford University), 'Living on the Edge: Anxiety and Identity in "British" Calcutta, 1780–1930'

Joanna Hitchcock (University of Texas Press), 'An Accidental Publisher'

Alan Friedman (English), '*A Midsummer Night's Dream*'

Antony Best (London School of Economics), 'British Intellectuals and East Asia in the Inter-war Years'

John Farrell (English), 'Beating a Path from Brooklyn to Austin'

Christopher Middleton (Liberal Arts), 'Relevant to England—A Reading of Poems'

Gail Minault (History and Asian Studies), 'Growing Up Bilingual and Other (Mis) adventures in Negotiating Cultures'

Wm. Roger Louis (History), 'Escape from Oklahoma'

John Trimble (English), 'Writing with Style'

Niall Ferguson (Harvard University), 'Origins of the First World War'

James Hopkins (Southern Methodist University), 'George Orwell and the Spanish Civil War: The Case of Nikos Kazantzakis'

James Currey (London), 'Africa Writes Back: Publishing the African Writers Series at Heinemann'

Sidney Monas (History and Slavic Languages), 'A Jew's Christmas'

Geoffrey Wheatcroft (London), '"In the Advance Guard": Evelyn Waugh's Reputation'

Spring Semester 2005

Katharine Whitehorn (London), 'It Didn't *All* Start in the Sixties'

Gertrude Himmelfarb (Graduate School, City University of New York), 'The Whig Interpretation of History'

Kurt Heinzelman (English and HRHRC), 'Lord Byron and the Invention of Celebrity'

Brian Levack (History), 'Jesuits, Lawyers, and Witches'

Richard Cleary (Architecture), 'When Taste Mattered: W. J. Battle and the Architecture of the Forty Acres'

Edward I. Steinhart (Texas Tech University), 'White Hunters in British East Africa, 1895–1914'

Don Graham (English), 'The Drover's Wife: An Australian Archetype'

A. C. H. Smith, (London) 'Literary Friendship: The 40-Year Story of Tom Stoppard, B. S. Johnson, and Zulfikar Ghose'

Paul Woodruff (Philosophy and Plan II), 'A Case of Anglophilia—And Partial Recovery: Being an Account of My Life, with Special Attention to the Influence of England upon My Education'

Toyin Falola (History), 'Footprints of the Ancestors'

Robert Abzug (History) 'Confessions of an Intellectual Omnivore: The Consequences on Scholarship and Career'

Deirdre McMahon (Mary Immaculate College, University of Limerick), 'Ireland and the Empire-Commonwealth, 1918–1972'

James Coote (Architecture), 'Building with Wit: Sir Edwin Lutyens and British Architecture'

Jay Clayton (Vanderbilt University), 'The Dickens Tape: Lost and Found Sound before Recording'

Christopher Ricks (Oxford University), 'The Force of Poetry: Shakespeare and Beckett'

Summer 2005

Blair Worden (Oxford University), 'Poetry and History of the English Renaissance'

Robert Bruce Osborn (British Studies), 'The Four Lives of Robert Osborn'

Alessandra Lippucci (Government), 'Perseverance Furthers: A Self-Consuming Artifact'

William H. Cunningham (former President of the University of Texas), 'Money, Power, Politics, and Ambition'
David V. Edwards (Government), 'Friendly Persuasion in the Academy'
Elizabeth Richmond-Garza (English), 'A Punk Rocker with Eight Languages'
Richard Lariviere (Liberal Arts), 'Confessions of a Sanskritist Dean'

Fall Semester 2005

Celebration of 30th Anniversary and Publication of *Yet More Adventures with Britannia*
Robert D. King (Jewish Studies), 'T.S. Eliot Reconsidered'
Round Table Discussion, 'The London Bombings': James Galbraith (LBJ School), Elizabeth Cullingford (English), Clement Henry (Government), Wm. Roger Louis (History)
Dolora Chapelle Wojciehowski (English), 'The Erotic Uncanny in Shakespeare's *Twelfth Night*'
Karl Hagstrom Miller (History), 'Playing Pensativa: History and Music in Counterpoint'
James D. Garrison (English), 'Translating Gray's *Elegy*'
Miguel Gonzalez-Gerth (Spanish and Portuguese), 'Another Look at Orwell: The Origins of *1984*'
Round Table Discussion, 'The Imperial Closet: Gordon of Khartoum, Hector McDonald of the Boer War, and Roger Casement of Ireland': Barbara Harlow (English), Neville Hoad (English), John Thomas (HRHRC)
Guy Ortolano (Washington University, St. Louis), 'From *The Two Cultures* to *Breaking Ranks:* C.P. Snow and the Interpretation of the 1960s'
Catherine Robson (University of California, Davis), 'Poetry and Memorialization'
Round Table Discussion, 'Britain and the Jewish Century': Lauren Apter (History), Robert D. King (Jewish Studies), Sidney Monas (History and Slavic Languages)
Hans Mark (Aerospace Engineering), 'Churchill, the Anglo-Persian Oil Company, and the Origins of the Energy Crisis: From the Early 20th Century to the Present'
Randall Woods (University of Arkansas), 'LBJ and the British'

Spring Semester 2006

Richard Gray (London), 'Movie Palaces of Britain'
Samuel Baker (English), 'The Lake Poets and the War in the Mediterranean Sea'
Thomas F. Staley (HRHRC), 'Graham Greene and Evelyn Waugh'
Gary Stringer (Texas A&M), 'Love's Long Labors Coming to Fruition: The John Donne Variorum Donne'
Caroline Elkins (Harvard University), 'From Malaya to Kenya: British Colonial Violence and the End of Empire'
Grigory Kaganov (St. Petersburg), 'London in the Mouth of the Neva'
Graham Greene (London), 'A Life in Publishing'
John Davis (Oxford University), 'Evans-Pritchard: Nonetheless A Great Englishman'
Barry Gough (Wilfrid Laurier University), 'Arthur Marder and the Battles over the History of the Royal Navy'
Ivan Kreilkamp (Indiana University), '"Bags of Meat": Pet-Keeping and the Justice to Animals in Thomas Hardy'

James Wilson (History), 'Historical Memory and the Mau Mau Uprising in Colonial Kenya'

Anne Deighton (Oxford University), 'Britain after the Second World War: Losing an Empire and Finding a Place in a World of Superpowers'

Steve Isenberg (Liberal Arts), 'Auden, Forster, Larkin, and Empson'

Harriet Ritvo (MIT), 'Animals on the Edge'

Peter Quinn (New York), 'Eugenics and the Hour of the Cat'

Dan Jacobson (London), 'Kipling and South Africa'

Fall Semester 2006

Michael Charlesworth (Art and Art History) and Kurt Heinzelman (English), 'Tony Harrison's "v."'

Peter Stanley (Australian War Memorial), 'All Imaginable Excuses: Australian Deserters and the Fall of Singapore'

Selina Hastings (London), 'Somerset Maugham and "Englishness"'

James W. Vick (Mathematics), 'A Golden Century of English Mathematics'

John O. Voll (Georgetown University), 'Defining the Middle East and the Clash of Civilizations'

James Loehlin (English), 'The Afterlife of Hamlet'

Daniel Topolski (London), 'The Life and Art of Feliks Topolski'

John Darwin (Oxford University), 'The British Empire and the British World'

David Cannadine (University of London), 'Andrew Mellon and Plutocracy Across the Atlantic'

John Lonsdale (Cambridge University), 'White Settlers and Black Mau Mau in Kenya'

Kate Gartner Frost (English), 'So What's Been Done about John Donne Lately?'

John Summers (Harvard University), 'The Power Elite: C. Wright Mills and the British'

Marrack Goulding (Oxford University), 'Has it been a Success? Britain in the United Nations'

Priya Satia (Stanford University), 'The Defence of Inhumanity: British Military and Cultural Power in the Middle East'

Don Graham (English), 'Burnt Orange Britannia: A Missing Contributor!'

Spring Semester 2007

Bernard Porter (Newcastle University), 'Empire and British Culture'

Paul Sullivan (Liberal Arts Honors Program), 'The Headmaster's Shakespeare: John Garrett and British Education'

Round Table Discussion, '*The Queen*': Elizabeth Cullingford (English), Karen King (American Studies), Wm. Roger Louis (History), Bryan Roberts (Sociology)

Martin Francis (University of Cincinnati), 'Cecil Beaton's Romantic Toryism and the Symbolism of Wartime Britain'

Susan Crane (Columbia University), 'Animal Feelings and Feelings for Animals in Chaucer'

Michael Charlesworth (Art History), 'The Earl of Strafford and Wentworth Castle'

Adam Sisman (London), 'Wordsworth and Coleridge'

Jenny Mann (Cornell University), 'Shakespeare's English Rhetoric: Mingling Heroes and Hobgoblins in *A Midsummer Night's Dream*'

David Atkinson (Member of Parliament), 'Britain and World Peace in the 21st Century'
Bertram Wyatt-Brown (University of Florida), 'T. E. Lawrence, Reputation, and Honor's Decline'
Wm. Roger Louis (History), 'All Souls and Oxford in 1956: Reassessing the Meaning of the Suez Crisis'
Indivar Kamtekar (Jawaharlal Nehru University), 'India and Britain during the Second World War'
Cassandra Pybus (University of Sydney), 'William Wilberforce and the Emancipation of Slaves'
Stephen Howe (University of Bristol), 'Empire in the 21st Century English Imagination'
Geoffrey Wheatcroft (London), 'The Myth of Malicious Partition: The Cases of Ireland, India, and Palestine'
Charles Rossman (English), 'D. H. Lawrence and the "Spirit" of Mexico'
Kenneth O. Morgan (House of Lords), 'Lloyd George, the French, and the Germans'

Fall Semester 2007

R. J. Q. Adams (Texas A&M), 'A. J. Balfour's Achievement and Legacy'
Robin Doughty (Geography), 'Saving Coleridge's Endangered Albatross'
Caroline Williams (University of Texas), 'A Victorian Orientalist: John Frederick Lewis and the Artist's Discovery of Cairo'
Susan Pedersen (Columbia University), 'The Story of Frances Stevenson and David Lloyd George'
Eric S. Mallin (English), 'Macbeth and the Simple Truth'
Mark Oaten, M.P., 'How "Special" Is the Special Relationship?'
Dan Birkholz (English), 'Playboys of the West of England: Medieval Cosmopolitanism and Familial Love'
Jeremy Lewis (London), 'The Secret History of Penguin Books'
Matthew Jones (Nottingham University), 'Britain and the End of Empire in South East Asia in the Era of the Vietnam War'
Martin Wiener (Rice University), '"Who knows the Empire whom only the Empire knows?": Reconnecting British and Empire History'
Book Launch: *Penultimate Adventures with Britannia* (Follett's Intellectual Property)
Hermione Lee and Christopher Ricks (Oxford), 'The Elusive Brian Moore: His Stature in Modern Literature'
Gabriel Gorodetsky (Tel Aviv University), 'The Challenge to Churchill's Wartime Leadership by Sir Stafford Cripps (the "Red Squire")'
Helena Woodard (English), 'Black and White Christmas: The Deep South in the Eighteenth Century'

Spring Semester 2008

Round Table Discussion, 'Tim Jeal's *Stanley: The Impossible Life of Africa's Greatest Explorer*': Diana Davis (Geography), A. G. Hopkins (History), Wm. Roger Louis (History)
Elizabeth Richmond-Garza (English and Comparative Literature), 'New Year's Eve 1900: Oscar Wilde and the Masquerade of Victorian Culture'
Robert Hardgrave (Government), 'The Search for Balthazar Solvyns and an Indian Past: The Anatomy of a Research Project'

Lucy Chester (University of Colorado), 'Zionists, Indian Nationalism, and British Schizophrenia in Palestine'

Michael Brenner (University of Pittsburgh), 'Strategic and Cultural Triangulation: Britain, the United States, and Europe'

Roger Morgan (European University, Florence), 'The British "Establishment" and the Chatham House Version of World Affairs'

Jason Parker (Texas A&M), 'Wilson's Curse: Self-Determination, the Cold War, and the Challenge of Modernity in the "Third World"'

Stephen Foster (Northern Illinois University), 'The American Colonies and the Atlantic World'

A. G. Hopkins (History), 'Comparing British and American "Empires"'

James Turner (Notre Dame University), 'The Emergence of Academic Disciplines'

Dror Wahrman (Indiana University), 'Invisible Hands in the Eighteenth Century'

Narendra Singh Sarila (Prince of Sarila), 'Mountbatten and the Partition of India'

Pillarisetti Sudhir (American Historical Association), 'The Retreat of the Raj: Radicals and Reactionaries in Britain'

Keith Francis (Baylor University), 'What Did Darwin Mean in *On the Origin of Species?* An Englishman and a Frenchman Debate Evolution'

Fall Semester 2008

Round Table Discussion, 'Ted and Sylvia': (UT English), Judith Kroll, Kurt Heinzelman, Betty Sue Flowers, Tom Cable

Roby Barrett (Middle East Institute), 'The Question of Intervention in Iraq, 1958–59'

John Kerr (San Antonio), 'Cardigan Bay'

Sue Onslow (London School of Economics), 'Julian Amery: A Nineteenth-Century Relic in a Twentieth-Century World?'

John Rumrich (English), 'Reconciliation in *The Winter's Tale:* The Literary Friendship of Robert Greene and William Shakespeare'

Richard Jenkyns (Oxford), 'Conan Doyle: An Assessment beyond Sherlock Holmes'

Theresa Kelley (University of Wisconsin), 'Romantic British Culture and Botany in India'

Sir Adam Roberts (Oxford), 'After the Cold War'

Geoffrey Wheatcroft (London), 'Churchill and the Jews'

Sir Brian Harrison (Oxford), 'Prelude to the Sixties'

Eric Kaufmann (London School of Economics), 'The Orange Order in Northern Ireland'

Robert McMahon (Ohio State University), 'Dean Acheson: The Creation of a New World Order and the Problem of the British'

Mark Metzler (History), 'Eye of the Storm: London's Place in the First Great Depression, 1872–96'

James Loehlin (English), Christmas Party at the New Campus Club, reading passages from Charles Dickens, *A Christmas Carol*

Spring Semester 2009

Margaret MacMillan (Oxford University), 'The Jewel in the Crown'

Bernard Wasserstein (University of Chicago), 'Glasgow in the 1950s'

Dominic Sandbrook (London), 'The Swinging Sixties in Britain'

Karl Meyer and Shareen Brysac (New York Times and CBS), 'Inventing Iran, Inventing Iraq: The British and Americans in the Middle East'

Albert Lewis (R. L. Moore Project), 'The Bertrand Russell Collection: The One That Got Away from the HRC'

Sir David Cannadine (Institute of Historical Research, London), 'Colonial Independence'; Linda Colley (CBE, Princeton University), 'Philip Francis and the Challenge to the British Empire'

George Scott Christian (English and History), 'Origins of Scottish Nationalism: The Trial of Thomas Muir'

Discussion led by Brian Levack and Roger Louis (History), 'Trevor-Roper and Scotland'

Warren Kimball (Rutgers University), 'Churchill, Roosevelt, and Ireland'

Ferdinand Mount (London) and R. J. Q. Adams (Texas A&M), 'A. J. Balfour and his Critics'

Dan Jacobson (London), Betty Sue Flowers (LBJ Library), and Tom Staley (HRHRC), Tribute to Betty Sue Flowers—'Hardy and Eliot'

John Darwin (Nuffield College, Oxford), 'Britain's Global Empire'

Saul Dubow (Sussex University), 'Sir Keith Hancock and the Question of Race'

Weslie Janeway (Cambridge), 'Darwin's Cookbook'

Julian Barnes, Barbara Harlow, Miguel Gonzalez-Gerth, 'Such, Such Was Eric Blair'

Cassandra Pybus (Visiting Fellow, UT Institute of Historical Studies), 'If you were regular black...': Slavery, Miscegenation, and Racial Anxiety in Britain'

Fall Semester 2009

Peter Green (Classics), 'The Devil in Kingsley Amis'

John Farrell (English), 'Forgiving Emily Brontë'

Samuel Baker (English), 'Wedgwood Gothic'

Louise Weinberg (Law), 'Gilbert and Sullivan: The Curios Persistence of Savoyards'

Elizabeth Richmond-Garza (English), 'Love in a Time of Terror: King Lear and the Potential for Consolation'

John Rumrich (English), 'John Milton and the Embodied Word'

Round Table Discussion, 'Effective Teaching': Tom Cable (English), David Leal (Government), Lisa Moore (English), Bob Woodberry (Sociology)'

James M. Vaughn (History and British Studies), 'The Decline and Fall of Whig Imperialism, 1756–1783'

Round Table Discussion, 'Bloomsbury': Betty Sue Flowers (English), Wm. Roger Louis (History), Lisa Moore (English), David Sosa (Philosophy)

Sir Harold Evans, 'Murder Most Foul'

Peter Cain (Sheffield Hallam University), 'The Radical Critique of Colonialism'

John Gooch (Leeds University), 'Pyrrhic Victory? England and the Great War'

Maya Jasanoff (Harvard University), 'The British Side of the American Revolution'

Maeve Cooney (British Studies), Christmas Party at the Littlefield Home, reading O. Henry's 'The Gift of the Magi'

Spring Semester 2010

Thomas Jesus Garza (UT Language Center), 'The British Vampire's Slavic Roots'

Marilyn Young (New York University), 'The British and Vietnam'

Daniel Howe (University of California at Los Angeles), 'What Hath God Wrought'

Roberta Rubenstein (American University), 'Virginia Woolf and the Russians'

Samuel R. Williamson (University of the South at Sewanee), 'The Possibility of Civil War over Ireland in 1914'

Steve Pincus (Yale), 'The First Modern Revolution: Reappraising the Glorious Events of 1688'

Selina Hastings (London), 'Somerset Maugham: A Life Under Cover'

Eugene Rogan (Oxford), 'Modern History through Arab Eyes'

T. M. Devine (University of Edinburgh), 'Did Slavery Make Scotland Great?'

Phillip Herring (University of Wisconsin–Madison), 'A Journey through James Joyce's *Ulysses*'

Alison Bashford (Harvard), 'Australia and the World Population Problem, 1918–1954'

Berny Sèbe (Birmingham University), 'French and British Colonial Heroes in Africa'

J. L. Berry (Austin, Texas), 'The Post-Twilight of the British Empire on the Zambian Copper Belt'

Bernard Porter (University of Newcastle), 'The Myth of Goths and Vandals in British Architecture'

Fall Semester 2010

Jonathan Schneer (Georgia Institute of Technology), 'The Balfour Declaration'

Larry Carver (Liberal Arts Honors Program), 'Reacting to the Past: How I Came to Love Teaching Edmund Burke'

Thomas Pinney (Pomona College), 'Kipling and America'

Donna Kornhaber (English), 'Accident and Artistry in *The Third Man*'

Doug Bruster (English), 'Rating *A Midsummer Night's Dream*'

Peter Stansky (Stanford University), 'Julian Bell: From Bloomsbury to Spain'

Crawford Young (University of Wisconsin, Madison), 'The British Empire and Comparative Decolonization'

Jeffrey Cox (University of Iowa), 'From the Kingdom of God to the Third World'

Roberta Rubenstein (American University), 'Approaching the Golden Anniversary: Dorris Lessing's *The Golden Notebook*'

Kenneth O. Morgan (House of Lords), 'Aneurin Bevan: Pragmatist and Prophet of the Old Left'

Robert Vitalis (University of Pennsylvania), 'From the Persian Gulf to the Gulf of Mexico: What We Know About BP'

James Curran (Sydney University), 'The Great Age of Confusion: Australia in the Wake of Empire'

Archie Brown (St Antony's College, Oxford), 'Margaret Thatcher and the End of the Cold War'

Phyllis Lassner (Northwestern University), 'The End of Empire in the Middle East and the Literary Imagination'

Spring Semester 2011

Tillman Nechtman (Skidmore College), 'Nabobs: Empire and the Politics of National Identity in Eighteenth-Century Britain'

Brian Levak (History), 'Demonic Possession in Early Modern Britain'

David Kornhaber (English), 'George Bernard Shaw: Modernist'

Lisa L. Moore (English), 'Sister Arts: The Erotics of Lesbian Landscape'

Bartholomew Sparrow (Government), 'Brent Scowcroft, Mrs. Thatcher, and National Security'

Philip Bobbitt (Law School and LBJ School), 'The Special Relationship'

Deborah Harkness (UCLA), 'Fiction and the Archives: The Art and Craft of the Historian'

Peter Clarke (Trinity Hall, Cambridge), 'The English-Speaking Peoples'

A. G. Hopkins (History), 'The United States, 1783–1861: Britain's Honorary Dominion?'

Reba Soffer (California State University at Northridge), 'Intellectual History, Life, and Fiction'

Joanna Lewis (London School of Economics), 'Harold Macmillan and the Wind of Change'

Andrew Lycett (London), 'Arthur Conan Doyle and Rudyard Kipling'

Geoffrey Wheatcroft (London), 'The Grand Illusion: Britain and the United States'

Priscilla Roberts (University of Hong Kong), 'Henry James and the Erosion of British Power'

John Higley (Government), 'Degeneration of Ruling Elites? Recent American and British Elites'

Fall Semester 2011

Round Table Discussion, 'The Oxford of Maurice Bowra and Hugh Trevor Roper': Paul Woodruff (Philosophy), Wm. Roger Louis (History), and David Leal (Government),

Marian Barber (UT Austin), 'The Scots, Irish, English, and Welsh in the Making of Texas'

Geoffrey Davis (University of Aachen), 'The Territory of My Imagination: Rediscovering Dan Jacobson's South Africa'

Nadja Durbach (University of Utah), 'Poverty, Politics, and Roast Beef: Poor Relief and the Nation in Early Nineteenth-Century Britain'

Leonard Barkan (Princeton University), 'What's for Dinner on a Desert Island: Feast and Famine in *The Tempest*'

Lindsey Schell (University Libraries), 'The Royal Wedding and the Making of a Modern Princess'

Laurence Raw (Baskent University), 'Shakespeare and Home Front during World War II'

Sir Brian Harrison (Oxford University), 'Surprising Resilience: Historians of British Conservatism since 1945'

Troy Bickham (Texas A&M), 'A New Grand Transatlantic Drama: Britain and the Anglo-American War of 1812'

Eli P. Cox III (Marketing), 'The Betrayal of Adam Smith'

Nicholas Rogers (York University), 'Crime, Punishment, and Governance in Eighteenth-Century Britain'

Donald Lamm (WW Norton and Company), 'The History of Oxford University Press'

Al Martinich (History and Government), 'Locke and the Limits of Toleration'

Spring Semester 2012

Philippa Levine (Chair), John Berry (Austin), Donna Kornhaber (English), Wm. Roger Louis (History), Elizabeth Richmond-Garza (English), '*The Iron Lady*'

Brian Cowan (McGill University), 'Henry Sacheverell and the Cult of Eighteenth-Century Personalities'

Ronald Heiferman (Quinnipiac University), 'Churchill, Roosevelt, and China'

Jeremi Suri (History and LBJ School), 'British Imperialism and American Nation-Building'

Susan Napier (Tufts University), 'Harry Potter and the Fantastic Journey'

Andrew Roberts (School of Oriental and African Studies), 'Poetry, Anthology, and Criticism: Michael Roberts and the BBC'

Michael Charlesworth (Art History), 'Derek Jarman and British Films: Paintings, Poetry, and Prose'

John Voll (Georgetown University), 'Britain and Islam in the Twentieth Century'

Sheldon Garon (Princeton University), 'Anglo-Japanese Cultural Relations, 1868–1950'

Anand Yang (University of Washington, Seattle), 'Convicts in British India'

George Bernard (University of Southampton), 'Editing the *English Historical Review*'

Selina Todd (St. Hilda's College, Oxford), 'The Problem Family in Postwar Britain'

Christine Krueger (Marquette University), 'The Victorian Historian Mary Anne Everett Green'

Jeremy Lewis (London), 'David Astor and the Observer'

Michael Winship (English), 'Napoleon Comes to America: The Publishing of Sir Walter Scott's *Life of Napoleon Buonaparte* (1827)'

Adam Sisman (London), 'Writing the Biographies of A. J. P. Taylor and Hugh Trevor-Roper'

Fall Semester 2012

Donna Kornhaber (English), 'Charlie Chaplin's Forgotten Feature: A Countess from Hong Kong'

Tom Palaima (Classics), 'The War Poems of Robert Graves'

Rosemary Hill (All Souls College, Oxford), 'Prince Albert'

Sucheta Mahajan (Jawaharlal Nehru University), 'Independence and Partition of India Reassessed'

Richard Davenport-Hines (London), 'Ivy Compton-Burnett'

Albert Beveridge III (Johns Hopkins), 'The Rise, Fall, and Revival of Anthony Trollope'

Philip Stern (Duke University), 'The Evolution of the City of Bombay'

Betty Smocovitis (University of Florida), 'Rhapsody on a Darwinian Theme'

Jad Adams (University of London), 'Tony Benn: The Making of a British Radical'

Steve Isenberg (Quondam Executive Director of PEN), 'Fathers and Sons: Edmund Gosse and J. R. Ackerley'

Paul Levy (*Wall Street Journal*), 'Lytton Strachey'

William Janeway (New York), 'Beyond Keynesianism: Maynard Keynes and the Good Life'

Dan Raff (Wharton School of Business), 'The Ancient University Presses Make Up Their Minds'

David Leal (Government), 'Method and Irrationality in the Traditions of Sherlock Holmes'

Spring Semester 2013

Kariann Yokata (University of Colorado, Denver), 'Unbecoming British? The Place of Post-Colonial Americans in the British Empire'

Brian Levack (History), 'The British Imperial State in the Eighteenth Century'
Anne Chisholm (London), 'Dora Carrington and the Bloomsbury Circle'
James Banner (Washington, D.C.), 'Academics, Intellectuals, and Popular History'
Selina Hastings (London), 'The Red Earl'
John Spurling (London), 'Sir Edmund Gibson and the British Raj'
Hilary Spurling (London), 'Pearl Buck and China'
Janine Barchas (English), 'Jane Austen between the Covers'
Wm. Roger Louis (History and British Studies), 'The History of Oxford University Press, 1896–1970'
Sir Christopher Bayly (Cambridge), 'Distant Connections: India and Australia in the Colonial Era'
Philip Waller (Oxford), 'Writers, Readers, and Reputations'
Jordanna Bailkin (University of Washington), 'Unsettled: Refugee Camps in Britain'
Geoffrey Wheatcroft (London), 'Assessing Margaret Thatcher'
Daniel Baugh (Cornell University), 'France and the British State and Empire, 1680–1940'
Richard Carwardine (Oxford), 'Lincoln and Emancipation: the British and International Consequences'

Fall Semester 2013

Henry Dietz (Government) 'British Sea Power and Napoleon in the Novels of Patrick O'Brian'
Christopher Benfey (Mount Holyoke College), 'The Myth of Tarzan'
Stephen Brooke (York University, Toronto), 'Photography and the Working Class in the 1950s'
Aram Bakshian (Washington, D.C.), '*The Economist*'
David Cressy (George III Professor of History, Ohio State), 'Gypsies and Cultural Tradition'
Stephen Weinberg (Josey Regental Chair of Science), 'The Last Magician: Isaac Newton'
James Scott (UT Statistics), 'Isaac Newton and the Birth of Money'
Lara Kriegel (Indiana University), 'Who Blew the Bugle? The Charge of the Light Brigade and the Legacy of the Crimean War'
Benjamin Gregg (Government), 'The Stasi and Secret Files'
Douglas Bruster (English), 'Shakespeare and Othello'
Miguel Gonzalez-Gerth (Founding Member of British Studies), 'Ian McEwan's Novels: Sex, Espionage, and Literature'
Allen MacDuffie, 'Dickens and Energy'
Walter Wetzels (Founding Member of British Studies), 'The Bombing of German Cities during the Second World War'

Spring Semester 2014

William S. Cunningham (UT Past President), 'Money, Power, Politics-and British Studies-at UT'
Michael Anderson (Government), 'Britain's Pacific Relations'
Rosemary Hill (London), 'Bloomsbury's Memoir Club'
Benjamin Brower (History), 'The Muslim Pilgrimage'
Margaret Jacobs (University of Nebraska), 'White Mother to a Dark Race'

Diana Solomon (Simon Fraser University), 'Seduction and Rape in Shakespeare'

Michael Stoff (History), 'Wilfred Burchett's "Warning to the World": An Australian War Correspondent Rewrites the Atomic Bomb Narrative"

Arthur Nicholson (San Antonio), 'Former Naval Person: Winston Churchill and the Royal Navy'

John Fair (UT Kinesiology), 'The Diverse Roots of Physical Culture'

Ian Hancock (UT Romani Studies), 'The Historical Identity of "Gypsies"'

Roy Ritchie (Huntington Library), 'The Advent of Beach Culture in Britain'

Bernard Wasserstein (University of Chicago), 'The Men Who Ruled Palestine'

James Vaughn (History), 'The Ideological Origins of the American Revolution Revisited'

Steven Isenberg (Visiting Professor of the Humanities), 'The Literary Legacy of the Great War'

William Whyte (Oxford), 'A Hotbed of Cold Feet? Architecture in Oxford Since 1950'

George Christian (History), 'Scotland's Independence?'

Fall Semester 2014

Stephen Enniss (Harry Ransom Center), 'The Ransom Center Looks Ahead'

John Gurney (Oxford), 'Nancy Lambton and Iran'

James D. Garrison (English), 'Gray, Johnson, and Elegy'

General David Ramsbotham (House of Lords), 'The Last Colonial War'

Elena Schneider (University of California, Berkeley), 'Perspectives on Revolution'

Roger Billis (London), 'The Reform Club: Its Creation and Traditions'

Max Egremont (London), 'Siegfried Sassoon: A Reassessment'

William Meier (Texas Christian University), 'Drugs in Twentieth-Century Britain'

Richard Davenport-Hines (London), 'The Death of General Gordon in Khartoum'

Leah S. Marcus (Vanderbilt), '*Much Ado about Nothing* and *The Taming of the Shrew*'

Kenneth O. Morgan (House of Lords), 'Wales, Lloyd George, and the First World War'

Round Table Discussion, 'The Link between Psychology and History': Robert Abzug (Jewish Studies), Randy Diehl (Dean of Liberal Arts), Wm. Roger Louis (British Studies)

Jane Ridley (Buckingham University), 'George V, the Tsar, and the British Monarchy'

Richard Cleary (Architecture), 'Well Played! Sports Settings and the Perspective of Architecture'

Sir Keith Thomas (Oxford), 'Army Life in Jamaica'

Archie Brown (Oxford), 'The Scottish Referendum'

Miranda Seymour (Brown), 'Germany and England: Romantic Connections'

Spring Semester 2015

Kurt Heinzelman (English), 'The Disappearance of Dylan Thomas'

Michael Brenner (University of Pittsburgh), 'Blair and Bush: Partners in Reaction'

Bartholomew Sparrow (Government), 'Legacy of Colonialism: America's Forgotten Class'

Bain Attwood (Harvard), 'Indigenous Rights in Australia and New Zealand'

Bernard Porter (Newcastle), 'Genocide in Tasmania?'

Ingrid Norton (Harvard Divinity School), 'The Poetry of Valentine's Day'

Ferdinand Mount (London), 'Harold Macmillan'

Thomas Meaney (Columbia University), 'The United Nations and Colonial Independence'

Lawrence S. Graham (Government), 'Northern Ireland's Continuing Troubles: Reflections on the Belfast Agreement of 1998'

Gabriel Paquette (Johns Hopkins University), 'Allies yet Adversaries? Portugal and Britain in the Age of Empire'

Molly McCullers (University of West Georgia), 'South Africa and the Question of African Independence: The Case of South-West Africa (Namibia)'

Robert D. King (Liberal Arts), 'British Studies and Liberal Arts at UT'

Jane Ohlmeyer (Trinity College, Dublin), 'Making Ireland English'

Dane Kennedy (George Washington University), 'Lost Expeditions, Lost Histories'

Round Table Discussion, 'Racial and Social Prejudice in British and American Universities': Holly McCarthy (British Studies), Wm. Roger Louis (British Studies), and Tom Palaima (Classics)

Andrew O'Shaughnessy (University of Virginia), 'The Men Who Lost America'

John Milton Cooper (University of Wisconsin), 'Colonel House and the British'

Lawrence Goldman (Institute of Historical Research, London), 'The *Oxford Dictionary of National Biography* and National Identity'

Fall Semester 2015

Round Table Discussion, 'The Falklands War': Wm. Roger Louis (History), Bartholomew Sparrow (Government), and David Leal (Latino Politics)

The Austin Brass Band, '40th Anniversary of the British Studies Program at UT-Austin'

Jonathan Schneer (Georgia Tech), 'Churchill and the Second World War: A Reassessment'

Simon Green (Leeds University), 'The Myth of All Souls College'

James H. Dee (Visiting Scholar, Classics), 'Whiteness and Color-Based Racism'

J. K. Barret (English), 'A Midsummer Night's Dream'

Reba Soffer (California State University, Northridge), 'Newer Women and Newer Men after the Great War'

Deidre David (London), 'Pamela Hansford Johnson: "And have you ever written, Lady Snow?"'

Hans Mark (Chancellor of the University of Texas System, 1984–92), 'The Falklands War'

Geoffrey Wheatcroft (London), 'The Difficulties of Writing about Winston Churchill'

Brian Levack (History) and Martha Newman (History), 'The Magna Carta'

John D. Fair (Kinesiology), 'George Bernard Shaw and Physical Fitness'

Round Table Discussion, 'The Story of Alice: Lewis Carroll and the Secret History of Wonderland': Carol MacKay (English), Jerome Bump (English), George Scott Christian (English), and John Farrell (English)

Philip Mead (Harvard University), 'The Unjustifiable and the Imaginable: Politics and Fiction in Contemporary Aboriginal Life'

Spring Semester 2016

Round Table Discussion, 'The Best and Worst Books of 2015': Wm. Roger Louis (History), Al Martinch (Philosophy), Elizabeth Richmond-Garza (English), and Steve Weinberg (Physics)

Caroline Moorehead (London), 'Writing about the Resistance in World War II'

Boisfeuillet Jones, Jr. (Washington, D.C.), 'British and American Newspapers: How Long Will Print Copies Survive?'
Luise White (University of Florida), 'The Lost History of Rhodesia: Race and the Decolonization of Central Africa'
Martha Ann Selby (Asian Studies), 'Everyday Life in South India and the Tamil Short Story'
Rosemary Hill (London), 'British Propaganda in World War II'
Michael Holroyd (London), 'Kipling: Early Years and a Clue to His Personality'
Steve Hindle (Huntington Library), 'Labor and the Landscape in the Eighteenth Century'
Kenneth Fisher (Beverley Hills, California), 'Cecil Rhodes: The Man, the Scholarships, and the Protest Movement: Rhodes Must Fall'
Ron Heiferman (Quinnipiac University), 'China and India during World War II'
Joseph Epstein (Northwestern University), 'The *Encyclopaedia Britannica*'
Laura Mitchell (University of California, Irvine), 'The Colonial Hunt: Collecting Trophies and Knowledge'
Steven L. Isenberg, (Visiting Professor, Liberal Arts), 'The Poet Keith Douglas in the Tradition of Siegfried Sassoon'
Martin Stannard (Editor of OUP's 43-vol. *Complete Works of Evelyn Waugh*) 'Evelyn Waugh: His Visits to the United States'
Daniel Foliard (Paris Ouest University), 'Cartography and the Making of the Modern Middle East'
Rand Brandes (Lenoir-Rhyne University), 'Seamus Heaney: Irish Poet and Nobel Laureate'

Fall Semester 2016

James H. Dee (Visiting Scholar, Classics), "Homo, Humanus, Humanitas—and the 'Humanities'"
John Prados (National Security Archive), 'British and American Intelligence Services'
Round Table Discussion, 'Brexit': Jamie Galbraith (LBJ School), David Leal (Government), Philippa Levine (History), and Wm. Roger Louis (History)
Round Table Discussion, 'Shakespeare's Richard III': Alan Friedman (English), James Loehlin (English), Elizabeth Richmond-Garza (English), and David Kornhaber (English)
Annamaria Motrescu-Mayes (Cambridge), 'Re-Illustrating the History of the British Empire'
Michelle Tusan (University of Nevada), 'Crimes against Humanity and the Armenian Genocide: How the British Invented Human Rights'
Andrew Lownie (London), 'Stalin's Englishman: Guy Burgess'
Barnaby Crowcroft (Harvard University), 'Britain's "Egyptian Allies" and the Suez Crisis of 1956'
James Scott (Statistics), 'Lost and Found: Bayes' Rule after 250 Years'
Geoffrey Wheatcroft (London), 'The Worst Thing since Suez? Tony Blair and Iraq'
Janine Barchas (English), '"Will & Jane": Shakespeare, Austen, and the Cult of Celebrity'
Richard Davenport-Hines (London), 'Jack the Ripper'
Terry Gifford (Bath Spa University) 'Six Stages in the Greening of Ted Hughes'
Steve Weinberg (Physics), 'The Whig History of Science'
John M. MacKenzie (Lancaster University), 'The British Empire: Ramshackle or Rampaging?'

David Edwards (Government), 'Post–November 8, Post-Brexit'
James Loehlin (English), 'Charles Dickens and Christmas'

Spring Semester 2017

Thomas Palaima (Classics), 'Bob Dylan and England'
Jane Ridley (Buckingham University), 'Harold Nicolson and the Biography of George V'
Wm. Roger Louis (History), 'Ernest Bevin and Palestine'
Jurgend Schmandt (LBJ School), 'Alexander King: Scientist and Environmentalist'
Caroline Elkins (Harvard University), 'British Colonial Violence and the End of Empire'
Al Martinich (Philosophy), 'Obedience and Some of Its Discontents'
Daniel Williams (Wales University), 'Assimilation and Its Discontents: Wales in British Literature'
Paul Kennedy (Yale University), 'Guglielmo Marconi and England'
James Epstein (Vanderbilt University), 'Writing from Newgate Prison, 1795: William Winterbotham's View of America'
Brian Levack (History), 'Trust and Distrust in Stuart England'
Kenneth O. Morgan (House of Lords), 'Brexit'
Sarah Beaver (Oxford), 'The Falklands Crisis: A Perspective from the Whitehall Operations Room'
John Rodden (Tunghai University, Taiwan), 'George Orwell's *1984* and His Subsequent Reputation'
Susan Napier (Tufts University), 'Where Shall We Adventure? Hayao Miyazaki Meets Robert Louis Stevenson'
Jason Parker (Texas A&M), 'The End of Empire: From "Divide and Conquer" to "Federate and Leave"'
Patrick French (Ahmedabad University, Gujarat), 'Writing the Biography of V. S. Naipaul'
Steven Isenberg (Visiting Professor, Liberal Arts), 'John Banville as Novelist and Critic: *The Untouchable*'

Fall Semester 2017

Jeffrey Meyers (Berkeley, California), 'Randolph Churchill and Evelyn Waugh in Yugoslavia'
Louise Weinberg (Law), 'A British Atrocity in American Courts'
James Loehlin (English), 'Measure for Measure: "Some rise by sin, and some by virtue fall"'
Abigail Aiken (LBJ School), 'Women in Northern Ireland'
John D. Fair (Physical Culture and Sports), 'Louis George Martin: Champion Weightlifter'
Paul Addison (University of Edinburgh), 'How Churchill's Mind Worked'
George Walden (King's College, London), 'Peter Carrington: His Long Career in Politics and International Diplomacy'
Geoffrey Wheatcroft (London), 'Presidents and Prime Ministers: From Wilson and Lloyd George to Trump and May'
Richard Davenport-Hines (London), '"Mr. Five-Percent": Calouste Gulbenkian and Middle East Oil'
Harry Lee Hudspeth (Austin), 'From University of Texas A. B. to Federal Judge'
Roby Barrett (Middle East Institute, Washington, D.C.), 'Crisis in the Gulf: An Echo from the British Past'

Nicholas Shakespeare (All Souls College, Oxford), 'Six Minutes in May: How Churchill Unexpectedly Became Prime Minister'
Jon Wilson (King's College, London), 'The Chaos of Empire: The Conquering of India'
Kate Dawson (Journalism), 'The Great London Smog'
Al Martinich (Philosophy), 'Four Books on Stuart England Plus One on China'
John Greening (Newnham College, Cambridge), 'Edmund Blunden and Undertones of War'
Jamie Galbraith (LBJ School), 'Rudyard Kipling's "Christmas in India"'

Spring Semester 2018

Mark Skipworth (London), 'An Englishman Looks at Texas History'
Elizabeth Baigent (Oxford), '*The Dictionary of National Biography*'
Krishan Kumar (University of Virginia), 'The British Empire Compared with the European Empires'
Lucy Collins (University College, Dublin), 'The Poetry of Louis MacNeice'
George Kelling (San Antonio), 'Cyprus and World War II'
Adam Howard (U.S. State Department), 'British Labour, American Labor, and the Creation of the State of Israel'
James H. Dee (Classics), 'Man's Inhumanity to Man: From Prehistoric Man to British Criminals'
Edward Mortimer (All Souls College, Oxford), 'Symbolic Names: Present Controversies in Historical Perspective'
David Leal (Government), 'Arthur Conan Doyle and Sherlock Holmes'
Tom Cable (English), 'Running with Shakespeare'
Carol MacKay (English), 'Subversive, Rebellious, and Genre-Busting: 18th- and 19th-Century Women Writers Move to Center Stage'
Antony Hopkins (Pembroke College, Cambridge), 'America's Global Empire'
Jane Ridley (Buckingham University), 'Reassessing Max Beaverbrook'
Karl Rove (Austin), 'Worldwide Consequences of American Expansion in 1898'
James Scott (Statistics and Data Sciences), 'Florence Nightingale, Artificial Intelligence, and the Future of Health Care'
Bernard Wasserstein (University of Chicago), 'How the British Left Palestine'
Round Table Discussion: 'A UT Ethics Center? The Oxford Ethics Centre in Comparison': Virginia Brown (Dell Medical School), Robert Prentice (Business School), Stephen Sonnenberg, M.D. (Plan II), Paul Woodruff (Philosophy)

Fall Semester 2018

George Scott Christian (English), 'Scotland and Brexit'
Jonathan Brown (History), 'Castro's Challenge to Britain and the United States'
James Loehlin, Alan Friedman, and Eric Mallin (English), '"To Be or Not to be" Through the Ages'
Rodolfo John Alaniz (History), 'Charles Darwin: *HMS Beagle* and the New Era in the History of Biology'
Robert D. King (College of Liberal Arts), 'Alan Turing: Genius, Patriot, Victim'
Joseph Epstein (Northwestern University), 'P. G. Wodehouse: Frivolous, Empty, and Perfectly Delightful'
Rhonda Evans (Australian Studies), 'Australia and the Non-Acceptance of Refugees'
Philip Waller (Merton College, Oxford), 'Light Reading for Intellectual Heavyweights'

Rosemary Hill (London), 'Ida John: The Good Bohemian'

Paul Sullivan (English), 'Martyrs and Mistresses in Restoration London'

Max Hastings (London), 'The Raj'

Kevin Kenny (New York University), 'Éamon de Valera and the Creation of Modern Ireland'

Stephen Enniss (Director, Harry Ransom Center), 'Seamus Heaney and the London Origins of the Belfast Group'

Hermione Lee (Wolfson College, Oxford), 'Tom Stoppard and T. S. Eliot'

Nigel Newton (Chief Executive, Bloomsbury Publishing, London), 'Bloomsbury and Harry Potter'

Paul Woodruff (Classics and Philosophy), 'Oxford's Battle for the Soul of Classics'

Michael Starbird (Mathematics), 'Lewis Carroll and the Jabberwocky'

Spring Semester 2019

Joanna Hitchcock (UT Press), 'Countess Noël, Heroine of the Titanic'

Round Table Discussion: 'Brexit!', Jamie Galbraith (LBJ School), David Leal (Government), Philippa Levine (History), Roger Louis (History), and Bartholomew Sparrow (Government)

Derek Leebaert (Washington, D.C.), 'Britain as a Superpower, 1945–1957'

Jamie Galbraith (LBJ School), 'Brexit: Portrait of a Cl*st*rf*ck'

Peter Stansky (Stanford), 'William Morris and the Arts and Crafts Movement'

Margaret MacMillan (St. Antony's College, Oxford), 'Warnings from Versailles, 1919, for 2019'

John Farrell (English), 'She Moves in Mysterious Ways: Jane Eyre's Journeys'

Ross Terrill (Harvard University), 'R. H. Tawney: Economic Inequality and Leftist Politics'

Mark Gasiorowski (Tulane), 'Britain, the United States, and the Iranian Revolution'

Round Table Discussion: 'Biographies: Research, Writing, and Reviews', Bill Brands (History), Bartholomew Sparrow (Government), and Ellen Cunningham-Kruppa (Harry Ransom Center)

David Edwards (Government), 'Fake News, Alternative Facts, and the Question of Truth'

Harshan Kumarasingham (University of Edinburgh), 'Brexits Past: Withdrawals from the Empire'

James Dee (Classics), 'Heroes of the Intellect: Unbelief and Enlightenment Values across the Ages'

Alan W. Friedman (English), 'Samuel Beckett: Joycean and Surreal?'

Geoffrey Wheatcroft (London), 'Brexit: An Historical Romance'

Sandra Mayer (Wolfson College, Oxford), 'The Novels of Disraeli and Oscar Wilde'

Round Table Discussion: '150 Highly Recommended Books': Randy Diehl (Dean of Liberal Arts), Kip Keller (British Studies editor), Lisa Lacy (Junior Fellow in British Studies), Meagan Bennett (Churchill Scholar), and Shane Wagoner (Churchill Scholar)